MASTERS OF TWO ARTS

Re-creation of European Literatures in Italian Cinema

In *Masters of Two Arts*, Carlo Testa demonstrates that pairings of famous directors and writers are commonplace in modern Italian cinema. Surprisingly, the study of the interrelation between Italian cinema and European literature has been almost completely neglected in film scholarship. Testa addresses and attempts to correct this oversight with nine in-depth analyses of the connection between an Italian filmmaker and a distinguished modern European author. Looking at combinations such as Pasolini and Sade, Rossellini and Stendhal, Fellini and Kafka, and Visconti and Mann, Testa uses theoretical as well as historical methods, showing how the respective text undergoes not 'adaptation' but full 're-creation' (as defined by Èizenshtein) in a different art form and, even more significantly, in a new cultural context.

CARLO TESTA is Associate Professor in the Department of French, Hispanic, and Italian Studies, University of British Columbia. He is also the author of *Desire and the Devil* (1991) and *Italian Cinema and Modern European Literatures* (2002), and the editor of *Poet of Civic Courage: The Films of Francesco Rosi* (1996).

MASTERS OF TWO ARTS

Re-creation of European Literatures in Italian Cinema

Carlo Testa

UNIVERSITY OF TORONTO PRESS
Toronto Buffalo London

© University of Toronto Press Incorporated 2002
Toronto Buffalo London
Printed in Canada

ISBN 0-8020-3640-6 (cloth)
ISBN 0-8020-8475-3 (paper)

∞

Printed on acid-free paper

Toronto Italian Studies

National Library of Canada Cataloguing in Publication Data

Testa, Carlo
    Masters of two arts : re-creation of European literatures in
    Italian cinema

    (Toronto Italian studies)
    Includes bibliographical references and index.
    ISBN 0-8020-3640-6 (bound).   ISBN 0-8020-8475-3 (pbk.)

    1. Motion pictures and literature – Italy – History – 20th century.
    2. European literature – Film and video adaptations.   I. Title.
    II. Series.

    PN1993.5.I88T47 2002   791.43'6   C2002-900608-2

This book has been published with the help of a grant from the Humanities
and Social Sciences Federation of Canada, using funds provided by the
Social Sciences and Humanities Research Council of Canada.

University of Toronto Press acknowledges the financial assistance to its
publishing program of the Canada Council for the Arts and the Ontario
Arts Council.

University of Toronto Press acknowledges the financial support for its
publishing activities of the Government of Canada through the Book
Publishing Industry Development Program (BPIDP).

Contents

ACKNOWLEDGMENTS   vii

Introduction   3

Part One: Epigraphic Re-creations

1 Goethe and Archibugi
    Italy, the Illegible Land: *Mignon Has Left* (1988)   27

2 Kafka and Fellini
    Soteriology, Cinecittà-style: *America* and *Intervista* (1987)   33

Part Two: Coextensive Re-creations

3 Gogol and Lattuada
    Fantastic Neorealism: *The Overcoat* (1952)   57

4 Tolstoy and the Tavianis
    The Interminable Path of History: *Father Sergius* and
        The Night Sun (1990)   77

The Re-creation to End All Creation

Sade and Pasolini
    Requiem for a Utopia: *Salò or the 120 Days of Sodom* (1975)   101

Part Three: Mediated Re-creations

5 Mérimée, Bizet, and Rosi
    The Consummation of Meridionalism: *Carmen* (1984)   125

6 Pasternak, Lean, and Moretti
   Hermits and Revolutionaries: *Palombella rossa* (1989)   143

Part Four: Hypertextual Re-creations

7 Stendhal and Rossellini
   The Masterpiece Fights Back: *Vanina Vanini* (1961)   161
8 Mann and Visconti
   One Sentry Falls: *Death in Venice* (1971)   183

Conclusion

On Readings: Perfect/Imperfect, Difficult, and More Difficult   205

NOTES   219

FILMOGRAPHY   321

WORKS CITED   327

INDEX   351

Acknowledgments

One section and one chapter in *Masters of Two Arts* are re-elaborated versions of already published articles: 'Francesco Rosi: *Carmen* et Imago,' *Romance Languages Annual* 7 (1995), 344–9; and '*Mignon è partita* and Francesca Archibugi's Illegible Land,' *Italian Quarterly* 33: 127–8 (Winter–Spring 1996), 43–7. I gratefully acknowledge the journals' permission to use these articles for publication here. An earlier version of chapter 2 is published in *Federico Fellini: Contemporary Perspectives*, ed. Frank Burke and Marguerite Waller (University of Toronto Press, 2002).

In North America and Europe, I owe more than I can say to my colleagues in Comparative Literature and in Italian Studies, among the latter particularly Peter Bondanella, Ben Lawton, Millicent Marcus, and Áine O'Healy, who unflinchingly encouraged me to carry on what at times – especially when wrong alignments of planets caused mental or financial resources to dry up – seemed to be a Sisyphean enterprise.

In Italy, I feel much obliged to the directors who kindly accepted to be interviewed, consulted, or in other ways exploited: Alberto Lattuada, Nanni Moretti, Francesco Rosi, and Paolo and Vittorio Taviani, all of whom generously provided me with insights and information on their work. Thanks also go to Lino Micciché, the Scuola Nazionale di Cinema (previously Centro Sperimentale di Cinematografia) in Rome, as well as the Cineteca del Comune di Bologna. I am also deeply indebted to my father, further family, and friends, who offered me moral and logistical support across the peninsula; to Alberto Bartolomeo at Casalini in Fiesole and Valter (with a V) Chierici at Videocavour in Milan, whose diligence allowed me to focus on some hard-to-spot material rather than spend my time looking for it; to signora Umberta Brazzini of the

Mediateca Regionale Toscana in Florence; to Alessandra Piovera; and, finally, to Graham and the friendly staff of Videomatica in Vancouver.

On the UBC campus, I wish to thank for their polymorphous support the Comparative Literature program, the interfaculty Center for Intercultural Language Studies (CILS), Keith Bunnell (Library Acquisitions), and the zealous, indefatigable, and friendly people at Interlibrary Loan Services: Moira Buckham, Patrick Dunn, Paul Lesack, Patrick Paterson, and David Truelove. I should also acknowledge receiving at a crucial time an HSS research grant from the UBC Research Services.

Closer to home, I will always be grateful to my late friend and confrere Annibale Noce for reading early drafts of some chapters and suggesting ways to improve them. My wife and colleague, Daniela Boccassini, receives analogous but deeper credit, in just proportion to her greater exposure to the slings and arrows of the outrageous fortune – endured by her with grace and caring – of having had to share her private life with *Masters of Two Arts* for so long.

This book is dedicated, with infinite gratitude, to all my teachers past and present.

Forgery (poddelka) *is repulsive. Re-creation* (vossozdanie) *is magnificent.*

SERGEI ÈIZENSHTEIN[1]

Never, so long as I live, shall I be illustrated – because the most beautiful literary description is devoured by the ugliest of drawings. As soon as a type is fixed by the pencil, it loses its general character, its concordance with a thousand familiar objects that causes the reader to say: 'I've seen that,' or 'It must be just so.' The drawing of a woman looks just like one woman, and that's that.

GUSTAVE FLAUBERT[2]

The illustrations of a literary work have an artistic value to the extent that they are not merely illustrative. It is the same with the cinema.

MICHELANGELO ANTONIONI[3]

MASTERS OF TWO ARTS

Introduction

The European Legion

Many, in fact potentially innumerable, are the variously overlapping subsets of which the corpus of Italian cinema can be said to consist. It seems to me that among these the Rusty Tin Lion (or Bear, or Palm) for the one most consistently neglected by scholars ought to be awarded to the large group that, as a first approximation, could be called the European legion in the peninsula: the films that directly or indirectly re-create works of European literature.[1]

One reason for this critical oblivion may not be particularly difficult to discern and, to an extent at least, to rationalize. Those diverse films clearly got caught in the crossfire among more immediately visible and more easily defined groupings: neorealism, the *commedia all'italiana*, political cinema, the spaghetti western, the film noir, neomythological or 'peplum' productions, the films on *incomunicabilità*, rediscovered works from the Fascist era, auteur cinema (Fellini, Antonioni), the *nuovo cinema italiano* of the 1980s–1990s, and so on. Yet the fact of the exclusion remains; and it is at times so brutal as to tempt one into considering some strange form of cultural xenophobia as its cause. Such a generalized prejudice can be seized nowhere better than in two works published in Italy during the last decade: Cristina Bragaglia's *The Pleasure of Narrating* (*Il piacere del racconto*, 1993)[2] and Giuliana Nuvoli's *Re-created Stories* (*Storie ricreate*, 1998).[3] From my viewpoint, a striking characteristic of these two books on filmic re-creations from literature is that they define their field of inquiry as comprising exclusively films inspired by, or related to, works of *Italian* literature. As for the first work, Bragaglia does not even take the trouble to mention that she is leaving out other cultures from her horizon of the events; Europe (and, for that matter, the rest of the world) simply do not exist. How, the author seems to take for granted, could foreign literatures be construed as in any way representative of states of mind, artistic impulses, or historical conditions genuinely native to the peninsula? With respect to Nuvoli, she is content with a hasty mention of 'Italian literature' and 'cinema made by Italian directors,'[4] as if it were a matter of course that no other sets need be considered. This is complemented, a few pages later, by a nonchalant reference to '*our* literature' and '*our* filmography'[5] – a wording that, I must confess, I could not help finding a little constraining, as I leafed through the freshly purchased book in a large Feltrinelli bookstore crammed with new arrivals from countries as far afield as Chile, Russia, Guatemala, the Caribbean, and Japan.

It is puzzling but true that, in the extant scholarship on Italian cinema, intellectual affinities between Italian directors and European authors, particularly of the modern era, have been treated in an entirely coincidental, unsystematic manner. I believe that we are denying ourselves the privilege of capturing a substantial area of Italian filmmaking – and, for that matter, of seizing adequately some of the fundamental vectors at work under the surface of the Italian polity in the second half of the twentieth century – if we do not move swiftly and without mental reservations toward giving this neglected terrain the status it deserves.[6]

From 'Adaptation' to Re-creation

Personally, as I shall explain in some detail in the conclusion to this book, I am of the opinion that a rigorously exact transposition from literature to film is not possible (or, indeed, desirable). Stubbornly, however, directors seem to have been practising it for many decades now: from Victor Fleming in *Gone With the Wind* to Stanley Kubrick in *Eyes Wide Shut*; from Luchino Visconti in *The Leopard* to Pier Paolo Pasolini in *Salò or the 120 Days of Sodom*; from Jean Renoir in *La bête humaine* to Max Ophuls in *La ronde*, to Jean-Luc Godard in *Le mépris* to Eric Rohmer in *La Marquise d'O*; from Vsevolod Pudovkin in *Mat'* to Nikita Mikhalkov in *Oblomov* and *Ochi chërnye*; from Friedrich Wilhelm Murnau in *Faust* to Rainer Werner Fassbinder in *Effi Briest*; and so on *ad libitum*. And what devils manipulated Robert Bresson into making *L'argent* out of Tolstoy's *The Forged Note*, or Sergei Èizenshtein into tackling Turgenev's *Bezhin Meadow*?[7]

In fact, *Masters of Two Arts* arose from my long-standing curiosity about the reasons that led so many film directors persistently to pursue an enterprise that, in theory, seems at best fraught with dangers, and at worst intrinsically self-defeating. *Masters of Two Arts* explores this puzzle in the case of some of the major Italian filmmakers of the past half-century, and of the French, German, and Russian literary interlocutors whom the Italians chose for themselves on those occasions. I consider myself fortunate that the former and the latter, the directors and the writers, belong to the group of my favourite masters of all arts.

However, I am thoroughly dissatisfied with the word 'adaptation,' as I am with the unquestionably condescending theoretical positions that can underpin it. (The Italian language has an even more ominous possibility, the truly reductionist *riduzione*. On a more cheerful note, the thought-provoking term *dislocazione* has most recently been put forward.)[8]

Over decades, the critical debate on the subject of what has most often been referred to as the cinematic 'adaptation' of literature has been so vast and articulated that I cannot hope to do full justice to its richness here. Or rather, any attempt on my part to engage with it exhaustively would make this a radically different book than the one I envisage. Suffice it to say – in full awareness of the fact that almost each of the words I am about to write could justify a very large footnote – that I share the misgivings of those for whom the very word 'adaptation' implies a logical or ontological hierarchy, according to which what came first in time automatically enjoys a primary status, and whatever happened to come later derivatively regested it. 'Adaptation' also rings ominous to my ears because it inevitably keeps us within a stone's throw of the F-word, 'fidelity,' which (unbelievably, but sadly true) is on occasion still uttered in the relevant literature. Granted, today hardly anyone who mentions F does so in order to argue that it be upheld as a criterion for aesthetic evaluation. But, it seems fair to remark that even *to allow for deviations from F* implies that deviations from F are still a subject worth debating. Viewing things in this manner clearly constrains the debate within the bounds of what to me are singularly sterile parameters. Such parameters I would term *separatist*: authors and auteurs are thereby separated from the respective contexts, synchronic and diachronic, in which they operated; and the form of their works is separated from its dialogical linkages, synchronic and diachronic, to other works in the same series.

My persuasion is that separatism reflects a very early historical stage in the development of critical discourse. Whenever articulated, such positions (and again, out of sheer goal-awareness I will not engage in lengthy one-on-one argument with them) hark back to a phase embodied to perfection in Viktor Shklovskii's *Literature and Cinema* (*Literatura i kinematograf,* 1923), an essay that included the famous, deliberately absurd, rhetorical question as to whether it was possible to 'play the Kazan cathedral' on a trombone.[9] In his times, Shklovskii of course had excellent reasons to write as he wrote, and his pamphlet is in many respects a jewel in the history of literary and cinema criticism. Besides, in a later phase during the 1920s the Russian Formalists – including Shklovskii himself – opened up to a wide array of hermeneutical stimuli that overcame their previous separatism altogether.

In the most essential terms, the 'adaptation'/F paradigm falls, to my mind, entirely within the realm of pre-Bakhtinian categories. This is not to imply that I regard Bakhtin as the new Aristotle; rather, I see him more as the new Galilei, who, having been preceded by Copernicus and Tycho Brahe, in turn paved the way for much useful research after himself – a fortunate circumstance being paralleled today in the latest development of textual criticism in the West. (While we are on the subject: however pleased by the fact that Bakhtinism is now a concept familiar to North American academia, I find it difficult to remain insensitive to the fact that few colleagues outside the field of Slavic semiotics have taken notice of the continuation and refinement of Bakhtin's research carried out by Yurii Lotman and his colleagues at Tartu University.)[10] How, then, to break away once and for all from obsolete paradigms and establish a satisfactory alternative?

In the wake of previous work done by Bazin and Andrew,[11] a much preferable solution has not too long ago been suggested by Millicent Marcus in an exemplary book on the dialogism between literature and film, in which she proposed and articulated the term cinematic *re-creation*: a movement of induction and deduction producing an appropriate cinematic 're-writing.'[12] However, her suggestion – formulated in completely uncontroversial terms – seems to have been received by the anglophone and anglo-centred academic community of film specialists with an interest not nearly comparable to that which it deserves.[13] In general, much effort seems to have been expended in the last few years to secure theoretical positions that would have been within much easier reach for the profession, had more of us read Marcus more carefully.[14]

Lest I be misunderstood on this point, I hasten to add that I in no way consider the aforementioned colleagues to be remiss in perusing their libraries. Rather, I am well aware that they work within a critical mainstream in which – not least because of its *Nouvelle vague* ancestry – literature and cinema have, until very recently, coexisted uneasily. By contrast, no such problem arises in the Italian tradition, where – not least because of its neorealist and/or Gramscian origin – the cooperation between the two art forms has led to some of the politically sharpest and artistically most splendid products of the national cinema tradition. When taken in North America, certain positions must clearly strike one as more novel than in the country of Lampedusa's and Visconti's *The Leopard* (*Il Gattopardo*, 1963).[15] What does this complex situation prove? It once more proves, I believe, that we always act and think *in a historical context*.[16]

To return to Marcus's *Rezeptionsgeschichte* (or, more exactly, relative lack thereof) in the anglophone world, I would like to mention at least one not untypical case in point. Robert Stam's position on film-and-literature matters is that

> one way to look at *adaptation* is to see it as a matter of a source novel's hypotext being transformed by a complex series of operations: selection, amplification, concretization, actualization, critique, extrapolation, analogization, popularization, and reculturalization. The source novel, in this sense, can be seen as a situated utterance produced in one medium and in one historical context, then transformed into another equally situated utterance that is produced in a different context and in a different medium. The source text forms a dense informational network, a series of verbal cues that the adapting film text can then take up, amplify, ignore, subvert, or transform. The film adaptation of a novel performs these transformations according to the protocols of a distinct medium, absorbing and altering the genres and intertexts available thorough the grids of ambient discourses and ideologies, and as mediated by a series of filters: studio style, ideological fashion, political constraints, auteurist predilections, charismatic stars, economic advantage or disadvantage, and evolving technology.[17]

All this is as true as it is exemplarily thorough. Nonetheless, it is presumably clear to anyone familiar with the history of the term in the anglophone world that Stam's formalization just quoted resolutely pours out the content of the 'adaptation' word *as criticism knew it* before, say, Bakhtin, and retains only its bottle. That bottle Stam fills with new and different concepts – concepts, for all intents and purposes, identical to those applied by Marcus to the idea of re-creation. Verily, there seem to be two separate and largely non-communicating film-and-literature traditions: the one that developed within the Gramscian-Viscontian context, and the one that didn't.[18]

Be that as it may, it seems to me out of the question that, in the circumstances, a new word will fit a new practice better. Re-creation has all that it takes to become the established successor to the 'adaptation'/F paradigm; and future readers might well look at occurrences of the old terms around the year 2000 as no more than quaint last flickers of a long-bygone era. Such impermanence is, after all, to be expected; we don't just write about cultural history, we live in it.

Last but far from least, it is important to note that the term *re-creation*, with its attendant emphasis on the role played by cultural contexts, is more viable than any of its older competitors at a time when, as is the case today, the history of cinema and the theory of cinema are rumoured to be getting along better than they have for decades.[19] Re-creation responds to both traditions; and it may not seem too optimistic to see it as well qualified to occupy a pre-eminent slot at the vanishing point where, one beautiful day, cinema history and cinema theory will converge.

Torito

One major reason why I am partial to the re-creation approach to literature and film is that it has been espoused by a fellow-traveller of the Formalists' critical revolution whose work I happen to esteem highly. This was a practitioner whose cultural-historical coordinates put him squarely in a position to qualify as Bakhtin's intellectual twin. However different their fields of specialization, a common co-inheritance is, in fact, what links Bakhtin to Èizenshtein. There are many good books on Bakhtin, and as many good books on Èizenshtein; but if there came along one that explored and elucidated the common genesis and parallel developments in their respective life works, what a book that would be![20]

Èizenshtein explicitly mentions re-creation in the sentence I have used as the first epigraph to *Masters of Two Arts*. Since I am using the concept as the nucleus of my own argument (I arguably re-create it in my own Italian and North American cultural context), it might be appropriate to spend a moment looking in some detail at his terms. In 'Diderot Wrote about Cinema,' Èizenshtein contrasts uncreative, debased imitation of pre-existing forms with an original appropriation of them that incorporates features inspired by a changed environment and adequate to it. For the first he uses the term *poddelka*; for the second, *vossozdanie*.

In Russian-English dictionaries, *poddelka* is straightforwardly rendered as 'forgery'; *Fälschung* is correspondingly used in German; and the Italian edition of Èizenshtein gives *contraffazione* (related to English 'counterfeit'). To exemplify the adjective *poddelnyi*, the monolingual Ozhegov dictionary adduces the fairly self-explanatory word combination *falshivyi dokument*. In and of itself, *poddelka* is made up of the prefix *pod-*, equivalent to our *sub-*, combined with the root *del-*, Latin *fac-*. Thus, if Western languages – English in this instance – had a direct equivalent to *poddelka*, it would be something like 'subfeit' – a transparent antonym to 'surfeit.' Clearly, the Russian word metaphorically implies that in the process of forgery the receiving end is being short-changed.

As for *vossozdanie*, Russian-English dictionaries will usually give different combinations of the following terms: 're-creation,' 'reconstitution,' 'reconstruction,' 'renewal.' Here, the prefix involved is *vos-* (in other contexts *voz-*), which generally indicates (a) rising, often repeated or renewed: *voskhod* '(sun)rise,' *vosstanie* 'uprising, insurgency,' *vospitanie* 'education,' *voskresenie* 'resurrection,' *vospominanie* 'recollection.' The rest of the stem, *sozd-*, means 'to create.' The Italian translators of Èizenshtein use *ricostruzione* ('re-construction'); but I assume this is because of an interference with the noun *zdanie*, 'building.' However, *re-creation* is unquestionably the correct word here. *Sozdanie* is not a direct compound of *zdanie*; it means 'creation' *tout court*. So much so, in fact, that non-Soviet dictionaries (the early-twentieth-century Dahl, for example) have no compunction about blurting out the inadmissible equivalence: the *Sozdatel'* is God – the Creator. Semioticians are equally unambiguous: 'Art acknowledges and experiences (*poznaët*) life by re-creating (*vossozdavaia*) it' (Lotman).[21]

With a firm grip on Èizenshtein's semantics, we may now proceed to take a look at how the director actually intended his terms to function in context. Though he did not articulate matters in neat treatise-like form (keeping Stalin at bay was but one of the many concerns that prevented him from meeting the exacting scholarly standards of our academia), Èizenshtein clearly viewed re-creation as hinging upon the elaboration of *cinematographic equivalents* for concepts and practices one could find prefigured in literature – most notably *chez* his all-time favourites from the nineteenth and the twentieth century.[22] While, in practice, the history of cinema did not always see it judiciously applied,[23] in Èizenshtein's terms the principle of cinema equivalents for literary devices strikes one as solid and promising.

In the short article 'Literature and Cinema' ('Literatura i kino,' 1928), the director wrote:

As for the 'mutual relations' [among arts] I can say that we have now completed the process of purging cinema respectively of:

1) Literature (primitive and operating only through plot: pure adventurism, *Rocambole*, *813*, *The Nibelungs* or psychological adventurism, for instance *The Parisian Woman*); 2) Theatre (the acted genre) ...

In our current tendency to search for forms that are really characteristic
of it, cinema finds its best *support* in what is happening in the field of the
renewal of literary forms.

This helps to understand better the series of problems that arise quite
independently from cinema's raw material by using the experience and the
analogy of a 'neighbouring' sphere.[24]

Leaving the sinister – or perhaps allusively ironic – term 'purging' to
one side, the obvious meaning I retrieve from Èizenshtein's words
quoted here is that he views a non-primitive, non-adventurist, non-
plot-constrained usage of literary stimuli as, indeed, *supportive* of the
worthiest efforts in contemporaneous cinematography.

According to Èizenshtein, the following are the prerequisite conditions for the relationship of cinema and literature, as well as its potential
prize:

You must force film directors to find the *cinema equivalents* of these works.
(When required.)

In this way we can conceive of both the renewal and the fertilization of
both the formal aspect and of the opportunities for cinema, and not just of
the thematic or plot aspect, which, in the final analysis, is successfully
implemented in other forms of literature.[25]

Èizenshtein is here particularly sharp in establishing the autonomy of
cinema as a salutary reaction against the encroachment of poor, reductionist 'adaptations' of literature to film (indeed, one could say 'adaptations' of cinema to Procrustean standards developed in wholly different
cultural-historical contexts). Clearly, he does so because such was the
most pressing need for him as a defender of cinema in his own context.
Still, he is completely open to a usage of literature that is respectful of
cinema's specific nature. It seems to be no coincidence that, shortly
after responding in the above manner to an official questionnaire,
Èizenshtein undertook the cinematographic re-creation of one of the
most difficult chapters in Turgenev's *A Hunter's Sketches*, the only deceptively serene *Bezhin Meadow*.[26]

The all-important notion that Èizenshtein develops on the subject is that of appropriation or assimilation (*osvoenie*) as conducive to, indeed identical with, cinematic re-creation. As is typical of him, Èizenshtein again writes on this subject unsystematically and in a text apparently unrelated to the one just quoted. I am alluding to an essay, the Spanish-titled *Torito*, deeply influenced by Èizenshtein's travel and work in Mexico (also home to a recent successful revolution at the time of the director's writing).

In *Torito*, Èizenshtein once more sets up the polar opposition we are familiar with. Here, however, he elaborates at some length on it. There are, Èizenshtein writes, two mutually exclusive paths that can be trodden by directors bringing literature to the cinema. The first is mise-en-forme (*oformlenie*) – which, by analogy with today's term 'word-processing' (Fr. *mise en page*), I suggest could alternatively be called *form-processing*.[27] This path, Èizenshtein argues, is good; it leads to appropriation/assimilation, and thus to the re-creation he elsewhere calls 'magnificent.' The second one boils down to mere external imitation. To him the latter is worse than awful, and doomed to artistic failure: doomed to crash spectacularly to earth in the attempt, analogically speaking, to duplicate birds' flight by external means alone.

Èizenshtein's style is so sharp and effective that I would rather present directly, rather than paraphrase, his views on cinema equivalents, his praise of form-processing, and his scorn for external imitation – especially because this part of *Torito* has not, to the best of my knowledge, been published in English to date. Èizenshtein writes:

> How many failed attempts were there in Soviet cinema to introduce, lock, stock and barrel, certain elements of American cinema – for example the typical situation in the ending of earlier cowboy films ... But the American situation did not in the least fit films that reflected our own social and ideological conditions. It did not fit them, because its principle manifested itself by means of a particular, specifically American reading.
>
> However, once that principle was reproduced according to our own reading, it was assimilated (*osvoilsia*) into our cinematography in a perfectly successful manner. True enough, it was necessary to recognize it under the guise of our specific form-processing (*oformlenie*). To recognize it in that new quality which, reflecting our social reality, it has taken on in our country ...
>
> The *finale* of *Battleship Potëmkin* was constructed 'according to the principle' ... of the last act of cowboy films.[28]

After some further elaboration, the director provides a fitting parallel to illustrate his point:

> To stress once more the universal, and thus not exclusive, nature of the phenomenon explained, it might not be pointless to bring up a further analogy in support.
>
> As an image of the borrowing (*zaimstvovanie*) of a principle ... I would like you to keep in mind the airplane ... The true victory of human beings against air undoubtedly began at the time when they moved from the imitation of the external form of the airplane's flying prototypes – the birds – to the acknowledgement of *form as a phenomenon-structuring law* (*forma kak zakon stroeniia iavlenii*).
>
> In other words, human beings' attempts to fly were doomed to failure for as long as the most important thing seemed to them to be the imitation of the external shape of birds' flight ...
>
> [This image (*obraz*)] will help you remember that the elements you 'borrow' will become part and parcel of your own invention, in a vital manner, only when they will be not fragments haphazardly drawn from another particular case, but rather, the result of the mature acquisition of a principle, appropriately applied in different or analogous circumstances.[29]

In other passages, particularly those derived from stenographic notes taken at his lectures, Èizenshtein develops – and applies – the theory of the elaboration of cinematic solutions adequate to render (*usvoit'*) corresponding literary features. Since more and more today such material is appearing in Russia, it is to be hoped that one day we will see the publication of a truly complete edition of his works, both in Russian and in other languages. Superseding the anyway very selected Selected Works – *Izbrannye proizvedeniia* – of Soviet times, this will at long last make it possible to cross-reference and analyse adequately any Èizenshteinian statement on the matter.

This should satisfactorily account for the reasons why in *Masters of Two Arts* I altogether discard the word 'adaptation' and consistently replace it with *re-creation*. To my mind, *re-creation* is able to acknowledge what 'adaptation' does not: *form as a phenomenon-structuring law*. Re-creation thus accurately labels the process of a thorough inter-media recasting of concepts and practices previously shaped by a given cultural-historical mould into another mould appropriate to a socially and technologically different moment.

Why, Why *Him?*

In an early stage of this project, a biographical component guided my first choices: having long worked on modern French, German, and Russian literatures, I was naturally drawn to examine their relationship to Italian cinema before others'. However, as my exploration turned systematic, and *Masters of Two Arts* gradually metamorphosed from nebula into solid object, I realized that covering the French, German, and Russian literary contexts does in fact offer a balanced and reasonably comprehensive picture of the influxes experienced by Italian cinema after the Second World War. While no combination of any (two? three? four?) cultures, European or otherwise, can account for 100 per cent of the external stimuli to which Italian cinema responded during the last half-century, choosing France, Germany, and Russia as priority targets does indeed turn out to maximize our scope. I would have been delighted to be able to include other nations too – Japan and Tibet, for example – but unfortunately I do not have the training for that.

Three is, of course, far from being a magical number. However, a single scholar cannot aspire to indefinitely ample coverage of any given subject; and among the aims of *Masters of Two Arts* I count not the impossible task of exhausting an almost inexhaustible field of research, but a more limited striving to obtain recognition for the fact that much useful work waits to be done in this area.

It seems to me that, in addition to its intrinsic interest, this approach has another advantage: it encourages us to strike out in a direction that leads us not only straight into the arms of some of the great classics of Italian film, but also into those of a few that, for a variety of reasons, never did attain (all the more so outside their country of origin) the coverage brought in its wake by canonical status. I think we have here a rare opportunity to explore and map in a new way a lode that, to judge by the extant catalogues of books published on the subject, might well impress as having been mined to death many times over.

To conclude the preamble to this section, I should now mention the reasons why I am not considering as part of my area of inquiry Italian literature *also*. It might seem that it would make sense if I did include Italian literature in *Masters of Two Arts*: specialists of Italian studies are, after all, privileged by a tradition of film-and-literature that, quite aside from Visconti's already mentioned *The Leopard,* can also count on such other Viscontian masterpieces as *The Earth Trembles* (*La terra trema,* 1948) and

Senso (*Senso* or *The Wanton Countess*, 1954); Pasolini's *Decameron* (1971); and the Tavianis' *Padre padrone* (*My Father My Master*, 1977). Still, this circumstance is neutralized, in my view, by at least two factors. First, many good books already exist on these films by Visconti, Pasolini, the Tavianis and their peers – and just about all the alternative ones that could be candidates for treatment on my part in an Italo-Italian context.[30] Second, I do not have any comparative advantage in this area; after all, any self-respecting Italianist who works in film knows Italian at the very least. It seems to me that I can be comparatively more useful elsewhere.

That said, even limiting myself to the Franco-German-Russian connection within Italian cinema, there still remained numerous possible options for each of the chapters in *Masters of Two Arts*. How, readers will legitimately ask, have I chosen the nine titles here collected? This is, of course, *the* question that in various guises haunts the author of any book, of criticism or otherwise. 'Why, why *him?*' famously cringed Henry James in confronting what to him looked like Flaubert's perversity in making a character James considered utterly insignificant, Frédéric Moreau, the protagonist of *Sentimental Education*.[31] Of course, the last impression I wish to convey is that the writers and film directors I am about to scrutinize are even remotely comparable to Flaubert's *homo superfluus*; quite the contrary, I feel confident that none of them will elicit Jamesian reactions among my readers. Nevertheless, the fact remains that a certain amount of preventive rationalization might render more perspicuous the choices I have made in the chapters to follow.

My primary concern has been to ensure as much diversity and representativeness as possible in a number of areas. With respect to the films themselves, I intended diversity and representativeness to relate to

- the approaches to re-creation practised by each film, and the solutions applied in it to each particular text-to-text conversion problem (style);
- the distribution of my test films over the decades in the history of post–Second World War Italy (cultural, economic, and socio-political context); and
- the profile and visibility of the directors, i.e., their specific importance in the history of cinema (their 'masterliness').

To rephrase the above in different but equivalent terms, my interest has gone to cinematic tasks and solutions whose importance lies in their *enduring* and *representative* nature for present as well as future filmmakers and publics. While, on the one hand, my chapters pay attention to the material and economic circumstances surrounding the films I discuss, on the other it is also true that almost exclusively market-oriented 'pop' genres (among others, peplums, spaghetti westerns, thrillers, even *commedia all'italiana*) remain beyond the horizon of the events of *Masters of Two Arts*. Why? First, there already is a substantial body of studies on these. Second, as I have discovered in the course of my research, rare – and, perhaps, logically so – are the 'pop' films that undertake to re-create classics of world literature. I realize that it could strike some readers as odd to read a book on Italian cinema that does not dwell on the likes of Sergio Leone, Dario Argento, Lina Wertmüller, or Sophia Loren and Marcello Mastroianni. Surely, what is well known is always more comforting and reassuring than the unknown; however, by the same token, what is well known also carries a lesser amount of significant information.

While I have used the terms 'enduring' and 'representative' to describe in a general manner the auteurs discussed in this book, I have no fetish about either; I would have been just as happy to adopt verbatim the three criteria (1, intrinsic excellence; *or* 2, influence; *or* 3, typicality) put forward and justified in detail by Kristin Thompson and David Bordwell in their *Film History: An Introduction*.[32] Needless to say, I am well aware that even Thompson's and Bordwell's principles still leave subjective latitude with respect to the actual make-up of what in Umberto Eco's terms could be called the *rosa* of possible specimens for study.[33] The good news is that, by combining 'masterliness' per se with my other categories mentioned above, one can narrow that *rosa* down to manageable and perhaps not too arbitrary options.[34]

While it might well take little less than a second book to justify each of my choices in detail,[35] at least one cluster of interrelated practical considerations could usefully illustrate my general *modus operandi*. To take Alberto Lattuada as a point of departure: I have opted to analyse *The Overcoat* rather than his later and commercially more successful *The Storm* (*La tempesta*, 1958), because *The Overcoat* is an accomplished example of Italian neorealism in its last phase; I have also preferred it to Lattuada's own *Heart of a Dog* (*Cuore di cane*, 1976), since *The Overcoat* is a far more powerful and original film. Conversely, I have devoted a chapter to Rossellini's *Vanina Vanini*, despite what I consider to be the film's artistic shortcomings, *because* this is Rossellini; and a Rossellinian failure can contain more instructive lessons than faultless execution by a lesser practitioner of cinema. The Tavianis' *The Night Sun* has imposed its presence in this book, despite the Italian public's partial – and the North American public's almost total – unawareness of its existence, on account of its topicality in Italy's (*and* North America's) post-ideological 1980s. And so on, and so on. Some of the films discussed here more visibly foreground formal-theoretical issues, while others emphasize cultural-historical ones; however, in each of them there is osmosis, rather than rigid separation, between the two aspects. *C'est la vie*; indeed, *c'est l'art.* 'The study of literary evolution is possible only in relation to literature as a system, interrelated with other systems and conditioned by them' (Tynianov).[36] My hope is that my readers will find in this book enough to heighten (I dare not say satisfy) their individual brand of curiosity toward that osmotic relationship.

Having said that, almost all of the many films I could not accommodate in *Masters of Two Arts* (over fifty items) are dealt with, albeit with proportionally shorter treatments, in my recent companion volume *Italian Cinema and Modern European Literatures.*

Diversity also guided my choice of films on the watershed of their respective literary prototypes. Aside from an obvious concern for *their* masterliness, the following are the criteria I took into consideration for my candidate prior texts:

– the genre to which they belong;
– the period in which they are set; and
– the country (national tradition) from whose culture they originate.

As far as literary genre is concerned, of the nine works re-created by our directors two are novels (Goethe's *Wilhelm Meister's Apprenticeship* and Kafka's *The Man Who Disappeared*, first published as *Amerika*); one is a novel as refracted through a film (Pasternak's *Doktor Zhivago*, revisited by David Lean's *Doctor Zhivago*); two are 'long stories' (*povesti*) (Tolstoy's *Father Sergius* and Thomas Mann's *Death in Venice*); two are short stories / novellas (Gogol's *The Overcoat* and Stendhal's *Vanina Vanini*); one is a novella re-created in opera (Mérimée's, later Bizet's, *Carmen*); and one is a philosophical work eager to murder genre among many other things (de Sade's *The 120 Days of Sodom*).

With respect to the historical periods portrayed, two are set toward the end of the eighteenth century (*The 120 Days* and *Wilhelm Meister*); three in the first half of the nineteenth century (*The Overcoat, Carmen, Vanina Vanini*); one in the middle of it (*Father Sergius*); two at the beginning of the twentieth century (*The Man Who Disappeared, Death in Venice*); and one between the early 1900s and the end of the 1940s (*Zhivago*). The time of their writing largely concides with these time frames, with the relatively greatest deviation – by about five decades – occurring in Tolstoy. In other words, almost all of this material was quite directly topical at the time of its conception and inception.

As to their cultural origin, three of the nine literary works here involved come from the German *Sprachraum* (*Wilhelm Meister, Death in Venice, The Man Who Disappeared*); three from Russia (*The Overcoat, Father Sergius, Zhivago*); and three from the francophone world (*The 120 Days, Vanina Vanini, Carmen*).

I must confess that in the course of my research I was taken by surprise in realizing the sheer extent to which the nine literary texts discussed in *Masters of Two Arts* in different ways stage geographical diversity, displacement, and cultural estrangement. Kafka's Karl lands in America and struggles in vain to establish himself there; Mignon, the frail personification of Italian artistry, is dispatched to a more ethereal world by the inhospitable climes and lifestyles of northern Europe; Saint Petersburg strikes – indeed, strikes down – Akaky Akakievich as a weirdly artificial, foreign, demonic location; Tolstoy's Sergius starts out as an aristocrat at the czar's court and ends up as a vagrant in Siberia; *The 120 Days* is imagined by de Sade to unfold in the insulated remoteness of a German castle; Carmen picks the French narrator's pockets in Spain, and herself hails from much farther afield; Zhivago (and not only he) is endlessly tossed around Russia by the Revolution; Vanina, though speaking the French of post-Napoleonic Restauration, blazes from hair to toes with an Italian Renaissance temper; and Mann's Venice is a disease-ridden Indian enclave on the Mediterranean coast, worlds away from Aschenbach's immaculate Munich. If our nine authors were by and large self-absorbed in the choice of their narrations' time frames, they thus proved to a remarkable extent outwardly projected in establishing their cultural and spatial coordinates.

With respect to the way the material in *Masters of Two Arts* is arranged, I have opted to organize it in four parts, sampling types of re-creation I term respectively *homological, epigraphic* or inscriptional (Part One), *coextensive* (Part Two), *mediated* (Part Three), and *hypertextual* (Part Four).

At one extreme of a hypothetical scale, in Part One, the term *homological* indicates re-creations that have a strong intellectual link to a prior text, but do no more than allude to it in their plot line. This group is here represented by Archibugi's *Mignon Has Left*. Archibugi's Mignon is recognizably an avatar of Goethe's Mignon, yet she acts in independent ways that are appropriate for her wholly different, late-twentieth-century Italian context.[37]

A second type of film, one that is more imbued with actual diegetic material from its prior text, consists of what I call inscriptional or *epigraphic* re-creations. The prior text is now directly evoked, although only isolated icons from it are put to fruition by the director. Kafka's *The Man Who Disappeared*, for example, appears in Fellini's *Intervista* in fragment form and as part of a compatible, yet largely different, orchestration. Fellini shows us many potential Karls and Bruneldas being, well, interviewed (shooting screen tests) for the job; however, he never does get round to making the Kafka film proper.[38]

Part Two deals with films that, bringing the game to a correspondingly higher level of explicitness, lie farther along the scale of the assimilation of prior material, and in some cases at the opposite end of it. In this group of *coextensive* re-creations I include films that show structural superposability with their literary counterparts in the sense of Èizenshtein's discussion in *Torito* already quoted. Here rightfully belong film-and-literature textual pairs that move from Beginning to Middle to End – or, alternatively, from Exposition to Complication to Peripety to Retardation to Denouement – by retaining a significant set of functionally equivalent devices. Some such devices include, variously combined, characters, plot, social background, point of view, and stylization. While films in this category are often *totally* coextensive with their predecessors, a few include an embedded shorter subunit with a strong coextensive link to a literary text; in this case they entertain what I suggest we call a *partially* coextensive relationship with that text.[39]

This part of the book accommodates two totally coextensive re-creations: Lattuada's *The Overcoat*, from Gogol's homonymous story, and the Tavianis' *The Night Sun*, from Tolstoy's *Father Sergius*. It was impossible for *Masters of Two Arts* to do without either of these films.[40] In a cultural-historical sense, they are too important, and technically they are simply too successful in providing cinema equivalents to literature, for the book to forgo them.[41]

In Part Three I explore two films from a group, relatively thin on the ground, whose approach differs in nature from the four variants covered so far. I am alluding to *mediated* re-creations. Among these I subsume films whose relation to their respective prior texts is filtered and to a large extent controlled by their choice to operate via an intermediate epiphany, be it from the theatre, the opera, or the cinema itself. (I am by definition excluding mere filmed theatre and filmed opera from this group.) In the case of Moretti's *sui generis* re-creation of

Pasternak's *Doktor Zhivago*, the much less than transparent go-between is David Lean's homologous love story – excerpts from which we are shown, five times, in *Palombella rossa*. For Mérimée and Rosi, the mediating intertext is Bizet's *Carmen*: an opera whose particular status, as we shall see, offers the director challenges and opportunities of a very particular nature.

The two *hypertextual* re-creations exemplified in Part Four of *Masters of Two Arts* belong to what may well be the least frequently attempted and most ambitious kind of all: the one in which directors deliberately strive to incorporate into their cinematic work a plurality of narrative texts by the same author. Thus, Rossellini's *Vanina Vanini* aimed at drawing upon, aside from Stendhal's novella by the same title, *Le rouge et le noir*, *The Charterhouse of Parma*, *Rome, Naples and Florence*, and *De l'amour* as well. Visconti's *Death in Venice*, for its part, 'contaminated' the fastidious Aschenbach of Thomas Mann's novella with the concerns – representationally speaking, the diseases – pertaining to Mann's own much later *Doktor Faustus*. It will be clear to readers perusing the relevant chapters why I believe that such a miscegenation was entirely successful in *Death in Venice* and disappointing in *Vanina Vanini*.[42]

And Pasolini's *Salò*? Pasolini's *Salò* was made, and intended, as perhaps the most inassimilable film by the most inassimilable of directors. I have given much thought to possible ways of 'categorizing' it, and have felt equally uneasy at each possible permutation. Eventually (not least in retrospective acknowledgment of the fact that κατηγορέω means 'to accuse') I have come to the conclusion that the best way methodologically to do justice to its irreducible status is to leave it *un-categor-ized*: on its own, in a space that does not undertake to assimilate or naturalize it. In that space, a space I will leave unmarked and unnumbered, *Salò* remains without common measure with anything else: certainly not with the generally constructive goals of artistic re-creation as we know it. May this be a homage of *pietas* to the one among the nine films in this book that it was unquestionably most painful for its director to make – the re-creation to end all creation.

I do not for a moment doubt that the material in *Masters of Two Arts* could have been arranged differently than it is. For, even leaving the scandal of *Salò* to one side, some attributions could have been decided in alternative manners. It can be argued, for example, that Rosi's *Carmen* has hypertextual characteristics that would also have made it reasonable to group it with the films of just that type.[43] And are *Vanina*

Vanini and *Death in Venice* not (total) coextensive re-creations as well? Furthermore, there is a strong component of cinema-within-the-cinema not only in *Palombella rossa* but also in *Intervista*, when a bedsheet doubles as an improvised screen to show us excerpts from the Trevi fountain scene in Fellini's own *La dolce vita* (1960).

My typology, too, could have been conceived differently.[44] In fact, why establish a typology at all? A straightforward chronological arrangement could have been just as revealing; it could have highlighted diachronic features in either filmmaking techniques or Italian cultural history, or both. Or why reject the conventionality of that very alphabetical order that we accept without demur from any of our dictionaries? Why not, *in fine*, an arrangement by the literary prototypes' nation? This, too, would have stressed particular cultural linkages. In sum, no one sequence is ideal, because no one sequence can univocally hierarchize all characteristics of each text, literary or cinematic. That hierarchy will always vary as a function of what it is one wishes to foreground in different contexts.

To conclude on the subject of contexts, I can never stress enough the paramount importance I attribute to the cultural context in which each of our films coalesced. Indeed, *Masters of Two Arts* could be described as being located at the juncture between two axes perpendicular to each other: one concerned with evolutionary issues (how the literary system and the cinema system have mutually interacted in several cases over the last half-century), the other interested in cultural-historical issues (how the cinema system has interacted with the social system – in our case, post–Second World War Italy). In other words, the sequence of my chapters groups films that share certain affinities, so as to highlight the literary-cinematic aspect of the questions raised in this book; but the chapters themselves include cultural-historical considerations that should help my readers make sense not only of *the ways* a literary text was re-created by a given director, but also of *the contextual reasons why* one particular re-creation occurred rather than almost infinite alternative possibilities. Cinematic re-creation never occurs as a random gratuitous act, but can only be explained in full by considering the entire context – the individual, artistic, and social continuum – from which it arises.

Most recently, Dudley Andrew urged film-and-literature scholarship to 'take a sociological turn.'[45] I think this points (I shall not say whether a mite too energetically) in the correct direction: film directors – as we all do – live and act in a complex historical situation, and they respond to cultural stimuli not in an abstract, purely idiosyncratic manner, but in one that is conditioned by intellectual, technological, social, and last but certainly not least economic circumstances. *Masters of Two Arts* may, of course, prove to be unequal to the task of attempting to pursue many concerns of this calibre at one stroke, but I feel the times and circumstances in the field are now at last ripe for an attempt. Human knowledge grows by accretion; other scholars will no doubt be able to improve upon *Masters of Two Arts* – a positive outcome that, in fact, I hope its appearance will call forth.

Conventions and Style

Now for some technical remarks about format. When indicating a title, I use English wherever possible (e.g., I write *The Night Sun* rather than *Il sole anche di notte*), with two exceptions: when a specific usage has already established itself (e.g., *Intervista* does not become *Interview*); and to avoid ambiguities between literary prototype and filmic re-creation, if the two titles translate identically into English. Thus, for example, I will henceforth set apart Gogol's *Shinel'* from Lattuada's *Il cappotto*, and Thomas Mann's *Der Tod in Venedig* from Visconti's *La morte a Venezia*, by calling each of them just that.

In my chapters, as a rule I quote in English translation (mine, if none was published as of my writing); the original-language equivalents can be found in the notes, along with bibliographical references. Wherever I have had to alter pre-existing translations in order better to render certain aspects of their respective originals, I have utilized brackets to mark off the modified wording.

In notes, reference to an English edition, if any, immediately precedes that to the corresponding original, with a simple semicolon between the two. If I give no bibliographical indication when I quote from the dialogue of a film, I am drawing directly upon the Italian-language dialogue of the video version currently available in North America or Italy.

Russian *ë*, always stressed, is pronounced [yo]. The book's bibliography (where originals are listed first) includes diacritics such as the Russian soft sign – e.g., Gogol', Pashen'ka – which I tend to ignore in my text (Gogol, Pashenka). However, I simply could not bring myself to drop the soft sign in the Russian word for 'overcoat,' *shinel'* (*l'* being very different from *l* – it sounds like the Italian *gl* of *luglio*). While in the text I adopt the most common scholarly system of transliteration into English, some established spellings (e.g., Dostoevsky) are retained. However, with the last name of perhaps the greatest film director of the twentieth century, I do the opposite: to make that name sound like something its human referent might have recognized, I transliterate it literally, albeit unusually, as Èizenshtein – a small effort on my part, and well deserved by its recipient. In notes, I use the technical system current in Slavic studies.[46]

A final annotation on the expository strategy of *Masters of Two Arts*. To the extent of my ability, I have striven to avoid applying a uniform, goose-step rhythm to the book. Some of my analyses are longer, some shorter; depending on circumstances, some provide an ampler rendition of narrative content, while others almost entirely dispense with it and focus instead on metatextual commentary. (In particular, I have devoted more space to a close, parallel/contrastive reading of literary and filmic texts in the cases where the film is simply not distributed in North America – *Il cappotto* – or can only be obtained with difficulty – *Vanina Vanini*). Some of the artists (Gogol, Visconti) receive greater attention with respect to *Sekundärliteratur* than do others (Kafka, Pasternak). Rather than explain each situation in pedantic detail, I prefer to stress preventively that such a variety arises from nothing more arcane than the varying relations which re-created texts may entertain with those that generated them – *and*, if I may confess to this, a certain inclination of mine in favour of expository variety for its own simple sake. Although by this procedure I may have caused uniformity and predictability to suffer, I am convinced that in the process *Masters of Two Arts* has gained other qualities no less desirable than uniformity and predictability. Could it be, in any case, that an aesthetic preference for symmetry is but one among our culturally conditioned prejudices?

Beyond a generic appeal to the non-adjudicability of taste, my own priorities in the matter of *ars poetica* avowedly go in the same direction as Verlaine's. Rejecting the symmetry of the even (*pair*) twelve-syllable alexandrine in favour of its odd (*impair*) poetic alternatives, nine- and eleven-syllable verses, the French poet argued:

> Music, music before all things,
> Uneven rhythm suits it well
> In air more vague and soluble
> With nothing there that weighs or clings.[47]

De la musique avant toute chose,
Et pour cela préfère l'Impair
Plus vague et plus soluble dans l'air,
Sans rien en lui qui pèse ou qui pose.[48]

It is for just such a mobility that *Masters of Two Arts* strives, aware of the danger of falling into the opposite extreme of a frozen artificiality: the artificiality of rhetoric, whose neck Verlaine invites us to wring only a few verses later in the 'Art poétique' just quoted. *Et tout le reste est littérature.*

PART ONE

Epigraphic Re-creations

Italy, the Illegible Land:
Mignon Has Left (1988)

Mignon

'Dost know the land where citrons, lemons, grow,
Gold oranges 'neath dusky foliage glow,
From azure sky are blowing breezes soft,
The myrtles still, the laurel stands aloft?
                              'tis there! 'tis there!
I would with thee, O my beloved one, go!'
...

On finishing her song for the second time, she stood silent for a moment, looked keenly at Wilhelm, and asked him, '*Know'st* thou the land' – It must mean Italy,' said Wilhelm: 'Where didst thou get the little song?' – 'Italy!' said Mignon, with an earnest air. 'If thou go to Italy, take me along with thee; for I am too cold here.' – 'Hast thou been there already, little dear?' said Wilhelm. But the child was silent, and nothing more could be got out of her.[1]

In whichever way we may wish to identify geographically the utopian region that serves as a background to *Wilhelm Meister's Years of Apprenticeship* (*Wilhelm Meisters Lehrjahre*, 1796), there can be little doubt that in Goethe's epoch-making *Bildungsroman* the Italian rarefied landscape acts as the ideally tractable and tameable space for the young protagonist's growth in apprehending and understanding life.[2]

As in every novel of apprenticeship, trial, and education, the conceptual basis for Goethe's pedagogical journey is what I would describe as a hermeneutic metaphor. The ideal balance between activity and passivity, between learning and guidance – or, in slightly more schematic terms, between the 'raw material' of life and the 'art' of living it – must be struck through a complex process of scouting and reconnoitring, which eventually leads to appropriate decision-making. In a word, the 'classical' concept of apprenticeship hinges on the protagonist's literacy in interpreting an essentially readable world. Indeed, *Wilhelm Meister*'s Italy is an archetypal land of legibility, in which, by the covert actions of a mysterious Tower Society, the imponderable workings of fate, and the protagonist's own fertile receptivity, an apparently incoherent mass of facts can be disentangled, organized, and utilized.

The culmination of Goethe's Utopia of readability may well be the moment when Wilhelm receives his 'Certificate of Apprenticeship,' whose last words summarize what could be termed the very paradigm of the mechanisms of growth: 'A true pupil learns how to [develop] the unknown from the known, and thereby [approaches] mastery.'[3] Mignon's land, Italy, is a fundamental step in the development of Wilhelm's status as a cosmic hermenut. After knowledge and understanding have been achieved, Mignon becomes dispensable. As a now superfluous symbol of a readable landscape, she can be caused to fade away; she can return to the ethereal world to which she had always belonged.[4] Once Wilhelm is ennobled with the diploma that consecrates him as an interpreter of praxis, Mignon can 'leave' – she can vanish and live forever in the world beyond,[5] guaranteeing from On High, *ne varietur*, her language: the language of art, cast as an absolute interpretive grid on the sound and fury of brute, uncontextualized facts.

Divorces, Italian Style

Francesca Archibugi's *Mignon Has Left* is a film about hermeneutic divorces. *Mignon Has Left* puts Goethe's canonic concept of readability exactly downside up: her Italy is a country in which signs have floated away from concepts, and the universe of legibility is radically disrupted. Today's Mignon, still the adolescent virgin that she was in Goethe (though now only possibly one by the end of the film), is sent to Italy against her will, irresistibly dislikes the peninsula's mindless cacophony, rejects the inauthentic consciousness in which it drowns, and, masterfully defeating deceit with deceit, finally manages to leave it by resorting to the no longer inadmissible semi-scandal of a (feigned) pregnancy.

What remains behind her is a substantially less than transparent landscape, in which most people are 'fulfilled' only in a material, survivalist sense. Here too – indeed, especially here – the dictum contained in Wilhelm's 'Certificate of Apprenticeship' holds true: 'He who works only with signs, is a pedant, a hypocrite or a botcher. There are many such, and they get on well together.'[6] In a perverse, limited sense, such people do 'get on well together' after all – if one doesn't demand too much of life, that is.

The extent to which Archibugi reverses Goethe in re-creating him is striking.[7] In synthesis, the Mignon of the film, far from being of Italian origin, is French-born and -raised; far from being an estranged child, she has, if anything, too many relatives in Rome; and far from being the quintessential *enfant du pays*, she remains a permanent linguistic, cultural, and existential outsider in the peninsula. Most importantly, of course, she conflicts with the local pedagogical principles and practices, or, rather, with the anarchic absence thereof.

Her main, and utterly un-romantic, trait is an ostentatious detachedness. Faced with banality and vulgarity in the everyday life of an almost timeless Rome's neighbourhood *proles*, it is easy for her to dabble casually in local forms of entertainment: an occasional party, or a fling with the bully in the group, which appear to leave no more dramatic traces than a fall from a scooter when riding in the rain. Numbed by her own sense of abandonment when she eventually realizes that her French relatives have merely 'parked' her in Rome for a few months during an embarrassing tiff with Parisian magistrates, she comes to the sad, but at least analgesic, conclusion that 'no one ever loves, no one,' as she rather melodramatically tells her friend and peer Giorgio after her motorcycle accident.

Giorgio is the second protagonist of Archibugi's *Bildungsroman*. If Mignon is that which probably every unwelcome child wishes to be in its own family romance (namely, extremely beautiful, extremely rich, and extremely indifferent to the petty turmoil of the world) and does that which every misunderstood child wishes it could do in its own environment, given the same circumstances (namely, get out of it with a ruse), in the film we find an alter ego of Mignon's in the form of yet another marginal person, who gapes at her haughty refusal with the envious frustration of a socially even more inarticulate outsider. This is poor Giorgio, none other than the film's first-person narrator, who happens to have no Parisian branch of the Forbicioni family upon which to fall back.

Giorgio and Mignon share the same uncomprehending glance of the fool that, in Bakhtin's words, 'makes strange the world of social conventionality': they are, in this sense, but one and the same character.[8] The radical difference between the two, however, consists in the fact that Mignon can in the end return to what she perceives as her original Eden, while Giorgio is mired in the intractable meaninglessness of the present world. Mignon manages to rise above *la storia* (understood as both 'history' *and* 'plot'), whereas Giorgio is steeped in its flow and can make no sense whatever of it. *Mignon has left* – and what is one to do to imitate her? *Mignon has left* – but not everyone is as wily a world-reader as she is. *Mignon has left* – but the dose of mothballs swallowed by Giorgio turns out to be grotesquely inadequate to assure the hoped-for parallel departure. So, he will have to stay.

'Bella ciao,' 'Good-bye My Beauty,' the song of the Partisans' 1943–5 *Resistenza* against the Nazi-Fascists that is ludicrously sung in the family car during a Sunday outing, symbolizes on more than one level Giorgio's un-Mignon-like epistemological obtuseness. The song eloquently testifies to the evacuation of meaning suffered by semantic systems: no longer tied to a legible history, such as the one practised in Italy during the times of neorealism, meanings now drift away and out of the Forbicionis' sight. The ensuing loss of guiding parameters for the generations whose Italy is no longer a Republic (as the official formula would have it) 'founded on the *Resistenza*' lead formerly anchored selves to *wave good-bye* to their Beauteous one – at the representational level, of course, Mignon, but conceptually history, alias the congruence between reality and our reading of it. Mignon and Giorgio convey an identical anguish about apprehending Italy; however, while Mignon need not bother for very long, Giorgio is in Rome to stay, and he is stuck without a way of coming to terms with his own world.

A main feature that Goethe's and Archibugi's Mignons have in common is that they are relatively unproblematic; as prime, elemental creatures, they could hardly develop. By contrast, Wilhelm and, for our purposes, Giorgio, are left to stand at the beginning of their own pedagogical novels, trying to match signs with meanings – de facto, Rome with its myth (or with its map, as the film revealingly does as early as its opening sequence). It is just here that trouble lies ahead for Giorgio.

In Giorgio's post-ideological, minimalist Italy, adults and adolescents alike seem to be cheating each other (and themselves) out of their true self, and are content, or at least tolerably content, merely to be what they appear to be. Is life then no more than a mirror of sorts, the dream of a mediocre ambition and of an ambitious mediocrity? Or *is there* even a 'true' self in those circumstances? Are we to take the *treason of signs* for granted – and call precisely such an acknowledgment the moment of transition to an adulthood whose supposedly ennobling trait would be the renunciation of all claim to any existential knowledge whatever? These are the questions that Giorgio implicitly asks, and on which he would need, at the very least, his co-protagonist Mignon's help and alliance. But Mignon leaves him behind: narratively halved, and lost in the constitutive stupidity (*bêtise*) of so many a Flaubertian character.

The epistemological loss symbolized by Mignon's departure, however, gives way to Archibugi's stubborn refusal to accept, for example, Frédéric Moreau's 'uncertain' rereading of his own sentimental education.[9] In a glimmer of hope, Giorgio at least bravely reacts to the disappointments of life by declining to give in to the hermeneutic illiteracy characterizing Frédéric's justly famous (or infamous) final, retrospective comment: 'That was the happiest time we ever had!'[10]

Illiteracy, Literal and Otherwise

The centre stage of *Mignon Has Left* is strategically occupied by the library, true vanishing point of the film's various allusions to the readability of reality – or, more exactly, to its maddening illegibility. The written text, which in Goethe amounted to no less than a material, tangible object guaranteeing Wilhelm's acquired dignity as a pupil (that is to say, as a reader and authorized interpreter of life), is here demoted to a shadow existence: the bookstore is simply a means for Mr Forbicioni Sr to earn a living. In the late 1980s, no longer does the spirit of the texts vivify the livelihood of a story's main characters; it is, conversely, the books' status as a commodity that is called upon to ensure a group of people's material survival.

Worse, the bookstore is the very locus where the betrayal of meanings is consummated: Giorgio's father improperly uses it as a convenient bachelor's apartment for an extramarital affair with his shop assistant. It is significant that the unreadability of reality extends to Giorgio's very inability to interpret facts he accidentally witnesses there: he thinks he sees Mignon lying on the floor and making love with her local boyfriend – although he may in fact be observing his father and the current employee similarly entertaining each other.[11] Archibugi's camera takes great pains to leave the question open, consistently viewing and describing reality through the undecidability of a non-committal glance. As a result the bookstore, experienced during the 1970s as a point of exchange of meaning in Italian society, loses its status qua moral hub and becomes the very epicentre of interpersonal failure. From the interpretation of signs to the arbitrariness of signs, the circle has been closed.[12]

Mignon Has Left stages the mad rebellion of signs against their systems. Or, to put the matter in more representational form: in the film, Italy is the *illegible landscape* of Giorgio's painful years of apprenticeship. Clearly, Archibugi's film is a work of the late 1980s, in which hermeneutic systems have crumbled; in it, any next best goal remaining after the demise of world-changing and world-building – whether pursued in revolutionary songs or elsewhere – is yet to be determined.

Furious at Goethe's nonchalant dispatching of Mignon after what he felt amounted to narrative exploitation, Novalis pronounced *Wilhelm Meister* 'a *Candide* against poetry.'[13] Should we take the cue from Novalis and interpret *Mignon Has Left* as a film about the difficulty of accepting the shrinkage of human aspirations from the all-encompassing ambition to rewrite the book of the universe (as the 1970s by and large attempted to do) to the comparatively narrow-minded goal of, to put it in Candide's wise words, cultivate one's garden – as the decade of the 1980s with obsessive insistence demanded?

Even that, however, may prove too rosy a view. The existential disarray in young Giorgio's adolescence reminds us that this peculiar sort of 'gardening' of the self requires protagonistic mastery over a highly sophisticated system of signs, social and otherwise; lacking which, success (i.e., happiness) may well be no easier to attain in selfish and monadic times than it was in the previous epoch, more absorbed by the task of correcting the spelling mistakes in the book of universal history. Thus it is that Giorgio's own apprenticeship leads him to reverse Goethe's confidence: exactly contrary to the biblical Saul alluded to at the end of *Wilhelm Meister*, the child in the film goes out into the world 'in search of a kingdom' and finds only 'she-asses' instead.[14]

But could that be the last word? *Mignon Has Left* is Archibugi's painstaking dramatization of a final refusal to accept Giorgio's, the outsider child's, gardening-style pessimistic statement about his own world and his own times: 'Cacti live happily, because they content themselves with little.'[15] It *is* true, it *cannot* be true – it must be a typo in the cosmic text.

Soteriology, Cinecittà-style:
America and *Intervista* (1987)

In the *république des lettres*, all artistic sympathies have equal dignity, but some seem to be warmer than others. It is, for example, hardly surprising to see with what love Francesco Rosi, a southern European to a fault, is attracted to the southern heritage that inspired his rendition of *Carmen* or of García Márquez's *Chronicle of a Death Foretold* (*Cronaca di una morte annunciata*, 1987). Likewise, the artistic affinity that led Visconti to go beyond the borders of Italian culture and delve into the inner struggles of the 'poor folk' of Dostoevsky's *White Nights* requires little hermeneutic effort, as does his personalized version of Thomas Mann's *Der Tod in Venedig*. Fellini's interest in the world of Petronius's *Satyricon* is another case in point among the many that could be mentioned. Some artists, it would seem, were simply born with a manifest destiny to meet each other and to shed light on each other in the realm of creation; and there seems to be something of the inevitable about the works of art that resulted from such encounters.

On the face of it, no such inevitability seems to arise when we compare Federico Fellini's artistic universe to that of Franz Kafka. On the one hand, we encounter a Prague intellectual, an introvert raised in the strict discipline of the conservative family of a Jewish merchant, a loner in a lonely group that attempted to acquire social recognition in a hostile environment but could rarely successfully interact with the Czech- and the German-speaking communities. On the other hand, we have a child of the archetypically exuberant Romagna, who later moved to the eminently social, cosmopolitan city of Rome (itself possibly the first and most significant cultural melting pot in the history of Western civilization) during one of the historical epochs when Rome was perhaps at its most social and cosmopolitan.

On the one hand, we have a stern world of perceived guilt and expected punishment, where the chain of logical causality is suppressed and replaced by the chains of an inscrutable necessity; on the other, we find a carefree atmosphere in which even sin smacks of pleasure – especially so, it goes without saying, for the sin par excellence of modern Christianity, the carnal one – because sin too, as an index of biological effervescence, is an instrument of nature, and thus ultimately a witness to the sanctity of Creation. On the one hand, we have a hidden God, who has vanished from the world and with his apophany has removed the key to the meaning of an orphaned universe; a God who has only left behind – whether by narratorial oversight, Freudian slip, or deliberate hint to readers in the future – a threatening sword where one would expect the flame of liberty: 'As ... Karl Rossmann ... sailed slowly into New York harbour, he suddenly saw the Statue of Liberty, which had already been in view for some time, as though in an intenser sunlight. *The sword* in her hand seemed only just to have been raised aloft, and the unchained winds blew about her form.'[1] On the other hand, we see a pliable God, utterly uninterested in punishment. Fellini's God seems to send a number of (often grotesque) representatives to earth – as Goethe's does with Mephisto – for the sole purpose of stimulating the Good by spurring it on through the thorn of Evil. He seems to act as though prohibition alone could endow human behaviour with the ultimate attribute in the exercise of freedom: transgressivity. In Fellini, the presence of guilt and sin, even when most keenly felt (I am thinking, to mention but one obvious episode, of Juliet-the-child's ordeal on the grill in *Juliet of the Spirits / Giulietta degli spiriti*, 1965), is never a reason for paralysis. Quite the contrary, in Fellini's world non-compliant behaviour is a powerful instrument on the way to assertion of the ego; and thus, among other things, ultimately also a device allowing for a lively, exuberant narrativity.

That Fellini should draw on Kafka for *Intervista* therefore strikes one as a bet running against many odds; and the discovery that the Japanese who turn up at the gates of Cinecittà for the eponymous interview find him engrossed in the shooting of screen tests for a film version of Kafka's American novel comes as a definite surprise to spectators who presumed they knew what Fellini and Kafka are all about. How to discern a way to reconcile and bring under a common sheet these two improbable bedfellows?

To be sure, Fellini knew and admired Kafka for reasons that are easy to explain within the cultural history of twentieth-century Europe. It was at a time when Fascism still stood that the Italian director, then only a relatively obscure journalist in Rome, became acquainted with the universe of the absurd created and popularized by the man from the Jewish-German-Czech 'freezing pot.' Fellini recalls:

> One day a colleague, Marcello Marchesi, came from Milan with a book, *The Metamorphosis* by Franz Kafka ... The unconscious, which Dostoevsky had used to probe and analyze emotions, became, in this book, material for the plot itself ... Here was the individual unconscious, a shadow zone, a private cellar suddenly clarified ...
>
> Kafka moved me profoundly. I was struck by the way he confronted the mystery of things, their unknown quality, the sense of being in a labyrinth, and daily life turned magical.[2]

At this time, however, we are still in 1941–3, almost half a century before the film *Intervista*, and fully in the shadow of the dictatorships that make Kafka's 'magical' (or nightmarish) anticipations seem perfectly adequate to, and in tune with, the European *Zeitgeist*. Furthermore, the text that came in from the cold – Fellini was in Rome, Marchesi brought the book with him from Milan – was not the novel about America, but the novella about cockroaches. So there must be more at stake in the broad Kafka/Fellini relationship than Fellini's extant statements on the subject reveal. What exactly?

The riddle can begin to unravel if we take a closer look at the information contained in two dependent clauses that Kafka's narrator adroitly ensconces in the opening paragraph of the unpublished manuscript that came to be known as either *America* (*Amerika*) or, in the most recent translation, *The Man Who Disappeared* (*Der Verschollene*, i.e., *The Lost One*) (published posthumously in 1927 [1912]):

> As the seventeen-year-old Karl Rossmann,
>   who had been sent to America by his unfortunate parents
>   because a maid had seduced him
>   and had a child by him,
> sailed slowly into New York harbour ...[3]

Ecce homo. The decisive link between Kafka and Fellini, between *The Man Who Disappeared* and *Intervista*, can be established, I surmise, not so much – or at any rate not only – by way of the aura of a 'daily life turned magical,' but also because of a specific thematic analogy between Kaf-ka's preoccupations in the novel and one of Fellini's favourite leitmo-tivs: namely, that of the coming of age of the (male) adolescent, an autobiographical double of the artist-director. Fellini's interest in Kafka's novel is overdetermined: it is in the field of existential edu-cation, especially sentimental education, in the area of the trials and apprenticeship of life undergone by adolescence, that they find a demonstrably commom theme. It is their shared interest in the *Bildung-sroman* that brings the two artists together.

Kafka's Novel of Education

'So then you're free?' she asked.
'Yes, I'm free,' said Karl, and nothing seemed more worthless to him.[4]

The fragments now collectively published and referred to as either *Amer-ica* or *The Man Who Disappeared* belong to Kafka's early works. They are the closest thing to a *Bildungsroman* that Kafka's works can offer us.[5]

In the novel we can observe tentative attempts on the protagonist's part to come to terms with the social dynamics of a comparatively (for Kafka) realistic-looking world, and to develop strategies aimed at evolu-tion and growth. On the basis of evidence from his letters, I believe that Kafka's ideal model – though not necessarily his immediate blueprint – was Flaubert's already alluded-to peculiar and somewhat perverse mas-terpiece in the genre, *Sentimental Education*.[6] The fame of *Sentimental Education* rests on the fact that it evacuates the traditional genre of the novel of education and consecrates an alternative tradition destined to great fortune in the twentieth century – a tradition in which the notion of the individual's meaningful insertion in a well-ordered society is even-tually exploded.[7] It surely was because of these salient features that it had such an impact on the avid young reader from Prague.[8]

The further development of Kafka's own artistic career could indeed be argued to have brought the descending curve of the modern novel of education to something very close to its terminal point: *The Trial* (*Der Prozeß*, 1925 [1914]) and *The Castle* (*Das Schloss*, 1926 [1922]) complete the subversion of the entire spectrum of premises on which the concept of growth through education and 'trial' (in an entirely different sense) had been predicated since the times of Goethe's *Wilhelm Meister*, Rous-seau's *Émile*, or Fénelon's *Télémaque*. Kafka's American text shows unequivocal signs that the disarticulation of certain historically connoted optimistic assumptions in Western culture(s) is about to enter its final stage; the novel's atmosphere is a recognizably 'Kafkaesque' one, in the sense that we lend the word today,[9] and the lack of a clear-cut thrust in the ending leaves Karl's fate, at best, in the balance. All that is certain is that, by the time he altogether discontinued work on his quasi-*Bildungsroman* in 1914, Kafka had drafted six numbered and titled chapters, followed by two more unnumbered and untitled ones that seem to be complete and in sequence, plus three fragments of unequal length that were probably destined to be part of the novel's conclusion. Unlike the canonical novel of education, Kafka's American text shows a protagonist whose development spirals increasingly downward as the plot thickens (or rather, thins out), with an only remote possibility of improvement in his situation in the last major fragment.[10]

At the beginning of the novel the protagonist, Karl Rossmann, lands in New York for the reasons already mentioned. Instead of pursuing certain family connections he has there, he moves on and decides to walk to the neighbouring city of Ramses. Always dragging with him a trunk that contains his clothes (along with money, documents, and food), he stops at an inn on the extreme outskirts of the metropolis, where he meets two youths, the Irishman Robinson and the Frenchman Delamarche. The two, who also are jobless, are slightly older than he. Wasting no time on scruples, they are able to use and abuse Karl at will, taking advantage of his complete social and financial naivety. During their march inland they steal Karl's money, take his parents' photograph, and exploit him in every possible way. At this juncture, Karl breaks up with the two and picks up a job as a lift boy in a hotel, working hard in a noisy and lonely environment.

One day, a drunken Robinson shows up at the hotel's elevators, once more harassing Karl and demanding money from him. Karl wants to drag him out of the hotel, but Robinson feels sick and throws up on the stairs. To avoid a scandal, Karl just about carries Robinson to his own bed in the elevator boys' room; in so doing, however, he abandons his post for a sufficiently long time to be found out. The head waiter and the head porter grill him at length for this lapse and put him on a full-fledged trial. Narrowly managing to leave the building, Karl literally runs away from the premises. Outside the hotel, he once more runs into Robinson, who has meanwhile been beaten to a pulp by the elevator boys he had insulted and challenged in his drunkenness, and is now being loaded into a taxicab. Karl boards the cab with Robinson and is driven off with him to the latter's place in a remote suburb.

These events, which make up the storyline of the six complete chapters in Kafka's American novel, set the stage for the situation rehearsed in Fellini's *Intervista*. When we first see Kafka's text at work in Cinecittà, its events are already well advanced; it is, in fact, the novel's paralipomena that are used by Fellini for his re-creation. What comes next is eagerly used by the director to screen young protagonists for the Kafka roles he has in mind.

Karl abandons all his personal belongings, including his papers, at the hotel. When a policeman attempts to stop him, he flees. Only Delamarche's intervention opens up an escape route for him – one, however, that entails the burden of permanent dependence on his saviour's hardly generously dispensed goodwill. The apartment that Delamarche and his lover, a buxom former singer called Brunelda, share with Robinson now becomes Karl's domicile too. The young Rossmann and Robinson take turns in serving and humouring the despotic couple, with Karl, the more recent acquisition in the *ménage à quatre*, sitting lowest on the hierarchical scale. Clearly, there is little logical or psychological consequentiality to this string of events (and the following ones); as is normal in Kafka, the *post hoc, propter hoc* relation is here systematically undone. With the abolition of causal development becoming the most distinctive feature in the novel's narrative universe, we now experience the surreal occurrences in Delamarche's apartment from Karl's nihiloscient viewpoint.

'Such a heat, Delamarche' are the first words of Brunelda's we hear. Lazy, capricious, vain, irascible – all characteristics she shares with her younger lover – Brunelda does little but sit or lie around on her sofa, complaining about the heat of an East Coast summer evening. True to their personalities, the two order their servants out onto the balcony so as to protect the privacy of a cooling bath for Brunelda. Robinson and Karl oblige, and, in a peculiar re-enactment of the Oedipal triangle, accept to remove themselves jointly to the liminal position of the observer, offering two complementary variants (respectively, the eager and the uncomprehending) of the voyeur's role.

Neurotic exchanges between the four tenants pepper evening life in Kafka's upstate New York – as does the hardly abundant repast consumed by the two outsiders, which consists of a hodge-podge of leftovers:

> Karl, getting up, watched as Robinson, without getting up, crept over on his belly, and reaching out his hands, from under the chair pulled out a silver-gilt dish of the sort that, say, visiting-cards are usually kept in. This dish, however, contained one half of a very black sausage, a few thin cigarettes, an

already opened but still rather full sardine tin spilling oil, and a mess of mainly squashed and caked together sweets. Then he produced a large piece of bread and a sort of perfume bottle, which seemed to contain something other than perfume ...'[11]

That open sardine tin is destined to travel very far indeed, as the ability to lick its contents with perverse abandon will be used by the Famous Italian Director portrayed in *Intervista* as the test of manhood for a string of applicants for the role.

Karl attempts in vain to make sense of the profusion of objects that has taken over Delamarche's and Brunelda's place. The apartment strikes him (and us) as repulsive not only because of the filth it harbours but also, or perhaps primarily, owing to the proliferation of the objects it includes.[12] Karl does undertake a flight attempt, but he meets with hard-nosed repression at the hands of both Delamarche and Brunelda. After two interludes,[13] the manuscript shows an interruption similar to that of a chapter ending – a chapter that could be said to amount to an unnumbered chapter 7. The end of this potential chapter 7 suspends and postpones Brunelda's cooling relief: she falls asleep, sighing and tossing about on her couch, 'apparently troubled by bad dreams.'[14]

The next, also unnumbered, chapter consists of Kafka's *pezzo di bravura* about Brunelda's bath, into which we are plunged as abruptly as Karl is: '"Up! Up!" cried Robinson, the moment Karl opened his eyes in the morning.'[15] In a thinly veiled allegory, the bath foregrounds the sexual act, which Delamarche and Brunelda interpret as an exhausting to-and-fro game of dominance and submission. Predictably, immersion into a bathtub looms as the parallel and equivalent test of womanhood for Fellini's extra-large hopeful Bruneldas in Rome.

Mere pawns in this comedy, in which they are in turn teased and rebuffed, Karl and Robinson prefer straightforwardly servile tasks. Such is the one, imposed upon them later on in the afternoon, to procure breakfast for the two tyrannical parental figures. This part, which could be termed chapter 8, comes to an end with the adult couple's ludicrous satisfaction with the breakfast the two youths have managed to scrape together for them by doctoring disgusting leftovers.

This is also the end of the continuous part of the novel in the manuscript. Two long fragments and a shorter one are appended in most recent editions.

The first fragment shows that a dramatic upset has occurred in the intervening blank space of narration. Robinson and Delamarche have both disappeared; in an about-face of paramount symbolic significance,

Karl and Brunelda are now a couple of sorts, united by their loneliness in their struggle for survival. Brunelda, who has by now lost all her residual professional dignity and self-respect, has swollen to monstrous proportions; no longer able to walk, she must be transported on a wheelchair, at the cost of stoical efforts on both her part and Karl's. In this fragment, she appears as a sweaty lump of flesh, covered with a cloth (why exactly, we are not told), resembling in size and shape 'ten sacks of potatoes' or 'a whole apple harvest.'[16] This situation too is explicitly evoked in *Intervista* as we witness preparations for the Kafka film getting under way.

Where is Brunelda so secretively being moved to? She is taking up residence in a mysteriously defined 'Institution No. 25' located in a narrow dark alley. It is significant that the normally unfocused Karl at once notices the dirt in the building – a dirt that materializes and objectifies the nausea that permeates his relationship to the world:

> What did alarm him as he pulled the wagon into the corridor was the dirt there, although he'd been expecting it too. It wasn't, when he looked at it more closely, any tangible sort of dirt. The stone flags in the passage had been swept almost clean, the whitewash on the walls wasn't old, the artificial palms only slightly dusty, and yet everything was greasy and repulsive, it was as if everything had been somehow misused, and no cleaning on earth could ever make it better.[17]

This closes the novel's section that could be labelled 'Brunelda's Departure.'

Our Kafkaesque novel of education then takes an even more enigmatic turn with what is presumed to have been the core of its concluding chapter, centred on the symbolical institution called in the manuscript 'The Theatre of Oklahoma.' The 'Theatre' fragment combines images of North American plenty, freely available to Kafka in contemporaneous travelogues for the benefit of hungry European would-be emigrants, with apocalyptic figures of a decidedly biblical inspiration.[18] In this gigantic *theatrum mundi* Karl finally gains some form of acceptance, albeit at an infinitesimal level. Though he still has no 'legitimation papers'[19] to prove his – hardly existent – qualifications, the immigration officers sign him up too: each and all are allowed to join the Theatre's fold. Karl does not want to reveal his true name to the institution; he chooses instead a pseudonym we recognize as highly connotated, that of 'Negro.' And as 'Negro' he enlists for the New World, the world of salvation for the harried masses. This section breaks off just as the train meant to take the newly hired employees to 'Oklahoma' is making preparations for departure.

The last fragment contained in the manuscript is barely one printed page long. It describes the journey (or, more precisely, the beginning of the journey) by which Karl and his fellow workers ride a train to the unspecified inland location where the Theatre's promise of unconditional acceptance – physical *and* metaphysical – is to be fulfilled. Only now, Kafka writes, does Karl realize the immensity of the American continent:

> On the first day they travelled over a high mountain range. Blue-black formations of rock approached the train in sharp wedges, they leaned out of the window and tried in vain to see their peaks, narrow dark cloven valleys opened, with a finger they traced the direction in which they disappeared, broad mountain streams came rushing like great waves on their hilly courses, and, pushing thousands of little foaming wavelets ahead of them, they plunged under the bridges over which the train passed, so close that the chill breath of them made their faces shudder.[20]

These are the last words in Kafka's text. It is on this train that Karl, having disappeared from the sight of, in rapid succession, his European family, his American relatives, and his sadistic 'friends,' vanishes from our view as well.[21] As foreshadowed in the original title of the novel, with the interruption of the manuscript he becomes 'the lost one' for us in name and in fact.[22] This train ride will reoccur in Fellini, in materially similar, yet deeply transformed, circumstances.

What, then, of Karl's education, sentimental above all? Kafka's American novel pushes to an extreme the paralysis of the *Bildungsroman* so convincingly carried out by Flaubert's *Sentimental Education* – minus, crucially, the Flaubertian irony. Kafka's novelty consists in his injecting into the world of adolescent experiences that tragic sense of life, that suffocating perception of powerlessness in the face of an inscrutable universe, that is the characteristic hallmark of his poetic world. Of the inherited literary form, only the structures remain; gone is the significant nucleus, the contents, vanished on the way to Oklahoma along with the concept of evolution ('*Entwicklungs*roman' as synonym of 'Bildungsroman') that had originally inspired the genre. In the experience of Kafka's Karl, work, friendships, politics, sex are no longer subject to a dialectical process of error and apprenticeship, but have instead become dehumanized spaces for other people's practice of unsubtle and at times outright brutal strategies of power. In the novel, the drive toward psychological depth is thus understandably replaced by the quest for a soteriological goal that remains ever invisible beyond the transcendent horizon.

Kafka's long-time friend and first posthumous editor, Max Brod, made strenuous efforts to inscribe the novel into a pre-existing nineteenth-century tradition, presenting it in the terminology familiar to his contemporaries. These, however, trained in the canonical hermeneutic criteria, were perforce unequipped to understand and appreciate either the effects Kafka was striving for or the artistic implications of his existential views.[23] To paraphrase Bakhtin, Max Brod did not know, or at any rate chose to ignore, the single most important thing about his late friend Franz Kafka – namely, *that he was Franz Kafka*, not a weird Theodor Fontane or a Charles Dickens gone astray; and that by merely being himself he had at one stroke rendered the nineteenth century's interpretive parameters obsolete.[24]

The American novel represented for Kafka an incursion into a symbolic land of freedom – a freedom promised, though not quite achieved in fact – that parallels the one undertaken during the same years, at a different metonymical level, by millions of European emigrants. A spiritual rather than an economic migrant, Kafka sought in the locus he calls 'America' an experimental space in which to test fictional ways of lightening, or possibly dissolving altogether, what can variously, but in the last analysis equivalently, be termed (to put the matter in theological terms) the crushing burden of guilt, or (to use the language of psychoanalysis) the Oedipal complex, or again (as deconstructionist theory suggests) the absence from the world, perceived as a system of signs, of an ultimate and certain guarantee for meanings. Finally (to couch the matter in terms of cultural history), Kafka could be argued to have sought to overcome in his metaphysical North America the intolerable prejudice of European nineteenth-century philosophical teleology, internationally adopted by the bourgeoisie, according to which all that is real is rational and all that is rational is real – a theory whose ultimate logical conclusion is that any form of thought criticizing the real amounts, by definition, to madness.[25]

It is in this hoped-for fictional testing ground that Karl Rossmann finally vanishes, trying to redeem the old world by travelling West. Surprisingly, he eventually resurfaces – if only as a tentative narrative space – in Fellini's Cinecittà.

Fellini's Novel of Education

Yes, I believe that, in the last analysis, everything one writes is of an autobiographical nature. But this can be said: 'I was born in such and such a year,
in such and such a place,' or 'There was a king who had three sons.'
(Borges)[26]

Literary autobiographies have become suspect since, at the latest, the
times of Rousseau's and Stendhal's; and older ones are almost daily
being taken to task. One of the complaints most frequently voiced
is that the more authors write and publish in an autobiographical
mode, the more difficult it becomes to disentangle fact from fiction
and to offer a reliable reconstruction of their actual experiences. At an
extreme, the genre of autobiography can perhaps be argued to be by
definition a forgery: after all, why would writers attempt to cajole us (or
their own superegos) into accepting one particular interpretation of
their lives, unless they had substantial reasons to distract us (or their
own superegos) from alternative ones that they wish to see left unem-
braced?[27]

If that is in fact the case, future generations may find writing a reliable
biographical account of Federico Fellini well-nigh impossible, for the
simple – and maddening – reason that, in one way or another, autobiography ostensibly is all we have in Fellini's filmmaking. We are, and will
ever be, in danger of confusing him with his protagonists, whatever their
names: Marcello Rubini, Guido, Sergio Rubini, or – Federico Fellini. It
is paradoxical, but true, that Fellini's penchant for exhibitionism on the
screen leads to a chaotic vanishing of his empirically verifiable self that
ultimately works out to the equivalent of a strategy of camouflage.[28]

Intervista is an outstanding contribution to this hide-and-seek game.
The structure of the film is made up of three different strands, of which
the first, the interview proper, represents the frame narration. The person to be interviewed is a Famous Italian Director (henceforward FID),
impersonated on stage by the actor Federico Fellini; the interviewers are
a group of Japanese film fans eager to see the FID at work and to ask
him questions about his art. The second narrative nucleus arises out of
the fact that the FID, ever creatively engaged, is now hard at work on a
rendition of Kafka's American novel (which, in accordance with the editions available to the general public at the time, he calls '*America*,' *tout
court*). He is engaged in the selection of the cast, the shooting of screen
tests, and the coordination of sundry organizational aspects of the

project. The third fictional core is the one centring around the FID's own recollections of his maiden trip to Cinecittà many years in the past and several episodes surrounding that visit. We thus have a triple source of narrative impulses that interact with one another – plus (as Bondanella rightly stresses) a wealth of cinema-within-the-cinema intuitions that make for a true cornucopian audiovisual experience.[29]

Yet, put this way, all looks entirely neat and clear; too neat and too clear, indeed, for our FID. First, it should be noted that the three narrative areas are not treated symmetrically. The interview (strand 1) and the reminiscences (strand 3) entail both a cinematic *and* a meta-cinematic component: that is, we get to see the final products along with the deictic gesture that unveils their respective modes of production. We witness the director's encounter with the Japanese visitors, as well as the events related to it; we enjoy the reconstruction of the director's memories, as well as the preparations necessary to shoot them (or rather, such preparations as the director deems artistically suitable for that purpose).

However, the same is not true of the film about America (strand 2), which is never presented to us. The slot to be allotted to Kafka's narrative – according to the interview conducted with the Japanese visitors, the generative nucleus of the whole project – remains an empty one (indeed it, too, disappears). There is, in other words, no final, solid Russian *matriozka* doll at the core of the penultimate hollow one.

The following is a possible way of charting these rapports:

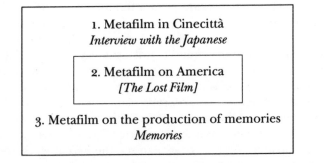

1. Metafilm in Cinecittà
Interview with the Japanese

2. Metafilm on America
[The Lost Film]

3. Metafilm on the production of memories
Memories

A second main complicating factor is that there are internal links between the three protagonists, and that these raise complex theoretical issues. For example, the FID plays the role of a classical Mentor vis-à-vis his younger self, the protagonist of the pre-war memories, whom he treats with paternal protectiveness. This entails a splitting of roles, a double personality of sorts, in which father and son are and yet are not the same person. The process re-enacts a duality fundamental to the symbolic world of poiesis – a world in which the art of narrating externalizes the artist's painstaking conquest of self-education by means of his or her fission into two separate entities: the narrator and the character.

Another point of theoretical relevance suggested by the film is that of the defamiliarization tangibly created by the presence of the uncomprehending glance of an outsider visiting the main scene of the events. In Western literature this role traditionally fell to the *pícaro*, the clown, or the holy fool;[30] in *Intervista*, a structurally equivalent urbane group of Japanese intellectuals perform that function. Almost proverbial in Italy for the (supposed) remoteness of its *forma mentis* from the local one, Japanese culture is here used by Fellini as an alternative vantage point from which to relativize that of the natives. Through such relativization, the experience of everyday life becomes available to the artist for fictional fruition, affording a passage through aesthetic representation that is essential to the process by which art lifts individuals, however temporarily, out of their time, allows them to suspend, however transitorily, their transitoriness, and presents them with a *sub specie aeternitatis* perception of their own impermanence.

Clearly, both the Mentor/character, trainer/trainee split, on the one hand, and the passage through representation by way of the outsider's glance, on the other, are strategies aimed at implementing something that could be called the artist's dream of omnipotence. It is in this sense, rather than in more accidental ones, that to my mind Fellini envisaged competing with the Creator when practising his own art.[31]

Third, the FID's film 'about Kafka' is enormously complicated by the fact that the director does not stick to his stated plan(s) and constantly trespasses on the boundaries between narrative areas in his film.

The most glaring and recurrent such transgression is one related to the would-be protagonist of the Kafka film. The situation is as follows: Sergio Rubini (an actor called Sergio Rubini who plays the role of an aspiring actor by the same name) is hired to play the adolescent FID's role in the Cinecittà film in preparation.[32] By contrast, the Kafka film does not yet have an assigned interpreter. Thanks to this preferential treatment, the film about the Cinecittà memories (or rather, parts of it) can be shot, while the one from Kafka's American novel bides its time. Betrayed by its own director, deprived of a protagonist, the fragment remains a fragment once more. Kafka's Karl, lost in America, resurfaces at the antipodes, but not as a solid semantic entity; he lives only potentially, as an empty space to be endowed with meaning. He 'exists,' and can be detected, only as a series of relations. It is in a long string of ironic digressions that the FID's film wanders about and along, spinning on to its conclusion.[33]

In *Intervista*, a certain type of autobiography thus wins out over the re-creation of literature in film – at the empirical level, that is. In a deeper sense, an immediate form of autobiography takes over from the mediated one that had been its pre-text (prior text). Ultimately, it is the self-unveiling, self-concealing ironic interaction between the two that lends to the narration the impetus necessary to proceed.

Fellini Interviews Kafka

All one puts in front of the camera is oneself. (Fellini)[34]

Do we really know for sure that Kafka is not a mere pretext for *Intervista*? After all, Fellini's opinion is explicit:

A work of art is its own unique expression. [Some] transpositions from one art to the other I find monstrous, ridiculous, off the mark. My preferences are for original subjects written for the cinema. I believe cinema doesn't need literature, it needs only film writers, that is, people who express themselves according to the rhythms and the cadences intrinsic to film. Film is an autonomous art form which has no need of transpositions to a level which, in the best of cases, will always and forever be mere illustration. Each work of art thrives in the dimension which conceived it and through which it is expressed. What can one get from a book? Plot. But plot itself has no significance. It is the feeling which is expressed that matters, the imagination, atmosphere, illumination, in sum, the interpretation. Literary interpretation of events has nothing to do with cinematic interpretation of those same events. They are two completely different methods of expression.[35]

Statements such as this show the extent to which Fellini was opposed to cinematic 'adaptations' of any sort. All the more reason to conclude that Kafka's Karl must have enjoyed a truly unique status with him, if he so exceptionally undertook to make the young man the object of a – however fragmentary – filmic re-creation.[36] Kafka obviously represented a meaningful, rich interlocutor for Fellini. What are the specific questions that, in *Intervista*, the director asked the writer? What are the answers he obtained?

The material in *Intervista* that is directly related to Kafka can be subsumed under three rubrics: (1) encounters with, and instructions to, individuals actually or potentially involved in the screen tests for what the FID calls *America*; (2) recognizable re-creations of situations present in the novel; and (3) allusions and oblique loans from the original – that is, micro-transpositions from Kafka that have undergone varying degrees of displacement, re-elaboration or camouflage.

(1) The references in the first group show an overall picture of how the FID perceives his Fellino-Kafkaesque characters. They are revealing because they allow us to see how the FID intends to transform verbal into visual and spiritual into physical.

For Karl, he considers signing on a young Englishwoman, whom he would cross-dress as a boy.[37] He then approaches 'two graceful and respectful youths' at the Rome music conservatory.[38] The director finally hires an agent, who shows up in Studio 5 of Cinecittà with a day's catch she thus peddles: 'I've been all over the place: music conservatories, libraries, religious institutions; Polish embassy, Hungarian embassy, Czech embassy, I've been through all of them, and well, if you can't find your character among these ones, then I sure don't understand what it is that he wants!'[39]

For Brunelda we have analogous episodes, which unveil the FID's reading of her character and the particular interpretation he gives of her capricious, lazy sensuality. To the person who brings him the first candidate, a brunette, he objects: 'Maurizio, Brunelda is blond, you know.'[40] (I will mention Brunelda's 'real' hair colour in a moment.) This does not prevent him from later opening up the search to all potential Bruneldas, as his assistant announces when the applicants are congregated in the studio for a general briefing session.[41] The (female) secretary of production gallantly remarks as she clarifies the character's personality: 'She eats, she sleeps, and she's always making love, no fool she!'[42] Two aspiring actresses object to the idea that they may be asked to pose in the nude for the bathing scene.[43] Maurizio, the assistant director, later explains to a potential Brunelda just what kind of sensuality is expected of her character:

Maurizio. 'Look at me! A frightening mask: a mask of perversity, of ferocity, but also of tenderness.'

He shows the expression to a gorgeous young woman wearing a white blazer jacket generously open on the front and a pair of sunglasses over her forehead.

'Listen to me – you have to be animal-like, beastly ... Ah, I've got it: the

quivering nostril is *absolutely crucial.* Trust me; the quivering nostril can make the whole difference.'
   The young woman nods as a sign of good will.[44]

(2) With respect to recognizable reproductions of situations from Kafka, for the reader of the novel the clearest modification undertaken in the film – a modification perceptible even before the Brunelda scenes are acted out in the screen tests – is that the FID intends to show the female leading character in full view, most notably during the bath scene.

Kafka's narrator not only studiously avoids mentioning the colour of Brunelda's hair (though he many times alludes to the red dress she invariably wears), he keeps her and Delamarche hidden behind a screen throughout what in his text is, literally, a steamy episode. *The Man Who Disappeared* engages in a sophisticated *Fort! – Da!* ('Here! – Gone!') game, in which garments and segments of bodies alternately emerge from behind the screen, appearing and disappearing in the haze under Karl's eyes. In sum, the novel gives the clear sense of a partition in the room's space: in the hidden half, Delamarche pants and sweats in the vain attempt to satisfy Brunelda's aquatic whims; from the part accessible to the reader, Karl observes the events, while a hypnotized Robinson glosses them for him. In the film, instead, the climactic scene is rehearsed with the entire room open to the youths' glance – and the public's.

The FID's screen tests introduce a further surprise for expert and less advanced Kafkaists alike: while for Kafka the four main episodes revolving around Brunelda (a., the sequence following the interjection 'such a heat, Delamarche'; b., Robinson's sardine-eating; c., Brunelda's bath; and d., her being rolled out by Karl on a wheelchair) occupy distinct moments of successive narrative articulations, in the film they are compressed into a rapid continuum. The novel's already scant evolutionary dimension is thus even further excised from the film.

A third change is just as telling. In the book, by the time Brunelda is carted off, the relationships obtaining at the beginning of the chapter with the bath scene have undergone a break that is not elaborated on further; concurrently, the nature of the 'Institution No. 25' to which she is transported remains undefined. By contrast, in *Intervista* the 'Institution No. 25' becomes a full-fledged brothel as a matter of course.[45] Clearly, the FID is, on the one hand, intrigued by the especially sensual visual opportunities offered by the multiple *ménage*; on the other hand, he is relatively uninterested in developing the diachronic shifts that occur within Kafka's plot, in particular those intervening between the main text and the fragments.[46]

(3) Among what I have called allusions and oblique loans (micro-transpositions from the original that have undergone various types and degrees of modification), there are five that seem to be particularly worthy of notice.

(3a) The subway taken by Karl to the open-air sign-up for the theatre of Oklahoma is referred to in *Intervista* as the 'elevated railway of an American city.'[47] The substitution may seem inspired by the mere desire to convey the urban skyline surrounding Karl. However, for Kafka's Karl it is indeed a liberating experience to emerge, after long ordeals, from the bowels of the earth into a realm of universal acceptance that has banished all discrimination. Disposing of the subway shows that the FID chooses to de-emphasize the soteriological element in the Kafkaesque atmosphere of the novel. In the film, furthermore, the foregrounding of Kafka's original material is entirely changed: *the subway we do get in* Intervista *is located in Rome instead.* It is haunted not by seekers of salvation, but by the FID's talent scouts on the prowl.

(3b)/(3c) During Sergio Rubini's impersonation of the young FID at the time of the latter's first streetcar ride to Cinecittà, a number of exotic, dreamlike landscapes arise – an obvious intrusion of cinematic fantasies into Rome's drab cityscape at the time of Fascist autarky. *These panoramas, which belong to the 'Cinecittà film,' are in fact covert interpolations from Kafka's novel.* They have been appropriated and reassigned from the America film, to which they should in principle have been destined.

> *Now the landscape changes. In the roar of tumbling water, we see the bright spray of a grand waterfall spread over the intense green colour of the vegetation. Sergio Rubini changes seats so as to admire the view from Antonella's window ... A veil of pulverized water reaches and fogs up the glass, behind which the young woman's face presently disappears ...*
>
> *Notarianni / Fascist bigwig.* 'Niagara, Niagara! As you can see, my dear young man, Italy is second to none! Even when it comes to waterfalls!'[48]

(The tongue-in-cheek stab at grotesquely misplaced nationalism deserves notice.)

> *The landscape has changed again. The jagged crests of a mountain chain flash past the windows.*

The little streetcar enters a kind of gorge, a narrow trench between two walls of bare rock ...

Driver (to the passengers). 'Ladies and gentlemen, look up there! The Indians!'[49]

Without a word of warning, Kafka's train has suddenly become Fellini's streetcar; and Karl's vistas have become part of the FID's fantasies. To be sure, the intertextuality of imagery is stressed by the specific references, added *ex nihilo* in *Intervista*, to Niagara Falls and to American Indians respectively; but even without them an obvious dialogical relationship recalls the storyline of '*America*,' and on occasion echoes its very wording.[50]

The circulation of images is so strong in *Intervista* as gradually to obliterate internal barriers between plots and to conflate protagonists: by way of one and the same process of daydreaming, the FID, Sergio Rubini, Karl Rossmann, Kafka's narrator, the obscure young journalist named Federico Fellini and impersonated by Sergio Rubini – all begin to blur and blend into one another.

(3d) The fourth substantial displacement that occurs between novel and film consists in the fact that *there is an ablution scene* actually shown in *Intervista*. This, however, occurs neither in the Kafka/America sequence (where sexuality is interrupted) nor in the Cinecittà sequence (where it is merely alluded to – on which more *infra*). The locus of liquidity's triumph is the autobiographical sequence, in which the clumsy FID-to-be is allowed to witness from as close as decency would allow the shower ritual enacted by a famous pre-war diva immediately before *her own* interview with the young man.

Next, perhaps, viewers may wonder in puzzlement, Will the mature FID be interviewed by his Japanese fans as he walks out of his morning shower? Not quite, but almost. At the time when he shows the FID entertaining the Japanese in Anita Ekberg's countryside villa, Fellini introduces footage from the famous sequence in *La dolce vita* where the FID's alter ego, Marcello, wades into the Trevi fountain in order to pursue the modern forest nymph Sylvia. In doing so, *Intervista* enacts a 'shower' scene no less sensual than those proliferating, *en abyme*, throughout the film.

And what about the dripping Sylvia of *La dolce vita*, in the world Anita Ekberg? When, after almost thirty years at large, the character she portrays welcomes the *Intervista* crew on her doorstep, she is wearing a bathrobe and a turban-like towel around her hair ...

(3e) This finally brings us back to Brunelda. The red-clad, archetypal literary 'man-eater'[51] simply cannot find her match among aspiring Roman actresses. Why? The reason is simple: the FID is looking for her in the 'wrong' narrative strand. He gets closer to the truth when, allowing himself to float on the waves of anamnesis, he enlists the magician par excellence, Mandrake (impersonated by Marcello Mastroianni), for a task so delicate he cannot even bring himself to articulate it.

It is out of this sense of shyness that a professional visit to the potential female leading character turns into an outright (though by no means simple) sentimental journey into the FID's – *and* the Famous Italian Actor's – past.

Accompanied by Sergio Rubini, the two travel in a car that eventually reaches a villa in the Roman countryside purportedly inhabited by Anita Ekberg (played by Anita Ekberg). As soon as we see on the screen our ageing but characteristically monumental acquaintance, her body and (blond) hair tightly wrapped in the bright orange of her terry cloth, we know that Brunelda's prototype had existed all along in a universe parallel to Karl's.[52] We then understand that finding her was merely a matter of breaking through the conventional barriers of narration, of abolishing the boundaries of time and self that artificially separate life from life and plot from plot. The reason why the FID does not ask Ekberg to star in his Kafka film may, in the end, simply be that (since here the distinction between one fiction and another is itself a fictional one) she *already* stars in it as it is.

'She's mythical!' proclaims the FID about her.[53] Myths have no beginning and no end; they are always, everywhere.[54] In the FID's poetic universe, there is little space for structured notions of time and identity based on the dualisms on which Western logic is posited: I–non I, true-false, before-after, centre-periphery, inside-outside.

Abolishing Boundaries of Self, Time, and Textuality

> To talk much about oneself can also be a means to hide oneself. (Nietzsche)[55]

While in his films Fellini constantly denudes himself before our eyes, contrary to what one might expect the final result of his self-spoliation is generally a rather sedative experience: there is no ultimate naked core to the sequence of *matriozka* dolls contained one inside the other – or rather, the multi-layered doll *was* the core we put aside in our expectation of a climax. Fellini's autobiographical strip is interminable; or, rather, it is always already contained in each of its increments.

After all, however, the hollow-dolls image may not be the most satisfying one among the many possible figurative renderings of Fellini's poetics. It is, in particular, another strip that I would like to suggest as a possibly less inadequate metaphor for his artistic method: the Möbius strip.

In its simplest form, a Möbius strip is a three-dimensional solid obtained by joining the two ends of a ribbon into a ring-shaped object after twisting the ribbon, end to end, by 180° around its longitudinal axis. (If a model is made out of adhesive tape, this entails twisting the tape so as to join one glued end against the other glued end.) The result is an approximately 8-shaped band on which an observer can move ahead and return exactly to the starting point after 'two' laps, having scanned the whole surface by moving continuously in the same direction. Put more simply, a Möbius strip is a three-dimensional object that has only one surface, and in which the notions of 'inside' and 'outside' are therefore non-definable.

Interviewing a Fellinian text, I maintain, causes an effect similar to that which an insect – or, for that matter, a character out of a novel by Kafka – would experience while crawling along a Möbius strip. As one progresses, one gradually moves from discourse to meta-discourse, from narration to meta-narration, from the 'inside' to the 'outside' of self, time, and text; and then back again. In fact, in the Fellinian universe outside and inside no longer exist as distinct concepts.

Each time we return to the starting point (let us assume, for the sake of simplicity, Studio 5 at Cinecittà) we seem to have just moved in one direction along the surface of a band; in reality, however, we have accomplished a complex three-dimensional journey. This is the journey through which *Intervista* takes us, loading us onto the scenic platforms of its trains/streetcars, and leading us alternately to the 'inner' and to the 'outer' side of, respectively, autobiography and novel, fantasy and cinematic re-creation. At the end of the film, we alight at the Cinecittà studio from which we had set out, and away from which we never really moved, having gone constantly ahead in one direction with each turn of the projector's wheel as we would have done on a hypothetical Möbius strip. This strip is *Intervista*, in which *Bildungsroman* and fantasy, autobiography and myth, are made to collapse and coincide, forming one and the same genre.[56]

What sort of *omiyage*,[57] then, do we – we strangers, we veritable tourists on a visit to Fellini's fantastic continent – bring back with us from this peculiarly stationary journey? Not much more than a sense of exhilarating playfulness; a meagre euphoria perhaps, nothing more than the thin, corny 'ray of sunshine' that a producer of old used to beg Fellini to include in his films as an antidote to what bothered him as an excess of pessimism on the director's part.[58] Yet it is clear that self-observation enacted through the prism of the mobilization of temporal and psychic boundaries can help achieve a certain levity and detachment from one's own impermanence, and thus ultimately serve as an excellent tool to carry out a form of training toward spiritual liberation; while the opposite is true of obstinate insistence on self-analysis mediated by the traditional Western parameters of dualism.

In the third of the notebooks published posthumously with the novella *Preparations for a Marriage in the Countryside*, Kafka's aphorisms engage in a prolonged, chain-like dialogue with the notion of evil, and at one point unequivocally argue: 'Only Evil has self-awareness.'[59] In interviewing Kafka, Fellini implicitly corrects him: 'In that Oriental tale of *The Sorcerer's Apprentice*, the book of knowledge that [the apprentice] arrives at after a long process of self-discipline is composed of pages made out of mirrors; which means, the only way of knowing is to know one's self.'[60]

Reflected and refracted through innumerable mirrors-sheets, Fellini's ray of sunshine (postmodernly portrayed in *Intervista* as emanating from Cinecittà's floodlights) bounces back all the way to us, the 'lost ones' in America. The simple-minded producer may now rejoice, unaware that the artificial ray he finally got may signify instead the doubtful ability of a certain type of art to save anyone or anything, in America or elsewhere.[61]

PART TWO

Coextensive Re-creations

Fantastic Neorealism:
The Overcoat (1952)

The Metamorphoses of the Puppet

It's horrible, yet it is not serious. (Ionesco)[1]

Something is definitely the matter with the protagonist of Nikolai Gogol's *The Overcoat* (*Shinel'*, 1842), Akaky Akakievich; and most of that matter, commentators concur, is fecal. But there is also another, opposite side to the facts: *A-kaky* is at the same time the Non-evil being, the meek victim of social persecution[2] – an innocent humanoid, degraded by his imperfect condition of contraption (one would be hard pressed to say creature), abandoned by the light of God.[3]

Over time, typically Gogolian contradictions of just this kind have created never-ending difficulties in our understanding of the great Russian author and made it problematic to disentangle the mix in his works of the humane and the grotesque: a mix that routinely courts demonic themes, and often trespasses into their sphere. Much of Gogol scholarship, not only on *Shinel'* but also on Gogol's most ambitious project, *Dead Souls*, is thus concerned with a diatribe as to whether in his prose there are more humaneness and compassion toward fellow human beings or, at the opposite extreme, social indifference coupled with an unmatchable obsession with the absurd and linguistic nonsense.

The political implications of the dilemma are obvious: should Gogol's position be read as the denunciation of identifiable historical grievances, and therefore understood as exposing a specific dysfunction? Or does it aim at depicting, in despair, something about the human condition that is universal and perennial – and therefore suggest one adopt quietism as the only appropriate response to an irreparable malaise?[4] Since the Russian 1840s, the struggle, in successive waves, between the humane interpretation and the formal one has caused critics to annex Gogol with gusto, pulling him in opposite directions. The trouble is that Gogol was, in fact, a torn and deeply 'romantic' soul, about whom it is arduous to tell whether he condoned or despised even himself, let alone the puppet-like government clerks he is fond of installing at the core of his stories.[5] In his youth Gogol relished a phantasmagoric narrative style richly drawing upon the demonic folklore of his native Ukraine, and he produced a type of literature that in the second part of his life (i.e., during and after his failure to extract himself *ex machina* from the provincial Hell of the first volume of *Dead Souls*) he repudiated as irresponsible and unworthy of the artist's sacred mission to preach the divine word. To be sure, the question of Gogol's inner contradictoriness is probably impossible to resolve in such polarized terms;[6] nor does it offer the desired, definitive help to suggest viewing spiritual duality as *the* constant and unifying trait of Gogol's personality – an easily true, but somewhat circular, squaring of the circle.[7]

Can the persistent inconsistency attributed to Gogol be explained, and his dualism resolved, other than by defining Gogol's state of cleavage as his ultimate, contradictory single nature? The dualism between self-contained linguistic virtuosity and humaneness can, I believe, be substantially resorbed if we assume that, in Gogol's implicit perception, the human species was *created by the devil*.[8] Applying this particular anthropogenic hypothesis would, at one stroke, explain why in Gogol's eyes humans are in fact 'demonic,' that is, defective artefacts, ever threatening to fall back into a sub- or pre-human state, and at the same time also a pity-inspiring bunch who ought not to be made responsible for an imperfect nature that is not of their own making. (Similar theories were known to Christianity since its inception. Gogol's intuitions could be classified as a variant of Gnostic-Manichaean teachings and, in particular, of Priscillianist thought.)[9] In synthesis, the hypnotizing attraction exerted by the devil-made puppet is, for Gogol, that it is *faulty without being at fault*; and that it can thus attract, in turn and without contradiction, sympathy and scorn, compassion and contempt.[10]

The situation is very different for Alberto Lattuada, who operates in the cultural-historical context of Italy's immediate post–Second World War reconstruction crisis. In accordance with the cultural tradition of Italian neorealism, the Italian director makes his own puppet, Carmine De Carmine, a character exclusively humiliated and offended by society.[11]

De Carmine's homelessness is not of a transcendent nature, but of a real one. He literally lacks a home of his own: he is a long-term renter in a *pensione*, with a claustrophobic view onto the neighbour's window across a narrow lane. All the world is not necessarily a *pensione*: many others live comfortably and have their own privacy – and overcoats aplenty. It is in an entirely new sense that *Il cappotto* portrays De Carmine as a representative of the human condition. Out goes a supra-historical devil; in come exploitation and abuse, which are always socially identifiable. In *Il cappotto*, the world is a *pensione* – for some.

Underdogs of the World, Unite

An anti-Fascist Milanese, raised behind the curtains of the Scala theatre, who nourished himself on the texts of the great European classics, Russian first and foremost, and who in his filmmaking turned to depicting the plight of the downtrodden. Surely a mini-portrait of Luchino Visconti? No, a succinct perspective on Alberto Lattuada – a Mitteleuropean *liberal-radicale* intellectual who grew up under Fascism and, as an adolescent and a student, did all he could to oppose the regime's cultural policy.[12]

Lattuada's long and prolific career as a director touched upon many genres and subjects, earning him, over the decades, a number of disparate labels: he was variously described as 'formalist' or 'calligraphic' in the 1940s, 'eclectic' in the 1950s and 1960s, 'intimist' or 'erotic' in the 1970s.[13] The breadth of the spectrum of Lattuada's production is indeed impressive, covering, as it does, renderings of turn-of-the-century and twentieth-century works of Italian literature,[14] soap operas,[15] neorealist-style explorations of provincial and urban Italy in the wake of the Second World War,[16] up to and including experiments in candid-camera reports,[17] socially critical *commedia all'italiana*,[18] thrillers,[19] spy stories,[20] classics of Renaissance theatre,[21] re-creations from the Russian,[22] as well as comedies perceptively depicting young women's sentimental education.[23]

It is understandably difficult, but not impossible, to condense such narrative wealth into a smaller number of significant headings. Lattuada's interest in broad historical frescoes is clearly discernible in his work, as is his keen eye for the conflict between private and public morality in both pre-industrial and industrial societies. His pedagogical focus on adolescents coming of age is also easily traced. A further major thread is the analysis of defeat in the single-minded pursuit of one's desire (money, pleasure, fame) in the face of an unforeseen disruption:

physical failure, the superior power of love, or fate. Last but not least, a theme that – freely combined with any of the above – often acts as a catalyst for Lattuada's filmmaking is the oppression suffered by the social underdog at the hands of privileged, calculating individuals.[24] The narrative attractiveness of Gogol's copyist for Lattuada is logical in the perspective last mentioned.

Il cappotto transports *Shinel'* to Italy with several modifications, the most perceptible of which consists in rendering Gogol's boorish outsider in mid-nineteenth-century St Petersburg with a contemporary Southerner employed as a humble scribe in a northern Italian town.[25] That town happens to be Pavia, on the banks of the Ticino River; but the film is careful to present it, with no further identification, as a cold location in a snow-clad northern landscape. In *Il cappotto* the neorealist heritage acquires a supra-temporal hue, intriguingly succeeding in encompassing both the historical and the perennial. This is entirely germane to Lattuada's own artistic sensitivity, as well as to his own brand of 'political' program.

The cultural homology among overcoats across societies and centuries provides the basis for the immediate transferability of Gogol's subject matter from Russia to northern Italy and from the mid-1800s to the mid-1900s. In case we are tempted to underestimate the high profile of the topic for its time and place, we should consult a lively diary entry that we are fortunate to have available from none other than the most conscious practitioner of Italian neorealism. Zavattini's candid *aperçu* explains in no roundabout terms what it meant to own a good overcoat in the impoverished Italy of the years immediately following the Second World War:

NEW OVERCOAT, February, 1947 ... This is the first item of clothing I've bought since the war, worn for the first time one March morning, happy but not entirely, because I had a pair of shoes unworthy of this coat. In the newspaper there were no dire events that day; I could enjoy the inauguration of the new coat in peace ...

All of a sudden I met Giuseppe Ungaretti. He was walking along calmly, with his assistant, Professor Barlozzini. 'Beautiful,' he said. Barlozzini agreed that the overcoat was beautiful. Ungaretti added that it was soft; and, in a very mild voice: 'I don't have one.' He said this without envy. I answered that he deprived me of the pleasure of owning it. I tried to deprecate the quality of the overcoat, saying also I had paid for it in installments. Meanwhile he kept passing his hand over the cloth as if he were patting a lamb. We said goodbye. Should I perhaps send a sleeve of it to his house, in true Christian spirit? How many poets have lived in poverty! Do they want glory? Let them have glory; glory plus an overcoat is too much.[26]

Five years after the date of this diary entry, Zavattini was to appear (alongside Lattuada, Luigi Malerba, and others) as one of the cooperative authors of *Il cappotto*'s script.[27]

So strong is the cultural value of vestmental analogies, through time and space, from *Shinel'* to *Il cappotto* that critics – encouraged, perhaps, by the director's statements[28] – seem to have taken for granted straightforwardly 'humane' intentions not only in Lattuada but in Gogol as well. Such an interpretation assumes unquestioningly that *Il cappotto* follows Gogol's *Shinel'* closely, re-creating the Russian text in the Italian situation with a minimum of changes necessary for it to take root in a new century and a new locale. Some critics stress the fact that the two plots are very similar, down to many narrative details.[29] This is true, but does not in and of itself prove that Lattuada's film as a whole cannot undertake a substantial departure from Gogol's spirit.[30] The issue can benefit from being examined in some detail – which, as the saying would have it, is precisely where the devil dwells.

The fireworks of *Shinel'*'s overture set the tone for the entire story:

> In the department of ... but I had better not mention which department. There is nothing in the world more touchy than a department, a regiment, a government office, and, in fact, any sort of official body. Nowadays every private individual considers all society insulted in his person. [It is said] that very lately a complaint was lodged by a police inspector of which town I don't remember, and that in his complaint he sets forth clearly that the institutions of the State were in danger and that his sacred name was being taken in vain; and, in proof thereof, he appended to his complaint an enormously long volume of some romantic work in which a police inspector appeared on every tenth page, occasionally, indeed, in an intoxicated condition. And so, to avoid any unpleasantness, we had better call the department of which we are speaking 'a certain department.' And so, in a certain department there [worked] a certain clerk ...[31]

This beginning tells us less about the empirical setting of the story than it does about a different kind of ambience: namely, the climate of the logical (or, more accurately, a-logical) universe we are about to enter.[32] A passage that may at first sight appear altogether bizarre seems in fact proper, if we only consider that what it aims at portraying is not St Petersburg, but a distant relative of it – Gogol's own St Petersburg, an archetypal *civitas diaboli*.[33]

Il cappotto wisely postpones until a later time its own modified indictment of the omnipotence of bureaucracy. Instead, the film presents the backdrop of the action, Pavia, under the snow, with its narrow cobbled streets, foggy arcades, and dark corners – and, most importantly (although we will realize this only later), its long covered bridge across the Ticino River.

What could be called the first act of the tragedy now begins, with the camera following our little man as he hurries to work in his threadbare jacket. Yet before Carmine De Carmine reaches City Hall, where he is employed, Lattuada's film manages to have him engage in a gesture that has no direct equivalent in Gogol: as, shivering with cold, he walks briskly toward his destination, he catches a glimpse of the steam condensing in the air from a horse's breath, and beatifically stops to thaw his hands in the warm vapour.[34]

Just after Carmine, at work, has disrobed, he is met by a crowd of postulants who throng around him with their written pleas,[35] while behind his back one of his colleagues clumsily rips his battered old coat as he hangs it on the clothes peg. At this time we also learn Carmine's name, which clearly qualifies him as an outsider in town.[36]

Shinel' now takes a perceptibly different tack. Instead of rushing into action, Gogol's narrator elaborates at length on how Akaky's not-so-noble, rustic house of the Bashmachkins (*bashmak* being a generic term for 'shoe') rose to ever more doubtful heights by virtue of the birth of the quintessentially harmless hero. Gogol's narrator then follows Akaky to St Petersburg. First, we are told that he was the butt of cruel practical jokes at work and enjoyed no respect whatever from his colleagues – who, in particular, called his diaphanous coat a *kapot* ('dressing-gown'). As an exception that confirms the rule, a workmate who had thus transgressed the bounds of human solidarity once came around and repented.[37] We also learn from the narrator about the almost passionate pleasure that the human puppet Akaky took in carrying out his job, transcribing documents for his superiors. In fact, on one occasion Akaky brought his calligraphic mysticism to the point of refusing an absorbing job – 'altering the headings of documents and, in places, changing the first person into the third'[38] – that would have distracted him from focusing entirely on the letters' curvaceous shapes, located in 'an interesting and pleasant world of his own.'[39]

Thus, day in and day out, Akaky would walk to and fro, copy, abstain from visiting acquaintances or entertaining them, dine swallowing his food 'with the flies and anything else that [God] happened to send him,'[40] go to bed early, wrestle with the 'mighty foe of all who receive a salary of about four hundred roubles [a year]: our northern frost ...'[41] until a specific event set in motion the narrative machinery destined to bring about his demise. On that day, Akaky *considered* whether there were 'any defects' (literally: sins, *grekhi*) in his coat; he *examined* it carefully; he *discovered* that it had turned into a sieve; he *decided* that he would have to take the overcoat to the tailor Petrovich – and thereupon made for the craftsman's place.[42]

Before Lattuada's Carmine can subject his own damaged garment to a thorough examination, only to find it frayed at the core, he has a considerable (and considerably different) way to go. Carmine, too, struggles with the local climate; he, too, abstains from socializing, and finds an almost mystical pleasure in his work. He, too, has colleagues, no more enlightened than their Gogolian counterparts – though these, at least, do not play cruel practical jokes on their marionette-like fellow worker. Still, the function of the tormentor is not abolished by Lattuada; it is merely reassigned to higher echelons in the social hierarchy. This change occurs by grafting onto the Gogolian story a deuteragonist, the Mayor of the city.[43] A crucial narrative displacement thus occurs between short story and film: with the shift to political bosses as the main embodiment of evil, the plot undergoes a deep re-accentuation in meaning.

The Mayor is a Fascist-style tyrant acting at the intersection of two subplots, both of which Lattuada introduces *ex novo* vis-à-vis Gogol's *Shinel'*. The more topical of the two consists of a tale of political corruption; the other one is the Mayor's erotic liaison with a glamorous woman-about-town called Caterina.

The political cabal in *Il cappotto* involves a sadly familiar story of real-estate speculation centred on the displacement, financed by public money, of low-income tenants for the purpose of private profit. The corresponding quid pro quo, in the film as in the historical reality of Italy at the time, are exchange votes; not the uprooted inhabitants', to be sure, but those that can demagogically be obtained from other citizens by packaging the deal in trendy rhetorical decoration. Hence, in *Il cappotto*, the Mayor's shrill nationalistic tone during council meetings as he peddles a zoning project that strongly resembles the EUR neighbourhood of Fascist Rome from the 1930s.[44]

Il cappotto, though, does not only voice the idiosyncrasies of a stylized ruling class; it also portrays the very real concerns of the working and the unemployed poor. The scene of the justice-seeking crowds that routinely congregate by Carmine's office at the time when city hall employees arrive at work is repeated many times in the film. Two befriended applicants stand out, one of whom – a veteran from Italy's 1911–12 Libyan war – has been waiting for his pension for forty years, because he is unable to prove that he served and fought with honour.[45] The poor folk at Carmine's drab boarding house also make themselves heard. When Carmine returns to his room after the city council meeting that has voted for new fees on yet another communal service, his fellow pensioners erupt into what amounts to an apartment riot against city-levied taxes.

As for Caterina, she is entirely oblivious to her keeper's machinations. This bestows on her an angelic role that causes our rag-clad human puppet to fall for her without afterthought. By a not particularly probable coincidence, it so happens that Caterina lives in a luxurious apartment located right across the alley from Carmine's spartan cell; their windows are exactly aligned. Thus it is that, after spending his day slogging through the political schemes woven by the Mayor and his secretary, Lattuada's humble clerk must, in his free time, go through the emotions of a disruptive, love-induced tachycardia: one beautiful evening, he suddenly beholds through the glass the generously endowed platinum blonde in a semi-transparent nightgown, who busily perfects her make-up to languid waltzing music. Akaky's infamous 'dressing gown' finds here a superbly ironic multiplication.

It is this one-way encounter that ultimately motivates our copyist's hopeful decision to become a new man. As he attempts to repair by himself the latest rip in his old overcoat, Carmine, distracted by the apparition beyond the window panes, inflicts further, irreparable damage on the fabric he is handling. Time to bring in the tailor.[46]

After such politico-erotic digressions, Gogol's and Lattuada's narratives now overlap again: our two scribes are about to show up on their respective seamsters' doorsteps. However, overlapping segments in two different plot lines need not have overlapping meanings, as our case clearly shows. Although Lattuada's self-conscious tailor, Andrea by name, considers himself an artist of dressmaking, he remains on a frank and reasonably comradely footing with Carmine. By contrast, the atmosphere is outright ominous in *Shinel'*, whose tailor bears many traits suggesting a devil's figure bent on a counter-creation that reverses what ought to be the cosmic order of things.[47]

In both *Shinel'* and *Il cappotto*, it is not until their third encounter that tailor and scribe seal their agreement on the overcoat; accordingly, the next narrative phase develops over the necessary negotiations. But how the two narratives attain the 'same' goal makes for substantial differences. Gogol emphasizes the puppetness of his protagonist, whose permanent physical and mental paralysis is exacerbated by his inability to clinch the ongoing sartorial deal. Lattuada's Carmine is shown instead to remain only too human in the development of his feelings (toward Caterina in particular).[48]

Soon enough, we comb the shops in the wake of the quadrille Akaky/ Petrovich and Carmine/Andrea, who are scouring their respective towns in search of the best deal for the material they need. The St Petersburg chums 'did not buy marten, because it was [really] expensive, but instead they chose cat fur, the [very] best to be found in the shop – cat which in the distance might almost be taken for marten.'[49] As for their peninsular counterparts, Andrea had already wrapped up the matter in almost identical terms during their previous encounter. The two tailors' attitude toward forgery puts the finishing touches on portraits that could not be more accurately harmonized with demonological tradition: as ever when it comes to demonic creation, objects are here *almost, but not quite* what they seem to be. One can apply to our story of vanishing, not-quite-real overcoats Siniavsky's brilliant dictum from his book dealing with 'the shadow of Gogol': 'All is *wrong and out of place*: right there is where the devil hides.'[50] To be sure, while by most indices demonism is the main point in *Shinel'*, it is not in *Il cappotto*, if for no other reason that there is a far greater amount of narrative material swirling around Carmine – and thus obliterating the devil – than just northern Italian snowflakes.

The two overcoats are finally completed and delivered; our puppet-like heroes are now, for the time being, home and dry. From the Russian original we know that we are in the middle of winter. The Italian film interprets this as meaning that we are approaching the celebrations for the New Year. The plot can now reach its narrative zenith.

Our two clerks' once-in-a-lifetime day of glory begins early, on the way to work. As they bask in the invisible sunshine of 'inward satisfaction,'[51] Akaky and Carmine parade about town for the duration of a brief – though unforgettable – splinter of eternity. Meanwhile, their respective tailors follow them into the streets and, from the sidelines, enjoy the spectacle. '*Bello! bello!*' Andrea cheers. Petrovich, for his part, ambushes his target by running ahead of him. Surely nothing can be more appropriate for a demonic character than his 'taking a shortcut through a [twisting] side street.'[52]

Once Carmine and Akaky are on duty, we witness parallel events: their respective colleagues have got wind that the old *kapots* are out and that two brand new overcoats are in. 'Sprinkling' them now becomes the buzzword, for two similar reasons: in Italy, it is New Year's Eve; in St Petersburg, it is the name-day of the assistant to the Head Clerk. How will the diabolical baptism of our scribes' overcoats turn out?

Akaky now reaches the home of the assistant to the Head Clerk: a man who, unlike our hero, knows how to live it up. Suddenly light, music, people, food, and drinks flash all around us. And, just as suddenly, they surround Carmine too. Our two heroes now again act in unison; feeling awkward and out of place, they both try to come up with ways of melting into the crowd.

Still, this is about the only analogy in two otherwise radically different soirées. The one in *Shinel'* is entirely uneventful: Akaky stares blankly at the card players, feels thoroughly bored, and starts to yawn (it is long past his usual bedtime). He is, in the end, forced by his jolly buddies from the office to wait until supper and drink two glasses of champagne.[53] When he finally manages to slip away from the hustle-bustle and go look for his overcoat in the entrance hall, our mechanical Cinderello cannot help cringing at the thought 'that it [is] twelve o'clock, and that he ought to have been home long ago.'[54] As for Carmine, the party is the locus where all the narrative threads of *Il cappotto* converge. First of all, the proletariat is very much present as a backdrop to the events: a group of complainants is waiting in the street under the falling snow, staring at the brightly lit windows. They are, as ever, expecting word from Carmine, to whom they have entrusted a written plea to be read out to the Mayor at His Excellency's first unguarded moment. Second, political intrigue is in full swing at the fancy gathering: in the fervour of the preparations for the Minister's impending visit, which is intended to release coveted government funding, both the Mayor and the secretary busily rehearse on their public their vacuous and hypocritical rhetoric. Third, and most important of all for Carmine, Caterina is in attendance.

As, starry-eyed, he contemplates his angel waltzing about the room in the Mayor's arms, Carmine attempts to put on the airs of a *viveur* by sporting a cigarette and drinking copiously from the trays proffered by the waiters. He becomes tipsy and, eventually, entirely incoherent. As a result, when midnight strikes and the crowd demands that he, the uncontested office jester, amuse it, Carmine puts in a performance even more impolite than could have been expected: he pulls the wronged citizens' plea out of his pocket. But reading out of a text, at the best of times a tall order for our stocky scribe, now becomes all the more difficult because of the doubly impairing rise to his head of Caterina and of French champagne. The concentric rings of Carmine's improvised speech soon expand to encompass criticism of the ills bedevilling the entire society in which he lives: 'There are 295 stamps and duties in this plea ... That's what it is – there are so many things that are no good. And outside it's snowing, and people feel cold, and they get wet. Pensioners with small children, the unemployed ... Take this, here's the plea. Please read it [Mr Mayor]. Because, if no one bothers reading pleas ...'[55]

In vino veritas: it is with Carmine's drunken address to the potentates of this world that *Il cappotto* most explicitly reinscribes the pre-realist grotesque of *Shinel'* into the Italian neorealist tradition of the twentieth century. Admittedly, the register of grievances is not allowed to unfold for very long; the innocuous fool was given the floor on account of his social irrelevance, but only conditionally. As the intolerable subversiveness of his oration becomes apparent, the Mayor's cronies hound him out of the room.[56]

This is as far as the two copyists will ever reach on the scale of full-fledged humanity. Already a premonition of doom had fluttered past them when, at the party, each of them had found his overcoat on the floor, dropped and trampled upon. The narrative peripeteia is nigh.

When, in *Shinel'*, the fateful moment strikes for Akaky, it hardly comes as a surprise to see him suffer a disquieting parody of Christ's Passion.[57] So far, the factors in the story that suggest a Golgotha *in sedicesimo* are the grotesque Last Supper we witnessed, which included Akaky's original unwillingness to drink from the bitter cup, and the first fall (of the overcoat). Further elements now being added are, in topsy-turvy, demonic disorder: Akaky's anguish and sense of solitude in the city's night; the ominous endless square that he has to cross; the blows he suffers when his overcoat is taken from him; the 'clap of thunder' (in reality, the voice of one of the robbers) at the time of the theft; and, lastly but most significantly, the abuse he endures after the fact from a watchman brandishing a halberd.

In *Il cappotto*, too, we are in the dead of night; and the equivalent to Akaky's feeling of loneliness and fear is well rendered by the lugubrious tolling of a bell. For Gogol's square is substituted the long bridge across the Ticino River; and a single aggressor metonymically takes the place of many. Later, Lattuada's version of the encounter with the guard renders *Shinel''*'s with an appropriate cultural equivalent. The Italian patrolman is a bicycle-mounted *metronotte* (a city sentry in charge of the nighttime security of shops). Carmine calls out to him:

> *Carmine.* 'Policeman, policeman, help! Catch the thief! If you chase him, you can catch him.'
> *Policeman.* 'Well ... I'm getting off right now. I've been pedalling for seven hours, my dear. Besides, I've got rheumatisms.'
> *Carmine.* 'But ... what kind of policeman are you?'
> *Policeman.* 'Maybe you don't know, but I'm a nighttime security officer. Go to the police station, all the way down there, to your right.'
> *Carmine (crying).* 'My overcoat!'[58]

Just as in De Sica's *Bicycle Thieves* (*Ladri de biciclette,* 1948), the police here, worse than being unable to carry out their duty, are utterly unwilling to do so.[59]

A first conclusion that can be drawn from Carmine's sorry story is thus that, under whatever national bureaucracy, the world is truly a devil's paradise.[60] The final sentence to another of Gogol's short stories sums up the matter as tersely as it can ever be put: 'It *is* a dreary world, gentlemen!'[61]

A phase of retardation follows. The vain and increasingly distressing attempt to recover their stolen possessions occupies what functions as the fourth act of Akaky's and Carmine's dramas – in different guises, as it turns out.

More dead than alive, Akaky goes to work the next day in his old *kapot*; and a few of his colleagues even have the bad taste to take pleasure in the sudden reversal of his fortunes. One of them, though, is touched, and provides expert advice: far better for Akaky, he suggests, to appeal on a personal basis to a certain Person of Consequence, entreating him to intervene behind the scenes. So far, so logical – at least in the logic to which we have become accustomed in Gogol's St Petersburg. Yet nothing told by Gogol's narrator is ever straightforward. First, the Person of Consequence is presented to us as a pompous bully;[62] then, with the next page, we are forced to tilt again the opposite way. This is how Gogol accounts for the Person of Consequence's mindset: 'He was ... at heart a good-natured man, pleasant and obliging with his colleagues; but his advancement to a [general's] rank had completely turned his head. When he received it, he was perplexed, thrown off his balance, and quite at a loss as how to behave.'[63] In reading what looks like one more narratorial about-face, we now realize that Gogol's *Shinel'* is not a simple defence of the little man, and a bitter satire on the sad state of Russian bureaucracy; it is a bitter satire on the sad condition of *all* of humanity – and an indirect reminder that such a fallen state is not, from the outset, of humanity's making. In Gogol's prose, as is the rule in his St Petersburg, the wind blows not from a single direction of the compass, but from all of them at the same time.[64] As for *Il cappotto*, by now Lattuada has his Person of Consequence already cut out for him: it is, of course, none other than the consistently and predictably authoritarian Mayor.

For both clerks, it is a very unpropitious moment to be appealing to their superiors, who are entertaining old acquaintances in their offices: the Person of Consequence, a friend from his childhood; the Mayor, a former comrade-in-arms.[65] Both find their respective subordinates' utterances inarticulate and their behaviour unacceptably offhand; both react to the intrusion with a frothy tirade on the paramount importance of proper procedure. Akaky and Carmine then have no choice but to vanish from the scene precipitously and with scant grace.

In the fifth act of the tragedy, agony and death come punctually to the rendezvous. Exposed to the devil's polar climate and incinerated by a merciless social order, Akaky and Carmine rush to rapid, feverish doom. A flurry of apparitions whirl before Akaky's and Carmine's eyes. Akaky sees thieves under his bed, and calls upon his landlady to flush them out; Carmine, who has absorbed the militaristic language of the Italian hierarchy surrounding him, invokes instead the intervention of 'the police, the army, the *carabinieri.*' Not that delirium weakens Carmine's devotion to his beloved: clutching his own portrait (in the now vanished overcoat, of course), which he means to send to Caterina, he addresses her tenderly in his ravings.[66] How does Lattuada visualize Carmine's painful last throes? Brilliantly, by making his shivers visible and audible through the hyperbolic rattling of his bed against the wall, and through the other pensioners' active role during the doctor's auscultation of his heart. The slowing down of Carmine's pulse into the silence of death is conveyed to the onlookers – and to us – by a compassionate witness's mimetic gesture showing a gradual loss of momentum, and eventually total standstill.

While falling far short of an apotheosis, Carmine's passing away is in some respects a bed of roses compared to Akaky's. Before he can finally 'give up the ghost,' the St Petersburg copyist descends into a comatose state in which his body seems to fall prey to the forces of evil that rule the earth: 'He finally [even] became abusive, uttering the most awful language, so that his old landlady [even] crossed herself, having never heard from him anything of the kind [in her entire life].'[67] And so Akaky and Carmine are easily dispatched, and their cities carry on as if the two copyists had never existed. Or do they? This is what their respective post-mortem epilogues proceed to test.

Akaky's funeral is celebrated by Gogol's narrator in five words – seven, in English: 'Akaky Akakievich was carted away and buried.'[68] *Il cappotto*, by contrast, has too many narrative channels open for the story to wind down as unceremoniously. Thus, before the 'fantastic ending' duly announced in its literary counterpart, the Italian film offers its protagonist a few moments in the limelight.

On the day when the Excellency from Rome finally visits the city and participates in the long planned pro-government celebrations, a large crowd is addressed by various political bosses. A pompous and nationalistic harangue by the Mayor echoes across the wide square (not without eliciting, in the process, the disbelief of some representatives of the working class). Suddenly, the vehicle that carries Carmine's mortal remains emerges from a side street; this forces the Roman politico to act in accordance with Christian piety, standing up and taking off his hat. Forestalled by his superior, the Mayor has no choice but to join him and temporarily suspend his speech. The tailor Andrea, also in (sceptical) attendance at the rally, asks about the identity of the person being led to burial – and, having found out about Carmine's death, decides to accompany him on his last trip. On the same lonely hearse, he and the undertaker vanish together from sight on the road to the cemetery.

When, subsequently, an anonymous nocturnal ghost starts to haunt the streets, the Russian and the Italian narratives again draw near each other. As ever, though, the differences in detail are all-telling – in fact, they are the very point of Lattuada's cinematic re-creation. In Italy, the locals chaotically interfere with one another, exchanging accusations of stealing buttons or even whole overcoats during their encounters. In this way, the film gives no indication whatever that the persecuted underdog takes revenge into his hands; and if Carmine's ignominious death seems to cause the social disruption we witness, that only occurs by the circuitous path of a Babel-like divine punishment.[69]

In Gogol's story we once again have events both more terrible and more laughable than those in its twentieth-century counterpart. In St Petersburg, rumour has it that a dead man (*mertvets*) roams the neighbourhood of the Kalinkin Bridge,[70] indiscriminately snatching coats of all sizes and styles from passers-by; someone even believes to have identified Akaky in this avenging apparition. So much for the terrible. As for the laughable, Gogol provides us with a masterpiece of the absurd within the absurd when he further informs us that 'orders were given to the police to catch the corpse regardless of trouble or expense, dead or alive, and to punish him severely, as an example to others; and they [even] very nearly succeeded in doing so.'[71] Arrested by tobacco-snuffing policemen, the corpse sneezes violently into their eyes – and, taking advantage of their confusion, speedily makes off.

Things can't get quite so fantastic in Italian neorealism: there, for the better or the worse of the story, the devil is not allowed to act as the (dis)organizing method behind the general madness. In *Il cappotto*, discord infects the evil camp by way of comparatively realistic-looking and -sounding developments. Blinded by hubris, the Mayor reproaches his secretary over what he perceives as the collapse of law and order in the city. This causes in the secretary a burst if not of honesty at least of self-respect, which belatedly leads him to resign from his post. As the previously monolithic cohesion of his gang begins to crack, the Mayor becomes increasingly isolated.

In the self-avowedly 'fantastic direction' taken by the ending of Gogol's 'anyway perfectly truthful story,'[72] the Person of Consequence is beginning to get cold feet: ever since he summarily dismissed the poor clerk, 'something not unlike [sympathy]'[73] has been gnawing inside him. When, his week-long scruples having finally forced him to inquire, he finds out about the copyist's tormented death, his entire day is ruined.[74] This is nothing we need to worry about: in yet another reversal, the Person of Consequence goes to see friends for supper and, inspired by – what else? – a couple of glasses of champagne, decides to drown his sorrows in pleasure by making a late-night detour to see his lover.

We can now for a moment leave the Person of Consequence gliding along in his sledge, smugly wrapped in fur and self-righteousness. The Italian Mayor has in the meantime arrived at Caterina's apartment. Here, remorse finally catches up with him, the person ultimately responsible for wrongdoing in the city. It does so, as is appropriate in cinema, in a number of objectified manners: a string of mysterious noises, inaudible to Caterina, haunt the Mayor; the copyist's touchingly comical portrait in the lost overcoat, which Caterina has left lying about her boudoir, catches the Mayor's eye, reminding him of his cruelty; and Caterina's lapdog acts up, affected by some unidentified vibration in the air. Exasperated, in the end the Mayor again puts on his coat and hat and takes leave, walking out into the night.

Gogol's Person of Consequence, for his part, never did reach his intended destination. While sitting in his sled, he

> all at once ... felt that someone had clutched him very tightly by the collar. Turning around he saw a short man in a shabby old uniform, and not without horror recognized him as Akaky Akakievich. The clerk's face was as white as snow and looked like that of a corpse; but the horror of the Person of Consequence was beyond all bounds when he saw the mouth of the corpse [twisted] into speech, and [smelling horribly like a grave] it uttered the following words: 'Ah, so here [thou art] at last! At last I've ... er ... caught you by the collar. It's your overcoat I want; you refused to help me and abused me into the bargain! So now give me yours!' The poor Person of Consequence very nearly dropped dead.[75]

Even this shock, however, hardly caused a Pauline conversion in the bureaucrat: 'He actually flung his overcoat off his shoulders as far as he could and shouted to his coachman in an unnatural voice: "Drive home! Let's get out of here!"'[76] No such mouth-twisting utterances occur in Lattuada's film; quite the contrary, *Il cappotto* makes it plain that neo-realist miracles may happen not only in Milan but even as far away as Pavia.[77] When, on the bridge, Carmine approaches the Mayor, the meek man's tone of voice is entirely conciliatory. Despite the Mayor's simmering ire (and in marked contrast to the brief and terrifying encounter in *Shinel'*) the dialogue here is amiable: the Mayor's early attempt to reproach the employee for his absence at the political rally in the morning[78] is defused by Carmine with disarming simplicity. I did attend, he says, and you even greeted me as I was riding by in the horse-drawn coach.

The coup de théâtre in the film, long in the making and yet not entirely expected, finally occurs when the Mayor, in seeing Carmine hovering a few inches above the roadway, definitively realizes that he is talking to a dead man. His hat falls off, his hair turns white, and he experiences a moral metamorphosis whose edifying impulse seems to know no bounds. He even promises to look for Carmine's overcoat. Though unimpressed by the Mayor's universal promises, Carmine nods ecstatically at this last one. The now white-haired man puts on his hat and takes leave, not without tipping it twice more to wish Carmine good night as he walks off homebound (*nota bene*, warm in his own coat). Carmine respectfully wishes good night in return. In his best suit, as befits a self-respecting corpse, he turns around and vanishes toward the opposite end of the bridge.

Now will the nightly mass hysteria among the citizenry die down? *Il cappotto* does not tell us whether the Mayor will keep his word; but the last scene in the film shows us, in the distance, the dead man as he approaches passers-by with an apologetic mien, checking their overcoats, just in case – and, despite himself, frightening them in the process.

Not unexpectedly, the slight final ambiguity of *Il cappotto* is justified by a much greater one in *Shinel'*, which keeps adding coda after coda to the events. There, after the (limited) change in the Person of Consequence's lifestyle, one could expect the return of peace to the community. But, the story continues, while it indeed appears that 'nothing more was heard of overcoats being snatched from anyone,'

> many restless and anxious people refused ... to be pacified, and still maintained that in remote parts of the town the dead clerk went on appearing. One policeman in Kolomna, for instance, saw with his own eyes an apparition [pop up] from behind a house ...
> [However, the policeman in question was of frail complexion,] so much so that on one occasion an ordinary grown-up suckling pig, making a sudden dash out of some private building, knocked him off his feet to the great amusement of the cabmen standing around, whom he fined two kopeks each for snuff for such disrespect.[79]

The pyrotechnic finale is, in many respects, a cameo of our own experience as readers of Gogol: it is *Shinel'* as a whole that turns us into weak guards trying in vain to police the circulation of meaning in its streets. As soon as we begin to think that, having followed all our clues rationally, we are about to identify our suspect in no uncertain terms and grab him by the scruff of the neck, we are invariably swept off our feet by a mischievous 'ordinary grown-up suckling pig' – obviously, Gogol himself – darting out of a private, only too private, home whose exact logical map (if any) is likely forever to escape our analysis. And, there being no spirited cab-persons around to fine in displaced compensation for our inane efforts, Gogol's ultimate joke is at any rate on us.[80]

Il cappotto reproduces most of the substantive conceptual features of its literary prototype, yet it does so with discerning selectiveness – and thus attains a life of its own that confers on it a solidly independent artistic value. Lattuada's film takes the padding out of Gogol's short story and replaces it with complex narrative material that, while appearing to have little in common with Gogol's Russia, in fact engages the same deep-level issues that generate the Russian plot, and thereby makes them available to us at a higher level of universality. By resolving the original narration in an Italian setting, Lattuada does not merely naturalize the surface-level story in a new country; he reveals – not through pedestrian duplication, but by thoughtful elaboration – what it is that makes *Shinel'* a classic of literature in the first place. If *Il cappotto* succeeds at the cost of a perceptible alteration of *Shinel'*, this is so because such is exactly the price at which cinematic re-creation can be artistically successful at all.

The Bridge of Forking Paths

It is possible, in the specific context of Italian society, to elaborate further on potential figurative readings of Lattuada's film ('anagogical' readings would be the term, borrowed from scriptural exegesis, that a critic of cultural ideology such as Jameson would probably apply here).[81] Such readings allow us to establish the relevance of *Il cappotto* as a first major cross-cultural marker in the artistic life of the then six-year-old Italian republic.

We have already encountered what could be called, in more than one sense, the first political meaning of the story: for some people, indeed for most, the world is not a home, but a cheap *pensione*; for a privileged few, it is a comfortable shuttle from impunity to privilege and then back again. To be sure, the film indicates that the exercise might involve some snags for the powerful: a certain amount of stress, perhaps a crisis, the occasional repentance. However, Carmine De Carmine's plight shows that, barring mysticism or sainthood, poverty does not usually lead to a more fulfilled lifestyle.

A second, important political reading of Lattuada's chilling apologue might be added. Considering that in 1952 the Korean War was still rumbling along (though bogged down not too far from where it eventually fizzled out), it seems logical to read the ubiquitous cold temperature in the film as a subconscious equivalent for the atmosphere of the cold war, and the acquisition of a coat as an attempt at 'warming up' toward one another – an attempt brutally thwarted by violence. Not that it should be surprising if at the height of the cold war Italy produced a film whose symbolism entirely centred on a bitter chill and on the failure of attempts at overcoming it. Simply, it seems paradoxical that, particularly at the time of its release, *Il cappotto* was read exclusively in the light of its surface-level representational component, when in fact – admittedly, with today's eyes – what strikes one most about it is probably its figurative value.[82]

The decade of Lattuada's film can be seen as a time gradually destined, on the one hand, to lift the cold spell blowing in from Yalta and, on the other, to ferry Italy over from the age of bicycle thefts to that of the first traffic jams. In this sense, a third and final metaphorical profile of *Il cappotto* can be sketched, in which the Pavia bridge stands for the transition to a new age beyond poverty, deprivation, and emigration – an age that appears ever within reach and is yet long in coming. Night and darkness seem to linger on endlessly, and the only crossing place on the way to the *miracolo economico* is haunted either by criminals or by ghosts. In 1952, the far side of the bridge is still far away indeed.

Complementary considerations obtain when we frame *Il cappotto* within the history of Italian cinema. From the film's pivotal position one can see three distinct paths depart and diverge, each prefigured in one of its narrative components: the denunciation of historical ills; the depiction of love and other mystical or transcendent experiences; and a comical rendering of reality.

During the years that followed *Il cappotto*, the three-way split among these constitutive elements was destined to lead to mutually alternative, less eclectic, and more 'specialized' artistic positions: for example, Fellini's oneiric universe, Visconti's historical and social engagement, and the *commedia all'italiana* of many others. There is no such *aut/aut* as yet in *Il cappotto*, and thus no need for an exclusive preference of the kind that would later divide critics' allegiances; for example, between the politically committed *Senso* and Fellini's uncommitted *La strada* (1954), or between the struggling migrants of Visconti's *Rocco and His Brothers* (*Rocco e i suoi fratelli*, 1960) and the failed mystics of *La dolce vita*. In 1952, Lattuada's film still represents a maximum common denominator among the anti-Fascists of various inclinations at a time when Italy struggles to cope artistically with the political implications of the cold war era. If in *Il cappotto* the three components just mentioned still hold together, this is because the neorealist atmosphere in which the Italian cinema of the time is still imbued allows them to coexist without apparent conflict.[83]

Coexist, I would argue, and no more; the differences even among democratic artists in those ideology-ridden years were such that *reporting and denouncing theft* was as far as the political agreement among them could go. Without a doubt, to some the Pavia crossing seemed important mainly as a symbolic bridgehead for a coming Revolution; to others, it was a bridge of dreams leading to the fog-covered lands of the self and the subconscious. Lattuada's film can be said to have, in spite of itself, concluded the epoch of neorealist open-endedness toward alternative democratic political options. In a sense, after *Il cappotto* not only De Carmine but neorealism too 'gave up the ghost.'[84]

For the four decades to come, Italians would then remain polarized along ideological lines. One of the unfortunate consequences of that political split was that, for the duration of what is now often referred to as the 'first republic,' Italians focused their attention on allegedly superior partisan objectives, and in the process devalued as inferior the ethics that governed (or should have) the everyday administration of the *res publica*. The history of Italian cinema makes no bones about what happened: for over forty years, theft became the filmic routine – the theft of bicycles (De Sica's *Bicycle Thieves*), of dreams (Fellini's *La strada*), of the *Risorgimento*'s heritage (Visconti's *Senso*), of one's life savings (Fellini's *The Nights of Cabiria/Le notti di Cabiria*, 1957), of public land and funds (Rosi's *Hands Over the City/Mani sulla città*, 1963) ... all the way to the moral wasteland around Amelio's *Stolen Children* (*Il ladro di bambini*, 1992).[85] As for the money grabbing, partisan or personal, of the non-artistic sort, it was to carry on unchecked in the background.

The Interminable Path of History:
Father Sergius and *The Night Sun* (1990)

Groping in the Darkness of Pride: *Father Sergius*

> It was a Russian film, *Father Sergius*, that during the last war gave me an
> inkling of the potential of this young art: Dream, Memory, Hallucination,
> Folly, the Splitting of personality! If cinematographers wanted to, there
> would be such great things to accomplish! (Pirandello)[1]

At the end of the TV-soaked 1980s and against the backdrop of a strikingly unengaged, 'post-political' Italian society, the Tavianis approach
one of the most revered literary figures in their private pantheon and
interrogate him on the subject of solitude. Contrary to what they had
done in their earlier *Saint Michael Had a Rooster* (*San Michele aveva un
gallo*, 1971), re-created from Leo Tolstoy's novella *The Divine and the
Human* (*Bozheskoe i chelovecheskoe*, 1906), the two directors now deal not
with a politically motivated solitude, but with an existential one, related
to the loneliness of a visionary individual in a frivolous society. This time
it is *Father Sergius* (*Otets Sergii*) that they re-create – another story about a
monk, a hermit, a 'saint.' A dilemma not unlike the one that the Tavianis' pupil, Nanni Moretti, sets in the small world of a water-polo game
(*Palombella rossa*, 1989, on which more in chapter 6) recurs in a far more
dramatic manner in the great world of *The Night Sun* (*Il sole anche di
notte*, 1990).[2]

Tolstoy wrote *Father Sergius* during the decade of the 1890s, alternating work on his hermit story with that on longer fiction, theatre, and
poetics. This was the last period of his life, a time when – after the turning point of 1878 – he espoused the cause of an unconventional, socially

critical form of Christianity. Tolstoy's faith was based on non-violence and strict adherence to the precepts expounded by Jesus in the Sermon on the Mount, and is best conveyed by such late texts as the novel *Resurrection* (*Voskresenie*, 1899), the novella *The Divine and the Human* just alluded to, the drama *And Light Shines in the Darkness* (*I svet vo t'me svetit*), and the essay *What Is Art?* (*Chto takoe iskusstvo?* 1897–8). (*And Light Shines in the Darkness* and *Father Sergius* remained without a final revision and were only published posthumously.) The immediate impulse for work on *Father Sergius*, as well as *Resurrection*, was Tolstoy's desire to raise funds for the emigration to Canada of the Dukhobors (or Dukhobortsy), a religious sect that held views similar to Tolstoy's and for that reason was being persecuted by the czarist regime in Russia.[3]

Tolstoy's last years were spent mostly at his estate in Yasnaya Polyana, among frictions and incomprehension within his own family, where the ageing artist devoted himself assiduously to his ethical mission. Yasnaya Polyana became a destination for visitors who appreciated Tolstoy's art and were sympathetic to his world view. During the last few years of the century, in particular, the painter Leonid Osipovich Pasternak – the father of Boris Leonidovich, the future author of *Doktor Zhivago* – would take his family on outings to Tolstoy's residence, both to pay homage to the religious man and to consult with him about his own forthcoming illustrations of *Resurrection*.[4]

Resurrection itself offers a practical condensation of the precepts considered paramount by Tolstoy, those contained in the Gospel of Matthew, 5:21–48.[5] *Father Sergius* reflects an identical outlook on the world and religion, and thus one is not surprised that the novella's artistic importance should have been downplayed in Soviet scholarship, in whose eyes Tolstoy was an important author only to the limited extent that his message could be made to prepare for and support Lenin's. Less comprehensibly, in the West *Father Sergius* is generally treated as a fungible minor item centred on sex and its evils, despite its being a magisterial work that contains in miniature all of Tolstoy's major themes.[6]

From the very first lines of *Father Sergius*, Tolstoy gives the life story of Count Stepan Kasatskii the intriguing features of a reversed novel of ambition:

In Petersburg in the 1840s a surprising event occurred. An officer of the Cuirassier Life Guards, a handsome prince ... left the service, broke off his engagement to a beautiful maid of honor, a favourite of the Empress's, ... and retired to a monastery to become a monk.[7]

Having captured his readers' attention by this anticipation of the story's plot (or, more accurately, of the first part of it), Tolstoy then picks it up again from the beginning. An impressively energetic young cadet from the Military Academy, Count Stepan Kasatskii, who entertains a form of near-adoration for his emperor, experiences a shattering disappointment when he belatedly learns that his fiancée, Mèri (Countess Korotkova),[8] was the czar's lover before the betrothal.[9] He decides to leave the world and become a monk. However, pride and ambition, which were Kasatskii's major motives at court both before and during his betrothal, continue to be the impulses that drive him. This is the original sin of Father Sergius's vocation; and it is an original sin destined to come back to haunt him.

Initially, Father Sergius spends a number of years in regular monasteries. In one of these he has an especially unpleasant experience when his abbot parades him like a trophy before an acquaintance, a visiting general. As if the famous Kasatskii were a rare animal, our monk is put on display, not for the greater glory of God, but for the prestige of men. Seeking more effective removal from politics in the hierarchy, Sergius withdraws to a hermitage in Tambino.

It is here that the next major incident in his life takes place. The cold days of Carnival arrive, the winter roads are butter-smooth and easy to glide on, and a group of merry party-goers happens to pass by in a sled.[10] One of the four, Makovkina by last name, is a divorced woman of great beauty. Her mind peculiarly combines perceptiveness with blindness: she fights off boredom and a certain amount of existential anguish by deliberately cultivating sensation-seeking behaviour. Upon a whim, Makovkina bets with one of the acquaintances in the party that she will spend the night with the handsome hermit Kasatskii in his cave in the forest.

Father Sergius need not wait for the visit of the oblivion-bearing Makovkina[11] to entertain doubts of his own: his faith is, as ever, an unsteady affair. Knowing himself, when the visiting beauty begs for shelter he only reluctantly lets her in; and he takes quick action when the going gets rough. As the sounds from the back of his cell become unendurably self-explanatory (Makovkina's feet are wet from outdoors, and she noisily undresses top to bottom to dry them up), he musters up the courage to cut the matter short in the very same way recommended by the Sermon on the Mount: '[I]f your right hand should cause you to sin, cut it off and throw it away ...'[12] While Father Sergius does not take Matthew altogether literally, he performs the next best feat for a right-handed person operating with an axe: he cuts off the index finger of his left hand. Makovkina, who even at first sight had been impressed by the hermit's powerfully severe looks, is shocked into shame and repentance.

Stories about Makovkina's conversion do the rounds of both aristocratic circles and less well-to-do society. As Father Sergius's fame spreads, people begin to besiege his hermitage with requests for miraculous healings. At first he recoils from performing such feats, considering it an act of pride to comply; later, though, he gives in, and even comes to treat such a healing practice as routine.

A dramatic change now occurs: Sergius's monastery steps in and markets the hermit's performances, turning out a profit in the process. This is of enormous importance to Tolstoy, ever critical of morally tainted institutions, religious or otherwise: '[T]he devil had substituted an activity for men in place of his former activity for God.'[13] In the service of the monastery Father Sergius is de facto a prisoner. The consequences on his morale are easily described: in his life, 'what was internal becomes external'; and he feels 'as if turned inside out.'[14]

It is this alienation that causes Father Sergius's despondency; and it is his despondency that causes his almost instant defeat on a warm evening in May.[15] A merchant accompanying his demented daughter arrives from a faraway province and leads her to Father Sergius's cave.[16] The very rudimentariness of the girl's seduction skills allows her to take Father Sergius by surprise.

The incident leads a shattered Sergius to the second-degree sin of despair. Before dawn, upon awakening, he flees. The path that descends from the mountain runs along a river. 'Yes, I must end it all. There is no God. But how am I to end it? Throw myself into the river? I can swim and should not drown. Hang myself? Yes, just throw this sash over a branch.'[17] It is only Sergius's fatigue that saves him in the end. He collapses in exhaustion and lies motionless on the ground for a while. Hovering between sleep and reverie, he has a vision of himself as a child, in the company of his male friends. They are making fun of Pashenka (Praskovia Mikhailovna), the only girl in the group, who is thin and shy and has big, round eyes. The group bullies her into doing something amusing (for them): showing them how to swim on dry land. She clumsily complies, becoming the boys' laughing stock. She blushes and smiles meekly.[18] Finally, Father Sergius sees an angel in his dream. The angel tells him to go to Pashenka: 'Learn from her what you have to do, what your sin is, and wherein lies your salvation.'[19]

Sergius does so. He sets out and walks hundreds of miles to the town where Pashenka lives. Almost thirty years after they last met, she now becomes the fourth and most beneficent woman in Kasatskii's life story. Pashenka welcomes Father Sergius to her run-down home; in sacred simplicity, she feeds him both physically and spiritually. She brings Stiva (Stepan) up to date about the further developments in her life, which have been harsh to her. Pashenka must support her whole extended family; and in order to do so she patiently submits to giving private music lessons in town. An ironic divine providence seems to have hand-picked the present profession of the aristocrat fallen on hard times: music, Pashenka confesses to Stiva, used to bore her to no end as a girl, and now it feeds her and her next of kin. This, however, she accepts in humility. Pashenka's life is unquestionably the closest thing to a saintly existence we get to read about in *Father Sergius.*

Kasatskii now awakes to the rueful final realization that for his entire life he has only 'lived for men on the pretext of living for God, while [Pashenka] lived for God imagining that she lived for men.'[20] Accordingly, Tolstoy's epilogue shows Sergius on a drastically changed quest for God: he wanders from village to village, serving the people and reading the Gospel in their homes. His progress in the paths of the Lord is finally attested to, one fine day, when he is stopped on a highway by a distinguished Russian couple who accompany a French tourist and find in the pilgrim a perfect specimen for the visitor to seize Russia at her most backwardly authentic. Far from resenting as demeaning an act that, to use his expression of many years in the past, 'exhibits' him 'like a wild beast,'[21] the vagrant now willingly accepts the show's ignominy for the alms he receives – which he promptly passes on to a fellow pilgrim. He is now neither Kasatskii nor even Father Sergius, but, as he says of himself to the strangers, an anonymous servant of God.

On the ninth month of his errancy, our penitent's resurrection to new life is fully accomplished: he is arrested, classed as a tramp, sentenced, and sent to Siberia. There, he settles down 'as the hired man of a well-to-do peasant, in which capacity he works in the kitchen-garden, teaches children, and attends to the sick.'[22] The epilogue of *Father Sergius* thereby merges with that of *Resurrection* not only spiritually but physically and geographically as well. Siberia is the final destination of the formerly ambitious hermit who has at long last succeeded in overcoming his pride, just as it is that of Prince Nekhliudov, who treads a similarly tormented path in belatedly seeking to redress injustices he has committed in his youth.

Siberia is the space of the seemingly interminable path following which both men come to see the light after the long darkness of their pride. That vast space is the backdrop for their purified, regenerated experiences. There, to quote the title of Tolstoy's posthumous drama, light shines in the darkness; and in that new life – according to the Tavianis' film on Father Sergius – one can find sunshine at night too.

A Voyage to the End of the Self: *The Night Sun*

As in Tolstoy's *Father Sergius*, in the Tavianis' story of Sergio Giuramondo a long quest for truth and self-discovery takes the protagonist on a voyage – both inward and outward – to the extreme limits of identity and society. To be sure, Tolstoy's Father Sergius is a practising Christian, while the Tavianis are not. However, a religious outlook and a non-religious one can arguably offer parallel itineraries to what is ultimately one and the same goal: testing the sense of Being by exploring the puny fraction of it called human history.

The only cultural history with which the Tavianis feel sufficiently acquainted to portray it in their art is that of their own country. Accordingly, the majority of their films, whether based on an original screenplay or re-created from a literary source,[23] either are set in Italy or transpose to Italy a situation originating in a different context.[24]

Their version of Sergius's story brilliantly illustrates this pattern. The Tavianis' film plays at the court and in the countryside of the Kingdom of Naples. The time frame of the events is correspondingly modified: in the film we are in the mid-eighteenth century, under the reign of Carlo di Borbone, the king of Spanish origin who held the Neapolitan throne from 1734 to 1759.[25]

While Tolstoy begins his novella by announcing in advance the failure of Kasatskii's experience at court, the Tavianis have more compassion for their Sergio. As a first sign of their kinder attitude, they permit him to retain his name throughout the story; Stepan becomes Sergio both for *barone* Giuramondo and the man of God. In fact, the Tavianis present their protagonist in an endearing prologue. Against the background of the vast open landscapes of Lucania, whose hills, ever-varied in shape, are enlivened by the alternating colours of vegetation and exposed clay, we see Sergio as a child, stretching out a hand toward a fruit tree in bloom, urging it to drop him a petal as a sign of benevolence.[26] The tree complies; Sergio clasps the gift, smiles, thanks the tree, and then leans against it, as if embracing it in gratitude. The prologue thus not only visually conveys the idea, expressed verbally by Tolstoy, that Kasatskii possessed a unique willpower; it also introduces the protagonist to us in a direct, almost intimate way.

The events and situations reported by Tolstoy's narrator – Kasatskii's pre-eminence in major disciplines and his immense pride – are rendered by the Tavianis by making them the object of dialogues occurring at court between the king and his ministers.[27] But a decisive change occurs in the transition: out go what could be called *cold* characteristics, and in come a wealth of *warm* ones. Tolstoy's Kasatskii almost throws a peer out the window because of the latter's sniggering comments about his collection of minerals; and, over a meal, flings a plate of cutlets at an officer who has lied to him.[28] How much more down to earth of the Tavianis' Sergio to have flung a plateful of cutlets at a peer making sniggering comments about his voracious appetite.

In a similar vein, there is no mention in the Tavianis of Sergio learning French. Most characters at court, indeed, speak Italian with a strong regional accent. Despite his German inflection, even the king goes out of his way to speak dialect: 'I studied it with love,' he says, 'so as to be closer to the people.'[29] And while, according to Tolstoy's novella, emperor Nicholas I 'plays with his cadets' – a skilfully ambiguous wording that avoids making a distinction between the literal (an innocent pastime) and the figurative (psychological manipulation)[30] – King Carlo quite literally invites Sergio Giuramondo to play with him. Arch-populistically, the game is not chess, which Kasatskii favours, but a round of cards: the *scopa* the young baron has 'learned from [his] nanny.'[31]

Because Sergio is soon to be promoted to royal adjutant, the sovereign expresses concern about the dejection to be experienced by the other forty-nine cadets who will see the fiftieth leap ahead of them. This point introduces a sensitive situation: unlike Tolstoy's, the Tavianis' protagonist belongs to the small provincial nobility. One of the ministers objects to the king's decision: 'He comes from the countryside in Basilicata! In that respect, the majority of the other cadets is worthier.'[32] This difference has a considerable impact on the protagonist's psychology. While in Tolstoy it is Kasatskii who, in order to satisfy his ambition, single-mindedly pursues the goal of a brilliant marriage at court,[33] in the Tavianis the situation is reversed: it is only so as to overcome the court's reluctance to see Sergio promoted that the king (upon defeat at *scopa*, though not necessarily because of it) decides to step in and find him a suitable bride. Sergio Giuramondo's portrait thereby begins to take a shape recognizably distinct from Kasatskii's: not only do we understand his personality better than his prototype's, we also understand that he has a better personality.

What about Kasatskii's intense devotion to his paternalistically inclined czar, of which Tolstoy makes so much? The Tavianis' cinematic re-creation of this feeling converts it into a secular confession to the king on Sergio's part. With a second flashback to Sergio's childhood, we are transported to the time when the king went south to plan the reclamation of a marsh near the child's home town. On that occasion, while the law of great numbers imposed conformity and mental torpidity upon the courtiers, exceptional individuals could ideally reach out to one another:

> 'Your ministers and the court were sceptical ... I was eight years old then, and I had no way of knowing this, but I sensed that Your Majesty was alone.
> When we went back home, I refused to take the coach, and covered the whole distance on foot.'[34]

A relationship that in Tolstoy entails subordination becomes for the Tavianis a bond between equals. What the two Promethean brothers of *The Night Sun* have in common (all reference to a possible personal empathy by Paolo and Vittorio being here, of course, intentional) is a shared solitude in the swamps of backwardness: a feeling of closeness based on a joint mission.

Viewers have by now begun to suspect that a monk's vacillations may not be everything – perhaps not even the main thing – about *The Night Sun*. At this precise time, the details of Sergio's flashback support with clarity the idea of a *lay* dimension in a religious subject matter.[35] Sergio's mother assists the limping child upon his return from the exceedingly long walk; she takes off one of his shoes, discovering inside it a bloodied sock and – a large pebble.

> *Mother.* 'What's this pebble for?'
> *Sergio.* 'I've made a vow ... When I'm an adult, *I* want to be the one standing at the king's side, so I can help him.'[36]

Vows are normally taken for reasons related to worship and faith, but the Tavianis propose one with an alternative rationale: the lone individual (little Sergio) is absorbed by the thought of a titanic task (eradicating malaria) and by the procurement of the means (an alliance of sorts with the king) for the implementation of his visionary utopia. A hubris-laden vessel, ever in danger of capsizing? To be sure, but no more so than that of many among the Tavianis' heroes, from Salvatore, the peasant and labour-union organizer in *A Man to Be Burned*, to the protagonists of *The Subversives*; from Giulio Manieri, who commits suicide in *Saint Michael Had a Rooster*, to Allonsanfán, to the Gavino of *Padre padrone*.[37] To this extent, the selfish ambition of Tolstoy's Kasatskii can be said to be reformulated in *The Night Sun* and to become functional to an entirely new, specifically Tavianian logic.

That said, *The Night Sun* differs from other films by the Tavianis on heroic solitude insofar as its introduction of the protagonist's dramatic confrontation with a particularly bleak reality occurs not at the end of a long lifetime, but at its outset. The film, in other words, compresses to a maximum the period devoted to visions of a golden age, and focuses instead on the agony that follows their collapse. *The Night Sun* is all about what could be called a post-delusionary time.

The *desengaño* I am alluding to obviously coincides with Sergio's discovery of the previous goings-on between the two people he loves most, the king and his own fiancée, Cristina.[38] Unlike Tolstoy, the Tavianis introduce the bride's family to us; they do so in order to visualize both the emotion and the ambiguity of the moment. (Their king sends Cristina gifts of considerable symbolic ambivalence: two mechanical birds in a cage, which sing upon command and cannot fly away; and two live turtledoves, which, when released, flap to freedom in the twinkling of an eye.)[39] The sad revelation eventually occurs in the palace of Cristina's family: not in the wing flooded with the ongoing marriage festivities, but, in stark contrast, inside a dimly lit, deserted ballroom. With remarkable perceptiveness, the Tavianis transfer Tolstoy's scene from the bright daylight of the park of Tsarskoe Selo to the spotty obscurity of a heavily curtained salon, where the two protagonists acquire and lose relief by sequentially entering and exiting luminous bands of sunshine penetrating the room through the windows – a figurative rendering of the checkered quality of good and evil in life unexpectedly revealed to Sergio by Cristina's confession about her past.

The Tavianis' dialogues largely correspond to Tolstoy's, from Cristina's broken-hearted admission to Sergio's final ire toward her mother: 'If only you weren't a woman!'[40] Some new lines are added (Cristina's 'Everyone knew ... and that's the only reason why my family accepted you')[41] to stress the factors liable to elicit Sergio's imminent, proud rebellion. However, unquestionably the most effective cinematic element here is the Tavianis' rendering of Kasatskii's immediate, stunned reaction to the painful news: 'Don't touch me! Don't touch me! Oh, how it [hurts]!'[42] These words are left out in the film. What we find instead is a rapid shot of the red coat of Sergio's uniform, which he drops on the elegantly decorated floor of the palace. In the filmic version, not only does the relinquished garment foreshadow Sergio's impending decision to let go of an entire lifestyle; by the manner in which it is laid out, mimicking the colour and shape of a large pool of blood, it also powerfully materializes the pain of the wound just suffered by Sergio.

The Night Sun now focuses on the days spent by Sergio at home with his family after he has renounced the world. Little in this part of the film is taken directly from the novella. The only element of an unequivocally Tolstoyan origin is the comment made by Sergio's mother: 'I know why he does this: because he wants to position himself higher than those who humbled him.'[43] Other incidents are instead entirely new; for example, Sergio's descent from the terrace of his home high atop the valley to the banks of the river Basento – an action that his mother misinterprets as a possible attempted suicide. When his sister Giuseppina finally re-establishes contact with him, Sergio shakes his head and pities her for the misapprehension, explaining: 'I would never drown myself in the water where we learned how to swim as children.'[44]

A third flashback to Sergio's childhood, falling somewhere between the two extremes of direct reproduction from the original text and entirely free creation, converts into cinematic sequence a comment on Kasatskii's deep religiosity made by Tolstoy's narrator. The film shows a sacred procession in Sergio's home town of Matera, in which the child zealously participates. As the Holy Sacrament approaches, he helps strew flower petals on the cobblestones in its path; and when, at last, the divine symbol fully offers itself to the boy's eyes, he offers himself in turn: 'Take me, my Lord, take me!'[45]

The farthest-reaching modification contributed by the Tavianis in this section, indeed in the novella's entire plot line, is the introduction of an elderly peasant couple that Sergio knows from his childhood. Living on a very poor farmstead by the Basento River, the two, Eugenio and Concetta Lauria, are destined repeatedly to allay Sergio's loneliness at uniquely difficult junctures in his life. (To stress the selflessness of their generosity, we are to learn their names only after their death.) The choice of leaving the *saeculum* behind is certainly one such moment for Sergio; and he now seeks their company, joining them in tilling the soil. The symbolic key to Eugenio and Concetta's role is their peculiar way of making ends meet: they not only work in the fields but also raise pigeons and collect their manure for sale. By submitting to the lowliest chores, they set the example of a viable alternative to Sergio's *superbia*. This is not to say that for them virtue is its own reward; dealing with their real, all-too-real birds (one of them delivers an unsolicited quantum of fertilizer on Sergio's head) at least allows them to stay clear of the gilded cage, cast in a brittle alloy of submissiveness and pride, that imprisons birds at the king's court.

The next episode, in which the Tavianis follow Tolstoy closely, shows to what extent Sergio is still a man of the world. The ceremony in church attended by top brass and aristocracy ends, as Kasatskii's had, with Sergio's encounter with an army general – not Kasatskii's anonymous commander, but a former peer of Sergio's, Prince Santobuono. As in Tolstoy, the meeting closes with a judgmental reproach made by the monk to his superior: 'I have renounced the world; why do you still want to put me on show?'[46]

Now Sergio, too, becomes aware that pride is the main obstacle between God and him. It is to fight this pride that he sets out on foot for the mountains of the Abruzzi.[47]

Above the timberline, a specifically Italian context of ascetic renunciation awaits Sergio. Not only is his predecessor and brother *in Christo*, Egidio, buried next to his rudimentary dwelling, but the mountains themselves seem to bear the spiritual traces of perhaps the most famous recluse in the history of the Church: fra Pietro da Morrone, who, having lived as a hermit on Mount Maiella, near Sulmona, was later elected to the papal see as Celestino V in 1294, and resigned after only a few months, in abhorrence of the moral compromises which his continued tenure would have forced on him. (Celestino V was the pope whom Dante stigmatized for having carried out 'the great refusal,' *il gran rifiuto*: an abdication clearing the path for his successor Boniface VIII's misdeeds.)[48] Next to Egidio's tomb, consisting of a mere pile of rocks, a skeletal tree against the backdrop of barren high-elevation pastures reminds Sergio that, while the paths of the Lord are infinite, the ones that pass through the comforts of the flesh are not those most likely to lead to Him. Contemplating such extreme surroundings, Sergio vacillates for a moment; and the Tavianis have him lean against the tree, repeating the imploration of his childhood: 'Take me, my Lord, take me!' With this, they effectively render, once and for all, Tolstoy's multiple allusions to the lapses and rebounds of Father Sergius's faith during prayer.

However, before returning to Tolstoy for the major narrative peripety of Makovkina's visit, the Tavianis have Sergio meet with Concetta and Eugenio again. More years go by; snow falls, accumulates, and then

melts again around the hermit's hut, until one day the two ageing peasants from the house with the pigeon-shed wander up the vast valley.
Smiling, they bring with them a woollen shirt made for Sergio by his late
mother; and, more disquietingly, a doubt that nags them. Would it be
possible, they ask *padre* Giuramondo, to beg the Lord for the grace of
dying together on the fateful day He will appoint? While remaining
non-committal on this particular wish, Sergio expresses in other ways his
affection for them.[49]

The moment of the two substitute parental figures' departure sup-
plies us with the information necessary to understand the film's title.
After they embrace and bid each other farewell, Eugenio wishes Sergio
'Many beautiful days!'; to this Concetta adds, 'With sunshine ... at night
too.' The Tavianis explain both the dialogue and the title as a reference
to a Tuscan idiom common in the area of their native San Miniato.[50]
The idea clearly appears overdetermined if we understand it as an addi-
tional homage to Tolstoy, echoing the title of his drama *And Light Shines
in the Darkness*.

It is now time for the Temptress to knock at the door. The Tavianis'
evening visitor, Aurelia, differs in two aspects from Tolstoy's Makovkina.
Nothing – least of all her young age – suggests that she is a divorcee; and
her dissatisfaction, while also rooted in the shallowness of aristocratic
routine, is exasperated by the limitations that etiquette imposes on her
as a woman.[51] (There is a further difference in setting: in Russia we have
winter and sleds, while in the Italian version carriages on wheels rattle
about, braving a summer thunderstorm.)

The interaction between the auditive and the visual is quite complex
in this filmic episode. Because Tolstoy's Father Sergius looks away
throughout the time of the temptation, Makovkina has to engage in the
pezzo di bravura of performing her seduction entirely by auditive means,
and Tolstoy's narrator must tackle the related one of turning her music
into words. In an audio-visual medium such as the one in which the
Tavianis operate, Tolstoy's efforts become unnecessary – and the facts
hit us (though not Sergio, who also looks away) altogether graphically.
Removing her wet stockings, giggling, brushing her hair, dropping her
clothes, stepping on the wooden floor, rubbing her feet with her hands
so as to warm them up: these are, in short, the six movements of Aurelia's chamber impromptu.[52] All the while, the soundtrack magnifies the
corresponding sounds to reflect the deafening resonance these attain in
Sergio's consciousness.

At the appropriate moment, the Tavianis even raise the stakes with respect to the original text. In Tolstoy, when Makovkina's friends come to pick her up she silently sits in the sled for the trip home.[53] By contrast, in the film the repentant Aurelia – as if to punish that part of her body that has sinned the most – shuns the coach and strides barefoot all the way to the bottom of the mountain.[54]

Unlike Tolstoy's, the Tavianis' exchanges in the hut are as unexpectedly secular as they are reticent about the magnetic spiritual force that brought Sergio to his hermitage. This is how monk and damsel converse, sitting back to back on parallel benches, almost touching each other with their shoulders:

> *Sergio.* 'Since you came into this room, I forgot the reasons why I am up here ...'
> *Aurelia.* 'I cannot see a single one.'
> *Sergio.* 'I can only remember the astonishment I experienced when, as an adolescent, I used to marvel at the indifference of people ... How is it possible, I would always ask myself, that nobody cares about anyone else, and that nobody wonders why? This is the reason why I told myself that if at least one man, one man only, removed himself from the whole world, so as to meditate on all others and for all others, we may perhaps still have a reason for hope.'[55]

As a theological argument, Sergio's words would be only half unassailable; the other half of their strength can only be grasped by interpreting them as the thinly veiled profession of faith of a lay character in line with an entire gallery of heroes portrayed in other Tavianian films. The Sergio of *The Night Sun* is evidently best understood as a cipher for the Tavianis' many visionary individuals who, despite the circumstances, uphold their faith in a future utopia. Granted, in their striving these characters take widely diverging paths: in *A Man to Be Burned*, Salvatore fights the Mafia; in *Saint Michael Had a Rooster* and *Allonsanfán* Giulio Manieri and Allonsanfán, respectively, organize revolutionary expeditions; and, in *Padre padrone*, Gavino seeks his own intellectual betterment against seemingly unsurmountable odds. Yet there is no mutual contradiction among such options, as there is none between them as a whole and Sergio's equally elusive ideal, an ideal he had described in a letter from the convent to his sister Giuseppina as 'the highest perfection, both inward and outward.'[56] The goals for which each of these protagonists strives differ; it is the striving that remains the same.

The directors, though – and Tolstoy with them – know better than to assume there is a butter-smooth path between man and God. And, in both Tolstoy and the Tavianis, a combination of diverse types of perversity brings Sergio to perdition. In both Tolstoy and the Tavianis, the superstition of the populace, on the one hand, and the even more inexcusable voraciousness of the church, on the other, consume the hermit physically and spiritually, until he ignominiously surrenders to sin.[57]

Before that moment strikes, however, the film injects a new element into Tolstoy's narration: raids by local brigands. There is a cogent logic to the addition, as the presence of bands of outlaws in the mountains of the *Mezzogiorno* corresponds to a well-known historical reality.[58] By reflecting this fact, the Tavianis prove the seriousness of their ongoing participation in the political vicissitudes of their country. The very choice of the predominant colours in these sequences illustrates the extent to which Italy is symbolically present in the directors' minds: the lush green of the pastures surrounding Sergio's hut contrasts with the whiteness of the grazing sheep and the bright red of the brigands' coats.[59]

A further means by which the Tavianis can be said to enrich Sergio's story at this juncture is their originality in building upon the opportunities offered by the visual component of cinema. In the instance, they foreground an element that Tolstoy seems unwilling to put to narrative fruition: Sergio's left hand, with the last two phalanges of the left index finger cut off. The Tavianis emphasize superstition among the uneducated masses in a sequence in which Sergio is forced at gunpoint to impose his hand on the head of a brigand's son. Believing the impaired hand to have magical powers that enable it to heal all manners of illnesses, the Tavianis' brigand insists that Sergio use the wounded limb, not the intact one, for his thaumaturgic practice. In the end, Sergio complies. Does this matter to us? Considerably. Thanks to the Tavianis' explicit visualization of the verbal, the viewers of the film can solidly retain something that tends to slip from the consciousness of the novella's readers: namely, the fact that Sergio's 'magic' hand is the *left* one. The realization that his miracles are being performed with the left hand immediately conjures up the vast folkloric context that links this particular side of the body with the devil. Clearly, what the Tavianis foreground by their cinematic re-creation of Tolstoy's story is the idea that the feats carried out by Sergio are 'left-handed miracles,' and could thus be called devil's prodigies.[60]

That demonic pride should eventually take the front seat, and Sergio fatalistically follow, is altogether consistent with Tolstoy's original story. This is precisely what occurs in *The Night Sun* with the triumph of the devil's hyperactivity: the building frenzy soon unleashed by the monastery around the monk. Sergio's hut, formerly nestled inside a ruined tower as a tangible reminder of the world's *vanitas vanitatum*, is cleared out by a team of masons, and the ruin itself built up again into a chapel eerily resembling a military structure. At the same time, Egidio's tomb is obliterated by an altar made out of expensive stone. Lastly and perhaps most importantly, Egidio's formerly denuded tree now 'blossoms' by means of countless suspended metal ex-votos that tinkle in the wind and blink in the sun in a manner decidedly recalling decoys for wild fowl. With a small loan from the Italian cultural tradition – the immediate subtext being the corresponding temptation not even remotely battled by Pinocchio – the Tavianis have a dejected Sergio observe the outrage and mutter to the invisible spirit of his predecessor: 'You can no longer help me, Egidio; they turned you into the Tree of Cockaigne.'[61] The chain of demonic miracles in the film lengthens by one link as the old tree so flourishes.

It is at this time that the merchant from afar starts up the slope of the hermit's mountain with his weak-minded daughter.[62] Before the two make it to the top, though, the directors create and introduce another apparent success of Sergio's. On the fifth anniversary of the brigand boy's healing, a band of outlaws swoops down on the encampment on horseback and carts, derisively dropping gifts for the holy man: 'Pigs for your poor, and prisoners freed for your sake!'[63] One of the liberated hostages turns out to be a good acquaintance: Prince Santobuono, the former comrade-in-arms whom Sergio last saw years before at the all-too-worldly Mass in Naples.

Santobuono's role now comes to further fruition. Not only does his emotion-laden appearance strengthen the narrative logic of introducing the brigands, it also offers Padre Sergio an opportunity to engage in heartfelt soul-baring with his friend:

Sergio. 'Mine is not a job, it is a mission ... except that now it is *becoming* a job.'
Santobuono. 'And yet, it should be less difficult to seek God in a place like this.'
Sergio. 'Those who seek God will not find Him, I fear. Perhaps those who seek truth will encounter God.'[64]

Thus truth, interchangeably with God, is the essence of the matter in 1990, almost a century after Tolstoy's evangelical version of the story.

Then the seduction of Sergio occurs. When comparing the literary episode to the cinematic one, we notice the Tavianis' originality in carrying out adjustments that both enhance the linearity of the narration and use the visual dimension to stress its spiritual component.[65] They leave out an upsetting dialogue that Tolstoy's Father Sergius has with a visitor (a young professor who, despite being an atheist, happens to be tranquil and at peace with himself), and add a novel incident in its stead: a pig is festively roasted by the miracle seekers outside the new chapel. Dishing out to Sergio a portion of that meal, an attendant overrides his moral objections by casuistically arguing, 'It's pork all right, but it's the pig of the miracle. It's going to give you strength.'[66] As for the merchant's daughter, the Tavianis re-create her by casting the twenty-two-year-old, extremely short woman described in the novella as one noticeably younger in age and of normal stature. Also, continuing their policy of modifying characters' names to suit new times and places, they change hers to Matilda.[67]

The specific form of the girl's mental derangement, described in Tolstoy as neurasthenia, remains generic in the Tavianis;[68] flashes of her instinctual behaviour are rendered by having her lap milk from a bowl like an animal. Father Sergius's original 'You are the devil' becomes Sergio's more tentative '*If you weren't ill, I would say that* you are the devil.'[69] Conversely, Matilda places Sergio's (right) hand not on her breast but directly on her *bare* breast – an appropriate deictic equivalent of Tolstoy's statement that Father Sergius felt 'that he was overcome and that his desire had already passed beyond control.'[70]

Upon awakening and becoming aware of his fall, the Tavianis' Sergio flees his cell, as Sergius had done in Tolstoy. He, too, is now ready for the corresponding angelic apparition. A cultural problem lurks here, however: a providential dream would poorly suit a late-twentieth-century film about the artist's and thinker's loneliness in a consumeristically minded society. Accordingly – and consistently with the directors' modus operandi in reading Tolstoy – Sergio's religious experience in overcoming the temptation of suicide is rendered by means of one that is secular in nature.

To this end, the Tavianis altogether discard Father Sergius's vision. Instead, they expand to a full episode Tolstoy's original half-liner: 'To throw myself in? I can swim and should not drown.'[71] Having fastened his hands inside his belt, their Sergio marches out into, and at first to the bottom of, a small, quiet mountain pond amidst open pastures.[72] As he disappears under the water and the ripples above his head slowly subside, a long uncertainty hovers over his fate. When Sergio finally darts to the surface, splashing about and gasping for air, we make sense of his return to life by recalling what he had told his sister many years before: that he would never be able to drown himself in the water where they had learned how to swim as children. Clearly, under water Sergio's consciousness develops a response at the borderline between the physical (a body struggling to preserve itself) and the emotional (a soul aching with the sorrow of 'betraying' its past as a child). It seems appropriate that what could be called the lay peripety of the Tavianis' drama should occur under water, in a no-man's-space hidden from our view. Here not only Sergio but, more pertinently, the directors themselves metaphorically find a way back to the world – to a human society in which life must go on despite all trials.

The Tavianis' denouement is both swifter and more uplifting than Tolstoy's. Swifter, because they have *already* re-created Pashenka's role in Eugenio's and Concetta's; and more uplifting, because thanks to the compassionate couple Sergio will soon be in a position to feel that not everything he has done was in vain.

For the third time, we now see Sergio, on his way home, approach the tree that presented him with a petal many years before. But it is late summer, both for the tree and for the man; and Sergio walks on until he reaches Matera. First, he sadly inspects his empty, untended home (his sister has in the meantime left too). Then, as he would often do in days of old, he takes the path to the Basento River, and once more hikes down to the two peasants' house. The farmstead with the pigeons, inhabited by a new family, acts as the catalyst for a symbolic summary of all that was good and bad in Padre Sergio's life. Instead of the couple, now deceased, there lives a mother with her three children. The young woman asks Sergio a question that seems certain to contain an authorial allusion: 'Did you need any pigeons' manure?'[73] Pigeons' manure is indeed something Sergio would have had use for during his youth – as a pedagogical tool, that is. Instead, his fanatic pursuit of honour and ambition blinded him to compassion (above all toward Cristina) and caused great suffering in him and others.

On the bright side, the young mother also announces to Sergio something that could justify a claim on his part to have performed at least one real miracle in his life. His two elderly friends have died, but

'[t]hey died beautifully, they died together! ...
They died at the same time – right there, behind you, while they were

collecting pigeon manure, within a minute from each other. Angela, do you remember? As if they had planned it out in advance!'[74]

Sergio seems to understand much as he hears this. When he reaches their tombs – two simple mounds of earth, with a single cross mid-way – he kneels and pensively imposes his hands on them. The same blessing he had grown accustomed to giving in pride is now imparted as an act of love.

The film ends with one of the childrens' balloon being blown away by the wind, while Sergio walks away and his silhouette slowly grows fainter against a sea of wheat-coloured hills. Meanwhile, the mother's voice-over retrospectively explains – as the narrator does in Tolstoy – that the monk then spent years on the land, going from house to house to help people, and finally vanished altogether from sight.

No matter how moving the film's end, though, the image in *The Night Sun* by which the viewers' minds may remain most indelibly impressed is one that shortly precedes it. I am referring to a freeze-frame at the time when Sergio is kneeling by the tombs. The mother stands next to him; behind her, the boys are playing a noisy game. To protect Sergio's contemplation, she makes a gesture meant to silence the children: she raises her left arm and hand back toward them, her fingers fanned out in a gentle sign that denotes a warning, a command, a plea for sympathy with human suffering. Why is the close-up shot, lasting a few seconds, so significant? Only accessorily because the woman's hand is as beautifully and elegantly disposed as an angel's in a Renaissance painting of the Annunciation; more importantly, because it is an *uninjured, intact* left hand. It is a hand blessed by the beauty of selfless simplicity, undefaced by the artificial efforts demanded by pride.

At Home in History

In Siberia, the far East of his country, Tolstoy's Father Sergius finds his freedom and his personal form of interrelation with humanity. Sergio Giuramondo finds them in the deep South of his own country, re-creating voyage with voyage and frontier with frontier.

It seems fair to say, however, that tilling the soil, collecting manure, and raising a family cannot be but figurative, ideal answers to Sergio's dilemma. What, then, is the meaning of the Tavianis' quest for truth and self-discovery? Their obvious starting point is that neither a king (representing political power) nor a church (symbolizing ideological allegiance to a group) allows any room to satisfy an individual's, let alone an artist's, need for inward development. Beyond this, and less intuitively, what the directors go on to show in *The Night Sun* is that even some of the alternatives to the above-mentioned paths of power eventually lead to aporias of their own: so, for example, self-absorption in blissful solitude, or the cultivation of one's own myth as a creator of miracles – if only of the artistic kind.

With Sergio's story the Tavianis argue that, while there are many reasons why life in society may seem to be a curse, there is no salvation in isolation either. The position of *The Night Sun* is that the answer to each individual's dilemmas can only be found by going back, in humility, to identifying and appreciating the interaction between a land and its people: a complex dialectic that the generally accepted cultural shorthand has, over centuries, become accustomed to calling history.

Sergio's answer is strikingly similar to that offered by Nikolai Nikolaevich, the most Tolstoyan character in Pasternak's *Doctor Zhivago*:

'Now what is history? It is the centuries of systematic explorations of the riddle of death, with a view to overcoming death ...

[M]an does not die [out of doors, by a fence] – but *at home in history*, while the work toward the conquest of death is in full swing; he dies sharing in this work.'[75]

The novel's narrator echoes Nikolai Nikolaevich by describing in words of his own the past in which our roots lie:

Every motion in the world taken separately was calculated and purposeful, but, taken together, [people] were spontaneously intoxicated with the general stream of life which united them all. People worked and struggled, each set in motion by the mechanism of his own cares. Yet the mechanisms would not have worked properly had they not been regulated and governed by a higher sense of a [fundamental] freedom from care. This freedom came from the feeling that all human lives were interrelated, a certainty that they flowed into each other – a happy feeling that all events took place not only on the earth, in which the dead are buried, but also in some other region which some called the Kingdom of God, others history, and still others by some other name.[76]

Pasternak's words describe with admirable precision the final station reached in the Tavianis' voyage to the end of the self.

As children of such an intricately defined 'history,' the Tavianis find a guide in Tolstoy, who believes that the interminable path of history consists of the sum of the countless paths taken by individual human stories. Thus, the path of *The Night Sun* – which begins with *Father Sergius* and ends with the Siberia of *Resurrection* and the title of *And Light Shines in the Darkness* – leads us through countless stories: Stepan Kasatskii's / Sergio Giuramondo's, and all those that it intersects.

Not that history must necessarily be a theme in films; it is films that are *steeped in history*. At the beginning of the 1980s, the Tavianis clearly expressed their awareness of this:

> *Paolo.* If our films have any meaning at all, that meaning corresponds to the various phases that have characterized our period of history, the years from 1960 on. Since we partook passionately, to the end, in these twenty years of history, these twenty years of our life, we had no choice but to express them ...
> *Vittorio.* Ideas ... do not arise by chance, much less from Jupiter's head. They are the shared heritage of each historical moment; and in each individual case they materialize, perhaps in unexpected ways, through individuals – the *auteurs*.[77]

To be sure, the 1980s ushered in difficult times for Italian cinema. A historical boom in the revenues of commercial television stations translated into a corresponding decline for filmmaking, permanently reversing (or so it seems) the traditional hierarchy in the relative economic ranking of cinema and television.[78] Just like Padre Sergio in *The Night Sun*, directors then began to seem like mystics who, in their lonely pastures, are suddenly flushed out of their huts by frenzied crowds: crowds that, while hell-bent for miraculous special effects, remain stubbornly insensitive to the artistic values that ought to justify producing those wonders in the first place. In such circumstances, are directors to take up the passes made by the merchant's demented, milk-lapping daughter, television – and thus lapse into an unforgivable sin, one that may lead to self-hatred and artistic self-destruction?[79]

On the whole, however, it is comforting to see that a host of Italian directors, having 'learned how to swim' in their youth, have simply proved unable to commit suicide. What should they do then? To the extent possible, imitate Sergio and resume exploring the self by exploring their own link with their fellow human beings. It is this broadly speaking historical vocation, this characteristic sense of symbiosis with its own society, that has enabled post–Second World War Italian cinema to produce – alongside items conceived for entertainment of a more ephemeral sort – the impressively high number of lasting masterpieces that justify the privileged position it now occupies on the world's cultural scene.

THE RE-CREATION TO END
ALL CREATION

Requiem for a Utopia:
Salò or the 120 Days of Sodom (1975)

Sade: Utopia/Eutopia, Dystopia, Blasphemy[1]

Sadism is only the coarse (vulgar) *contents* of the Sadean text. (Barthes)[2]

Klossowski and Barthes have made such strong cases for viewing the Marquis de Sade as a utopianist/eutopianist that it has by now become almost obligatory to read the divine Marquis in that transcendent context. For Klossowski, Sade pursues the ideal of the 'integral man,'[3] in which the height of freedom can only be attained by a paroxysmal 'corruption taken to its limit'[4] that leads to the splendidly flourishing utopia/eutopia of a 'permanent insurrection.'[5] For Barthes, Sade is to be inscribed in the visionary-regulatory tradition that stretches from Loyola to Fourier. Systematically unleashing the senses within a minutely codified ritual – the goal of which, subverting the title of one of Sade's most famous works, could be called his 'philosophy in the *un*dressing room' (*La philosophie dans le boudoir*) – is for Barthes a symptom of Sade's somewhat oxymoronic materialistic mysticism.[6] For both critics, Sade's position is that of a frustrated 'totalitarianist,' who, disappointed by reality, turns from the pursuit of totality within the Good to the phantasmatic quest for a perverted totality of an opposite moral sign – a search most notably carried out in texts such as *Les 120 journées de Sodome*.

Nevertheless, as an eighteenth-century rationalist, Sade could also be a utopianist/eutopianist of a more conventional kind, matching and in some sense outbidding what could be called the contractual-constitutional obsession of his own place and time. In a cultural atmosphere in which almost every author considering himself to be worth his salt, from

Rousseau to Restif de la Bretonne, made it a point of honour to flex his intellectual muscles by drafting novel social covenants for countries near and remote, real or imagined, Sade too tested his mettle by producing full-fledged literary utopias/eutopias of the kind usually recognized by the public as such. Two examples of this kind are at hand for us when Sade incorporates two extended digressions, 'The Kingdom of Butua' and 'Zamé, King of the island of Tamoé,' into *Aline and Valcour, or Philosophical Novel* – a long and complex text whose subtitle telescopes, thus partly obfuscating, the book's double identity as an adventure *novel* and a 'conte *philosophique.*'[7]

We know that Sade's a-moral endorsement of *jouissance* met with systematic repression by both the old regime and the new one, and eventually also by the one that was to be the newest of all, Napoleon's. The causes for this are not difficult to rationalize. The pre-revolutionary monarchic system could certainly tolerate the privileges and even the debauchery of the aristocracy, but only so long as they could be supported by ideological props of a moralizing nature: power by divine right, the subjects' duty of Christian obedience, the good of the nation as a symbolic organism, and so on. But Sade's unmediated and unapologetic defence of hedonism threatened to (and, with the Marquis's scandalous raids through the provincial countryside, did in fact) tear away the veil from the reality of violence as a class privilege – and thus also, by implication, from the reality of all class privilege as violence. It is one thing to savour one's delicious morsels in a golden ghetto tucked away from the envious glances of the populace, and quite another to turn an exclusive *petite cuisine* into a publicly advertised banquet exposing to all and sundry the arbitrariness of a partition that, generation after generation, cordons off the brow that sweats with toil from the brow that perspires with pleasure. The moralism of pre-revolutionary power (brandished, it should be noted, first and foremost within Sade's own family) was dogged but by and large rational in repressing the Marquis's mania to divest his own and other people's bodies: it correctly identified such a drive as a force destined to show the working classes that, quite literally, emperors are always naked.

By a no less transparent opposite logic, it was also impossible for Sade's materialistic hedonism to be adopted by the revolutionaries struggling against the aristocratic regime. These leaders were a group of intellectuals for whom a republican upbringing within the scope of classical antiquity went hand in hand with the need to develop an anti-monarchic set of principles. The archetypal human quality of the

Roman republic, that of *virtus*, embodied for most of them the desirable traits of the *civis/citoyen* – and included the notion of a sensual restraint (if not outright moralism) that flew in the face of Sade's obsessively regulated *dérèglement de tous les sens*.[8]

As for the Napoleonic period, which saw Sade's imprisonment continue in all but name at the insane asylum in Charenton, it is obvious that the new-but-old monarchic regime, with its emphasis on law and order, would have made the public advocacy of debauchery untenable even if it had not chosen – as it in fact did – to seek a reconciliation with the Catholic church by the Concordat of 1801.

From prison, Sade responds to what he perceives as a wicked, repressive social order by taking refuge in a writing practice that turns his yearning for utopia/eutopia into the self-contained prison of his private dystopia. As the social mediations built into the conventions of narrativity fall by the wayside, the Sadean text disrobes itself more and more of characters and plot line, and, shunning a representation of pleasure achieved through power and the submission of others, adopts the portrayal of orgasm by way of the Other's annihilation. In *Les 120 journées* the destructive function is embraced with such force that it ends by undermining pleasure and almost altogether hollowing it out. As I will argue more in detail later, Sade's book thus remains virtually deprived of pleasure in the sense we would normally expect the word to have in a piece of fiction ostensibly 'about sex.'

As is clear from even the most cursory glance at the work, dystopia is indeed the ground from which *Les 120 journées* arose. The long scroll left to us (a product of Sade's wile against his jailers) contains 600 micronarratives, illustrating as many forms of perversion distributed over a 120-day period. The events are supposed to occur in the fictional castle of Silling during the months of November, December, January, and February of a no further specified year in Sade's own century. There are various narrators, who tell the 600 stories to libertines/executioners and their many victims. At irregular intervals and in unpredictable patterns, some of the narrated stories are 'tried out' by the debauchers onto the debauchees, generally causing – among other things – the latters' painful deaths. The manuscript, which Sade never completed and was published only posthumously, finds a conclusion of sorts in a synoptical tabulation of how many people survive and how many have died by what means, with notes about the book's next planned draft.

Les 120 journées combines both imitation and inversion of certain structural and thematic features contained in Boccaccio's *Decameron*.[9]

Like *Decameron, Les 120 journées* consists of a cycle of narrations by story-tellers for the benefit of a public gathered in a location hermetically sealed from the outside world. (Boccaccio writes of a *palagio*; Sade has a castle.) The content of Sade's stories, however, has nothing to do with the themes broached in *Decameron*[10] and focuses instead on complex combinations of what are today referred to, not without reason, as S/M-istic practices. Also unlike *Decameron, Les 120 journées* proudly exhibits   an encyclopaedic penchant for taxonomy that seems inspired by a deranged rationalism: the text promises an exhaustive treatment, no less, of *all* passions – the '150 simple or first-class passions' (month of November, narrator La Duclos), the '150 double or second-class passions' (December, La Champville), the '150 criminal or third-class passions' (January, La Martaine), and finally, the '150 murderous or fourth-class passions' (February, La Desgranges).

Clearly, in *Les 120 journées* the eighteenth century can be said to show through the fabric of Sade's text by way of its obsessive attention to mechanical-combinatory details (the number of stories is adjusted to total exactly 150 per unit, irrespective of the length of the month; the months themselves are chosen so that the number of days will total exactly 120). Its altogether palpable ambition is to emulate in the sexual realm the systematic and exhaustive treatment of Nature already offered by the scientist Linnaeus. However – and this is the crucial point – the scientific thrust is here reversed: it is not a cosmic *order* that Sade intends to scan, but rather, the natural *dis*-order that alone, in his view, makes life worth living.

Sade defiantly challenges the prevailing notion that Nature is good, and that human beings can and should act virtuously, accepting its commands. Pleasure is also natural, he (reasonably) points out; yet its pursuit invariably conflicts with the practice of virtue as society understands it. Hence, inevitably, one of two possible conclusions: either Nature is evil – and so are we human beings, qua consubstantial with it; or we are, at the very least, ignorant of her true intentions – and thus unnatural in practising the 'goodness' we mistakenly attribute to an entity on whose behalf we have no authorization to speak.

The introduction to *Les 120 journées* is explicit on this point:

Imagine that all pleasures, both honest and prescribed by that beast which you incessantly talk about without knowing it, and which you call Nature – that such pleasures will specifically be excluded from this collection of stories.[11]

In this framework, the reasons why Sade replaces the centesimal articulation of Boccaccio's *Decameron* with a centivigesimal one appear relatively obvious. Most likely, the Marquis rejected the neatly ordered teleological construction in base 10 because in Boccaccio such a structure was just that, a sequence of accurately dovetailing episodes that implied the expectation of a flicker of light at the end of a long tunnel: in the instance, the plague of 1348. In Sade, the plague that hovers over the earth, the criminality of Nature – human nature, as well as biological nature – is with us to stay, and no arrangement is justified that may lead us to think that there is any method to her madness.

It is, accordingly, far from coincidental that within its narrative subunits Sade's text should display an erratic fabulatory pattern. While in *Les 120 journées* crimes are meant to be narrated first, and only later perpetrated *in corpore vili* on the victimized audience, no regularity can be detected in the actual implementation of that rule – so much so that Sade himself notices this retrospectively.[12] Furthermore, beginning with Part Two, the 'double track' pattern (*past* stories intercut with *present* practices) yields to an unadorned, sketchy plan of the subject matter, which leaves aside the trappings of indirect speech and represents all manners of 'passions' in a direct, demonic mimesis of sorts.

Another major reason for Sade to avoid the number 100 was clearly the popularity that arrangement had acquired over centuries, largely due to its association with the one hundred cantos of Dante's *Divina commedia*, itself arrived at by a systematic reiteration of the ternary principle enshrined in Christian dogma ($1 + 3 \times 33 = 100$). In order to subvert to the end all possible association with Christianity, Sade's dystopian storytelling adopts here a consistently quaternary basis: in *Les 120 journées*, the events stretch over four months, there are four narrators, four 'Messieurs,' four studs (*fouteurs*) at a time, and four old women to wait on the crowd as priestesses.[13] Intriguingly, this transition from a ternary distribution to a quaternary one lends itself to being described in Jungian terms as the addition of a fourth component previously repressed – an addition parallel to the Jungian one of a fourth element, the Shadow, to the conventional trinity as a fundamental constituent of an integrated godhead. Whatever the reasons behind the perverse chaos of his combinations, Sade here appears to be groping in the same direction as that taken centuries later (minus the sadist intention) by depth psychology.[14]

To be sure, presenting Good as Evil and Evil as Good strikes one as a fairly simplistic approach to seizing the cosmic interaction between Light and Darkness. In other words, the fact that *Les 120 journées* belongs to a not particularly refined subgroup within the category of the blas-phemous can, in my view, be the subject of hardly any uncertainty. While all of Sade's work to a greater or lesser extent bears a similar imprint, the most visible characteristic of *Les 120 journées* seems to be that its God-denying vocation is articulated without the finesse one can find in other Sadean works – for example, *Dialog of a Priest and a Dying Man* (*Dialogue d'un prêtre et d'un moribond*) and parts of *Philosophy in the Dressing Room* (*La philosophie dans le boudoir*), *The New Justine* (*La nouvelle Justine*), and *Juliette's Story* (*Histoire de Juliette*).[15] In *Les 120 journées* blas-phemy is, to my mind, comparatively impervious to further elaboration because it is acted out rather than reasoned to any extent.

One can admittedly make sense of *Les 120 journées* by contextualizing the work within the entire Sadean corpus. The latter as a whole shows us that for Sade (to summarize the matter in the extreme) the blasphemous gesture is, first, an act of challenge against the power of religious dogma-tism; second, a passionate defence of individualism in the face of all sys-tems and self-interested preachers of 'virtue'; and thus, third, in the last analysis a denunciation of the internal inconsistency – worse, the utter moral nihilism – of any religion that purports to extol divine Creation by humbling its creatures. For Sade (and we shall see how relevant this is to our Pasolinian context), systematic blasphemy can be described as a device useful in the representation of a dystopian literary counter-universe that is intended to ape and parody the dystopian universe in which we live to our day. In Sade's intention, novels are useful reminders of just how grim the natural *and* the human spheres are:

> We must respond to the perpetual objection made by some bilious minds who ... never cease to query: *What is the use of novels?*
>
> What *is* their use, you hypocritical, perverted beings? since you are the only ones who ask this ridiculous question: their use is to depict you such as you are.[16]

We may agree or disagree with the particular view of utopian/eutopian desire that Sade has in mind, but there can be little doubt that for him dystopia is the world of a historical past that perniciously lingers on into the present; and that his most extremely 'sadist' books – *Les 120 journées* first and foremost – are a mirror held up to that world for the purpose (in the pursuit of which few will deny that the Marquis met with extra-ordinary success) of duplicating in the reader the very same disgust that Sade himself feels toward our present historical condition of instinct repression. In more enlightenedly sadist times, times that yet have to dawn on an imperfect humanity, Sade hopes for the introduction of better social institutions that would allow for a full liberation of desire. (Very important *nota bene*: this 'full liberation' would not affect *everyone*'s desire. To the bitter end, the Marquis is an aristocrat of hedonism, and simply cannot countenance the idea that all desires might be born equal.)

Sade's texts imply some imaginary framework in the future when a constructive utopian/eutopian society inspired by new, healthy principles would finally supersede the rule of obscurantism denounced in his own destructive literary dystopias. Today, that liberation is made temporarily impossible by ideological repression; hence, until a more favourable moment, propaganda by blasphemy, curse, and God-hatred. However paradoxical this may seem, it could be argued that Sade's convulsively tormented prose is in fact the product of his faith in *sui generis* Good Tidings: namely, the announcement to the entire world that Judaeo-Christian religions are doomed because they contain both a logical impossibility and a moral self-contradiction in setting up an opposition between the human and the divine, rather than a congruence of the two. The eventual victory of a Sadean/sadist liberation is, on this view, but a matter of time and perseverance.

Having, so far, focused on *Les 120 journées*, we should now turn our attention to the issue of how Sade's Sade relates to Pasolini's Sade, and to the often hardly linear ways in which the Marquis's work influenced *Salò or the 120 Days of Sodom*.

Pasolini and Blasphemy: 120 Variations on a Death Fugue

> Suffocated by all the *life* there is in my body, I am seized by the decision *to give death in order to die.* (Pasolini)[17]

In 1968, the graffitists of the Parisian *Mai* quite graphically argued for imagination to grab power as a mighty ally of utopia/eutopia. Yet, the sovereign freedom of imagination can just as easily work in reverse – the very word 'freedom' being, after all, just an empty slot, which speakers routinely fill with content according to their own condition.

Imagine, for example, a world that has turned into a concentration camp, with the best and brightest subjected to endless tortures on the part of a small clique of decaying, repulsive, cruel *apparatchiki* of both sexes who have arranged their environment in four different 'circles' reminiscent of Hell.

Imagine the hapless victims being brainwashed, homogenized, and stripped of their identities. Imagine them being blinded, muted, and used as objects by zealous angels of death in the guise of prison guards with skull-and-bones collar badges on their uniforms, while the puppet-masters either participate in the orgy or, with no lesser glee, spy on the spectacle from a distance. Imagine, then, the defenceless crowd being forced to lap up whatever mass of disgusting bodily byproducts may be put out by the torturers.

Furthermore, imagine that the villa hosting this pocket concentration camp is adorned by masterpieces of avant-garde art: a sumptuous collection of 'revolutionary' paintings that the tormenters, far from rejecting as politically subversive, thoroughly enjoy, in fact elevate to the rank of a canonical aesthetic standard.

Imagine, amidst these, a piano player whose task it is to entertain the merry company by her art. Imagine that, in a moment of crisis, she eventually commits suicide in despair over her despicable profession.

Imagine that, in this inferno where God is all but silent, one of the prison guards is an almost pubescent Dante who turns on the radio and maladroitly engages in a few steps of dance with Virgil. Imagine that, holding each other, the two spin around the room in an unassuming, innocent manner – much as boys used to do in the days before the Fall, when the sexually segregated conventions of rural societies still caused simple-minded youths to practise their social skills within their own gender before they could try them out on the almost fabulous Other one.

Imagine, finally, that in this self-contained nightmare the only moment I shall not say of redemption but of respite is encapsulated in the two lines that Dante and Virgil exchange during their shared rotations. Imagine that Virgil asks Dante Jr: 'What is your girlfriend's name?' and that Dante Jr answers: 'Gretchen.'

If I have solicited imaginative participation on my readers' part, this is clearly because my introductory rendering of Pasolini's *Salò* wishes to be an interpretive effort, rather than a summarily reductive one; and the events I have described do not occur in the film literally.

What does happen in the film literally is that we see dozens of youths being rounded up and locked away to serve as human puppets in the sex-and-death games eagerly engaged in by the perverts I mentioned; and their ordeals are structured by Pasolini in four infernal narrative phases (*Ante-inferno*; *Circle of Manias* or *Girone delle manie*; *Circle of Shit* or *Girone della merda*; *Circle of Blood* or *Girone del sangue*.) Then, mass murder; and, as a conclusion, the two young dancers' epilogue of sorts.

In sum, I should now begin reversing myself by saying that the victims I mentioned 'are' not contemporary consumers who lose their identity, psychological and ethical, to the ugly rule of the anonymous laws of capitalistic markets; they are specific individuals, who are quite individually stripped, beaten, raped, or castrated (or a combination of the above), and finally killed off. Just as their being muted and blinded is portrayed altogether mimetically in *Salò*, so, too, is their absorption of the excrements mass-produced by modern capitalistic industry (a production referred to in economics, with unintended and unsurpassable ambiguity, as 'physical output') – thus yielding a certain number of coprophagic shots that, not unreasonably perhaps, have seemed unpalatable to viewers untrained in Pasolini's aggressively insouciant management of figurative levels of narration.

I shall furthermore admit that we cannot be absolutely certain about the real motivations behind the pianist's leap to her death from a window in the villa of opprobrium. To be sure, her fate suggests the notion (confirmed by the presence of 'revolutionary' Dada-Futurist art in the concentrationary villa) that anything appreciated and consumed by Power, however subversive in its original intention, becomes by its nature as merchandise a support for that very power; and so much the worse for the artist unwilling or unable to cope with this.[18] Still, it was my initiative to articulate Pasolini's principles with such direct explicitness.[19]

I must finally confess that the two hesitantly dancing youths 'are' not Virgil and Dante, but two simple rookies in the Salò army; and that Pasolini's adolescent Dante has presumably not read Goethe – not in the original, anyway – since he does not literally say 'Gretchen.' Yet there is no doubt that Pasolini was haunted by the *Divina commedia* (on which more below); that the two dancers are tiptoeing at the bottom of Hell; and that the question as to the girlfriend's identity is in fact answered by the name 'Margherita.'[20]

The allusion is too heavily loaded for us to ignore. First, there is one association that inevitably comes to mind when a poet, such as Pasolini was, mentions any variant of the name 'Margarete' within the barbed-wire bounds of a concentration camp. I am referring to 'Death Fugue,' Paul Celan's poem about life and death in the suspended existence of the inmates (*Häftlinge*) ever expecting to reach their 'grave in the air':

Black milk of daybreak we drink it at sundown
we drink it at noon in the morning we drink it at night
we drink and we drink it

we dig a grave in the breezes there one lies unconfined
A man lives in the house he plays with the serpents he writes
He writes when dusk falls to Germany your golden hair Margarete
he writes it and steps out of doors and the stars are flashing he
                                                            whistles his pack out
He whistles his Jews out has them dig for a grave in the earth
he commands us *strike up for the dance*.[21]

While I cannot do justice here to the aesthetic and symbolic richness of Celan's poem, suffice it to say that in 'Death Fugue' Margarete and her blond hair act as unattainable icons of normalcy and fulfilment.[22]

Celan's Margarete is, in turn, intertextually linked to the diminutive Gretchen of Goethe's *Faust*. It is not, however, the transfigured Gretchen made famous by the last few lines of *Faust II* that I have in mind here; after all, she is by then no longer called 'Gretchen' by Goethe.[23] Rather than evoking the no-longer-human being embraced by divine Grace, who sets in motion soteriological horizons that are simply nowhere to be detected in *Salò*, Pasolini's finale seems to be alluding to the Gretchen of *Faust I*. How so? Because, as is clear from early on in *Faust I*, Gretchen is the catalyst of a fatigued Faust's desire to return to a more tranquil, normal life than he was allotted in the time preceding the events we witness. When offered by Mephisto the opportunity to give free rein to his desire, the Faust of the first part of Goethe's tragedy deliberately abstains from the glamorous worldly exploits sought by his literary predecessors and opts instead for what he believes will be fulfilling interaction with the archetypal Everywoman. It is Gretchen's unintellectual and unassuming personality that, in Faust's eyes, best qualifies her as the object of his own ill-fated attempt to replace speculative research in an ossified paper world with real-life relations among people of flesh and blood. Thus, when the two adolescent guards in *Salò* start their dance, the outcome of their dialogue almost tangibly materializes the theme of the polarity *intellectual desiccation / folksy simplicity* already well known to readers and viewers familiar with Pasolini's *oeuvre*.

I should probably add that the connection I established between *Salò*'s all-male dance and the good old times before heterosexual promiscuity, when boys used to learn how to dance by practising with boys, is not in the least imaginary, but proven. A book on which Pasolini worked throughout the 1960s contains a photograph that presents two young men in the same attitude as *Salò*'s guards, under the heading '*Ragazzi*, the way they were toward the end of the 50s.' This work, under the general title *The Divine Mimesis* (*La divina mimesis*), among other things explicitly rewrites in modernized form parts of Dante's *Inferno*, with Virgil in the lead and Pasolini in the position of the Florentine poet.[24] The (hellish) circle could hardly be more tightly closed.[25]

This said, in writing about *Salò* I have admittedly trod lightly on facts in the film and attempted to describe some, mostly metaphorical, truths about it instead. The reason for this course of action is, I hope, intuitive: *Salò* is a film that, no matter how detached the observer, is almost as intolerable to write (and read) about as it is to watch.[26] The irrecuperability of *Salò*, in a sense, simply proves the success of its blasphemousness: here you have an attack, Pasolini seems to reason, that no system of power will ever be able to appropriate and neutralize. With *Salò*, Pasolini promises more than most of us can take; and he certainly does deliver upon his promise.[27]

Nonetheless, I feel that there are certain facts that need to be established about Pasolini's 120 variations on a death fugue and require explicit verbalization. First, in the transition from Sade's systematization of the art of blasphemy to Pasolini's re-creation of it, a Dantean model is superimposed upon a Boccaccian narrative structure, without entirely replacing it.[28] Hellishness is the defining feature of *Salò*, and the Dante of *Inferno* seems to exert a major cultural influence on it – more so than Boccaccio does, and perhaps no less than even Sade himself. (It is probable that the same public walking out in disgust at Pasolini's cinematic tortures would be willing to accept them if they were presented as endured by the damned ones in the first cantica of the *Divina commedia*. It is not Pasolini's rendering of sadism that is repulsive, I believe, but his deliberate intention to keep that sadism mimetic in his film.) I have already mentioned Pasolini's publishing *La divina mimesis* shortly before his work on Sade. For almost two decades, he circled around Dante's *Inferno*, toying with the temptation to rewrite and update it. *Salò* was the implementation of that dream.

Second, there is no depiction of pleasure in *Salò*. However counterintuitive, this observation seems to me true of *Les 120 journées* as well. A revealing spelling mistake by Sade unwittingly confirms this impression. The entry for 13 February of *Les 120 journées* lists as no. 68 of the 'murderous, or Class Four passions' a fairly complex homicidal phantasy whose details are beside the point here.[29] Almost as an afterthought, Sade then comments that the debaucher (*le paillard*) deals with this particular passion *de sens froid*, a non-existent expression literally translating as 'in cold sense' – an obvious mistake for the common *de sang froid*, 'in cold blood.'[30] A slip of the pen of this kind is, I believe, instructive because it exposes some of the subconscious tensions repressed at the empirical level of the text. Why such tensions? Because Sade's rationalization of all possible forms of passion is a perhaps necessarily self-contradictory balancing act between his stated aim of *jouissance* and an attempt at an exhaustive codification that – in cold sense – ceaselessly works against that goal.

The atmosphere of a glacially un-orgiastic universe is even more tangible in *Salò*, where the characters portrayed by Pasolini as hopeful masters of orgasm are a pretty sorry bunch, plagued by an impotence for which they mostly seek compensation in voyeurism, and in general haunted (though for reasons exactly opposite to those of Goethe's original) by Faust's lucid comment to Mephisto: 'But thou hast heard, 'tis not of joy we're talking.'[31] One need only recall the hyperbolical physical performances with which Sade endows his protagonists to realize, by sheer contrast, that the point Pasolini wishes to make is the utter sterility of a power doomed to extinction by its very self-referentiality. If *Les 120 journées* is written 'in cold sense,' *Salò* is shot in an even colder one, with innumerable rhetorical and intellectual buffers.[32] Sade's blasphemy is directed at God; Pasolini's blasphemy is not directed against God at all, but against a self-sustaining regime of death where the godhead, if it exists at all, resembles the skulls worn on Fascist uniforms.[33]

This contrast leads us to what seems to me the third and most important consideration of all: namely, the fact that while Sade identifies with the puppet-masters, Pasolini (with an important proviso to which I shall return later) sympathizes with the victims.[34] I can think of no better way to illustrate this pervasive perception than by referring to a sequence in *Salò* in which Pasolini almost literally remakes one of the episodes from his own *Decameron*. In *Salò*, two young prisoners of opposite sexes decide to offer whatever resistance they can to the bloody pack of their guards. They manage to escape to a secluded room, where, at nighttime, they consummate their love entirely according to nature. In the morning, they are reported and discovered. Since their behaviour contravenes the rules, they are shot dead on the spot. The director thereby metes out to them an idiosyncratically mild punishment in an idiosyncratically cruel environment – one, above all, that allows them to die in dignity and self-awareness: the young man even has the time to raise a clenched fist in a Communist salute before he is showered with bullets.[35] The parallel episode in Pasolini's *Decameron* is the one where Caterina and Riccardo, caught by the girl's father at daybreak *in flagrante delicto* on the roof of her family's dwelling, are let go scot-free.[36] Not exactly a bulletproof sympathy, one may think in viewing *Salò*. Yet the fact remains that, despite modifying the setting from fairy tale–like novella to nightmare, Pasolini's position is worlds away from the Sadean one. It is in the *differential* between Sade and Pasolini that we can perceive the solidarity that *Salò* intends to express.

For Sade, blasphemy is a routine reminder that we need to leave behind us (or at any rate, that the happy few among us need to defeat) a dystopian legacy of obscurantism, and that we ought to aim for the pan-orgasmic, radiant future utopia/eutopia that lurks beyond that barrier. For Pasolini, instead, blasphemy is a statement directed at the present; it is a form of mourning over the fact that the fairy tales of the past have by now been exterminated – and that dystopia is already upon us.

Pasolini and Dystopia

> You are talking about facts, not truth. (Mishima)[37]

In 1971, Pasolini was sufficiently impressed by the public suicide of the Japanese poet, novelist, and playwright Yukio Mishima to mention it twice in his own *Heretical Empiricism.*[38] It is not unreasonable to assume that Pasolini knew at least some of the works by a fellow intellectual whose fame was sufficiently broad to have made him a nominee for the Nobel Prize for literature.[39] This seems all the more probable because Mishima shared many an important trait with Pasolini himself: a particular brand of what could be called militant homosexuality; antimodernism; and a strong endorsement of age-old cultural traditions (especially religion) among the People as a living entity. In these last two features at least, both poets could be described in terms of what the nineteenth century knew as 'conservative romanticism.'[40] With his nationalism and militarism, Mishima fit the overall bill to a T; Pasolini deviated from it by preaching a highly personal form of Communism.[41] The enemy was, in both cases, a globally accelerating process of massification and cultural homogenization.

Among Mishima's works, it would be most tempting to assume that Pasolini knew at least the drama inspired by the life of our ill-famed Marquis. 'You are talking about facts, not truth,' poignantly ripostes Renée, the Marquise, in Mishima's *Madame de Sade* as she defends her unfaithful husband against her own fact-obsessed mother.[42] The same lack of interest in Machiavelli's notion of 'facts as they are' (*la verità effet-*

tuale) and the same fascination with symbolic truths can be seen at work as the organizing principles of *Salò* – a film in which there arguably remains, if anything, a mite too much realism (beginning with the inaugural, confusing impression that *Salò* may consist of factual statements about the historical republic of Salò in 1943–5).

Below a violence that is still too naturalistic and not symbolic enough for most audiences, there lies the level of truths in which alone *Salò* is interested. Pasolini himself went as far as telling us clearly what critics have by now (some twenty-five years later) absorbed and integrated, namely, that the ultimate message behind the tortures is his own rebellion.[43] This rebellion was directed against what I have called the extermination of fairy tales, and Pasolini described as 'the death of the fireflies';[44] against the cultural genocide perpetrated on peasant cultures by late-twentieth-century capitalism; against a debasing massification induced by television and by mandatory schooling; against the homogenization due to consumerism, particularly typical of partners in a (heterosexual) couple; and, last but not least, against materialism and hedonistically 'liberated' positions on issues such as divorce and abortion. Some of these positions would not set Pasolini significantly apart from the views taken, especially under John Paul II, by the Catholic church; but what about his Communism? and his homosexuality? Pasolini's Catholicism being a subversive one that could not forgive the Roman church for its millennial history of compromise with – and contamination by – political officialdom, it was clearly impossible for our Christian poet to find a position with which to identify on the Italian political spectrum of the 1970s.

Not surprisingly, Pasolini was fascinated by the figure of Saint Paul, to whom he devoted considerable attention in the 1960s and early 1970s, going as far as drafting the script for a film that never came to fruition. From the extant versions we know that what attracted Pasolini to Paul of Tarsus, the persecutor later turned enthusiastic Christian convert, was the ongoing dualism between the zealot's mystical side and his organizational skills – a dualism that, however tensely, allowed Paul to combine within himself the two polar opposites of spiritual vision and political savvy. As illustrated especially in the collection of poetry appropriately titled *Trasumanar e organizzar* ('To transcend the human vs. to organize society'), Pasolini always viewed these two aspects as mutually exclusive.[45] His posthumously published *San Paolo* script appears as a sustained exploration of the issue – I dare not say a resolution of the dilemma – of how to accomplish the survival of the man of God within the shell of the man of power.[46]

The film on Saint Paul was left to one side, however, and Pasolini chose to devote himself to Sade instead. It is thus chiefly as a symptom of his solitude (as well as a statement of a strictly personal nature)[47] that we ought to read the public confession he wrote shortly before working on Salò, his 1975 'Repudiation of the Trilogy of Life,' where he condemned as excessively optimistic his three great box-office hits, Decameron, The Canterbury Tales (I racconti di Canterbury, 1972), and The Arabian Nights (Il fiore delle mille e una notte, 1974).[48]

It is difficult to deny that Pasolini's perception of contemporary Italian polity possesses a high degree of internal consistency. Yet, even open-and-shut cases, in which everything we will ever need to know seems to have already been spelled out in advance by the authors themselves, should not be taken uncritically. Pasolini's choice of Les 120 journées as a master text, for one, is peculiar, even problematic. Granted, Salò aims at conveying the urgency of its author's disgust for the dystopian 'Cowardly New World' of Pavlovian consumerism that he sees closing in on us from all sides. Still, leaning on Sade for support does strike one as a contradictory gesture of Pasolinian desperation – a renunciation of one's faith, however unconventional. There is no God in Sade other than as the butt of defiant jokes; hence no redemption, and above all no hope. It is Sade's prerogative as an atheist to write as he best deems fit; but it is quite another matter for Pasolini to draw upon him for inspiration. Abjuring one's past films as inadequate, excessively rosy, and out of touch with worldwide hard facts is one thing; it is an altogether different enterprise to act upon that statement by choosing for one's later works an approach to the subject matter that is radically at odds with one's world view. Sade's dystopia has very little in common with Pasolini's, and it could only prove of little poetic and conceptual use in shaping Salò: not because the empirical contents of the two plots are not similar (at a superficial level they are), but because the goals of the two narratives diverge substantially.[49]

Hence the inevitable question: why Sade? It seems that after all Pasolini would have been artistically better advised to finish his long-standing San Paolo project first. Unless, of course, the choice of Sade arose in Pasolini from some powerful drive that did work against his spontaneous Christian feelings – from some urgent impulse, that is, of which Pasolini himself may have been only dimly, imperfectly aware. Unless, that is to say, Pasolini chose Sade because in Les 120 journées God is denied and because of the book's rage against youth. What would be the hypothetical cause for Pasolini's throwing overboard, if only temporarily and in a fit of rage, a Christian faith that had been his defining trait as a person and as an artist ever since his earliest poems in Friulan dialect? There is only one conceivable reason I can propose for this choice: namely, that through sadism he symbolically wished to *punish* a much-beloved youth by whom he felt betrayed. The only explanation I can find for *Salò*'s obsession with the destruction of the cherished object, for its endless 120 variations on the theme of death, is that the exercise might function as a form of revenge. In witnessing the inexorable drift by which heretofore sincere and spontaneous Italian youths snubbed his calls for simple-minded authenticity and chose instead a presumptuously vapid (not to mention politically dangerous) identity as 'sophisticated' postmodern consumers, Pasolini's solidarity with their plight as victims must have suddenly crumbled, opening a breach for identification with their torturers instead.

I am, in other words, suggesting that what Pasolini's *subconscious* – as opposed to his self-conscious artistic persona – is up to in *Salò* is the following: in the first place, he is punishing the youths he used to love, because they spurned his cultural-ethical advances; and second, he is also punishing himself retroactively for having loved them. (He need not be physically on stage for that; he can punish himself indirectly by destroying the beloved object.)[50] One only has to compare *Salò*'s treatment of youth with the conclusion of *Mamma Roma* (1962), where the death in prison of a very modestly consumeristic, unassuming, good-hearted young Ettore is presented by a camera work and with a soundtrack that fall imperceptibly short of suggesting his martyrdom as a duplication of Christ's passion.[51]

Thus *Salò*, a film potentially susceptible to circle around the apotheosis of Gretchen, deliberately chooses instead to orbit within a Sadean apotheosis of despair, in a mournful gesture that denies all hope for an exit. Just as was the case for Gogol, the author of *Dead Souls* about whom Pasolini jotted down in one of his notebooks that he was to be taken into account '*tutto*,'[52] the Hell of *Salò* never managed to metamorphose into a purgatorial continuation, let alone a paradisian redemption. Pasolini's dead souls remain dead, 120 times over riveted to the dystopia of God's permanent disappearance.

Sade did not look with anxiety to the dawning age of materialism; quite the contrary, he feted the death of God as his most fervent hope, attacking the nihilism of historical religions and predicting their doom. A century later, with a keen historical sense, Nietzsche too denounced the nihilism of established religions, announcing the death of God at our hands. Unlike Sade, however, Nietzsche recognized that the transition from the theological to the post-theological age is not necessarily a smooth one, and that it can only act as a liberation if human beings understand the new possibilities that it contains – if they can, that is, turn the panic about their cosmic solitude into Panic enthusiasm for their newly acquired freedom.[53]

Painfully for Pasolini, both Sade's and Nietzsche's positions are denied to him. Because he blames God's murder not on us as whole beings, but only on what could be called the Stranger among us (i.e., that fraction of the present times called industrial capitalism), Pasolini has no way to recuperate for social use a change that, rudimentarily in Sade and more elaborately in Nietzsche, entails a liberation, a difficult but exciting *Eu-angelion* of sorts. Pasolini's *Salò* is a *Dys-angelion* that announces not the utopia/eutopia of the future but the dystopia in which we live, lonely in a universe studded not with stars but with the market's star performers imposed by a totalitarian, neo-'fascist' form of consumerism.

Pasolini and Utopia/Eutopia: Death of a European Dream

A little over a year before his death, Pasolini spelled out an apology of his world view in an open letter to Italo Calvino originally published by *Paese Sera*. Pasolini reproached Calvino for having stressed what he, Calvino, perceived as Pasolini's backward-looking utopianism/eutopianism, and went on to argue:

> Me, regretting the Italy of old [*l'Italietta*]? If that is what you think, you haven't read a single verse in my books *The Ashes of Gramsci* or *Calderón*, you haven't read a single line in my novels, you haven't seen a single shot in my films, you know nothing about me! Because all I have done, all I am, by its very nature *rules out* that I may feel nostalgic about *l'Italietta*.

Pasolini then reminded Calvino that the *Italietta* of old waded in a 'petty bourgeois,' 'Fascist,' and 'Christian Democrat' provincial mire, and went on to argue:

> What I do feel nostalgic about is the unlimited, pre-national and pre-industrial peasant world, which survived until just a few years ago. (Not by chance, I spend as much time as possible in the countries of the Third World, where it lives on, although the Third World too is now beginning to enter the sphere of so-called Development.)

The people of that universe did not live in an *age of gold*; likewise, they were only nominally involved with *l'Italietta*. They lived in what has been called ... the *age of bread*. That is to say, they were consumers of goods that were necessary in the extreme. And this may well have been what made their poor and precarious life extremely necessary. Whereas (just to be extremely plain and to put the issue to rest once and for all) it is clear that *superfluous goods make life superfluous*.[54]

I have no record of a further answer by Calvino to Pasolini's objections. However, having reread for the occasion both *Calderón* and *The Ashes of Gramsci*, I must confess that while I indeed could not trace anywhere in them Pasolini's 'Italy of old,' I nonetheless found them as reminiscent of utopian/eutopian dreams as any literary text can be. From Fra Dolcino to Savonarola and on, there have been plenty of Communist, or at least communitarian, utopias/eutopias in Italian history – none of which was petty bourgeois, Fascist, Christian democrat, provincial, or at the margins of history, and a number of which were no less keen on Christian ideals than Pasolini's own. The argument that Pasolini could not be himself *and* look backward for inspiration simply does not hold.

The point is that Pasolini just *did not wish to appear* utopian/eutopian. This irritability was largely understandable. The embarrassing circumstance, of which he may not have been lucidly aware, lay in the fact that, well before him, the Italian proletariat had a historic tradition of being aestheticized (in two opposite variants: the ideal *and* the demonic one) by European visitors. Did Pasolini sympathetically depict slum-dwellers in his Roman works, and then cheerfully lead the Neapolitan mob to the colonization of Boccaccio's *Decameron*? Hardly news: centuries before him, Goethe, Madame de Staël, Byron, Stendhal, Lamartine, and countless other Northerners who visited the peninsula (and even quite a number of those who never made it there) were only too eager to feel ecstatic about – or, in the case of Thomas Mann's Aschenbach, sick with – the local population's mischievous simplicity, unrefined directness, and physical impulsiveness. Their archetypal Italians just had to have a certain *tutto tondo* lack of self-reflective introspection even as they bent the rules of polite, civilized interaction for the sake of their own survival. The Italian as the sun-baked, impulsive Child of Nature, the Innocent Animal, the Crook with a Heart – are Vittorio/Accattone in *Accattone* (1961), Ettore in *Mamma Roma*, Stracci in *La Ricotta* (from *Rogopag*, 1963) not of that same ilk? By his view of the 'natural' Italians on the verge of an extinction wrought on them by cultural homogenization,

Pasolini returns in a substantial way to an early-nineteenth-century romantic stereotype of the Italian; *except that he would never admit it.*

The laudative assumption of just this stereotype was perhaps nowhere more poignantly expressed than in an aphorism by Nietzsche in *The Joyful Wisdom* significantly titled 'The Animal with Good Conscience':

> It is not unknown to me that there is vulgarity in everything that pleases Southern Europe – whether it be Italian opera ..., or the Spanish adventure romance ... – but it does not offend me, any more than the vulgarity which one encounters in a walk through Pompeii, or even in the reading of every ancient book. What is the reason of this? Is it because shame is lacking here, and because the vulgar always comes forward just as sure and certain of itself as anything noble, lovely, and passionate, in the same kind of music and romance? 'The animal has its rights like the human being, so let it run about freely; and you, my dear fellow human being, are still this animal, in spite of all!' – that seems to me the moral of the case, and the peculiarity of southern humanity.[55]

This 'animal with good conscience' was the creature on whose qualities – whether in the political or the moral arena – Italian intellectuals pinned their hopes in the wake of the post–Second World War regenerative rediscovery that, after phoney imperial Italy had bitten the dust, the Italian *populus* still existed, undaunted and uncorrupted. The nineteenth-century northern romantic tradition of what could be defined as an exoticizing meridionalism was thus continued in neorealism, whose explicit source of inspiration in Verga's disenchanted naturalism somehow coexisted with a celebration of southern vitality that, in retrospect, seems to have been no less perspectival than romantic idealization. Visconti's *The Earth Trembles* was the cinematic prototype of this genre, later continued by Rossellini in *Voyage to Italy* (*Viaggio in Italia*, 1953), and further developed, with different twists, in Visconti's own *Rocco and His Brothers* and Pasolini's works just alluded to.

As Pasolini was only too painfully aware (though he did not himself express the issue in these terms),[56] the *miracolo economico*, the 1960s, and the conflictual 1970s all made a serious dent in the neo-romantic belief that the soul of the Italian people was destined to remain immune to the attractions of a calculating and dissimulating modern rationality.[57] The last nail was put in the coffin of ideal figures such as Stracci, Ettore, or Accattone by, I would argue, the students' rebellion in 1968 and the following years – a rebellion that, despite Pasolini's failure to see in it anything more than an internal affair within the existing establishment and a reshuffling of power among the bourgeois, did in fact change the social make-up of the educated classes in the country.[58]

On this critical view, one realizes that the only way for Pasolini to survive the impact of a fast-changing Italy would have been to shift or reconsider entirely the focus of his preoccupations – much as, not by coincidence, Visconti or Rossellini themselves were doing in their late years. Pasolini did explore the paths of the *aggiornamento* of ancient mythology in, for example, *Oedipus rex* (*Edipo re,* 1967), *Teorema* (1968), *Porcile* (1969), and *Medea* (1970), but he must have experienced some difficulty in the fact that the more he did so, and thus the more he ostensibly removed himself from the present features of modernization, the more he symbolically kept returning to contemporaneous Italy. Delving over and over again into the conflict between *muthos* and *logos* is, after all, but another way of scrutinizing ever anew the modern historical pattern by which the latter (as a 'bourgeois' feature) arises from the former (with its traits typical of 'heroic' times). In sum, Pasolini's suffering and despair in the 1970s arguably arose from the fact that – unlike Visconti vis-à-vis the fishermen of Aci Trezza – he simply never grew out of what could be called his Accattone complex.

Pasolini, I would argue, was the last great European utopianist/eutopianist. Even after – as De Seta aptly expressed himself – 'swordfish hunting was over' in Italy, 'because the swordfish all but disappeared from her seas,'[59] Pasolini continued with genuine sympathy (rather than imperialistic possessiveness) the meridionalist tradition of love toward a hoped-for land untainted with the plague of generalized commodification. Although, as he put it, 'the fireflies' had died out, Pasolini upheld his devotion to a vanishing rural simplicity that no longer warranted belief in the survival of extant marginal cultures, let alone in that of the dawn of a millennial day when, as the biblical topos would have it, the aloe tree will bloom. It was Pasolini's destiny to suffer and to bear witness to the end, however masochistically (S/M-istically), in the name of the naturalness that Italians gradually lost as they forfeited their blessed innocence in exchange for the curse of a consumerist Mammon. He died in an age now almost inconceivably remote, that of the Vietnam War: an age of which, only one generation later, the world barely seems to have any memory.

Pasolini did not live to see the age of the personal computer; in his times, 'PC' still read in Italian as 'PCI,' 'Italian Communist Party.' He knew nothing about the coming age of private TVs and global telecommunications. Our postmodern, post-ideological, post-national and, I would certainly argue, post-cultural status puts us in a position drastically changed with respect to his; whether we like it or not, we must today cope with a situation in which, as a North American Nietzsche could reasonably claim, it is up to us to determine whether we want to understand the death of God as a bereavement or as a challenge and an opportunity.

Largely as a consequence of these circumstances, we do not suffer as much as Pasolini did. We do not blaspheme, or mourn, as he did (or as romantic fundamentalists of sundry national origins could do), because, having absorbed our Nietzsche, for better or worse we accept our cosmic solitude – or, at least, we take it for granted.

PART THREE

Mediated Re-creations

The Consummation of Meridionalism: *Carmen* (1984)

1845–1875: Forgetfulness and the *Carmen* Case

He that can forget, is cured. (Nietzsche)[1]

The novella *Carmen*, published in 1845, was a product of French romanticism – and of Prosper Mérimée's idiosyncratic literary taste. Inspired by travels through Spain undertaken by its author in the 1830s, and spiced with his ever-present wit, *Carmen* is a novella about Spanish mores, a gypsy *femme fatale*, the ultimate impossibility of assimilating passion into social coexistence, and thus ultimately about the irredeemable dangers of desire. The text's combination of a 'centripetal' pull toward its subject matter, which led to identification, with an only too obvious 'centrifugal' vector, creating ironic distance from it, caused Mérimée to be viewed, in the course of the decades, alternatively as a romantic author and as a proto-naturalist one, offering insight, in sequence, to colleagues or literary critics of opposite theoretical persuasions.

That said, there no doubt is a sense in which Mérimée's *Carmen* proves a boundlessly romantic piece of fiction. I am alluding to the fact that it shares with a large section of northern European literature the presupposition that something special, something 'natural' and authentic characterizes the peoples living south of the great European mountain ranges (the Pyrenees, the Alps, the Caucasus) in the areas broadly definable as 'the South' and 'the East.' I have already briefly treated this phenomenon in discussing Pasolini; it is none other than the well-known orientalist/meridionalist complex – a complex arising out of a certain type of discourse of power that, although through and through ideological, represses its own status as ideology, and projects onto an ethnic and geographic otherness certain qualities that it finds convenient to 'create' for purposes of cultural control.[2]

Not that Mérimée's *Carmen* – or Georges Bizet's corresponding opera, for that matter – fit the cultural-imperialist bill to perfection; more would have to be said in order to refine the argument and apply it to the two works.[3] Special consideration should, in particular, be given to the fact that European romantic literature responds to a deeply utopian impulse, which is neither necessarily directed abroad (the thrust toward the Middle Ages, on the one hand, and on the other the cultivation of the 'mysterious way' of interiority testify to this) nor always imbued with an unchallenged sense of moral superiority on the part of the northern conscience. This is especially true, I maintain, of that particular brand of orientalism that in fact ought to be called meridionalism, and that leads northern Europeans, from Winckelmann and Goethe to Tieck, Byron, Stendhal, Pushkin, Heine, and countless others (on some of whom more in a moment), to wander along literary paths to Greece, southern France, Andalusia, and of course the Italian peninsula, all blessed locations 'where the lemon trees blossom.'[4]

Almost identical expressions of just such a kind come in triplicate from the pens of no lesser authors than Goethe, Byron, and Pushkin. In *Wilhelm Meister's Apprenticeship*, Goethe's Mignon sings about Italy:

Dost know the land where citrons, lemons, grow,
Gold oranges 'neath dusky foliage glow,
From azure sky are blowing breezes soft,
The myrtle still, the laurel stands aloft?
   'Tis there! 'tis there!
I would with thee, O my beloved one, go! ...[5]

The first verses of Byron's 'The Bride of Abydos' celebrate Asia Minor in similar words:

Know ye the land where the cypress and myrtle
Are emblems of deeds that are done in their clime?
Where the rage of the vulture, the love of the turtle,
Now melt into sorrow, now madden to crime?

Know ye the land of the cedar and vine,
Where the flowers ever blossom, the beams ever shine ...?[6]

Pushkin, too, evokes the Southern beauty of Italy in the following verses of 1828:

Who knows the land where the sky shines
With ineffable blueness,
Where the sea's warm waves
Softly splash around the ruins;
Where, evergreen, laurel and cypress
In proud freedom spread their leaves;
Where the great Torquato sang,
Where, in the darkness of the night,
The Adriatic's waves
To this day repeat his stanzas;
Where Raphael painted ...[7]

Unless we decide that these authors, and their likes, do not 'really' mean what they are saying, whereas *we* know better, we ought to admit that the attitude at the core of meridionalism – Mérimée's *Carmen* first and foremost – is less a straightforward imperialism than a profound ambivalence about the *Naturkinder* of the Mediterranean. If a certain sense of superiority there is (and one can undeniably find it in many real or fictional accounts of life in the lands of the beautiful savages), it is also accompanied by a genuinely utopian sense of envy for a spontaneity and directness that has been forever lost to the tamed lands of *politesse*.[8] Perhaps the most intriguing feature of much of northern European romanticism is precisely the fact that the balance sheet of its meridionalist enterprise is anything but a zero-sum game in which what is charged to others accrues to oneself; colonialist though meridionalism may be, in its utopia there is no final word on right and wrong, and no civilization can thus be said to be definitively 'inferior.'

This much – or this little – having been said on romantic meridionalism, the fact remains that by 1875, when Bizet finished his opera, romanticism was a thing of the distant past. Whether in an ironico-realist variant or in a tragico-rhetorical, Hugoan version, romanticism belonged in the museums by the time *Carmen* was staged, a full generation after the original literary version. And a dramatic generation this certainly was for France. In between, there had occurred the two 1848 revolutions and the brutal reaction that ensued; Louis Bonaparte's *coup d'état* of 1852; the Second Empire; wars across Europe; the 1870 defeat at Sédan; the Prussian invasion; the Parisian Commune, with attendant replay of the 1848 repression; and, finally, the establishment of the Third Republic. The original *Carmen* could have been, and likely was, read by Balzac; when Bizet chose it as the basis for what was going to be his last opera, Flaubert's life was approaching its end, and Zola's fame was on the rise. Wagner had already composed most of his operas (only *Parsifal* would be performed later, in 1882); and Offenbach's *opéra bouffe* was an established genre.

The cultural atmosphere surrounding Bizet's *Carmen* was thus characteristic in two ways. On the one hand, growing masses of bourgeois public wished to increase their wealth while entertaining themselves to oblivion – to oblivion, in particular, of the bloody political convulsions only recently incurred by France during and after two major popular uprisings. On the other hand, precisely the unleashing of a laissez-faire, primal sort of capitalism caused the spread in their country of social ills such as those that Zola and other writers of the naturalist school (Maupassant, the Goncourt brothers) unflatteringly revealed. Around the corner lay Zola's exemplary *Nana* (1879–80), a novel about a corrupted and corrupting woman from the working class who succeeds in rising to the highest level of wealth in French society, and in the process exposes the ruling classes' moral quagmire. It was forgetfulness that the public found in Bizet's *Carmen* – though, to be sure, one of a less philosophical kind than that we shall detect in Nietzsche's meridionalist speculations.

The first impact *Carmen* had on the Parisian public in March 1875 was an unsuccessful one: the Opéra Comique that staged it catered to a family-oriented audience, and was understandably loath to appreciate its piquant subject matter;[9] some of its musical innovations seemed technically objectionable to a conservative-minded constituency;[10] and the critics could not, for various reasons, be persuaded to praise the opera. Nonetheless, the ingredients for success were there, and the potential of Bizet's *Carmen* was quickly fulfilled – interestingly, on the rebound of enormous success in Vienna just a few months after the Parisian fiasco.[11] Thus it was that the *Carmen* case had a happy ending; happy for everyone, that is, except the composer, who had died at the age of thirty-seven without being able to savour the Escamillo-like triumphs being granted to his work throughout Europe.

This positive outcome hinged on the opera having cleared to perfection specific requirements with the public of the time. Bizet and his librettists had felicitously left Mérimée's smelly, savage Spain to one side; elevated Carmen to a mythical, archetypal dimension of femininity; purified her sexuality from the morbid (and politically explosive) connotations such matters acquired in naturalistic novels *à la* Zola;[12] ennobled both her and her lover Don José, martyrizing them for breaking certain conventional barriers; celebrated an entirely non-nationalistic form of militarism (the *corrida*) in a war-fatigued Europe; and, last but not least, waved innocuous, escapist red flags in the safely sealed-off space of the bullring at the precise time when more dangerous ones were being hoisted in other arenas. In sum, Bizet's *Carmen* extolled the 'purity of passion' in a reassuring manner that proved unproblematically enjoyable to the public.

The most southern-minded of all German philosophers saw through to the core of *Carmen* when he opened his musical and philosophical pamphlet entitled *The Case of Wagner* with a review that would have been Bizet's (or, for that matter, any composer's) dream:

Yesterday – would you believe it? – I heard *Bizet*'s masterpiece for the twentieth time. Once more I attended with the same gentle reverence; once again I did not run away. This triumph over my impatience surprises me. How such a work completes one! Through it one almost becomes a 'masterpiece' oneself.[13]

These few words sketch out the better-known part of Nietzsche's argument. But some of what follows has an even more direct relevance to our subject:

Bizet's work also saves; Wagner is not the only 'Savior.' With it one bids farewell to the *damp* North and to all the fog of the Wagnerian ideal. Even the action in itself delivers us from these things. From Mérimée it has this logic even in passion, from him it has the direct line, *inexorable* necessity; but what it has above all else is that which belongs to the sub-tropical zones – that dryness of atmosphere, that *limpidezza* of the air. Here in every respect the climate is altered. Here another kind of sensuality, another kind of sensitiveness and another kind of cheerfulness make their appeal. This music is gay, but not in a French or German way. Its gaiety is African; fate hangs over it, its happiness is short, sudden, without reprieve. I envy Bizet for having had the courage of this sensitiveness, which hitherto in the cultured music of Europe has found no means of expression, – of this Southern, tawny, sunburnt sensitiveness ...

Perhaps you are beginning to perceive how very much this music *improves* me? – *Il faut méditerran[é]iser la musique.*[14]

We have explored some of the background against which Nietzsche's opinions were formed; and his peremptory words deserve being retained as a significant hermeneutic key as we ourselves venture out to the Mediterranean. However much he may have liked to pose as an 'untimely' observer of society, Nietzsche was in fact (in operatic matters at any rate) perfectly attuned to the tastes of a large segment of the European public: witness the fact that there *were*, within a short span of time, twenty performances of *Carmen* he could choose to attend. Nietzsche may, just possibly, have suffered from a particularly intense case of utopian meridionalism. Still, one thing should be clear: he was not the only one.

Francesco Rosi: *Carmen* and *Imago*

It is now time to turn to other Southerners who lay claim to a special relationship with Andalusian cigarette-makers, and to examine the legitimacy of their pretension. While Carmen as a character has, by our time, moved so far into the mythical and supra-national realms that no exclusive access route to her ultimate truth can be secured, in Francesco Rosi's interpretation she remains closest to her operatic prototype.[15]

Several years ago, in reviewing Rosi's *Hands Over the City* and *Salvatore Giuliano* (1961), a critic disparagingly wrote: 'Both are technically brilliant. As human dramas, both are hollow ... Mr. Rosi is wonderful with crowds, as in a sweeping massacre sequence. As we await simple, meaningful human drama from him, let's hail his graphic wizardry.'[16] Literary *querelles* seem to have a peculiar way of teaching us that even the most improbable charge is worth examining, since it usually contains some subverted truth deserving to be restored to its original upright position. There can be no doubt that the *sweeping massacre* of Rosi's films carried out in the review just quoted is, if nothing else, absolutely truthful when it admits that Rosi 'is a graphic wizard' and that he is 'wonderful with crowds.' There might be a definite heuristic value in following up on these principles and allowing them to guide us through a close reading of important scenes in Rosi's *Carmen*.

There are three perspectives from which I think it is fruitful to look at Rosi's *Carmen* as a pivotal film of the Italian 1980s. The three groupings can be described as follows: first, naturalistic effects; second, auto-correlated references to previous Rosian works; and third, symbolic strategies pointing to a philosophical substratum.

What I propose to call Rosi's naturalistic effects are, prima facie, the features that over and over again have caused commentators to state – often with no further elaboration – that Rosi brings 'realism' to the Carmen tradition.[17] Pursuing representational aesthetics is Rosi's principal way of celebrating the South in general and declaring a special form of love for it.

Crowds appear in the film not only, as is to be expected, at the obvious locations: inside the bullring, in and around the cigarette factory, and – in the guise of bands of street urchins, the ever-present *gamins* – swarming around the dragoons.[18] It was bonded will, however enthusiastically embraced, that led the director to show them there. Yet he also exercised free will by putting them where they were not obligatory: at the encampment near the bulwarks of Seville (during the day, as the dragoons ride by, and at night, when we witness Escamillo's first public appearance); and at Lillas Pastia's inn, which for Rosi virtually takes on the atmosphere of a full-fledged county fair. In all these cases, there is beauty in numbers, and the crowds' exuberance conveys a sense of *joie de vivre* that aptly counterbalances – if the compensation can ever be said to be a successful one – the permanent threat of death in Carmen's story.

The obverse of the crowd is the hero. To Rosi, as a Neapolitan, it must be obvious that, from Masaniello to Maradona, the two are necessary and complementary to each other. Few works of art, literature, or music are centred on a character more hyperbolically self-conscious than *Carmen*'s bullfighter. A personification of victory, he is defined by his name and trade with no margin of error: 'Je suis Escamillo, toréro de Grenade.'[19] Escamillo's hubris is so exaggerated that at times it comes close to self-parody. It is precisely then that the presence of a cheering crowd next to him helps retain a sense of verisimilitude: discourse is accepted as authoritative when seen to be guaranteed, if not by authority, at least by popularity. (The counter-example is Don José, who loses ascendancy over Carmen to the same extent that he allows himself to lose his rank – the paradox here being that he does so precisely in order to follow his lover.)

Along with the presence of the crowd/hero pair, the locale counts among the fundamental devices used by Rosi to naturalize his *Carmen*: the director chose to shoot at all times on location, and with practically no touch-up in the mediterranean land- or cityscape. Everything in Rosi's *Carmen* is authentic; purists may raise doubts about the solidity of Bizet's Micaëla, but not about the backdrop against which she appears in Rosi.[20] Even opting to shoot in smaller Spanish towns, I believe, adds to, rather than subtracts from, the credibility of the film: the size of Ronda or Carmona reproduces more accurately the historical character-istics of the Seville of old than today's Seville would.

Animals do not lag far behind location and people as prime factors in rooting Rosi's *Carmen* in a realistic setting. Bulls and horses in the arena obviously rank first; however, they were part of the story. Likewise, Rosi's choice to have horse-riding smugglers was influenced by pre-existing iconography.[21] But it is the dispensable presence that carries the most contrastive weight – as, for example, in the director's decision to ani-mate the streets of his Seville with dogs and donkeys.

A striking example occurs as Don José and Micaëla are concluding the duet 'Ma mère, je la vois,' during which the angelic girl delivers Don José a letter from his mother. The slowly pacing couple is about to disappear in the background, at the exact point where the perspectival lines (roof and base) of a dilapidated cottage converge. Suddenly the screen is crossed by a man who, riding a horse loaded with hay, trundles past the same building in the opposite direction. The hoofbeating, market-bound pair dwarfs the two vocal turtledoves and eventually eclipses them as it grows in apparent magnitude. Moments before, two stray dogs had appeared in a corner of the screen, on furlough from the child's play in which they had been participating during the previous sequence.

In treating objects, too, Rosi doubles the melodramatic action with a visually naturalistic exploration. It is precisely because examples of this principle are diegetically inconsequential that they become willed and thus artistically relevant.

First let us analyse the end of Act One, with Don José's feigned fall from his horse that allows Carmen to escape. When the other two dra-goons pursue her in a fruitless horseback chase, the ensuing commo-tion disperses the populace originally going about its business. As each person runs for shelter in a different direction, tools of various trades are cast off. Rosi shows in the upper half of the frame the legs of the people on the run, while the lower half consists of a close-up of an empty segment of the street surface. Èizenshtein-like, the sequence ends with a close-up shot of a dropped basket of vegetables, which falls, rolls, and finally stops in the middle of the street (and of the frame), while human beings disappear – in another tribute to the representation of reality that has come to be considered one of the hallmarks of realism in cinema.[22]

Second, at the beginning of Act Three, before the *cuadrilla* marches into the bullring, the *alguaciles*, picadores et al. cross themselves – something that, though real enough, is expected. The same cannot be said when the first *alguacil* who opens the procession stubs out his cigarillo butt and thoughtlessly throws it across the space framed by the screen.[23] This is not meant to deny that cigarettes may accompany an announced death but to stress that a *casual* practice of smoking is at odds with the rhetoric of festive rituals.[24]

A third striking mark of Rosi's style can be detected during the final duet 'C'est toi! – C'est moi!,' at the end of which Don José stabs Carmen to death. In scanning the small courtyard in which the scene is enclosed, the camera reveals Carmen's red scarf abandoned in a far corner, standing out sharply as a vivid spot against a white wall. Here, the enduring presence of an object that has become superfluous to the events is an index of a deliberate poetological intention – again an *effet de réel* characteristic of real life.

Finally, there is a fourth element that I find especially striking in the context of *Carmen*'s naturalistic effects: dust. The street urchins (and the dragoons' horses, and the participants in the bullfight, both animal and human) raise storms of it as a matter of course. Dust also pervades the entire final duet between the two ex-lovers: their shoes are covered with it as, oblivious to such matters, they excitedly argue. A myriad particles rise as Carmen falls to her knees (or rather, as Don José's emotional momentum translates into kinetic, and he pushes her to the ground). A whole suffocating cloud is then kicked up with the belated arrival of Carmen's friends and other women, who, in despair, can only witness her agony.

It is difficult to see any diegetic necessity for this element. If anything, showing a dispute between lovers with full coverage of their dusty shoes seems more likely to destroy than to enhance the conventions we hold concerning what (melo)drama ought to be all about. My suggestion is that we construe the apparent conflict as a deliberate emphasizing of real historical coordinates. While not renouncing its poetic vocation, Rosi's film on Carmen is able to remain naturalistic from top to bottom – from head to shoes – and to anchor itself not only in the history of music and of cinema, but in that of European culture as well.

The latter aspect comes to full fruition in that feature of the film to which I intend to turn next: namely, the fact that *Carmen* uses narrative elements or, more frequently, images to refer us to other works by Rosi and to add up to the equivalent of a multi-film cycle. Rosi's texts are linked by a network of occurrences in which not the same characters, but the same situations reappear or recall one another.[25]

Thus, the crowds in Carmen's Seville can be seen as a reminiscence, in a more cheerful key, of the Montelepre women who protest against the Italian army's intervention in *Salvatore Giuliano*; they also echo the scenes in *The Mattei Affair* (*Il caso Mattei*, 1972) showing the welcome offered to the oilman Enrico Mattei in the Sicilian village of Gagliano. And the narrow streets of Ronda and Carmona, where *Carmen* was shot, replicate those in Craco that had been the backdrop for the plight of Italian peasants in *Christ Stopped at Eboli* (*Cristo si è fermato a Eboli*, 1979).[26]

The shapes of individual buildings also recur from film to film. Lillas Pastia's inn outside Seville, where smugglers, gitanas, and idle soldiers congregate, has a floor plan similar to that of the ancestral Apulian farm in *Three Brothers* (*Tre fratelli*, 1981): a central courtyard is surrounded on three sides by a two-storey, whitewashed stone structure, whose upper level is reached by an outdoor flight of stairs located inside the courtyard itself. The reminiscence is almost hallucinatory. Couldn't old Donato Giuranna suddenly peer out of one of the windows of his home?[27]

Landscapes also feature prominently as visual links between *Carmen* and Rosi's earlier oeuvre. In *Carmen* we witness the recurrence of certain Sicilian vistas that appear in the tragedy-laden reversals of *Salvatore Giuliano* and in those of the Lucanian fields that in *Christ Stopped at Eboli* receive the derisive news of the conquest of an Italian empire in Africa. Mediterranean landscapes are especially perceptible in the entr'acte preceding Act Three, which plays in an arch-romantic wild location. The rugged mountain area is haunted by smugglers, who commute to and from Gibraltar, as well as – by melodramatic coincidence – by Escamillo tending a herd of bulls. Because the entr'acte is exclusively instrumental, the choice of this particular illustration was Rosi's own, and so suggests links between his re-reading of *Carmen* and his own artistic sensitivity toward southern landscapes.[28]

Before we move to the *plaza de toros* for the denouement in Act Four, another one of the opera's instrumental entr'actes allows Rosi the time to expatiate on Escamillo. Sunk in almost trance-like concentration, the bullfighter goes through the ceremony of the clothing, then betakes himself to an adorned chapel to pray. These elaborately baroque settings are reminiscent of the opening scene in *Illustrious Corpses* (*Cadaveri eccellenti*, 1976) when Varga, also deep in meditation, wanders about the skeletons in the Capuchin cemetery, confronting the ever-present reality of death. No less baroque is the prelude to the opera, during which the musical theme that adumbrates death is visualized by Rosi with a nightly procession of black-hooded *confrères*, bearing candles and penitential crosses, and with the appearance of a group of veiled women who, heading in the opposite direction, chant and implore the Virgin as they carry a tearful statue of her.

One last association needs to be mentioned here. Few intertextual references are likely to strike the viewer of Rosi's *Carmen* as more deliberate, shocking even, than the film's final duplication of Salvatore Giuliano's position in death with Carmen's own. The variation introduced by Rosi a quarter of a century later is a 180° rotation of the image around its vertical axis: with an identical position of the limbs, Giuliano is prone, while Carmen lies supine. The bodies of the two outlaws face and mirror each other, and across the boundaries of history (as well as those of gender and genre) Carmen and Giuliano are thus symbolically joined.

The picture of Rosi's own *Comédie humaine* that crystallizes out of these elements is one of a vast fresco set in the South of Italy and of Europe – in that mediterranean area that, since romantic times, has historically been the object of the defamiliarizing glance of the Northerner. In this cultural chain, Bizet's *Carmen* (and, well before it, the novella by Mérimée that inspired it) is only one link, however important. I shall return in concluding to the pivotal importance of Rosi's contribution to this line, and in particular to the significance of the move by which a culture that was a traditional object of exoticism reappropriates its own exotic quality and becomes a subject of desire.

As we turn our attention from individual elements to the ways in which they interact to form larger units, the thematic level of analysis blends into the philosophical. It is in this latter sphere that some of the symbolic strategies employed by Rosi's *Carmen* call for scrutiny.

A first such nucleus in the film is related to vertical displacements and to the polarity they create. In the North-centric *Weltanschauung* of European romanticism, sex and the South have one obvious thing in common: they both happen *down there*.[29] This world view, so characteristic of the northern discourse of power, is brilliantly translated into image by Rosi from the very opening scenes of his *Carmen*. Unlike previous re-creations of the novella, Rosi's film organizes the landscape in a charged way: it positions the seat of reason and self-control – the locus of Don José before the Fall – atop a hill that dominates the city, far above the factory where Carmen works. She and her fellow workers, by contrast, congregate at the bottom, and are subject to thorough examination on the part of the observing glance that stands guard above them.[30] Thus,

Don José's 'descent' into the realm of the senses, in which he is to lose his reason, appropriately begins with a quite literally physical descent down the steep slope that leads from the fortress to a shadowy patio by the cigar factory below it. Moreover, Rosi has the visual further metaphorize the psychological by insisting on the fact that Don José's narrative place of origin is indeed a military post: an effective transposition of the constraints and repressions intrinsic to civilized society.[31] In sum, Rosi's *Carmen* can be said to formulate in many mutually reinforcing ways the process by which what is 'up' goes 'down,' and what is controlled becomes uncontrolled, as the organizing glance loses its commanding view.

The beginning of Carmen's and Don José's affair in Act Two is significant in more than one respect. It will be remembered that in Bizet's opera the gitana tries hard to seduce the dragoon – who, though in principle happy to oblige, is nonetheless reluctant to be late for the nightly roll call. Carmen's task, then, is not so much that of persuading José that she is valuable company for one evening, but the more arduous one that she is worth, in effect, deserting for. These circumstances prompt Rosi's Carmen to initiate what is for all intents and purposes a thinly veiled strip-tease scene.[32]

In Rosi, Carmen's undressing is not presented directly, but hinted at. While in the film the fiery dancer retains on her body the bare minimum of clothing that is admissible within the conventions of – as Bizet's critics had put it over a century ago – the tastes of families on a Sunday outing, it is her room that strikes the eye for the almost complete nudity it exhibits. In sharp antithesis to the decor that adorns not just churches and mansions, but, in its own way, even the humble tavern immediately below the two lovers, all Rosi puts into Carmen's room is the following: two candles, two baskets and a rudimentary coat hanging from the walls, a mattress with sheets lying directly on the floor, and two chairs. This seems, indeed, very little, especially because the bedroom itself is larger (about twice the size) than any of the other ones we are allowed to peek into. A not unintended further consequence of this process of re-emphasis on Rosi's part is that the room's naked walls can act as screens of sorts on which Carmen's gyrating shadow uncannily multiplies the shapes of her body.

The gypsy equivalent to a seven-veils dance in which Carmen engages is important, because it stirs up a series of cultural antecedents that have a long tradition in the history of nineteenth-century European (particularly French) meridionalism, to which both Mérimée and Bizet belong.

The obvious parallel is with the Egyptian dancer Kuchuk Hanem, whom Gustave Flaubert patronized during his 1850 trip to the Orient, and about whom he writes in his letters and travel notes. After reporting on the charms of the artist, whose skills he hired for both an evening performance and the night following it, Flaubert goes on to mention that he engaged in romantic reverie during intermittent lapses in his nocturnal rest; and then entirely unromantically adds: 'I amused myself killing the bedbugs that were crawling on the wall, and this created long, red-and-black arabesques on the whitewashed surface.'[33]

The key concepts that accompany sex are here, on the one hand, (E)'gypsy'anness, and, on the other, dance and *song*: the Latin word for which is, not coincidentally, *carmen*. To spice this comfortably triangular constellation with an added pinch of *couleur locale* and bring it to a consistently coherent whole, bedbugs and other pests come in handy, among nineteenth-century travellers, as concretizations of their feelings. Unlike Flaubert's Kuchuk Hanem, Mérimée's and Bizet's Carmen need not have extra (indecent) animals on her walls, since the implicit – and not-so-implicit – agreement between her (decent) authors and their (decent) public is that she is little short of an animal-like creature herself.[34]

Let us now return to Rosi's film and its narrative strategies. Through Carmen's mouth, Bizet's opera lays great store by the tragic inescapability of fate: fatalism being, once more, one of the characteristics attributed to the 'children of Nature' exotically and charmingly, though dangerously, living around the Mediterranean. There is a brilliant equivalent by which the film succeeds in rendering the original story's sense of impending doom. When, at the climax of the tragedy, Don José and Carmen are face to face with each other in the final duet, Rosi, contravening the opera's stage directions, does not position them 'in front of' the *plaza de toros*: rather, he places them near a lateral entrance, enclosing them within the high walls of a courtyard. They are here quite literally imprisoned by their own destinies. Don José is trapped by his only too obvious passion; Carmen, for her part, is ensnared by the somewhat less visible, but clearly perceptible, excess of nonchalance with which she has, in sequence, committed herself to different lovers.[35]

A little-noticed statement of hers interestingly reveals the contractual self-contradiction of her position. During the brief exchange in which she and Escamillo engage before the bullfight, and immediately before a dishevelled Don José beckons for a final reckoning, she answers Escamillo's declaration of love with the following words:

I love you, Escamillo, and may I die
If I ever loved anyone as much as you.[36]

By the logic of Carmen's own statement, the fact that the optative clause in her sentence is later fulfilled suggests the retrospective conclusion that there *was* in fact someone she had loved as much as Escamillo. Surely, lovers' casually formulated if-then clauses shouldn't always be taken literally; but, on the other hand, would the extra-sensorially endowed Carmen ever mention death haphazardly? She is perfectly aware of the mortal danger looming over her – and declares herself willing to accept it. Whatever the reason for her words at this juncture, Escamillo's importance as a diegetically significant element is undercut by them, and the option of reading his role as a mere 'pretext unto death' correspondingly strengthened.

The stage is now definitively set for the appearance of the Grim Reaper, who is no less eager to strike in Don José's and Carmen's very private *corral* than Escamillo is in the larger one next door. There is an eerie, hypnotizing ambiguity to the chorus's lines that accompany the appearance of the bullfighter in the ring.

Here's the *espada* [the Sword], the sharp blade,
Who comes to put an end to all,
Who appears at the end of the drama
And who strikes the fatal blow.[37]

These lines create a distinct gender ambiguity through the use of the synechdoche 'the *espada*': a bullfighter (masculine) carrying a sword (feminine) becomes *the* Sword. Thanks to the metonymy, the grammatical subject of the sentence acquires a perceptibly 'feminine' dimension. The main poetic effect of this is an extension of the field of possible semantic associations to include, primarily, death itself, which in French is feminine and thus faultlessly bears being called 'the sharp blade' ('*la fine lame*') *tout court*. The result of this allusive personification of Death strengthens the notion of *Carmen*'s availability for a baroque reading – which, as we saw, is part and parcel of Rosi's re-creation of the opera.

Among the farthest-reaching poetological implications of Rosi's *Carmen* I would finally count one that cannot but oppose it sharply to the previous Carmen stage tradition. I am alluding to what could be called Rosi's choice of a metaphysics of presence over one of simple substitution. While other filmmakers choose to collapse the story to its presumed conceptual nucleus, Rosi opts for the opposite tack, that of consolidating the narrative tradition of *Carmen* by building into its representation a full visual account of its semantic centre of gravity: the heretofore elusive violence of bullfighting. What other *Carmen*s only verbalize, Rosi's proceeds to show. No view-from-the-walls in his film: we *are* inside the ring.[38]

It is thus not only metaphorically that the space inside the arena features as full, rather than empty, in Rosi's *Carmen*.[39] Cinema is, of course, an artistic medium that makes the adoption of a metaphysics of presence particularly feasible: unlike literature or, all the more so, theatre, cinema can put (seem to put) things – even bulls – right *there*. Still, a possibility is not a necessity; making use of it remains a free act of artistic volition.

The overall effect of Rosi's narrative strategies, enacted at the three different levels I have examined, is that in his film we can sense a concerted reappropriation of *Carmen*'s text on the part of the observing glance: the director's glance, and consequently our own. In Rosi's *Carmen* we no longer feel the exotic distance or mythicization perceivable in Bizet's pages; nor can we find the sardonic irony that Mérimée's original had interposed between itself and a band of charming but, at bottom, smelly savages. A southern Italian himself, Rosi is able to eschew resentment toward conventional views of a desirable mediterranean South, and to embrace instead a South that is lively, homey, with flesh and bones ... and dust. Rosi's *Carmen* is an ideal example of a sovereign reoccupation – I am tempted to say, paraphrasing Saïd, *decolonization* – of a literary tradition. The full import of Rosi's aesthetic shift can only be grasped if we consider how deeply romantic literature is imbued with the 'northern' longing ever to press for a space beyond what is known to us. It is only by questioning our almost automatic assumption that a main goal of artistic creation is to achieve *de-*familiarization that we can appreciate the way in which, by the return of a real South to a real South for purposes of narrative control, Rosi's *Carmen* sanctions the practice of an exquisite *re-*familiarization.

A discussion of the *Carmen* case in the light of (neo)colonialism and its vicissitudes would, of course, not be complete if the analysis of the intellectual aspects of the film were not complemented by an at least cursory look into their obverse, the economic ones. Rosi's *Carmen* was made and distributed at a time of chaos and crisis on the Italian film market: a chaos and a crisis largely due to the sudden emergence of a Wild West situation on the Italian TV scene. Bolzoni aptly reminds us that by the time *Carmen* was released in 1984 the flood of second-hand

American serials and films beamed out by a jungle-like canopy of antennas, private especially, had already *colonized* the Italian public to the point of obliterating all but the narrowest spaces available to Italian filmmakers.[40] Our context has, hopefully, shown how appropriate his use of the C-word is; although, to be fair to foreign 'cultural imperialists,' objectivity demands that we exonerate them from direct intervention in this field. While Hollywood did provide the weapons for colonization, the actual campaigns were waged by the media armies of entirely Italian *condottieri*.

The Consummation of Meridionalism

With Rosi's *Carmen*, the South can be argued to be returning to the South, and is no longer examined by a northern alterity. The narrative voice feels everywhere at home and irradiates everywhere a sense of belonging.[41]

Rosi's fictional Seville is a place his spectators have already visited, where – unlike Don José – they can feel at home. We can recognize in its winding roads the familiar alleys of *Christ Stopped at Eboli*. We meet in it the same women, assembled in similar mass displacements, with whom we became acquainted in *Salvatore Giuliano* or *Hands Over the City*. In it we visit the same arena, a backdrop for blood and heroism, as we do in *The Moment of Truth* (*Il momento della verità*, 1965). We witness sensual duets that echo those in *The Challenge* (*La sfida*, 1957). However different the historical frame, in Rosi's Seville we are confronted with a process scrutinizing the same ultimate goal of military obedience that was questioned in *Just Another War* (*Uomini contro*, 1970). Last but not least, in the interconnection of love and impending death Rosi's images collectively chronicle one more death ominously and many times foretold: Carmen's own. *Carmen* summarizes so much of Rosi's life work that it can be seen as the deliberate condensation of a coherent cinematic poetics, as an artistic recapitulation that was many years in the making.

Carmen – and *imago*. While the opera fuses image and song, Rosi's film goes one step further in the merger, in that it not only reconciles two artistic media with each other, but also enacts a reappropriation and identification of the narrating glance with its subject matter. The dichotomy observer/observed is shattered. Orientalism-meridionalism vanishes as a world view and as a representational system when the artist from the South finally takes the Other Land's *imago* – and its *carmen* – into his own glance, into his own hands, into his own camera.

By a process I suggest we define as a veritable *consummation of meridionalism*, in Rosi's *Carmen* the South becomes an aesthetic object for itself. By mirroring itself in Spain as its alter ego, the modernized Italy of the mid-1980s looks back at 'the way we were' and finds that she has come full circle: having shed the passive hetero-erotic aura received from northern Europe during the nineteenth century, she has become auto-erotic: the subject-and-object of narcissistic desire.

During the nineteenth century, Italy was long viewed as 'the Egypt of Europe' – by implication, as its Kuchuk Hanem: sensual, but with bed-bugs on her walls.[42] Alternatively, the greasy palms of her civil servants were mentioned condescendingly: not the palms de Musset refers to when he writes, 'Romanticism! that's the water tank under the palms' – the *other* palms.[43] With Rosi's *Carmen*, the exotic country (Egypt, Spain, Italy in particular) now comes on stage autonomously, reappropriating for herself her own seduction. That can be no coincidence: the time when Rosi's film was made marked the precise moment of mutation when Italy, already looking ahead to a promising future in an ever more closely knit Europe, was at the same time about to become an object of lust for an entirely untraditional set of would-be Europeans: no longer the rich ones up North, but the poorer ones in eastern Europe, the Balkans, and Africa.

This is a crucial historical transformation. Gradually, during the 1980s Italy turned from 'the lusty woman down South' into 'the prosperous woman up North.' With a short lag, as of the 1990s Italian cinema testifies to this transformation by a wave of films on immigration, ranging from certain sequences in Giuseppe Tornatore's *Everybody's Fine* (*Stanno tutti bene*, 1991) to more concentrated treatment in Michele Placido's *Pummarò* (1990), Maurizio Zaccaro's *The Article 2* (*L'articolo 2*, 1993), and Gianni Amelio's *Lamerica* (1994).[44]

Francesco Rosi's *Carmen* marks a watershed in this transition. The film may well be the (literal) swan song of the mythology of the 'land of the lemon trees,' while potentially foreshadowing an epoch of lament over an inhospitable 'land of the tomato fields.' No longer a duplicate of the (northern) *conquistadores*' mythical Eldorado/California, the peninsula now becomes the equivalent of what California may mean to (southern) migrant workers from across other borders and from over other waters. Soon the troubles of the mid- to late 1990s (wars in ex-Yugoslavia, uncontrollable mass migrations, civil war in Albania, and economic slowdown to boot) will cast long shadows over the presumed brightness of a united Europe's future; and the very dreams that Italy feeds on its own far shores will threaten to turn the peninsula into the locus of clash between racism on one part and bitter disappointment on the other. In a word, Rosi's *Carmen* immediately precedes the rude awakening by which Italy is to discover that being an object of desire may involve undesirable side effects and impose unpredicted responsibilities in the cohabitation with visitors other than the traditional romantic ones from the North.

Hermits and Revolutionaries: *Palombella rossa* (1989)

The Hermit

I may well be gnashing my teeth as I joke. (Fĕdor Dostoevsky)[1]

Very much like the Sacher-Torte of which so many Morettian protagonists are inordinately fond, *Palombella rossa* consists of the stratification of diverse components.[2] The film alternates personal and autobiographical layers with others of a social and political nature, and glazes them over with a third (albeit uncommon) object of addiction: water polo. In the process of portraying the tantrums of an unusual Italian Communist, it particularly delves into an intriguing exploration of what I would like to call, with an oxymoronic expression, the dilemmas of 'antidogmatic faith': in the historically polarized Italian polity, an article as rare among artists as among politicians and the citizenry at large.[3]

In *Palombella rossa*, Nanni Moretti once more impersonates a long-established alter ego of his, Michele Apicella. The Michele of *Palombella rossa*, however, is only loosely related to the homonyms that preceded him. No longer the revolutionary student of *Ecce Bombo* (1978), the film director of *Sweet Dreams* (*Sogni d'oro*, 1981), or the math teacher of *Bianca* (1984),[4] our water-polo-crazed protagonist is now a Communist MP, eagerly and seriously attempting to help his party forge a new identity in the rapidly changing times that are soon to lead to the vertical collapse, economic and political, of the Italian Communists' traditional Soviet lighthouse. Only, he is an MP with a twist – or two, or three, as it turns out.

Michele's most obvious peculiarity is his non-mainstream, self-questioning identity. Within the party, his individualistic deviance is constantly threatened by the ever-scandalous 'temptation' of monolithic thought. How exactly does he fight off the temptation of dogmatism?

As he plays in the match that Monteverde, his water polo team, is destined to lose, Michele is distracted, indeed harassed, by several unwelcome apparitions. First, a born-again Christian named Simon attempts to obliterate his individuality by assuring him that the two of them 'really' are 'the same';[5] then an ambitious journalist assails him for an interview without possessing the slightest qualification to comprehend the historical and cultural matters at hand; later still, the referee of the match falls out of his role and begins to pontificate in Michele's face, extolling, as he paces back and forth along the poolside, the thaumaturgic virtues of his own brand of psychiatry.

That people embodying the competing existential models just mentioned – fundamentalist Christianity, rampant yuppie-ism, pop psychoanalysis – should fail to elicit apostasy in Moretti's hermit is not altogether unexpected. The situation becomes proportionally more novel when comrades of Michele Apicella's intervene, as they repeatedly do. In one such episode, a pair of agitated populists chase Michele around the pool, reproaching him for his alleged refusal to talk to them. As they do so, they throw in improbable claims to a high degree of lucidity and make loud statements about the extreme intensity of their impatience at 'the current state of affairs.' (What affairs, exactly, they leave unsaid.) All along, they carry in their hands trays with pastries and glazed cakes of various sorts, which they attempt to force on Michele even as they vent their frustration at him. A second type of abuse Michele must recurrently face from surreal comrades is the one he must endure each time he encounters a bearded labour-union leader. Over and over again, the bossy old man corners Michele in order to preach to him aggressively about the growing difficulty Italian unions experience in fighting successful battles and retaining the support of the masses. Are these meant to be comic characters out of a *grand guignol*? Does their apparition perhaps aim at reviving, in a leftist variant, Ionesco's theatre of the absurd?

Neither is the case. These seem to me entirely logical personifications of two opposite but ultimately equivalent aspects of a temptation that haunts our stubbornly autarkic 'saint' Michele: that of political extremism. The imposing paternalism of the hirsute leader and the vapid, self-righteous victimism of the two cake-bearing *poseurs* send a common message to Michele Apicella: namely, that it would be easier for him to let himself slip into the passive duplication of inadequate patterns of thought pre-established for him by others, rather than uphold his quest for a personal alternative path.[6] In other words, they represent the temptation – no word other than the time-tested religious one can here adequately convey the concept – to acquiesce in the 'sinful' comfort of the well-known ghetto of defeat, rather than setting out on new paths and braving the challenge of devising previously unthought-of strategies of victory.[7]

In refusing time and again to give in to the blandishments of intellectual sloth, and reiterating instead his choice of mental independence, Michele duplicates in modern times the (self-flagellatory) stubbornness of the hermits of early Christianity. The word *eremita* occurs, in fact, quite explicitly in the film during a flashback that covers an earlier political debate on TV (*Tribuna politica*) between Michele Apicella and a group of journalists. These press him about the ways and means the Italian Communist party considers appropriate to bring about the societal changes it wishes for. At a loss for a precise reply, Michele answers in increasingly broken and increasingly mystical sentences that eventually lift off into rapturous chant: '... to act as a hermit, who renounces his own self ...'[8]

Perhaps all hermits behave in similar manners, perhaps not. For our purposes it is at any rate striking to note just how much there is in common between Michele's attitudes and those of easily the most famous early Christian hermit in modern European literatures, Flaubert's Saint Antony.[9] In particular, during the onslaught of the temptations that assail him Saint Antony seeks support in the bittersweet solace offered him by reminiscences from his childhood; and Moretti's Michele does likewise.

Michele's recollections from childhood and adolescence are, indeed, a locus where the allegorical and the symbolic planes in *Palombella rossa* interface seamlessly.[10] The allegorical plane – Michele the athlete as a substitute for Michele the militant Communist – is activated by original footage we are shown from a 1973 super-8 film by Moretti himself, in which an adolescent revolutionist (played by Moretti) appears on the screen, against a Roman backdrop, endlessly and sometimes comically debating with his friends the reasons for their shared Communist convictions.[11] A separate set of memories, on the other hand, engages the symbolic level of narration, on which Michele stands for the lonely soul: the sickly but at least hyper-rational thinker unable to accept the worn-out linguistic clichés shared by bourgeois and proletarian masses alike.[12] I am alluding to the Dostoevsky-style oneiric reconstruction of the time when a four-year-old Michele, having been caught by his parents stealing (he has, of course, appropriated a cake), is summarily ordered to pack his miniature suitcase and wander off to jail. As was the case for Dostoevsky, the paternal threat (there, execution; here, incarceration) is stayed at the last moment. Dostoevsky's capital punishment is commuted; Michele wakes up from his nightmare.[13] But, in both cases, loneliness and a sense of exclusion ensue; and, with them, a keen interest in studying – for Michele, indeed, furthering – one's own pathological state. 'Come on, let us continue like this, let us hurt each other more,' Michele had pleaded during an earlier appearance of his in *Bianca*. His kinship with the diseased Man from Underground is transparent.[14]

If, as I suggested, Michele metaphorizes the masochistic position of the ascetic loner, who basks in the sun of his intellectual pride even as he suffers the torments of gnawing self-doubt, by a quite natural transition the concept of masochism will now lead us to the third anti-naturalistic feature in the athletic/asketic/amniotic/psychotic politician's life: namely, the film's availability for a reading in which Michele's Monteverde water polo team rather directly signifies the Italian Communist party in its history up to the time when the film was made, 1989. In that year, the collapse of the Iron Curtain set in motion something unforeseen by both friends and foes: the break-up process by which the Soviet Union simply ceased to exist. The allegorical aspect of the film – one permeated with humour, at the surface anyway – is reinforced by the presence of a Hungarian player called Imre, who plays for Monteverde's opponents (Acireale) and inflicts a disastrous score upon Michele's boyish troops.[15] It seems clear to me that such unusual damage can only stand for the dramatic setback in public support that the Italian Communist party suffered in and after 1956, when it failed to draw the appropriate conclusions from the Soviet invasion of Imre Nagy's Hungary, and lost credibility by sharing the responsibility for it. (Nagy was head of the provisional government that had declared Hungary's short-lived neutrality, i.e., her de facto independence from the Soviet bloc. After the tanks rolled in, Nagy was – in breach of an explicit promise to this effect – put on trial for treason and shot.)

The figurative chain then winds on as, during the game, Monteverde at the last minute manages a miraculous near catch-up (from 2–9 to 8–9). This, it seems to me, transposes the outcome of the 1975 and 1976 almost-but-not-quite successful elections that brought the PCI within a whisker of overtaking the ruling DC and qualifying to supplant it in government. The political opportunity for renewal, however, was wasted in Italian history; and in much the same way Michele fails to score the penalty he has the chance to shoot during the last few seconds of the game. Hence – on either level of signification – crisis, doubts, and soul-searching in the team. To put *Palombella rossa* in a nutshell: in the pool, Michele Apicella's dimension as a solitary mind coexists with that of the Monteverde equivalence with the Italian Communist party.

The allegorical level of *Palombella rossa* leads to the altogether political question that implicitly sustains the entire film: namely, the long sequence of failed bids for power made by the Italian Communist party in its history. By what form of pleasure in self-punishment did the largest leftist party in Western Europe fail to tap what seemed to be inexhaustible human resources and manage to fritter away its potential for success? The diegetic hint in *Palombella rossa* seems to be that nothing short of a perverse determination to lose must have come into play. While it remains for historians and political scientists to work out the social causes for the self-defeating stubbornness that took the upper hand in this process, what *Palombella rossa* illustrates with the utmost clarity is that by 1989 the Communist 'sun of the future' had simply failed to rise.

Two corollaries on Moretti need to be appended to this statement, one related to the Communist MP Michele Apicella, the other to David Lean's *Doctor Zhivago*, which *Palombella rossa* abundantly excerpts (thereby securing, if not a revival of revolutionary fortunes, at least its own inclusion in *Masters of Two Arts* in just this location). First, in pointing out all manner of insufficiencies in Michele Apicella's political and private life, I am not implying that they are also Nanni Moretti's; quite the contrary, I believe that Nanni Moretti *produces* Michele Apicella largely as an externalization of what he is not, no longer is, or does not wish to be.[16] Second, it is a fact, by the director's own avowal, that Moretti is not conversant with Pasternak's *Doktor Zhivago*;[17] that is to say, Moretti's use of Lean's film within his own, to which we will soon turn, cannot be interpreted as a deliberate tool of his critique of Michele's behaviour. But this, I believe, is far from undoing Michele's own stand against naive political positions; indeed, his point will be proved a fortiori by the fact that he is much closer to his comrades than he would ever himself suspect.

The concluding sequence in *Palombella rossa* shows us Michele with his daughter Valentina crawl out of their car's wreck. (Did Michele suddenly lose control during a brief blackout in his rational functions? Was the accident a disguised suicide attempt? We never find out.) As, dazed, they stumble back toward the highway and hesitantly walk up a grass-covered levee, a crowd suddenly materializes around them and accompanies them in their silent ascent toward the ridge. Suddenly (the camera is at a distance, below the crowd) all stop in a precarious pose, their right arms stretched out before them and their left legs raised in the opposite direction for balance. But, with one foot only as a base, equilibrium is elusive; everyone quivers in visible and perhaps intentionally exaggerated titubation.

In the film's last shot, the camera moves up and around to face the crowd from the top of the levee. Thence it once more focuses on those in the front row – most notably the four-year-old Michele and his mother. This final *tutti* is at one and the same time an allegorical representation of the predicament of the Italian Communist party in 1989 and a metaphorical rendition of an individual soul's struggle against doubt.

What, then, of the egalitarian millennium awaited by the PCI? It is precisely toward such a radiant dawn that the *popolo comunista* stretches its arms in the ending of *Palombella rossa*. Yet, significantly, the sun they stretch their arm toward is an artificial one made out of cardboard. In typical postmodern fashion, that sun is little by little ratcheted up a scaffolding (one uncannily resembling those cherished by Fellini), and it thus provokingly exhibits its own contrived nature. Meanwhile, the *real* sun rises on Moretti's scene. Its rays shine at a narrow angle, almost blinding the camera and the viewers – emphatically *not* from the position where the mechanical sun is located. The consequences are obvious: the Communist rank-and-file, whose *tableau vivant* closes *Palombella rossa* with little Michele at their forefront, are looking into the wrong sun.[18]

The final pseudo-sunrise in *Palombella rossa*, and the existential instability by which it is accompanied, position face-to-face Flaubert's ascetic hermit and Moretti's athletic one, linking the two in an endlessly productive cultural homology. Considering that in the etymological sense the word *askêsis* simply means 'training,' it seems fair to conclude that the parallel between faith and water polo is far more water-tight than a first spectatorial glance at *Palombella rossa* might have induced us to assume.

Italian Communists and the Wrong Revolution: *Doktor Zhivago* and *Palombella rossa*

This leads us to the conceptual core of *Palombella rossa*: the conflict in the film between the reality of the Russian revolution and the reception allotted by Italian Communists to its fictional representation. In a different context, the ambiguity of mainstream Communists following the 'wrong sun' (or, which is to say the same, staring into the sun of the wrong future) could possibly be argued away as a joke of no particular consequence on a director's part. But, if we consider the abundant material that Moretti's film contains on Russia, it becomes difficult to deny that – whether by authorial design or a revealing coincidence – some substantial misperception is indeed afoot in the minds of the Italian revolutionists depicted by Moretti.

Five times in *Palombella rossa*, Moretti quotes David Lean's 1965 *Doctor Zhivago* by inserting original footage from it. How so? The bar next to the swimming pool where the water polo match is taking place has a TV screen for the entertainment of its public. Viewers of *Palombella rossa* are shown the five excerpts at different times when Moretti's camera pauses on *Zhivago* as it follows athletes and public wandering to and fro.[19] While there is no reason to pursue here a full comparison between Pasternak's novel and its re-creation by Lean,[20] I shall now identify and comment on Moretti's quotes with the specific goal of drawing some conclusions about the light the footage sheds on the Italian Communists' view of the Russian revolution.

(1) Komarovsky and a sixteen-year-old Lara appear. They are having an argument. The lecher says to the girl from the working class, whom Pasternak calls 'a girl from another sphere':[21]

Komarovsky. 'There are two types of men – two only. Your fiancé [Antipov] is one of them. He is noble and pure. He is the type of man whom the world feigns to admire, but whom in reality it despises. He is the type of man who causes unhappiness, especially among women. That your taste, for the time being anyway, should favour that type of man, I find understandable. However, it would spell disaster for you to marry that young man. Because, it so happens that there also are only two types of women ...'

(Lara instinctively shields her ears with her hands. Michele, who is watching the film at the bar by the pool, imitates her, shielding his own.)

Komarovsky. 'There are two types of women; and, clearly, you do not belong to the purer of the two ...'

(Lara slaps Komarovsky; then Komarovsky slaps Lara.)
Komarovsky. 'You, my dear, belong to the kind for the bed.'

Not a word of this occurs in Pasternak's *Doktor Zhivago*. The above is – one assumes – an attempt to render at one go subtle psychological processes in individual characters that the novel intermittently describes in parts II and III of Book 1 and intersperses with elements of the social, political, and religious currents of thought moving toward boiling point in the valve-less pressure cooker of Russia between 1905 (part II) and 1911 (part III).

Pasternak, if anything, flaunts the indirectness of the way he conveys the beginning of the affair between Komarovsky and Lara. Part II, section 4 refers to a glamorous ball, and in an airy paragraph written in free indirect discourse alludes to waltzing as 'the root of all evil': 'It was all this waltzing that had started it ...'[22] The outcome of Komarovsky's strategy of corruption can easily be inferred. Also in free indirect discourse, Pasternak later writes simply (and, for the intuitive reader, predictably): 'How had it happened? How *could* it happen?'[23]

To put the matter bluntly: in *Doktor Zhivago*, Pasternak's novel about the failed passion between the revolution and the Russian *intelligentsiia*, we find no date rape, no violence, no argument, and no theorizing about genders and their subspecies. In other words, we hardly have any Komarovsky at all in the whole process. In Pasternak, Komarovsky is an entirely fungible feature, a little blood-sucking parasite whose presence points to certain dysfunctions in society, but who has no ontological substance in and of himself; he only has a structural function, and is thus a *mosquito* in name and in fact.[24] In Lean's film, the mosquito is instead promoted to the rank of Main Villain.

This abusive reshuffling transforms the narration from a collective drama to an individual one; and Russia's tragedy becomes the sad story of a Western-looking girl with a hairstyle like Brigitte Bardot's. Lean reduces the main characters of *Doktor Zhivago* to the level of sentimental puppets, depriving them of all philosophical, religious, and political significance; conversely, it elevates a quintessential irrelevance (not grand evil, but petty evil, evil turned stupid) to the sphere of Being.[25] By contrast, if the original *Doktor Zhivago* could at all be described as the story of a shipwrecked love, then it was the story of the shipwrecked love between the Russian liberal radicals and an ideal of social redemption that the revolution originally contained but, in the end, shockingly betrayed.

(2) The second Lean quote in Moretti's *Palombella rossa* portrays the

dismantling, in 1917, of the First World War field hospital where Yurii and Lara, who had briefly crossed paths in Moscow, have coincidentally met again. The doctor hugs a departing (male) nurse. Then Zhivago tenderly takes leave of Lara, who also boards the outbound carriage. In the soundtrack, 'Lara's theme' begins to play, *crescendo* and *sforzando*. It is autumn, and the music, the leaves blowing about in the wind, the farewell atmosphere, etc., amount to a heart-rending recapitulation of a great love – thus suggesting that some apocalyptic event might be nigh.

This cinematic sequence is counterfeit from beginning to end. In Pasternak's novel about Russia, we are in 1917 all right, but it is springtime (Zhivago will go back to Moscow during the summer; see Book 1, part V, section 13). We do not read about the field hospital being dismantled and moved. There is no farewell scene. Previously, there had been a discussion between Zhivago and Antipova (Lara's name after her marriage to Pavel Pavlovich Antipov), but its content was of a philosophico-religious rather than amorous nature. While ironing, Lara had said to Zhivago:

'Such a thing [as a revolution] happens only once in an eternity ... It makes you think of the Gospel, doesn't it?'[26]

As for 'Lara's theme,' Lara's departure, the blowing wind, and suchlike, Pasternak's facts and Pasternak's atmosphere are the following:

They had no more talks of this kind. A week later Larisa Fëdorovna left.[27]

Sentimentalization and, more importantly, banalization of the tragedy of the Russian revolution are the inevitable result of Lean's modus operandi. In and of itself, this would not matter much to us – if, that is, the Italian Communists who in *Palombella rossa* uncritically gobble Lean's *Doctor Zhivago* weren't such a sentiment-prone bunch, feeding on Lara's sugary misfortunes with the same recklessness as many a Morettian protagonist does on chocolate cakes.

(3) The following dialogue occurs in David Lean as Yurii and Lara enjoy the swan song of their happiness in a Disney-like crystal palace located in improbably sunny and barren flatlands (rare in Siberia, but common in Spain, where the film was made):

Lara. 'We would have gotten married, we would have had a home ... You – what would you have preferred, a boy or a girl?'

Yurii. 'We'll go crazy if we think about this.'
Lara. 'But I, I will always think about it.'
(They wear warm clothes. She has a woollen turtleneck on; he huddles in an overcoat of Gogolian size.)
Lara (into the next room). 'Katia!'

This is gibberish. Lara and Pasha Antipov marry in 1912, at a time when the young woman has had only a fleeting acquaintance with Yurii Andreevich (who is anyway even younger than she). Having obtained two teaching jobs in the same town in the Ural mountains, Lara and Pasha move there and enjoy a brief but unclouded time of happiness, inspired by ideals going back all the way to the *narodniki*.[28] This blissful moment is then devastatingly interrupted by the outbreak of the First World War.

Lara loves Antipov deeply. This occurs not least out of a sense of solidarity between two persons of the same class, who know how to support each other in the face of persecution on the part of the upper classes or of its parasites (*Komarovsky*). To the end, Pasternak's Lara makes it utterly clear to her 'younger brother' Yurii that, while she certainly loves him too (Russia loves her intellectuals, when they are honest, good-looking, and poetic), her ultimate idol, the beacon in life she looks up to, is Antipov. In 1905, all she had to say about the incipient Russian revolution, destined to shoot at the likes of Zhivago, was

'Oh, how splendidly [the gunshots crackle] ... Blessed are the downtrodden. Blessed are the deceived. God speed you, bullets. You and I are of one mind.'[29]

This is brief, sharp, and unequivocal. Highly equivocal, by contrast, is what 'if' underlies the 'would' contained in the insipid filmic dialogue already quoted. Whatever the conditions, it is clear that the consequences it formulates are impossible, both socially and psychologically: there was simply no way for Yurii and Lara to get married and have children, 'if ...'. *Doktor Zhivago* could, indeed, be described as a novel about the *enormity* of the social cataclysm necessary to bring about an inherently improbable and labile (mis)match such as the one between Lara and Yurii.

The *poshlost'* (petty-bourgeois corniness) of the ideals expressed in the lines of Lean's Lara is sufficient to deprive of all seriousness her entire cinematographic entelechy. In Lean's film, the humiliated and offended are humiliated and offended once more.[30]

(4) Nanni Moretti's fourth pseudo-Pasternakian quote occurs when Lara abandons the prairie with Komarovsky, on Komarovsky's sled, due for some faraway place in the Far East – beyond the Spanish Sierra Nevada:

(Zhivago hands Lara a balalaika. *'Lara's theme' roars. The sled glides away as Zhivago waves adieu.)*

(As if following an invisible Pied Piper, the players in the pool – Michele being the first among them – and the entire public in the water polo stadium converge en masse around the TV screen in the bar).

From the sublime to the ridiculous there notoriously is but one step: a step here boldly taken by Lean. In Pasternak's novel about the Russian revolution there is, of course, no *balalaika* – which is possibly the most stereotypically perverse one among the many conceivable emblems of what *Doktor Zhivago* is all about.

Yet the spurious addition is perhaps not even as revealing as one surreptitious subtraction. Something the novel has that the film has not is *an abyss* – a deep ravine, located right next to the forest house where Yurii, Lara, and Katia have taken up lodgings.[31] As a symbol, an abyss may not be particularly subtle (and Pasternak has been accused of all kinds of compositional naivety by some critics); but it is one that is consistent with the book's chosen theme, the events it narrates, and the personality of the characters it portrays. The fact that the tearful Italian Communists of Moretti's *Palombella rossa* fall for the *balalaika* business and thus, by virtue (if such is the word) of their credulity, 'miss the abyss' of the revolution may, at this point, begin to shed some substantial light on the reasons why they lose all their water polo games – especially the ones they play against executed Hungarian revenants.

(5) Appropriately perhaps, diegetic invention in Lean's *Doctor Zhivago* reaches its climax in the depiction of Yurii's death.

(Many years later, Zhivago has returned to Moscow. One day, he believes he sees Lara walking in the street as he rides past in a streetcar. She is not aware of him. He in vain attempts to draw her attention by banging against the sealed windows of the vehicle. The doctor staggers out at the next stop and tries to run in pursuit of her. However, his heart fails him, and he collapses on the street.)

(All the while, Moretti's Italian Communists have been cheering on.)
'Turn around! Turn around!'
(To the driver) 'Let him off! Let him off!'
'Run! Run [after her]!'
(A cry of horror rises from the crowd when the TV screen finally shows the doctor tumble over and die.)

How does this episode occur in the novel that tells the story of how and why Russians of all classes and persuasions, having first fallen for the idea of the revolution, were then bitterly disappointed by its reality? There, the situation is different beyond recognition.

First, in Pasternak the woman walking along a Moscow street in 1929 *is not Lara*; Yurii has met that woman, but *does not recognize her*; and he collapses on the stone paving without having entertained *the least intention* of talking to her.

Second, the massive myocardial infarction that floors the doctor has *no rapport whatever with his feelings* – not with those that relate to women, anyway.

In Pasternak, the circumstances are of an exquisitely political nature. This is why:

(5a) The woman walking along the street is Mlle Fleury, a Swiss national whom the readers of the book (though certainly not the audience of the film) remember from the Meliuzeevo field hospital we already know about. For its part, the Soviet streetcar on which Zhivago is riding lurches along in a series of transportational hiccups due to mechanical failure:

> Yurii Andreevich had already lost sight of [the woman] several times, whenever the trolley had started up after a stop for repairs and passed her. [And, a number of times,] she again came back into his field of vision when it [again] broke down and she caught up with it.[32]

The Swiss citizen and the Soviet streetcar are interrelated, and in a moment I shall say why.

(5b) The disease to which Yurii succumbs is nominally an ailment of the heart; but it is, in fact, a moral ailment – the physical manifestation of the malady of the times, fostered by a regime of 'permanent soul-twisting.'[33] Of such 'permanent soul-twisting' we have ample illustration throughout that part of Pasternak's novel that is set under Stalin's regime – and which Lean conveniently decided to ignore in his film, perhaps because it would have forced him to face the thorny issue of how to deal with Stalinism ... and, last but not least, with Zhivago's third life companion, Marina.[34]

These apparently diverse elements in fact interlock as tightly as those of a puzzle. Lenin's famous slogan that 'Communism is the Soviets, plus electrification,' clearly acts as a cultural subtext to denote Zhivago's electric streetcar as a symbol for a revolution that, its claims notwithstanding, only barely manages to keep up with a walking West (here, Switzerland) it has triumphantly promised to overtake.[35]

As for Zhivago's illness, I have already mentioned its true nature. The one element needed to complete the picture is that in the novel the doctor's fatal crisis is triggered by a claustrophobic panic related *not* to Lara, but to an attack of nausea that seizes him inside the hermetically sealed revolutionary vehicle.[36] It is thus utterly clear to any reader interrogating the only serious extant *Zhivago* that the conclusion of Yurii's life is not something like the last episode in a syrupy love story, but the altogether unromantic indictment of the bloodthirsty catharsis called Russian revolution – love, rats, blood, mosquitoes, hunger and typhus and all.

While none of these facts is kept particularly secret by Pasternak's text, and I can thus advance claims to no special talent for pointing them out, doing so at least has the merit of offering an interpretation that inscribes personal events in *Doktor Zhivago* into the greater historical picture with a certain degree of consistency. The feat of Pasternak's novel is, indeed, precisely to arrange internal resonances between individual tragedies and a nation's tragedy in such a way that by the end of the book the reader feels there has been mutual illumination between two complementary aspects of the same issue. At the end of Lean's film, by contrast, the only lights that go on are the ones in the movie theatre.[37]

To repeat myself: all this would be only indirectly related to our subject if Nanni Moretti's *Palombella rossa* did not zero in on the predicament of the Italian Communists, portraying them as electrified and transported in enthusiastic sympathy by the vicissitudes of people they take for Russian revolutionists and an incident they imagine to be the Russian revolution. Were that *not* their assumption, why would Michele raise his left arm with a clenched fist at the precise moment when 'Lara's theme' starts and Lara's carriage rolls out of the field hospital in the Spanish highlands? Yet that is exactly, and strikingly, the case.

The inability of Moretti's Communist crowd to come to terms realistically with the reality of the Russian revolution comes across, in the last analysis, as a consequence of their refusal to deal head-on with evidence available from direct sources, and thus is a result of their dependence on sentimental political lullabies about it. Moretti is, as a Communist, sufficiently self-critical to illustrate Michele Apicella's political difficulties; but he fails to expose what is perhaps Michele's gravest inadequacy. Being naive about what Pasternak has to say on Russia automatically defeats any attempt of Michele's at being truly sophisticated about what needs to be said on Italy.

To translate explicitly *Palombella rossa*'s ultimate implications from the artistic level to the political one: the main reason why the Italian Communist party was a permanent loser, particularly in post-1956 political battles, seems to me to have been that it entertained a deleterious ambiguity vis-à-vis a mythicized Russian revolution, with which it was fascinated (much as young Lara was with waltzing), without (unlike Lara) ever being able to wean itself away from it. True, at the time of the Polish military coup in 1981, the mountain did give birth to a mouse of sorts: in a public statement, Berlinguer admitted that the propelling thrust of the 1917 October revolution had exhausted itself.[38] But the PCI then left the matter at that, and was thus disastrously overtaken by the events of 1989, when the Wall crumbled on top of it.

I would argue (as Apicella, and Moretti, fall short of doing) that the identity crisis in the PCI that *Palombella rossa* both expresses and attempts to exorcize is but a predictable consequence of the Italian Communists' failure – I shall not say to foresee the unforeseeable, but at least to draw explicit lessons from an ominously circular past. If, theoretically speaking, the lesson of Pasternak's *Doktor Zhivago* had been absorbed, and the logical consequences drawn, by Italian comrades (and, e.g., the transformations undergone under duress in 1989–90 had been undertaken squarely at an earlier time, perhaps in the wake of the Afghan war), their party would later have been perceived as having intuited and dominated the events. Because in politics perception is everything, it may well have been rewarded beyond its political merits, thus forestalling the occurrence of the very crisis around which *Palombella rossa* revolves – to be precise, not just a plain 'crisis' but, to quote the words ironically lent by Moretti to the journalists who interview MP Michele Apicella, a 'crisis, worsening, decompensation, fit, paroxysm, modification, perturbation, difficulty, disarray, recession, depression, ruin, disequilibrium, disturbance, bewilderment, restlessness, *dis-con-cert*!'[39]

To be sure, as we all realize, history cannot be rewritten with 'ifs.' And thus it was that, by a combination of different varieties of ignorance, David Lean's political line was allowed to triumph in the end.

Nonetheless, no karma is ever embraced without a degree of acquiescence. While offering no hint of a critical distance between the Italian Communists and a grotesquely flattened cinematic parody of *Doktor Zhivago*, *Palombella rossa* provides us with a profusion of episodes in which Michele exercises a radical critique of language: a critique that pushes linguistic skepsis to the point of questioning the validity of textuality as we know it, especially in the media and in literature. The peculiar fact is that the Ockham razor brandished by Michele falls asymmetrically: it spares cinema (at least David Lean's cinema, which he passively accepts as conveying certain truths about the revolution), while it cheerfully savages other types of relations between signifiers and signifieds.

Michele has a truly restless relationship with signs. First, as I have alluded, he mounts violent verbal attacks against the clichés that deface everyday language and obscure communication. Second, the entire 'plot' (if such a word can be granted) of *Palombella rossa* is constructed as a string of desperate efforts on his part to overcome a bout of amnesia, that is, to match a sign ('Michele Apicella') with its meaning (the elusive biographical and psychological content to be attributed to just that label). Third, and perhaps most important, the source from which *Palombella rossa* as a whole sprang in 1989 was a historical process of self-renovation by which Italian Communists attempted to reinvent their identity. They called this process 'the Thing' (*la Cosa*) – and most of their effort actually went into, and was subsumed by, the creation of an appropriate sign, symbol, or logo for whatever the new 'Thing' was to be.[40]

From Socrates to the *nouveau roman*, by way of Hofmannsthal's Lord Chandos, mistrust toward the codes of the transmitted word represents a recurring concern; and it is especially understandable that similar preoccupations should surface in the course of Nanni Moretti's protracted cinematic essay about how best to take political shots in water polo. By a coincidence that seems too coincidental by half, Monteverde's downfall in the very last seconds of the game is shown by Moretti as being brought about by Michele's failed penalty throw – an incident that uncannily resembles the ending of Peter Handke's best-known *nouveau roman*, *The Goalie's Anxiety at the Penalty Kick* (*Die Angst des Tormanns beim Elfmeter*, 1970):

'The goalkeeper is trying to figure out which corner the kicker will send the ball into,' Bloch said. 'If he knows the kicker, he knows which corner he usually goes for. But maybe the kicker is also counting on the goalie's figuring this out. So the goalie goes on figuring that just today the ball might go into the other corner. But what if the kicker follows the goalkeeper's thinking and plans to shoot into the usual corner after all? And so on, and so on.'

Bloch saw [that] all the players gradually cleared the penalty area. The penalty kicker adjusted the ball. Then he too backed out of the penalty area.

'When the kicker starts his run, the goalkeeper unconsciously shows with his body which way he'll throw himself even before the ball is kicked, and the kicker can simply kick in the other direction,' Bloch said. 'The goalie might just as well try to pry open a door with a piece of straw.'

The kicker suddenly started his run. The goalkeeper, who was wearing a bright yellow jersey, stood absolutely still, and the penalty kicker shot the ball into his hands.[41]

As in Handke's novel, Michele too shoots the ball into the goalkeeper's hands. End of the game. Defeat for Monteverde. Why defeat? I suggest this is because Michele's potentially victory-bound linguistic skepsis is only imperfectly applied: he attacks everyday language, journalism, and literature, while taking misleading films at face value.

At the end of the first half-time, Michele's laudable faith in the redemptive value of a truthful use of language had grown into a blanket condemnation of all written testimony. While recovering from the physical effort, he had panted from the pool: 'One mustn't read! One mustn't write either! ... Because then, right away, a notion becomes a lie ... I *hate* the written word!'[42] Why did Michele and the Italian Communists neglect the original Zhivago of Pasternak's book? Probably because books are written stuff, and as such, according to Michele, should not be read.

Moretti would, of course, have made Michele's political position stronger if he had endowed him with a more flexible iconoclasm, able to include cinematic re-creations of world literature into his scepticism. On the other hand, Michele's argument against the dangers of buying into cultural clichés is in fact reinforced, rather than weakened, by Moretti's recourse to a film that neither Michele nor his comrades adequately criticize. The essence of the matter remains the same: the ignorant always lose out. Which is why I would recommend, by way of conclusion, that good books be carefully read for guidance; or else, someone will misread them for us, and we will misguide ourselves by means of the bad films into which others may have 'adapted' them.

PART FOUR

Hypertextual Re-creations

The Masterpiece Fights Back:
Vanina Vanini (1961)

Stendhal's *Vanina*: or, On Energy

Contrary to a widespread misperception, Stendhal's *Vanina Vanini* does not belong to the collection *Chroniques italiennes*, the latter title being appropriately reserved for a cluster of *récits* that Stendhal re-created in the 1830s on the basis of original Italian manuscripts obtained from the Caetani family. These stories, and these only, are a homogeneous unit derived from Italian Renaissance sources. *Vanina Vanini*, which had been written and published at the end of the previous decade (1829), stands apart from them in a twofold sense: the setting of the events was for the author a contemporaneous one; and the core of its subject matter reached Stendhal directly when he was in Rome. While this real-time quality can easily be overlooked today, it does testify to Stendhal's responsiveness to the culture and historical climate in his host country – a responsiveness that ought to be as shocking as though, *mutatis mutandis*, a French visitor to the peninsula had, in the 1970s, fictionalized some incident surrounding activities of the terrorist groups active at the time.

The only real link between the *Chroniques italiennes* and *Vanina Vanini* is Stendhal's enduring quest for the primordial Italian soul: a soul (in Stendhal's view, at any rate) often cruel, but passionate and authentic, descended from the magnanimous Romans of the Republic and still alive underneath layers of corruption deposited by time and tyranny. 'The Romans being depicted here do not have the honour of being French,' Stendhal sarcastically comments in a footnote to the novella.[1] To him, Italians are characterized primarily by their vitality; it is 'superb' that Romans have '*energy*, that is to say, the quality most lacking in the nineteenth century,' he comments in *Promenades dans Rome*.[2] In sum, the original *Vanina Vanini* stands entirely under the sign of Stendhal's infatuation for what, with truly Beylian concision, Nietzsche once called 'acts of sublime madness.'[3] Stendhal's story is told – to use the trenchant words of *Beyond Good and Evil* – 'in Napoleonic *tempo*.'[4]

Fast-paced the novella indeed is. We encounter Stendhal's Vanina at a ball arranged by her father, the prince Asdrubale Vanini. There, she dances with Don Livio, her fiancé, whom she finds unspeakably boring – as boring, indeed, as the whole society that fatuously whirls around her. Suddenly, the dance hall is abuzz with an astonishing rumour: disguised as a woman, a *carbonaro* (a member of a pro-unification, nationalistic secret society) has just escaped from Castel Sant'Angelo. He stabbed a guard, was himself wounded, fled toward the river, and eventually vanished into the darkness.

The next day, Vanina notices something unusual in her family's *palazzo*. Glancing across the courtyard and glimpsing the wide-open louvres of the rooftop apartment located there, she thinks she discerns a woman in a violet dress lying on a bed. Quivering with curiosity, Vanina betakes herself to the attic. After several visits, it eventually dawns on her that the person before her is none other than Pietro Missirilli, the daring patriot she has heard about.

Thrilled to no end by the discovery that she is facing a dangerous subversive, Vanina arranges for Pietro to stay on and be discreetly treated for his wounds. During Pietro's convalescence, the two young people fall head over heels in love. They enjoy a protracted, undisturbed bliss high above the roofs of Rome. When good health returns, however, Pietro once more hears the call of the Italian revolution, and he goes back to his native province of Romagna.

Forfeit happiness after such a short experience of it? Never. Her wits sharpened by love, Vanina decides it is high time for her to do some long-term vacationing at the Porretta spa in the Apennines. This is conveniently located between Missirilli's home town and the Vaninis' castle of San Nicolò, close to the town of Sant'Angelo.

Here the inevitable happens: Vanina discovers that, although passionately in love with her, Pietro is nonetheless committed to full-time work for the unification of Italy. After much fruitless pushing and pulling, Vanina's aristocratic heart can no longer endure this affront on the part of a commoner. Impulsively, she denounces Pietro and a number of his fellow conspirators congregated in Cesena. These are duly arrested and imprisoned.

Now that Pietro's political exuberance has been brought under control, it remains to be seen how to snatch him from the papal gallows. Not a problem for Vanina: the perfectly well-bred young woman that she is, she gives her father her consent to marry Don Livio – and then enlists the latter's powerful uncle, *Monsignor* Savelli-Catanzara, to look into ways to have Pietro freed. By the same means she also obtains a secret rendezvous with her revolutionary sweetheart in a jail outside Rome.

Yet the supposedly climactic encounter fails to jolt Pietro into the reaction desired of him. Far from that: in solitary confinement, he has lost all will to live, developing both a marked lack of interest for Vanina and a crushing sense of guilt toward his comrades. Clearly, he lacks the information necessary to make sense of what happened on the fatal night in Cesena. Thereupon Vanina, carried away by her own shock at Pietro's withdrawal, cannot help putting forward the strongest argument she knows to exonerate him: I am the one who reported you, she avers – the blame is on me, and on me alone.

Pietro does not take kindly to this revelation. Enraged, he hits Vanina with the chains that constrain him. End of the love story, and thereby end of the story too: Vanina comes back to Rome empty-handed from Città Castellana – 'and the newspaper reports that she has just married prince don Livio Savelli.'[5]

We shall see in a moment how topical Stendhal's novella on the Italian *Risorgimento* must have appeared to Rossellini on the eve of Italy's first centennial in 1961.

Mythicizing the Nation

At the beginning of the 1960s, Italy was a young country indeed; if one takes as a starting point her democratic rebirth in 1945, she had only just turned fifteen. On the wings of the *miracolo economico* and with ebbing cold-war conflict and agrarian-patriarchal control on societal mores, significant numbers of Italians became able to live in a climate of confidence or relative euphoria, and to afford a bottle of *spumante* in order to toast the adolescent Republic's coming of age. A rejuvenated Italy could not possibly find a better occasion than that of her one-hundredth modern anniversary to ponder and reassess her identity as a republic and as a developed, industrialized democracy.

Just a brief time had elapsed since Fascist propaganda had ceased to drum into Italians' heads the concept that there were only three 'Italies' to be proud of: that of ancient Roman times; that of the Communes and of the Renaissance city-states; and the country led to renewed glory by the Leader *tout court*, the Duce. Given that at least the third of these historiographical abstractions had tangibly proved itself so disastrously imaginary, the present moment seemed to offer an ideal opportunity to find out what the unified, modern 'third Italy' really was meant to be. To paraphrase D'Azeglio's commonly quoted 1861 slogan 'Italy has been made, now we have to make Italians,'[6] the Italians of 1961 were *making themselves Italian* with remarkable zeal. Whether by way of mass migrations, increased rates of literacy, or simple exposure to the state-owned TV broadcasts, for the first time citizens from disparate regions could actually understand one another, linguistically if not always culturally, and quite naturally carry on their musings about the discovery of the Other into the exploration of their new homogeneous self.[7]

If it wasn't the Fascist one, *what* then really was the much-touted 'third Italy'? Whence did it come, and where was it going? To most Italians, the empirical answer was obvious: the best Italy around in a long time had, at long last, materialized with the Republic born of the *Resistenza*. Yet existing materially, politically, and (to a NATO-defined extent) militarily – the attributes of any sovereign state – was not, and could not be, quite good enough. The demise of the Savoy monarchy in 1946 had not amounted to a slight constitutional change; it had meant the disappearance, after many years of ineptitude, compromise with the Fascist dictatorship, and in the end (September 1943) sheer cowardice, of the only national entity that had survived the comparatively recent clean sweep of 1861. How often can a flag be replaced before the people behind it come to suspect that they may well outlive it? The question about Italy's identity at the time of its centennial was clearly related less to material issues than it was to cultural needs.

There was even more for the Italians of 1961 to contend with. The post–Second World War publication of Gramsci's notebooks had stimulated an open discussion of what could previously only be whispered: namely, that the Fascist propaganda of a strong, unified *Risorgimento* rooted across the country and across social classes was no more than just that, propaganda. In particular, at least since the *querelle* surrounding Visconti's *Senso* in 1954, it had ceased to be uncommon knowledge that, in the North, the Savoy monarchy had been so obsessed with the supposed dangers of democratization that it opted to smother popular support for what it conceived as its own dynastic war against Austria, rather than take the risk of giving Garibaldi's Red Shirts and other left-leaning groups a share of power equal to their contribution to the common cause. As for the South, Tomasi di Lampedusa's enormously successful historical novel *The Leopard* (*Il Gattopardo*, 1958) had, among other things, definitively debunked the conventional, grade-school notion that Garibaldi's southern expedition of 1860 had pitched brave and enlightened 'Italians' from all regions against a mercenary bundle of foreign stooges.[8] Quite the contrary, by the 1960s a truth began to surface that a variety of successive *raisons d'état* had previously not allowed to circulate for a full century: namely, that the unification of 1860–1 was a military conquest made possible, on the one hand, by European political circumstances and, on the other, by the tremendous social pressure accumulated in the southern kingdom, vis-à-vis which Garibaldi's behaviour succeeded only by dint of a skilful ambiguousness. On this more sober view, Garibaldi made it from Marsala to Naples as a victor largely because – to eschew all euphemism – he received support from a dejected populace who believed to recognize in him the first-ever brigand with a fighting chance to succeed against the powers-that-be.[9] Symmetrically, for their part the overwhelming majority of the northern intellectuals who made up the bulk of the Red Shirts' expeditionary corps saw in 'Italy' mainly a romantic concept, a literary reminiscence right out of the *Odyssey*, with Sicily a jewel in the wine-blue sea where Poseidon shook his trident.[10]

Because no society is solid unless it is able to generate a cultural discourse (a mythology, an ideology, an imaginary universe) adequate to cement it, over and above its de facto existence the adolescent Italian Republic of 1961 also needed a post-Fascist narrative about its own origins endowed with an aura – moral, political, intellectual – with which it would be able to identify. After all, during the last two centuries romantic fictionalizations of history had proved to be smashing hits in those countries where they had been systematically pursued: France, with its revolution, and the United States, with its Wild West, had been market leaders in this particular industry. (Germany had tried hard via Wagnerian opera, though with mixed results.)[11] What could Italy turn to for a comparable foundational myth? The Second World War should have been her natural source for one; and to an extent it was, producing several novels and films about the *Resistenza* that deserved attention and praise. Still, myth and politics, lyricism and civil wars, do not mix well; memories of recent bloodshed cause pain, not hazy dreams – and, to put the matter as neutrally as it can reasonably be, whether applauded or loathed the fall of Fascism promised to belong for a very long time to the realm of the real. When it came to creating the young and attractive Republic's letters patent of nobility, then, what better approach than to move further upstream by many decades and mythicize its proto-history, the *Risorgimento*?

The advantages for the Italians of 1961 of taking the *Risorgimento* as a neutral mythopoietic terrain were obvious. First, one could treat the subject according to an anti-Fascist (i.e., realist) aesthetic by presenting the period and its most famous characters in their full creatureliness. This trend is clearly exemplified in Rossellini's own *Viva l'Italia!* (1960–1), whose true-to-life portrayal of Garibaldi accomplishes a thorough humanization of the hero.[12] As importantly, one could embrace intellectual sophistication and take into account the harsh social and political realities denounced by Gramsci, while at the same time enjoying the freedom to downplay their stridency by way of fictionalization. This was the path that, in the 1960s, would be taken by some deserving but less well-known films (to mention but one, Camerini's *The Italian Brigands / I briganti italiani*, 1961) that adopt as background for their stories the social circumstances of the times around Italy's unification.

It did, of course, help the ideological nation-founding process of the Italian centennial that the 'bad guys' of 1860–1 happened to have been almost exactly of the same nationality as those ejected in 1945 from the motherland's sacred soil – Germans. Furthermore, it proved no less convenient for mythopoiesis that the *Risorgimento* itself had been an essentially romantic movement born at a date when romanticism was already *the* mainstream European cultural movement.[13] Mythicizing the *Risorgimento* thus amounted, in essence, to the hardly formidable enterprise of romanticizing romanticism – a job already half done to begin with.

The particular attractiveness of Stendhal's *Vanina Vanini* as a source for a film on the *Risorgimento* was that it offered abundant material on Italian unification *and* on a paramount love story too. Visconti's *Senso* had already shown how great an impact the mix of love and politics could have; by means of recently developed large screens and vivid technicolour, mass displacements of armies in battle could alternate with prodigiously blown-up, tear-wrenching scenes of passion.[14] Surely, *Senso*'s central historical argument, that the Savoy dynasty mistrusted Garibaldi just as much as it disliked the Austrians, had been received (in right-wing circles, that is) as politically dangerous. But no such risk existed for a Stendhalophile director: along with youth and passion, the story of Vanina's affair with a *carbonaro* contained only an utterly uncontroversial love for one's motherland. *Vanina Vanini* must have seemed inexhaustibly promising to Rossellini, a director interested not only in the intricacies of sentimental relationships – to which his Ingrid Bergman films had attested in the late 1940s and 1950s – but also, increasingly, in the illustration to the public of historical situations begun with *Viva l'Italia!* one year earlier.

There was a specific Rossellinian context for this state of affairs. After never-ending attacks by the critics not only on his cinema, but even more viciously, on his private life (his relationship with Ingrid Bergman was among the top tabloid scandals of the Italian 1950s), in the last phase of his artistic career Rossellini opted for the creation of pedagogical works on major historical issues, and in particular came to focus on the theme of the eon-long technological and scientific struggle carried out by humanity for its survival.[15] Along with *Viva l'Italia!*, *Vanina Vanini* belongs to the gestation stage of Rossellini's new phase; only gradually would the director develop a full awareness of his own ideal – an ideal he eventually came to identify in Comenius's pedagogical theory of Pansophy. To Comenius's concept of 'total education' Rossellini's book *A Free Mind*, published in France shortly before his death, is indeed a touching homage.[16]

Taking into account all of the above, we can say today with a fair degree of certainty that, by an ironic twist in both private and historical circumstances, the last period of Rossellini's production was largely a struggle *for his own* survival: in part, to be sure, in an economic sense, but primarily in the artistic one.[17] In the course of the 1960s Rossellini reached the certainty that virtually nothing worthwhile could be achieved within the pre-established, narrow bounds of commercial cinema. Reversing the attitude of the then fashionable films on *alienazione*, which aimed at showing how the growth in technological prowess creates a world of increasing powerlessness for the individual, Rossellini argued that progress lays the basis for liberation from physical need, without thereby necessarily subordinating humanity to its own mechanical creations.

With a lucidity equalled, before him, only by Tolstoy, Rossellini realized that art was sadly failing its mission by restricting its focus to narrow-minded lamentations over humanity's allegedly alienated status.[18] This realization had immediate, far-reaching repercussions on his view of the artist's work: 'I noticed that [in focusing on individual problems] I was carrying on debating the drama of an ant, while in the universe a galaxy was exploding. That's when the ant's drama ceased to interest me.'[19] Our horizon ought to be far grander: 'The Himalaya has risen, and we're still staring at the dust in the valley!'[20] The only genuinely absurd thing about the age of the absurd in art – Rossellini tirelessly argued in books, articles, and interviews – is that today's abdication occurs precisely at the time of the greatest triumphs ever celebrated by human beings over their inescapable condition as vulnerable and exposed to the whims of Nature.[21]

Despite a misunderstanding lingering on since the time of *Rome Open City* (*Roma città aperta*, 1945) and *Paisan* (*Paisà*, 1946), Rossellini had never thought of himself as a political *auteur*, and had been exploring many new paths since the period of his neorealist masterpieces. In fact, while the spectacular (i.e., commercial) potential was inevitably what most attracted the producer to the idea of a film from Stendhal, Rossellini eyed the project as a potential conduit for the new type of pedagogical cinema for which he yearned, and the subject matter was intended by him to provide specific historical information for the masses. The director seems to have been sufficiently intuitive to grasp (though he never said so in such stark terms) that, having forged too far ahead with his misunderstood Ingrid Bergman films, it was advisable for him to go back to the drawing board and lead the general public to aesthetic appreciation by a gradual learning process. His *Vanina Vanini* arose from a desire to break the deadlock of self-centred contemporaneous books and films about incommunicability, and to roll into one the commercial, the poetic, and the didactic potential of a love story inspired by one of the great classics of European literature. In fact, the film specifically endeavoured to be a hypertextual conflation of inspirational elements drawn from many Stendhalian sources.[22] Combining all these promised to deliver the best of many worlds; yet it was all going to prove more easily planned than done.[23]

Rossellini's Vanina: or, On Fear

I will first devote some concentrated attention to Rossellini's handling of Vanina's and Pietro's feats, so as to supply readers with solid evidence to buttress my subsequent contrastive comments on novella and film.

Against a blue sky, we see the churches of Rome, and we hear their bells ring. The year is AD 1823; Pius VII has just died, and a new pope must be elected. Rome begins to teem with cardinals' carriages converging on the Eternal City for the conclave.

Among the vehicles that go through the gate at Porta del Popolo, there is a stagecoach carrying characters with important roles in our story: Countess Vitelleschi and Pietro Missirilli, a young physician from Romagna. The gendarme at the gate is suspicious of the young man's lack of references in the city. To help Missirilli, the countess testifies that she knows him, although this has only been true for a few hours. After they alight at the coach terminal, Missirilli follows the noblewoman to her residence, only to see the profuse manifestations of his gratitude summarily curtailed by her. Countess Vitelleschi is distracted by other thoughts: once in her rooms, she receives the visit of a stocky man in his fifties, dressed in black and with a crew-cut hairstyle, who speaks with a heavy *romanesco* accent. This is her lover, Prince Asdrubale Vanini.

Meanwhile, Pietro has gone his way, to a secret meeting in a lower-class neighbourhood. (The viewer is treated, in passing, to a flash visit through a peculiarly spotless brothel.) By means of a coded exchange, he finally identifies in a café the contact person he is seeking, and is allowed to join the group of *carbonari* who are expecting him. After witnessing a detailed reconstruction of the *carbonari*'s initiation rites, we realize that Missirilli's task for the evening is more than that of a mere spectator: he has been instructed to dispatch a spy in the group. This task Missirilli performs with exemplary diligence.

There follows a strong narrative caesura: a series of wide-angle shots show a magnificent reception in a *palazzo*, with dozens of couples dancing to waltzing music. Among them, Vanina dances with her fiancé, Don Livio – a young man whose greatest claim to attractiveness lies in his wealth and connections to his uncle, the powerful Cardinal Catanzara-Savelli. Unlike her suitor, Vanina is deeply bored: all these people are happy, she tells Livio, because everything can be bought in Rome, including a cheerful mood.

The dance is temporarily interrupted by a visit by none other than the cardinal, generous enough to exchange with the young couple a few words about the art of dancing. Don Asdrubale follows the prelate on his heels, then trots away behind him, without forgetting to reward his daughter for her politically precious role. He caresses her and proffers what seems to be his favourite term of endearment: 'Cutsie ... sugar-daddie's sugardaughter!'[24] When the music and the dancing resume, a desperate-looking Livio again inquires about the reasons for Vanina's coldness, as well as about any means by which he could conceivably overcome them. Without so much as uttering a word in reply, Vanina moves to another room.

Then the news about the wounded *carbonaro* spreads. Our curiosity about him is satisfied by the film even before it has the time to build up: in a matter of seconds, the ball disappears from sight, and we are at the Vitelleschis. There, an elegantly cross-dressed, visibly white-bled Missirilli is lying on a couch, while before him a heated argument between the countess and Don Asdrubale is under way. Having overcome his knee-jerk jealousy and reluctantly accepted the countess's impulse to shelter the wounded fugitive, Don Asdrubale finally carries home Missirilli on his shoulders, muttering darkly: 'Eh, I wish I too were twenty years old! C'mon, honey, c'mon!'[25]

Back at the Vaninis', Vanina observes her father's mysterious manoeuvres as he leaves one of the apartments in the attic. She then tries the door, but cannot get in. The next morning Vanina's chambermaid, Clelia, brings to her mistress's room a cage with two canaries, a present only just delivered by the servants of *casa* Savelli. Having constrained in a dressing gown her fully developed body (the lead actor in *Vanina Vanini* is the noticeably adult Sandra Milo), our would-be romantic adolescent reaches to the window and hangs the cage from the open frame. This allows Vanina to catch a glimpse of an unknown woman in one of the attic rooms.

Later on in the day, Vanina climbs secret stairs in order to find out more about the mysterious presence. Already, she feels sympathy for the poor person, who, she says, must be suffering deeply over her loneliness.[26] By way of the terrace, she then reaches the desired flat and knocks at the shutters. When she finally walks into the room, it takes her only a fraction of a second to realize that the guest before her is in fact a young man. Passionate words are soon exchanged between the two, alone in their *tête-à-tête* – alone, that is, except for the accompaniment of about forty violins in the soundtrack.

The next day brings the maximum blossom, and the rapid withering, of the lovers' Roman bliss. During Vanina's morning visit, the revolutionist is slightly more passionate than he was heretofore. The idea of being healed, having to leave Rome, and no longer being able to see her is a new source of suffering for him. Dismayed that they belong to two different worlds, Vanina tells Pietro that she can't promise him anything, and bids him farewell. The two sigh, in each other's arms. Both are turned toward the camera, their eyes rolling heavenwards.

Pietro leaves on the same night, thanks to Don Asdrubale's complicity (the nobleman, who has bought a passport for him from a foreign embassy, comments aloud that luckily one can buy anything in Rome). End of the Roman idyll; Missirilli is off to Romagna. The love story could now easily fizzle out before it has even seriously started, but Clelia keeps the plot going by presenting the disconsolately sobbing Vanina with a brilliant idea: how about vacationing for a while at the Porretta? Vanina accepts with relief. Soon the two women leave the capital and take up lodgings there. Rome is now far away, and Rossellini's film duly informs us of local political circumstances by strategically devised dialogues between a messenger from the capital (Giovanni, one of the Vaninis' servants, who happens to be an active *carbonaro*) and subversive *romagnoli* sporting peculiarly spotless buckskin waistcoats and puttees.[27]

At the castle, Vanina wishes to see Pietro at once. However, organizing this takes time; and she must meanwhile receive a more embarrassing visit, that of the new local chaplain – a young man with nothing more challenging to dwell on than the religious zeal of his predecessor.

The second cluster of encounters between Vanina and Pietro, which in the film spans four days' time, is about to begin. Each presumed 'morning' is now signalled by what could be described as a postcard view of medieval Sant'Angelo atop its hill. The function of these shots – sheep, shepherds, and all – is to act as sundials for the spectators' benefit, while also throwing in a bit of local colour for good measure.

The four days in the San Nicolò castle allow Vanina's and Pietro's amorous dream to be fulfilled. Many more times, the two lovers pose next to each other and, facing the camera, arch-sentimentally gaze past it into the distance. However, their diverging, in fact clashing, priorities gradually become obvious, as Pietro waxes lyrical in his devotion to the national cause: 'How I wish I were free, rich and powerful ... I feel that I could be much more useful to the cause of freedom ... And when Italy were to be free from her oppressors ... I would stay forever with you!'[28] Upon hearing these words, Vanina pants, breathless, on the verge of incoherence. When she can finally control herself, she manages to propose marriage to Pietro. All it takes to erase their sin, she argues, is to call in the chaplain; she will later make sure that her father accepts the *fait accompli*. Pietro, however, expresses perplexity at the idea: at present, he is an outlaw, and he will have to stay in hiding for several years. This lapse of time he intends to put to use by working, in secret, for the national cause.

Before long, the two lovers have clearly identified a stumbling block that divides them: politics. Their dialogue impresses as a primer on European history, with Vanina accusing the Jacobins of having 'soaked the world in blood,' and Pietro retorting that at any rate 'the old world is destined to disappear.'[29]

When the chaplain pays a second visit, he directs at Vanina a torrent of arguments whose key words and concepts include 'perturbations,' 'creatures being loved ... instead of the Creator,' 'friendship, love, audacious words,' 'young body,' 'impure impulses,' and much else in that spirit.[30] Soon enough – and Rossellini's strategic zooming bears this out – Vanina is too shaken to endure such a verbal barrage. She declines to comply with its stated purpose, which is to obtain a full confession, and retires to her rooms. When she is again alone with Pietro, her mood is understandably at an all-time low; fearing eternal damnation, she feels shame for the pleasure she has experienced with him. According to her, she and Pietro can no longer live in sin, and they ought to confess their guilt. Pietro, however, believes that the confessor's true aim was simply to obtain from Vanina names of subversive *carbonari*; political repression is all they can expect.

The reaction predicted by Pietro is not slow in coming. Amidst great display of troops, we now see a *Monsignor* Benini arrive from Rome with the mandate to crush the rebellion in the region. When Pietro learns about this, he concludes that he must leave the castle at once. Vanina finally consents to his leaving at nightfall.

The ideal time for the lovers' next stealth encounter is the Cesena county fair; and that is just when Vanina shows up in town, with deep rings under her eyes and dressed in long, mournful attire. Pietro is, meanwhile, coordinating a meeting of the pro-unification conspirators in one of the houses that look out onto the square. The news is bleak: a member of the group has just been executed; below, the papal police prepare the public flogging of two of the dead man's accomplices. Since this information needs to be circulated in the province, Pietro and the others call an emergency session for the next day. Whoever, for the sake of security, wishes not to leave the house until then may do so.

Vanina, aware of the goings-on, instructs Clelia to go to Cesena in order to pass on to Benini detailed information about the planned gathering, and then she returns to Pietro. Temporarily removed from her familiar frame, the ubiquitous alcove, she now tries to involve him in some serious romanticizing about their common future – in America perhaps? Pietro, the exemplary patriot, rejects the idea.[31]

As early as the following morning, Pietro's affection for his fellow countrypeople is sorely tested. While Vanina, once more in her nightgown, is in bed, he, fully dressed, sits on its edge, uneasily waiting to leave. Giovanni reports that the *carbonari* have been betrayed and arrested in the house in Cesena where they were assembled. One of them has committed suicide so as not to be captured. The town is occupied by the military. Upon hearing this, a stunned Pietro – to prove that it was not he who gave away his comrades, and out of solidarity with their plight – decides to rush to Cesena to turn himself in. He thereby precipitously vanishes that of our sight, as well as that of his dumbfounded mistress.

The focus is now on Vanina: drawn by eight white steeds, her carriage – with the customary countless violins – speeds past us. Without even deigning to answer sugardaddy's tentative approaches about the possibility of her marrying don Livio (this being the last we hear about him in the film), Vanina heads straight for the brave young man's uncle. Soon she shows up in the sumptuous Renaissance study of Cardinal Catanzara-Savelli.

To the cardinal, Vanina confesses that she harbours a love that disturbs both her conscience and her heart; but she also reiterates that she is a good Catholic. The only way to redeem her sin, she insists, is marriage. Catanzara-Savelli decides to give her a second chance at trying to persuade the young man gone astray, and allows her to betake herself to a church to meet Pietro for her great gamble over his body and soul.

The prisoner eventually wanders in, heavy with chains that run across his chest and constrain his arms down to the waist. Trembling with emotion, Vanina explains to Pietro that all trouble can be over as if by magic, if only he consents to tie the invisible knot. But Pietro, aloof, does not even listen. Why? *Coup de théâtre*:

'The two of us! And what about the others? Why wasn't I at my post that night? I wasn't there, because I didn't love only Italy. Luckily, I too will now be able to die for my motherland.'[32]

Hence Vanina's explosive counter-argument:

'I will go to your comrades to humble myself before them, to tell them that I was mad with love for you ... and that it was I who reported them ...'[33]

This information proves, alas, destructive: reacting like a fury, Pietro starts a movement to hit the kneeling Vanina with the loose ends of his chains. The extremely quick scene cuts him off in this gesture, while we hear Vanina's hysterical screams pierce through the music of the usual battery of violins.

After the denouement, two parallel, rapid epilogues ensue. In an almost empty square, Pietro is led to capital execution; in ascending the gallows, he stops for a moment and turns around, as though he could see Vanina in the distance. Finally, Vanina is shown runnning along a path on a wooded hill overlooking the city; she leaps to a large, secluded portal and rings the bell. Soon a nun appears at the entrance; Vanina sinks to her feet. Just before vanishing behind the gate, she casts one last glance behind her, as if attempting to discern Pietro in the city below her. Innumerable violins rage, deafeningly.

What now follows is an annotated synopsis of the dramatic changes wrought on Stendhal's story – and, more to the point, on its atmosphere (i.e., wrought on the latter *by way of* the former) – in Rossellini's re-creation.

First, in Stendhal there is no prelude presenting Missirilli's arrival in Rome and embroiling him in a possible Donjuanesque exposure to Countess Vitelleschi's charms. This is a perhaps necessary, but certainly awkward expository mechanism that, in the film, casts a potentially less than heroic light on the male protagonist.[34] Second, the novella does not bother to meander from brothel to bar to free-masonic lodge in quest of instructive *effets de réel*; a grand ball is all we need, and a grand ball is all we get. Third, Stendhal's *récit* has no use for Don Asdrubale's platitudes, the languid trivia that Livio and Vanina exchange past each other, or the cardinal's paternalistic comments on waltzing. Instead, we have just a few sharp lines:

[Vanina] seemed to relish more in tormenting the young Livio Savelli ...
    'That young *carbonaro* who just escaped [has] at least done something more in his life than taking the trouble of being born.'[35]

This line, an allusion to Beaumarchais's *Marriage of Figaro* entirely lost on Livio,[36] marks the farthest a well-bred young woman of the times could venture in criticizing her social environment.[37] For its part, the film does nothing with the Beaumarchais connection, despite its being so hot.

Fourth, there are zero chances of survival in the film for a further Stendhalian detail: Vanina's two Jesuit brothers who died insane. Fifth, the novella has no squabble between Countess Vitelleschi and Prince Vanini about the dangers of picking up young revolutionists; or, sixth, any grumblings by Don Asdrubale about having to take *honey* home; and, seventh, no interaction – cages, birdies, or stools – with a maternal-minded chambermaid, least of all one called Clelia.[38]

Eighth, the encounter between the two young people is, in quantity and quality of detail, far more developed in the novella than it is in the film: Stendhal's Vanina goes to the terrace many times and peers into the room on many days in a row;[39] she observes the in-patient's beautiful eyes; and she sees 'her' dress thrown onto a chair. By counting the rips in the fabric, Vanina can even surmise the number of times 'she' was stabbed. The literary Vanina's final comment is more sympathetic than sentimental: the poor 'woman' must have truly fearsome enemies, she concludes.[40] Admittedly, in this particular sequence it is not easy for a necessarily deictic medium such as cinema to replay literature's power of abstraction. Indeed, Stendhal's text deliberately plays with the ambiguities built into the gender structure of romance languages in order to camouflage Pietro's masculinity until such a time as Vanina is herself in a position to notice it.[41]

Precisely because it takes Stendhal's Vanina not a few seconds, but about two weeks, to realize that the presumed young woman is in fact a young man, readers can – ninth – savour at length the amazing lightness of touch with which the novella carries on the *équivoque* between the two partners, dancing on the razor's edge that divides the sublime from the ridiculous. Tenth, when the misunderstanding is at last cleared, the novella richly portrays the struggle of two proud souls, each of whom, though attracted to the other, deems it unseemly to admit as much openly. Stendhal's Vanina and Pietro share the concern that being the first to avow one's love might be taken by the other as a sign of submissiveness and inferiority that will automatically devalue that love in the beloved's eyes. To complicate matters further, both contend with an acute sense of class consciousness: despite her eagerness to break away from the deadly boredom that haunts a spineless aristocracy, Vanina never becomes oblivious to her superiority over the bourgeois hero ('If I see him, it's for myself, it's to treat myself to a pleasure').[42] Pietro, for his part, is excited to joust with a strong, beautiful young woman so far above his station, but precisely for that reason remains ever cautious not to expose himself as the less dignified of the two.

Readers familiar with *Le rouge et le noir* will be able to recognize the unique 'Napoleonic *tempo*' of Stendhal's 'acts of sublime madness' in transitions such as the following: 'One evening, having spent the day hating him and resolving to be even colder and stricter than usual, she told him that she loved him. Soon she had nothing left to deny him.'[43] In the film, however, all this turns into something more akin to the opposite: sobs about social differences.

Eleventh, in the novella the account of the lovers' eventual happiness in Rome (of which there is no trace in Rossellini's film) intensely renders an almost dizzying stupor – the stupor that sets in during the development of carnal passion as a process only accomplished by *spiritual* disrobing:

> Great though Vanina's folly may have been, one has to grant that she was perfectly blissful. Nor did Missirilli any longer concern himself with what he thought he owed to his own dignity as a man: he loved as one loves for the first time at nineteen years of age, and in Italy at that. He exercised all the care of passionate love, to the point that *he confessed to this young and so haughty princess the very strategy he had used to make her love him.* He was astonished by the plenitude of his bliss.[44]

Twelfth, the novella alludes to Napoleon's scepticism about the Italians' love of liberty; it also includes Vanina's cold and calm offer of weapons and money to her departing lover. It is at this dignified time, and not in the context of bitter reciprocal recriminations, that we find Pietro's original declaration of duty toward his motherland: the nobler Vanina's heart, he pleads, the more she ought to understand and support his commitment.

Thirteenth, Stendhal's lovers talk marriage without mentioning their families at all. Thus, while some of their exchanges are seemingly echoed in the film's dialogues, the conclusion one draws from the novella is that the two young people are in fact fully devoted to each other. By contrast, in the film we find Missirilli's hyperbolical-sounding proclamation that, to him, Vanina is 'like a wife, more than a wife ... the woman [he] will be able to love and protect': dangerous stuff, considering not only what Stendhal's Vanina thinks of bourgeois attitudes toward marriage but, even more pertinently, what we have been taught to think about Roman family-building by some of the dialogues we overheard at the ball. In the novella, by contrast, Pietro's words are not in the least petty-bourgeois or demeaning; they simply aim at reassuring Vanina when, in a moment of dejection, she perceives herself as 'a fallen young woman.'[45] Pietro furthermore makes it clear that, far from loving Vanina less than he loves Italy, he loves Italy *even more* than he loves Vanina – an alternative formulation of the concept not without a definite impact on its substance. Fourteenth, in direct opposition to his Rossellinian alter ego he also adds that, if only Italy were freed from barbarian rule, he would be quite happy to emigrate with his princess.[46]

Fifteenth, when the time comes for Pietro's planned departure, and Vanina collapses, begging him to give her three more days' happiness, 'as he would pay any poor woman from the countryside who had cured and healed him,' the atmosphere is anything but one of decadence and corruption; and her words strike readers as exactly the opposite of what in the film can seem to be semi-prostitutional advances.[47] Within the societal conventions described in the novella, Vanina's smiling, beggarly offer of her body acts as a sign that she has gone full circle, and that a class-blind tenderness has entirely replaced her previous class-conscious hubris. Stendhal is altogether lucid that *this* is the ultimate proof of love – the kind of nudity most ferociously guarded in the otherwise cheerfully promiscuous society he depicts.

Sixteenth, when Stendhal's Missirilli leaves Rome, he is spared Don Asdrubale's filmic tirade on pan-Roman venality; he gets home and back to his family, quite simply, 'thanks to a passport purchased from a foreign embassy.'[48] Seventeenth, at the castle frictions between the two lovers do eventually arise, but in a manner entirely different from that portrayed by Rossellini. Coming second to the motherland hurts not Vanina's possessiveness, but her pride;[49] and the abyss that separates her feelings from narrow-souled corniness is obvious from the way Stendhal writes about her:

'In truth,' she told him, 'you love me as a husband would; that does not suit me.'
    Soon her tears started to flow; but *out of shame of having lowered herself to reproaches.*[50]

This is the exact opposite of Vanina's course of action in the film, where reproaches are all she is able to direct at Pietro.

Eighteenth, in the novella the central reversal matures suddenly and unsentimentally. In a moment of discomfiture, the young rebel clumsily lets on that he could give up the struggle altogether, if the *carbonari's* plans were to be quelled yet again. Upon hearing this, a sinister light goes on in Vanina's mind: if only that could be the case! Hence her demented calm in suggesting a little stroll in the country. Contrary to the film's plot, it is thus an entirely self-generated internal process that leads Vanina to her fatal error: there is no trace of religious scruples, or of a confessor's meddling, in the young woman's miscalculation. Nineteenth, after Vanina goes back to Rome it is not Christian repentance, but calculated temporization that motivates her; twentieth, she does not propose, but accepts (with full mental reservation) the idea of marriage; twenty-first, the bridegroom-to-be *is not Pietro, but Livio* (Don Asdrubale has in the meantime arranged the transaction for his daughter).[51]

Twenty-second, Stendhal's aristocratic heroine now manipulates her dull fiancé into arrangements that allow her to have access to the private offices of *Monsignor* Savelli-Catanzara, governor of Rome and minister of the police.[52] To exploit this opportunity fully, she disguises herself as a man, and secretly examines the papers related to the ongoing Missirilli trial.[53] Twenty-third, she shortly thereafter duplicates the same feat – and her ensuing nightly encounter, pistol in hand, with Savelli-Catanzara is unimaginably different from the self-deprecating *auto da fe* shown in Rossellini's film; it consists, rather, of a spirited conversation in which a playful tone masks very serious threats.[54] Stendhal takes little trouble to obscure the gallant component of the encounter: Vanina is 'ravishing' in her unaccustomed livery, and she rewards with a kiss the old man for the support he promises.[55] Twenty-fourth, unlike Rossellini's ideologists, Stendhal's Italian prelates can be shrewd politicians, finely attuned to the new political realities of the nineteenth century: *Monsignor* Catanzara throws his weight behind Vanina's request because he senses that he may well live to see 'a time when the blood spilt today will be a stain'[56] – a prediction literally fulfilled thirty-two years after the publication of Stendhal's story.

Twenty-fifth, in the novella the scene in the chapel takes place not on a bright Roman afternoon but at the transit police station in Città Castellana, in the middle of the night and in the dim flicker of a lamp. Twenty-sixth, over and above lay guilt Stendhal's Pietro also feels a religious sense of remorse hanging over him. Confronted with this unexpected peripety – a reversal that, ironically, would be sure to fill Rossellini's Vanina with joy – Stendhal's agnostic heroine remains speechless.[57] Twenty-seventh, when Vanina, desperate for anything more effective to say, reveals her denunciation, thus causing Pietro to hit her with his chains, Stendhal gives us not only Vanina's shrieks but also adequate information about Pietro's mental processes. The contrast between media is especially revealing at this juncture. Vanina's outcry goes down a treat in the novella, tucked away in a dependent clause, while in the film it confusingly overpowers everything else. The film, in particular, neglects to have Pietro call Vanina a monster and forever forswear all help from her; the screams are all we get for sure.[58]

Twenty-eighth, in Stendhal no rolling drums and no scaffold eventually await Missirilli; in fact, there is no indication at all of his fate.

Twenty-ninth, there are no violins for Vanina, and no desperate dash of hers for a nunnery's doorbell. And – thirtieth – the close of the novella is not dramatic but tongue-in-cheek: it transparently mocks the very source it is citing. Having learned to its full extent the unofficial side of the story, Stendhal's (French) readers are in an ideal position to appreciate the ludicrous inadequacy of the (Italian) newspaper's report: some prince, some don, some marriage. Which, of course, in no way means that Stendhal believes the jaundiced Italian public to be taken in by the pomposity of the piece of news: his narrator's last gesture amounts to a complicitous wink he exchanges with us about the events on which he has just let us in.

On Art and Its Institutions

In an ecstatic review of *Vanina Vanini*, Fieschi mentions the trials suffered by the film as a consequence of the clash of interests intervened between producer and director, and defines Rossellini's work 'a mutilated masterpiece.'[59] Somewhat more soberly, Baldelli calls it 'an exemplary case of a deviated masterpiece'[60] – attributing the responsibility for such a deviation from masterliness to all and sundry, except Rossellini himself: a greedy producer, a clumsy lead actor, inflexible left-leaning scriptwriters who attempt to pull Missirilli toward an orthodox revolutionary line, ideologically rigid Catholic watchdogs who manage to plant a fanatic confessor in the middle of a great would-be historical fresco, and more in this vein.[61] What I would suggest instead is that we give up on any attempt to see Rossellini's *Vanina Vanini* as a masterpiece, hedged with whatever number of qualifications or extenuating circumstances. To my mind, there is only one masterpiece in the whole Vanini saga, and that is unquestionably Stendhal's. The masterpiece – the real masterpiece – successfully fought off a motley army spurred by conflicting motivations that in the end unfortunately cancelled one another out.

As is often the case in many art forms, financial and political factors did play a decisively negative role here: Ergas, the producer, was determined to duplicate on command the success obtained not long before by himself and Rossellini with *General Della Rovere*;[62] Sandra Milo, at the time Ergas's significant other, wished (or was perhaps persuaded) to make an unreasonably daring bid for the once-in-a-lifetime role that seemed to loom on the horizon for her;[63] and Rossellini's own right-leaning advisers were eager to anchor firmly the artistically and existentially scandalous director within the admissible bounds of Catholic doctrine[64] – whereas his Communist scriptwriters, Solinas and Trombadori, were interested, come what may, in repeating for the year 1823 the Marxist reconstruction of Italian history carried out by Visconti's *Senso* for 1866.[65] The pain brought about by such conflicts left a deep mark on Rossellini, to the point of precipitating in him the new, pedagogical approach to filmmaking he had been considering for some years.

Nevertheless, the director himself was not entirely innocent, since he applied a scarcely commendable hermeneutic approach to his sources. His overconfidence shines through in statements about his cinematic re-creation:

> Being a Roman, I could easily understand a character belonging to the period of the rise of romanticism: an intense girl, who has only to give her hand to someone to feel herself swooning ... Stendhal's character is so cynical ... she's a Roman noblewoman who believes in absolutely nothing and satisfies specific instincts, so this is where there is a substantial change in the character. With a different actress the character would have been different.[66]

There is some laudable common sense in this, but also too much interpretive hubris: by and large, Rossellini's Stendhal is a figment of the director's own imagination. In fact, Rossellini candidly admitted that he had, for all intents and purposes, given up on the novelist and merely intended to use him as 'a pretext'[67] to carry out the work of historical research that, after his revelatory voyage to India in 1957, had become dear to him.

After *Vanina Vanini*, and to a significant extent because of *Vanina Vanini*, Rossellini's educational work for television consolidated and applied in practice the intentions he had long been developing theoretically. Gone then was his earlier focus on the Western perception of an ongoing existential crisis, and gone was also the artistic and ideological enslavement ever implicit in a director's dealings with Hollywood or its many avatars across the globe. By working for television, Rossellini could finally undertake what he assumed to be the un-ideological and unconditionally liberating task of using the power of modern technology for the sake of education.[68] One of his favourite maxims was: 'We must democratize knowledge.'[69]

In light of Rossellini's subsequent evolution during the 1960s and

1970s, *Vanina Vanini* appears as a well-meant but inevitably ill-fated early attempt of the director's to make the film industry work against its own priorities. Having set out to conquer Stendhal with all sorts of inappropriate appurtenances – the wrong producer, the wrong lead actor, the wrong soundtrack, the wrong team of advisers and scriptwriters, and, last but not least, the wrong approach to Stendhal's deceptive simplicity – the ragtag band of disorganized assailants led by the director to the conquest of high prizes in art and education could not but come away with a bloody nose on both counts. Although (and in a sense because) Rossellini's views were in many respects some thirty years ahead of his time, *Vanina Vanini* was for him worse than an artistic error, it was a *strategic* one – an error he incurred in the mistaken belief that compromise would allow him to enrich Italian cinema by an at least partial expression of his new ideas.

Vanina Vanini was a mistake that Rossellini need not have committed – and that perhaps he would not have committed, had he read more carefully his great predecessor, Tolstoy, in whose crisp and enlightening preface to *What Is Art?* the outcome of Vanina's tribulations could already be found prefigured:

> I have narrated all this in such detail because it strikingly illustrates the indubitable truth that all compromise with institutions of which your conscience disapproves – compromises which are usually made for the sake of the general good – instead of producing the good you expected, inevitably lead you not only to acknowledge the institution you disapprove of, but also to participate in the evil which that institution produces.[70]

To be sure, obvious technical reasons make forsaking institutions considerably easier for writers than for filmmakers – perhaps.

One Sentry Falls:
Death in Venice (1971)

Death in Italy: Sex, Lies, and Stereotypes

An ageing intellectual from Munich, Gustav Aschenbach – or 'von' Aschenbach, a particle earned by his rise as a canonic literary figure in Kaiser Wilhelm's Germany – takes a trip to Venice, dislikes Italy and Italians, but cannot bring himself to leave because of his attraction to Beauty: in the instance, the beauty embodied in a fellow tourist, a Polish boy vacationing on the Lido with his family. Aschenbach eats Italian strawberries, becomes ill, and eventually dies, possibly of cholera (but causality is left ironically imprecise by the narrator). 'And later that same day a respectfully shaken world received the news of his death.'[1]

As a novella about Asian epidemics, set against the backdrop of Byzantine churches and involving a venerable German author's relation to an East European boy, *Der Tod in Venedig* can effectively be described as the combination of two long-standing literary topoi (Oriental sensuality; the plague) controlled by a third, binding element: *Haltung*, that is to say, countenance – and its gradual loss.[2] Venice and, in general, Italy are ideal catalysts for Aschenbach's fictional passion, because they are elements in a literary orientalist-meridionalist tradition uniquely able to encode the manner in which foreigners interact with their exotic environment. By broaching the theme of the slippage of self-control in a Northerner who visits the South, Mann ultimately engages the dichotomy between exteriority and interiority, order and chaos, the desire for the God of Beauty and the attraction to the God of the senses, and thereby – so the standard interpretation of *Der Tod in Venedig* runs –

blends its components into the well-governed, seamless, smooth narrative with which we are familiar.

However, is Mann's text truly as smooth as all that? What about the disruptions caused by the long string of Italophobe situations in it? In the manner of E.A. Poe's purloined letter, these stand out as clearly against their context as they are easily overlooked by the casual observer.[3]

On the steamer to Venice, a decrepit *viveur* approaches and almost lecherously accosts Aschenbach (a foreboding of what Aschenbach is himself to become under Italian skies); a despotic gondolier ferries him from the centre of town back to the Lido (a prefiguration of his impending death); a group of street-singers – one of them in particular – tease him well beyond the limits of decent manners; a hairdresser makes him up like the parody of a dandy. In sum, throughout his stay in Venice, the German writer is constantly encircled, as Dante is in Hell, by a crowd of shady, venal, mellifluous petty devils.[4] Does this *basso ostinato* not point to some sub-textual friction underlying the Form-abiding, single-minded self-control with which the novella focuses on Aschenbach's Form-obsessed malaise? What, for example, if the narrator's Italophobia were *itself an ingredient in Aschenbach's discomfort*?

Sections 1 and 2 take place in Munich. As the writer takes a stroll near a suburban cemetery, he is seized by a sudden desire to travel to exotic wetlands. A bizarrely-clad mysterious stranger, with reddish hair and brows, grins at him menacingly from the steps outside the Byzantine-style mortuary chapel across the street. We then obtain, in flashback, an annotated biography of Aschenbach, which mentions the (fictional) titles of his works, his thirst for fame, his 'rejection of the abyss,' his 'rise to dignity,' his favourite motto: 'Endure,'[5] his obsession with Beauty, and, most importantly, his artistic canonization – in short, all that makes him the quintessential self-assured foreigner on a visit to the sunny peninsula.

It is with the third section of the novella that the Italian plot begins to thicken. Already the ship from Pola, however feeble in steam, vigorously whistles up extra-classical preoccupations that situate *Der Tod in Venedig* within an unmistakably *Kaiserlich-Königlich* cultural atmosphere:[6]

It was an aged vessel, long past its prime, sooty, and gloomy, sailing under the Italian flag. In a cavernous, artificially lit cabin in the ship's interior – to which Aschenbach had been conducted with smirking politeness by a hunchbacked, scruffy sailor the moment he embarked – sat a goateed man behind a desk. With his hat cocked over his brow and a cigarette butt hanging from the corner of his mouth, his facial features were reminiscent of an old-time ringmaster.[7]

As is to be expected, the meal served on board is wretched.[8]

The made-up old fop on the boat and the Charon-like gondolier who surface a little later in front of Aschenbach have already caused so much critical ink to be shed as to make it unnecessary to dwell here any further on the repulsiveness that *Der Tod in Venedig* attributes to Italy. Similar considerations also apply to the not-much-better impression conveyed by the eel-like polite manager whom Aschenbach meets as he finally arrives at the Hôtel des Bains.[9]

Aschenbach meets Tadzio and, for an irresistible reason, instantly develops a crush for him: 'The boy was perfectly beautiful.'[10] Munching on what could be called the symbolic equivalent of Eve's apple, 'large, fully ripe strawberries,'[11] he watches Tadzio play on the beach and bathe, rising from the waters of the Adriatic in a re-enactment of the 'birth of the Gods.'[12] The high-minded visitor thus falls in love with another foreigner – a foreigner, that is, not only to himself but to the locals as well. For him, opaque Italy may be the perfect procurer, but clearly does not warrant direct concupiscence.

Bad smells, the scirocco, humidity, and local beggars unpleasantly haunt Aschenbach. A few days later, he feels feverish; as he leans for support against a wellhead in a small square in the centre of Venice, he comes to the conclusion that the local *aria* has a malignant effect on his health. 'To remain stubbornly in place obviously went against all reason.'[13] On the same day, therefore, he prepares his luggage, which is soon 'perfectly ready for departure.'[14]

As one might have feared, Italian devils strike again. Polish boys, created by the Gods, and German trunks, packed by German poets, can attain a perfection that is denied to inefficient, unreliable (and probably mischievous) local hotel managers; and, not altogether unexpectedly, Aschenbach's luggage is mis-sent to Como rather than Munich.[15]

The further events ironically throw into reverse the *Haltung* attributed to Aschenbach earlier in the novella. Forced to stay on, the magisterial artist so relishes the opportunity to see Tadzio again that, at the very thought, he has an infernal time controlling his joy and retaining his countenance. He takes the fast shuttle boat back to the hotel; the wind blows through his hair with the same cheerful briskness as if he were a romantic hero sitting high in the box of a coach bound for the charmed South.

Section 4, suspended in a timelessness of sorts, ushers in an idyll on the beach between the voyeuristic author and the narcissistic youth. Aschenbach whispers to himself excerpts from Platonic dialogues, imagining himself to be ugly Socrates who intellectually seduces beautiful Phaedrus. The narrating voice, too, becomes involved in the classical atmosphere: fragments from the Greek intertext are directly reproduced,[16] and a parallel between work and play is suggested.[17] Above all, hexameters and quasi-hexameters are pervasively used in the narration, rendering in free indirect discourse Aschenbach's mood and the environment that surrounds him. This very nearly paradisical section begins with a crypto-verse that refers to the God of the Sun, Apollo ('The god with fiery cheeks ...'),[18] and closes with the *coup de théâtre* of Aschenbach's whispered 'eternal formula of longing – impossible under these conditions, absurd, reviled, ridiculous, and yet holy and venerable ... – "I love you!"'[19]

The fifth section of the novella leaves the Greek world behind, never to return. The god Apollo becomes Tadzio 'the idol';[20] the outside world, that is, Italy, takes over, and so does the reality of its cholera. The attraction for Tadzio and the repulsion toward Italy grow in unison.[21]

The foreshadowings contained in sections 1 and 3 now come to fruition. The exotic-looking chapel in Munich is mirrored in St Mark, and the mysterious stranger on those steps – already twice reflected in the ruffian-gondolier and the seasoned playboy on the steamer – now finds a third avatar in a repulsive *virtuoso*, with traits of a beggar and of a mountebank, who leads a street performers' group onto the terrace of the Hôtel des Bains. True Latin lover that he is, the street musician accosts Aschenbach with a demeanour that is not only outright vulgar but, more specifically, sexually ambiguous.[22] Nor does the doubtful character fail to endorse the doubtful official story about the epidemics: namely, that the medical precautions ordered by the police are no more than 'a preventive measure.'[23] In case any delusions remain about Italians' moral fibre, shady *gondolieri* then appear again, openly conniving with Aschenbach in his increasingly hopeless gondola-chase after Tadzio through the canals of the plague-ridden city.

In almost providential contrast to the Italian hotel manager in the French-style frock coat, a British employee at Thomas Cook finally steps in, revealing not only (as readers had long intuited) that the police version of the cholera story is a mere cover-up, but, as important, that – in *Der Tod in Venedig* at any rate – the Germanophone imperialism and the English-speaking one can engage each other in global conflicts of interest not *despite* the truth-based language they share, but *because of* it:

> The Briton [was] possessed of that steady, trustworthy bearing that stands out
> as so foreign and so remarkable among the roguish nimble Southerners ...
> And then, in his candid and comfortable language, he told the truth.[24]

Translation: Italians (and French) speak neo-Latin, *welsch* languages,
which impede truthfulness; but Britons speak English, a Germanic language
that, in the circumstance, offers the only possible source of rational
behaviour for Aschenbach. The scholar eventually passes up on his
chance, but not for lack of reliable advice.

Why does he fail to act? Because, I would like to suggest, *he is himself
about to become Italian.* Without realizing the extent of his own transformation, Aschenbach shuns the impervious path he had earlier envisaged (warning Tadzio's mother about the danger) and takes the
downward-sloping, southern-exposed one instead (conniving with the
falseness of his situation, in the hope that the Poles will stay on). Thus it
is that, duplicating the pitiful fop's disguise on the steamer, Aschenbach
falls like an overripe strawberry for the gooey rhetoric of a local barber,
caving in to the temptation of seeking an artificial physical attractiveness
with which to seduce Tadzio.[25]

The circle is now fully closed: his face plastered with make-up, his hair
dyed black, and his lips brightened with lipstick, Aschenbach observes
Tadzio's games from his chair in the last moments of his life. On an
unseasonably cold summer morning at the beach, Aschenbach is ready
for the final dissolution that will lead him to a death signifying the final
collapse of his composure and moral sense.

That, again, is the official story. Nevertheless, has his moral demeanour
tangibly caved in? Ultimately, that does not appear to be the case. The
potential for that is certainly there; the text spares no effort to describe the
crumbling of Aschenbach's great-bourgeois façade,[26] judiciously juxtaposing the sandcastles erected by the boys with the barely more permanent ones inhabited by a person who has built his entire life on the
foundation of worldly fame.[27] Yet that is only one half of the picture.

It must be granted that on occasion the famous man's emotions do in
fact run riot. Aschenbach's loss of control becomes perhaps most acute
a few days before the Polish family's departure and his own death. Then,
we are told, the writer stalks Tadzio and his family through the labyrinth
of Venice's alleys and canals, in a cloud of smells emanating from rot-
ting refuse and disinfectant. After eating more strawberries, 'overripe
and soft,'[28] he starts again in pursuit. Finally, he loses contact with the
object of his desire, and, finding himself without bearings, stops per-

plexed. 'A little piazza that was quite deserted and seemed enchanted opened out before him. He recognized it, for it was here that weeks ago he had made his [desperate] plan to flee the city. He collapsed on the steps of the well in the very middle of the plaza and rested his head on the stone rim.'[29] It is here that the decadent/decaying intellectual, having misplaced both fame and name, and having all but lost his German identity, must give up his yearning for what could be called a decent (*anständig*) union with Beauty's body. In a long dialogue-monologue with the image of his beloved, he goes over a number of statements already made by himself or by the narrator, and (to borrow a term later used by Mann in *Doctor Faustus* / *Doktor Faustus*, 1947) 'takes back'[30] a serenity anxiously postulated but evidently not established on a firm enough existential footing. In Nietzsche's sharp words, 'and lo! Apollo could not live wihout Dionysus!'[31]

That said, the crucial point is that Aschenbach is in no way on the verge of approaching Tadzio *as if* the boy were Apollo, Hyacinth, or Narcissus. Motionless on the beach, he does not commit the (to him) unforgivable methodological error of coalescing real with ideal, confusing the body of Beauty with a beautiful body. I would argue that it is precisely the enormous strain of such a double allegiance that causes his death.[32] Aschenbach is eventually killed by the two-pronged conflict, not by the one-sided triumph of (homo)sexual temptation;[33] for the self-controlled author, death is precisely *a bodily response to the danger of losing control.*[34]

In sum: better dead than definitively, irretrievably Italian.

Significantly, Mann's text persistently refuses to accompany Aschenbach's fatal dilemma by a formal loosening of its own. In fact, the opposite occurs: the more the text invites reflection on the ecstatic dimension of artistic creation and the hidden catabolic obverse of Art, the more rigid its formal structures become. This is obvious at the time of Aschenbach's death, when the writer's self-eliding immobility in the leaning chair is mimicked in Tadzio's body's exasperatingly slow rotation inviting to descent into the elemental.[35] While by the end of the novella Aschenbach's instincts are going native, the narrator clearly is not[36] – quite the contrary, his German meta-discourse is then busier than ever containing and constraining the fallacious, lethal logorrhea of Italians in Venice. One hardly needs to stress that, however brilliantly reinterpreted, these are and remain stereotypes.

To summarize: the rapport between *Der Tod in Venedig* and Italy shows two important aspects. First, Thomas Mann's text is far from being ethno-culturally neutral; it is, in fact, eager to exploit the potential for subtle, and less subtle, demarcations between 'him' (the Northerner who loses his grasp on rationality) and 'them' (the Southerners who, qua Southerners, have no Logos to give up in the first place). Second, Aschenbach abandons himself very much less to self-abandonment than he is often described as doing. His loss of control over Form seems, at most, partial (to say nothing of his narrator's), and anyway occurs not only in the terminology but altogether within the cultural horizon of classical grace and dignity.[37]

Within about thirty years of the publication of *Der Tod in Venedig*, the global context changed dramatically. By the time the Second World War had ended and Thomas Mann's apocalyptic *Doctor Faustus* was in the works, provincial, folkloric Italy – however bad her merchants and her *buffi*, or even her Cipolla-like magicians[38] – was mercifully out of the picture as a breeding ground for the disruptive forces creeping out of the abyss. In 1945, Aschenbach's Dionysian dangers at the Hôtel des Bains might have seemed to Thomas Mann, then artistically confronted with portraying the demonic forces unleashed by Nazism, eminently tame and perhaps even entirely and healthily aerobic. Who knows whether the spiritual, intellectual, and political bankruptcy ultimately experienced by the land of *Kultur*, Germany – its failure, that is, at taming the beastly and the bloody within itself by ways of education and self-education – could not have been forestalled by seeing in the mobilization of the self a stimulus toward spiritual integration, rather than (as Aschenbach does) a mere nightmare.[39]

The Formless and Its Representation: Visconti's Cinematic Quest

When the credits of Visconti's film evaporate like early-morning mist, the images of the sunrise over the lagoon fade. As soon as the Mannian steamer from Pola appears before St Mark square, we sense that something quite fundamental has changed in the transition from German novella to Italian film. The first symptom of reaccentuation is obvious: the Italian vessel now has a name, and that name is 'Esmeralda.' What does that name signal?

In *Doctor Faustus*, the horizon of the events is the bleak, bombed-out skyline familiar to viewers of Rossellini's *Germany Year Zero* (*Germania anno zero*, 1948). The Second World War is nearing its end, and the fictional narrator of the novel, Serenus Zeitblom, retrospectively recounts how his late friend, the musician Adrian Leverkühn, throughout his life struggled against the exhaustion of artistic forms experienced by

Europe during the twentieth century. In his defiant attempt to regenerate Western art against all historical odds, Leverkühn came to pursue the demonic dream as a last resort against sterility. Subverting, in his hubris, the paradigm of decency he was expected to uphold as a good citizen and good artist in turn-of-the-century Germany, Leverkühn deliberately pursued contact with a prostitute, whom he designated by the exotic-sounding name Hetaera Esmeralda, and contracted syphilis from her. As a consequence of his illness, he later developed certain hallucinations; once, for example, as he was travelling in Italy, he struck up a spirited conversation with the devil on things both personal and universal, as well as specifically related to musical technique. This very special encounter confirmed the subjective conviction in him to be bound to the devil by a pact, in which he anyway found a source of renewed artistic inspiration. Spiritually emboldened, but also physically undermined, by demonic exchanges of this sort – Serenus Zeitblom's report continues – Leverkühn could thus proceed to overcome what amounted to personal and societal desiccation, literally writing revolutionary pages in the history of Western music. Finally, early on in the Second World War, Leverkühn died of last-stage syphilis.

Hence, Visconti's hypertextual usage of the name 'Esmeralda' for his ship amounts to an abrupt announcement that the sphere we have now entered is no longer the inward-looking one of *fin de siècle* aristocrats, but the fully, retrospectively aware one of a postbellum narrator, who has one eye on *Der Tod in Venedig* and one on *Doctor Faustus*.[40] Corollary: out goes Thomas Mann's impalpable irony on, for instance, the low temperature of the glacial protagonist's German showers; in comes a fiery sense of urgency in dealing with an abyss that is much less individual, as well as much deeper, than heretofore assumed.

And much more international, too: in the film's images, as opposed to the novella's words, the steamer is neither particularly sooty nor exceedingly gloomy – and thus, when all is said and done, not very 'Italian' at all. Obviously, cinema does not use culturally connotated implements such as adjectives to define its objects, whereas with language we are always already, as an existentialist could put it, *embarqués*. Still, the fact remains that Visconti's Esmeralda lacks a repulsive film of Italian grime, and therefore she no longer comes across as unpleasantly, threateningly foreign to the northern tourist.

On the other hand, the ferry's funnel does belch a cloud of black smoke into the air. Suggested decodification of the director's choice to combine that particular subtraction with this particular addition: in Visconti, no longer do ob-jects (*Gegen-stände*) layered with Italian unclean-liness close in on the immaculate self-respect of a visiting German intel-lectual. Rather, the intellectual in question travels on a vessel that, by virtue of its very name, belongs as much to the German tradition as it does to the Italian government – the two now being jointly answerable for the polluting emissions. In *Morte a Venezia* the dualism Germany/Italy is superseded from the very beginning; from the very beginning, Aschenbach is a relatively conniving passenger on an international demonic ship.[41]

Visconti's Aschenbach thus carries a cultural passport perceptibly dif-ferent from Thomas Mann's. His protagonist is as much at home in the world as he is in Munich, and thereby minimizes the polarity that was so perceptible in his original circumstances and identity.[42] It is logical that Aschenbach's celebrated works, and the rise to fame that accompanies them,[43] should fall by the narrative wayside in the film; these are too specifically German (to be exact, too specifically pre–First World War German) to elicit anything but an illustrative, historical interest. In his endeavour to re-create Mann across boundaries of culture and time, Vi-sconti discards a literary heritage that would have placed Aschenbach squarely within the parameters of a single nation, and he seeks instead a supra-national tradition for his protagonist. Hence a further innovation that strikes the viewer right away in *Morte a Venezia*: Aschenbach is now a composer.[44]

The comments made by Visconti, who was himself an accomplished musician, on the matter of this substitution are persuasive enough: first, Thomas Mann had in any case drawn part of his inspiration for *Der Tod in Venedig* from Gustav Mahler's life; second, a writer's text tends to get embarrassingly in a film director's path, whereas music can come to fur-ther fruition in the soundtrack.[45] Yet Visconti expressed only in a very roundabout way something that appears to me of even greater substance: signing up Aschenbach as a practitioner of Adrian Leverkühn's trade allowed the director to absorb into the film some issues that only Leverkühn's music had developed to their ultimate consequences. More-over, Visconti did not say at all what seems decisive from my perspective – namely, that his redirecting Aschenbach from literature to music pow-erfully contributes to the celebrated artist's de-Germanization. This ulti-mately permits the musician to focus on what (in Visconti at least) is his main concern: dealing not with Italian devils, but with his own.

All devils, of course, by definition spell trouble; and the trouble with those of the spiritual kind is that they are difficult to personify and show on screen. So long as they appear in Mann as already precipitated in human form, Visconti's film can absorb them with minimal structural adjustment. This is exactly what happens with the novella's unholy triad, whose members (the decrepit playboy, the infernal gondolier, the mountebank–pimp–street singer) all appear in *Morte a Venezia* in just the guise and capacity one would expect from perusing *Der Tod in Venedig*. For his part, Tadzio is made more filmic, as well as slightly more disturbing, than his prototype by being cast as quasi-pubescent.[46] But some chimeras are more elusive than others. What about the thoughts and anguished feelings that Thomas Mann's boy inspires in Aschenbach; what about the novella's hexameters? That is to say: in the transition from text to film, what happens to a style whose function (as is the case in *Der Tod in Venedig*) is not a decorative but a structural one? In the final analysis, how can cinema adequately render the struggle of language – in fact, of any art form – to articulate the Formless through representation?

Morte a Venezia's answer to this question is to have recourse above all to dialogues, which the film encapsulates in a series of narrative flashbacks.[47] In these, we witness Aschenbach argue, at times bitterly, with a friend (whose existence we owe to Visconti's re-creation of Mann), espousing positions that portray him as the canonized embodiment of dignity we know from *Der Tod in Venedig*. His friend Alfried, in contrast, personifies the Old Enemy – on the point of artistic theory, at any rate.

As Alfried, sitting at his piano, trenchantly points out, Gustav's works are ineluctably contaminated with the seeds of what a commonly accepted symbolic shorthand calls the forces of the demonic:

'Art is always ambiguous ... And music is the most ambiguous of all arts ... Yes, Gustav, it is ambiguity made into a system.

Wait ... Listen ... Take this chord ... or this one ... You can interpret it as you deem fit ... You have before you an infinite series of mathematical, unpredictable, inexhaustible combinations ... A paradise of double meanings, in which you yourself wallow more than anyone else, like ... like ... a seal in its aquarium ...

Can you hear this? You recognize it, don't you? ... It's yours ... it's your music.'[48]

The ambiguity of art is not merely discussed in the film; it is portrayed. With a further hypertextual link to *Doctor Faustus*, Visconti has Aschenbach recollect only too well the occasion on which, earlier in his life, his path crossed with Hetaera Esmeralda's in her brothel.[49] The memory is triggered in the composer's consciousness by the association arising between his recollection of Beethoven's 'Für Elise' played by the young woman many years in the past and the same piece hesitantly tinkled away at by Tadzio in the hotel lounge. It is altogether appropriate, as well as exquisitely ironic, of Visconti to have introduced a scene of physical contamination between people by means of what is metaphorically referred to as literary contamination between texts.

This particular connection requires pausing for a moment. Beyond the intradiegetic establishment, through the musical leitmotiv, of a crystal-clear erotic equivalence between Esmeralda and Tadzio,[50] the Beethoven flashback seems to accomplish something conceptually more far-reaching: namely, a devastating extradiegetic questioning on Visconti's part of the normalization of great art carried out in and by the process that frames it as 'canonic.' Beethoven's genius used as aesthetic fodder for entertainment in literal bordellos (Esmeralda's) or metaphorical ones (the Hôtel des Bains)? Far from impossible in the real world, but no doubt provocative when so manifestly displayed in a work of art – a display ironically indicting[51] the ever-recurrent process of sterilization that makes the demonic tame and the abyssal superficial.[52]

In Mann's novella, the last thing of which one could accuse 'the poet of all those who work on the edge of exhaustion'[53] is a lack of awareness that great art has little to do with commonsense bromides, and that its goal is to complicate, rather than simplify, one's experience of the world. However precarious and fragile his conclusions, the German Aschenbach is solidly aware of the premise: namely, that the art we get to see at the end of any creative process is but the visible result of the clash of concealed forces, and 'that nearly everything achieving greatness did so under the banner of "Despite" – despite grief and suffering, despite poverty, destitution, infirmity, affliction, passion, and a thousand obstacles.'[54] Whatever the empirical circumstances that originally caused 'Für Elise' to be used as a bridge between the novella and *Doctor Faustus* for the double leap Aschenbach-Tadzio-Esmeralda, the cultural implications of Visconti's choice amount to introducing forcefully into *Morte a Venezia* the sensual equivalent of the fundamental 'Despite' concept from *Der Tod in Venedig*.[55]

The ultimate impact of Aschenbach's accumulated fears and doubts is portrayed in the nightmare that shortly precedes his death. This offers Visconti the opportunity to engage in a paramount example of re-creation across media: the Dionysian orgy of *Der Tod in Venedig* becomes

Morte a Venezia's fiasco at the first public performance of one of Aschenbach's works. Accordingly, the victory of unregulated, animal-like demons that, in *Der Tod in Venedig*, exude blood, sweat, and music as they go[66] becomes in *Morte a Venezia* the revenge of a demonic principle now embodied in Alfried's less than kind criticism of the music written by his friend:

> 'Swindler! My dear swindler! Pure Beauty ... absolute rigor ... the morality of Form, perfection, the abstraction of the senses! ... What has remained of all this? Nothing ... nothing, nothing! Your music is stillborn! And you have been exposed! ...
>
> Wisdom, truth, human dignity ... it's all over now! Now, if you want, you can climb into the grave with your music. You have attained a perfect equilibrium ... Man and artist are but one ... They went to the bottom together.
>
> You never had chastity in you. Chastity is a gift of purity, not the pitiful product of old age; and you are old, Gustav ... And there is no impurity in the world as impure as old age.'[57]

The reasons recommending the literature-to-film substitution of a Panic orgy with a critical orgy of reproaches and self-reproaches are transparent: physical excesses can be comparatively easy to evoke in the selectively lit sphere of verbal communication (in particular if strictly policed hexameters dictate what can be 'seen' by the readers), but they are too tall an order for *bon goût* in the show-it-all world of images. Accordingly, Visconti at first intended to shoot in a Munich nightclub the cinematic equivalent of Thomas Mann's Dionysian rites, but in the end decided otherwise.[58]

There may well be something that is intrinsically Form-destroying, and therefore by definition mocks representation, about the portrayal of the dissolution of Form. It is just possible that (*pace* the dreams fleetingly pursued by Aschenbach in the mediterranean South) a fully Dionysian art is a contradiction in terms; and, consequently, it makes little difference whether it is from an Italian or a German tradition, with words or from behind a camera, that one attempts the poietic process aiming at the most arduous re-creation of all – the one meant to convert into the *Kosmos* of Form the artist's visionary *Chaos*.

Visconti Two and a Half

At the time of *Morte a Venezia*, Visconti was no beginner in the artistic treatment of the city calling herself *Serenissima*; in fact, in his Venetian filmography *Morte a Venezia* numbers two-and-a-half. *Senso* had included his first depiction of 'this most improbable of cities,'[59] with interwoven motifs (the rising nationalistic view alternating with the late-imperial one of an impending *finis Austriae*) that solidly interlaced cultural elements from both south and north of the Alps. *White Nights* (*Le notti bianche*, 1957) then gave a reasonably close approximation to an encore by virtue of its in-studio reproduction of a cityscape crisscrossed by canals.[60]

Italy along with Germany, Germany along with Italy. That Venice was to Visconti a sovereignly available space, not occupied by a single national cultural tradition, was indeed already clear over fifteen years before *Morte a Venezia*, when viewers of *Senso* could witness Countess Lidia Serpieri and her lover-to-be Franz Mahler (a Mahler not unrelated to the musician, in spirit anyway) rest together by a wellhead identical to that where a dejected Aschenbach would one day burst into sardonic laughter about his own demise.

Gallantly broaching the subject of German literature, the Mahler of *Senso* asks the countess whether she knows a poem by Heine that he quotes as follows: 'It is the Day of Judgment; the dead resurrect to joy eternal, or to eternal suffering. We alone remain embraced, caring for nothing, neither Paradise nor Hell.'[61] Lidia, who doesn't know her Heine by heart, may be excused for not finding the reference particularly revealing; but revealing it is in its own right – not least, of the acquaintance Visconti has with his sources and of the skill with which he employs them. The quote is almost exactly authentic; it is a paraphrase from Heine's 'Lyrical Intermezzo' (1823).[62] The extent of Visconti's (diabolically Italian?) sleight-of-hand in lending Mahler these particular lines can be fully appreciated if one considers their precise wording and original context:

My own sweet love, when you are dead
And the grave's dark shadows face you,
I shall go down to your earthy bed
And cherish and embrace you.

I kiss you, clasp you wildly athrob,
You cold, unmoving, white-eyed!
I tremble, I thrill, I softly sob –
I become a corpse at your side.

The dead stand up as midnight booms,
They dance with airy grace;
We two remain within our tombs,
I lie in your embrace.

The dead stand up, the Judgment Day
Calls forth the damned and the blest;
We two sleep undisturbed for ay
And lie in love and rest.[63]

The poem is, in fact, not about love, but about death; it is not joyful, but morbid. Its full text reveals the exact opposite of what an excerpt from it appeared to mean.

What this shows once more is that the intertextual complexities in *Morte a Venezia* are enormous from the start – from many years before the start, in fact. In Visconti we not only sense a constant interchangeability between Italian and German cultural lineages, but even develop the feeling that *Morte a Venezia* may 'quote' and refer back to, first and foremost, its director's *personal* tradition: a self-generated Viscontian reservoir of sorts.[64] Through the water of one and the same well, intuitions of death by the musician Aschenbach, who borrows Leverkühn's fictional musical gift and the historical Mahler's real one, mirror themselves in the funereal visions previously cultivated by a soldier named Mahler. In both cases, the larger picture of ultimate undoing is only temporarily obscured by a deceptively restricted focus[65] on immediate figures of love.[66]

Fallen Masters, Lost Sentries: Politics and Wars of Liberation

In recent years, a great deal of attention has been focused on Visconti's homosexuality. The critics who wrote on *Morte a Venezia* specifically contrasting it with *Der Tod in Venedig* almost unanimously commented on the fact that the ultimate result of Visconti's re-creation amounts to a foregrounding of Aschenbach's homosexual desire for Tadzio.[67] It seems to me that, given Visconti's circumstances, a re-accentuation of homosexuality in *Morte a Venezia* makes the most sense – personal and historical circumstances, that is, which can fully be understood only by going beyond the narrow approach of a one-on-one examination of novella versus film and drawing upon broader contexts for an assessment.

Around 1970 there undoubtedly was an urgent need, subjective as well as objective, to read Thomas Mann afresh if one wanted to turn him into film. After *Der Tod in Venedig*, almost sixty years had elapsed that had resulted in far-reaching upheavals in the global system of alliances, international cultural relations, and the sphere of personal relationships. It was under the influence of such factors that Visconti chose to discard the outdated literary link between Italy and savage primeval drives that it is incumbent upon Graeco-German rationality to tame and control. He thus reasonably fortified the somewhat fragile persona of Mann's Tadzio, reassigning to it a correspondingly larger quota of the film's attention and interest. The director had, after all, only just dealt with Nazi demons in *The Damned* (*La caduta degli dèi*, 1969),[68] which may explain why in *Morte a Venezia* he left to one side the full-fledged demonism he could find represented in Adrian Leverkühn, concentrating instead on the comparatively meeker one traceable to the Heine-Aschenbach-Tadzio lineage. Out of sheer lack of hexameters, Visconti may well, in the process, have disappointed the auspices – or, in other cases, perturbed the sense of *Anständigkeit* – of some critics who expected him to produce no more than a richly irrelevant visual footnote to Thomas Mann; but films are not footnotes to literature.[69]

If there is one generalization that can be made about philological comments on Luchino Visconti's approach to Thomas Mann, it is that more than a few scholars have viewed *Morte a Venezia* under the puzzling methodological presupposition that cinematic re-creation is but a crippled younger sister of philology. Yet it seems obvious that the main goal of great artists re-creating other great artists ought to be loyalty not to someone else, but to themselves first and foremost. Paradoxically perhaps, a critic's charge of 'mis-adaptation' may thus be no more than a symptom signalling the *successful* occurrence of the adoption of a master on another master's part, in the spirit of Nietzsche's sharp 'Vademecum-vadetecum' aphorism in *The Joyful Wisdom*:

> Attracted by my style and talk
> You'd follow, in my footsteps walk?
> Follow yourself unswervingly,
> So – careful! – shall you follow me.[70]

It is precisely the paradoxy of the *vadetecum* principle that Visconti addresses with his plea to be left alone while he pursues a path that is distinctly his, rather than an ancillary of Thomas Mann's – alone as the Hermetic camera that, after Aschenbach's death, remains abandoned on the Lido, enigmatically facing the Infinite of the sea and the sky.[71]

Visconti freely admits that he is presenting a personalized reading of the relationship between Aschenbach and Tadzio. In an interview, Micciché comments to the director that he has 'to an extent, turned Tadzio into a prostitute, and the prostitute into Tadzio.' Visconti's answer is adamant:

> That's what I wanted. As a matter of fact, my urge was to unify and at the same time split the component of the 'contamination' and of sensual attraction, as well as that of infant purity. Anyway the young woman in the brothel looks a bit like Tadzio ...
>
> In sum, in establishing a link between Tadzio's presence and the memory of the prostitute ... Aschenbach perceives fully the most 'sinful' aspect of his attitude toward Tadzio.[72]

Visconti then goes on to offer a broader context for *Morte a Venezia* by staking a lucid claim to artistic and personal autonomy. In a statement of well-founded pride, he protests that he has in the past already paid his dues to expectations of social engagement, and demands for himself and others the right to be left free to undertake more personal voyages to Italy:

> [W]e have got a past behind us, and, in a sense, we have [already] made the point we wanted to make. I made mine from *Ossessione* [1943] to *The Damned*, and when I allowed myself a break, as I did in the case of *White Nights*, it was by no means a demeaning one. Now we may well be grappling with more particular and personal themes, but behind us we have a record of political struggle that can justify this belated and temporary return to a 'privacy' we rejected for years. Will you argue that ours, too, is a crisis, a state of laziness? Let's assume. Still, it took us forty years to get there.[73]

Political escapism? No, at the most refocusing due to old age.

The hiatus between *Der Tod in Venedig* and *Morte a Venezia* must thus be rationalized by contextualizing it within another chasm of a higher order in our story: that between the early Visconti, who made politicized masterpieces such as *The Earth Trembles*, *Senso*, *Rocco and His Brothers*, and *The Leopard* and the inward-looking *auteur* who followed.[74] But there is more. This state of affairs, in turn, was not merely a contingency due to Visconti's personality; to a large extent, it was a repercussion of the historical events through which Italians lived between the 1940s and the early 1970s.

The very author of *Der Tod in Venedig* had, after all, set an outstanding example of intellectual metamorphosis over the momentous central decades of the twentieth century. The first part of Mann's career was eminently unconnected with politics, and – as both *The Buddenbrooks* (1901) and *Der Tod in Venedig* show – more absorbed in scrutinizing the fragility of the old world than concerned with thinking beyond its impending downfall. As late as *Observations by an Unpolitical Man* (*Betrachtungen eines Unpolitischen*, 1918), Thomas Mann explicitly reiterated his distaste for politics; the latter seemed to him a charlatanesque cancan typical of the Western lands of *Zivilisation*, unredeemed by the composure of German *Kultur*.[75] However, the subsequent developments in the history of his country would fast turn the unpolitical man into a passionately committed political refugee, transforming Mann into an outspoken anti-Fascist, and thus ultimately into a reverential figure for what was to be post–Second World War democratic Germany.[76] In a peculiar twist of fate, even the Marxists whose world view he had explicitly rejected eventually came to see in him no less than a quintessential example (to use a concept favoured by Lukács) of an 'honest bourgeois.'[77] Thus, over time historical and personal experiences worked together to disrupt and subvert beliefs that Mann had earlier considered permanent anchors in his life.

A symmetrical transformation – though for reasons not nearly as tragic – may be said to have occurred for Visconti: exploring Thomas Mann's path in reverse, a former champion of public political commitment focused with increasing intensity on individual and private issues, especially those pertaining to the demise of the self-contained, aestheticizing world of old.[78]

Between the end of the Second World War and 1968, Italy had changed almost beyond recognition, as a sudden flush of affluence – both of the real and the perceived kind – turned a country of bicyclists into one of motorists and beach-goers. Along with this socio-cultural mutation (and, to be sure, largely as a consequence of it), by the time the Soviet tanks rolled into Prague (1968) the old-style, dual Italian political scenario had become quite complex.[79] In particular, there had appeared at least one other major agent, difficult to categorize in terms of the received paradigms: the student movement.[80] The demands made by the students on what then went by the name of 'the system' notoriously concerned questions of lifestyle as much as they raised political issues; they had far-reaching consequences through the 1970s, and eventually came to fruition in new attitudes – some of which are now altogether uncontroversial – according an important political status to the personal sphere. 'The personal *is* political' (*Il privato è politico*), pointedly asserted a now famous slogan that was coined in those years.

It is not difficult to see how the increasing political and ethical mobilization practised by youths, Italian and otherwise, in the years running up to *Morte a Venezia* would naturally encourage, perhaps even prompt, a parallel act of liberation in an ageing intellectual; one who, like Aschenbach before him, had in effect 'risen to canonic status' by virtue of his entire life work but, in the process, had had to leave unaddressed in his art what the repressive conventions of the times – left, right, and centre – often designated by the simplistic (and homophobic) misnomer 'forces of the abyss.'[81] There can thus be little surprise about the master eventually loosening the *Haltung* he had long imposed upon himself in matters of sexuality, and claiming instead his right to project himself freely into the fictional figure of an artist with whose life his own bore resemblance.[82] As Italy changed and her young people changed, Visconti changed too. In his Mannian film the director allowed himself to relocate the political from the explicit to the implicit; or, better yet, *to express the political in personal terms*, thus ultimately anticipating a position that later on in the decade of the 1970s would become the norm.

Morte a Venezia's entirely unambiguous message is that, if others feel so inclined, they may tread where Visconti has already trodden before them – but it is now their turn to pick up the banner of the war of liberation, allowing an artist haunted by death (as the musician Aschenbach is in *Morte a Venezia*) to retreat quietly from the front line. He is not deserting from a life's task; rather, the time has come for him to abscond.

No less strenuously engaged in the battle for social and political progress, Visconti's beloved Heine had nourished similar feelings toward the end of his own life. Close to death, he wrote 'Enfant perdu,' a poem that used wars of liberation as a metaphor in which to inscribe the meaning of his entire life:

> I fought to hold positions that were lost
> In Freedom's war for thirty faithful years.
> Without a hope to win, despite the cost
> I battled on, expecting only tears.
>
> In vigil day and night, I could not sleep
> Like all my friends in my own tented squad –

(The way these good lads snored sufficed to keep
Me wide-awake when I began to nod.) ...

My wounds are gaping wide – A post's unmanned! –
One sentry falls, another takes his part –
And yet I fall unvanquished, sword in hand –
The only thing that's broken is my heart.[83]

Of this poem the Italian freedom fighter, unaccounted for in the shallows and sandbars beyond the beach of the Lido, must have heartily approved.

CONCLUSION

On Readings:
Perfect/Imperfect, Difficult, and
More Difficult

Reading, Perfectly and Otherwise

Let us assume that the re-creation of literature in cinema were an exact science, with operations characterized by a set of properties allowing for univocal equations of the type 2 + 2 = 4, in turn susceptible to undergo univocal reversibility as 4 − 2 = 2. Would such a type of convertibility between texts be *desirable*? The answer might well be a matter of tastes – philosophical tastes, that is. Would we *want* to bind ourselves to what would then be a definitive reading of any given text? In some very real sense, the lack of ambiguity that science pursues as beauty could be perceived as ugliness in existential terms. Probably no one ever made this point more forcefully than the narrator of Dostoevsky's *Notes from Underground*, who protests that, as a human being endowed with free volition, he wishes to be able to claim that 2 + 2 = 5. For something as banal and mechanically reproducible as 2 + 2 = 4, he caustically argues, no human beings are needed: any machine can produce that result.

And then there is the small matter of social and historical change, of which we are reminded by the fact that texts keep getting translated over and over again through the centuries between natural languages – whenever, that is, the language of a nation has evolved to the point that its speakers no longer feel comfortable with the wording (often, indeed, with the concepts) favoured by their ancestors. How many times has a canonic text such as the Bible been re-translated into one and the same national tongue? What has it meant each time for the nation in question to translate it anew? Clearly, even a scientifically exact textual conversion could only be desirable for a limited time and space: the historical and cultural context from which it arose.[1]

At any rate, the cinematic re-creation of literature is nowhere near the neat simplicity of $2 + 2 = 4$, $4 - 2 = 2$. The conversion between the literary system and that of cinema is characterized by a complexity of the highest level. Here, there simply cannot be any question of creating an algorithm that establishes the bi-univocal equivalences necessary for us to move from Text A to A′ and then back from A′ to the original reading in A.

To elaborate further on the views of Lotman and the Tartu school of Soviet semioticians that I have so far been paraphrasing: thankfully, the above situation does not mark the end of the story. Let us resume the Man from Underground's $2 + 2 = 4$ argument: certain interpretive operations might well be *perfect* – but if any machine can carry them out, what kind of truth are they liable to reveal to us as human beings? None, evidently. It is not the single, ideal language of perfection that human beings understand, but their many imperfect, humane ones.[2]

In terms of cinematic practice, on this view the task of film directors is *not* to aim for a target that is anyway going to elude them, but to act in such a way that the new equation they are setting up holds according to its own internal logic. In some sense, for masters of cinema who re-create works produced by masters of literature it is *necessary to ensure* that $2 + 2 = 5$; or, more precisely, that 5 is the only solution consistent with '$2 + 2 =$' as defined on the basis of the operations and properties of their own new, re-created universes.[3]

I am far from implying that it is easy to replace an artistic system endowed with its own consistency by a new one with a logic of its own. This is an enormous challenge, a challenge to tackle which there seems to exist no standard procedure: no hyper-algorithm, as it were, to tell us which hypo-algorithms will work best in each particular situation. The nine re-creations we have examined (anyway only a small subset of those carried out even within Italian cinema) testify to the width of the spectrum of possible approaches. In the following synthesis of the films analysed in the course of this book, I will review what it was in each individual case that represented the greatest challenge for our nine masters of cinema in re-creating the narrative systems of their literary counterparts.

Beyond Words and toward the Inexpressible

Part One: Homological and Epigraphic Re-creations

It is hardly news, and certainly no misdeed specific to the late twentieth century, that – to use a famous adage's words – classics be thought of as those great books that everyone mentions but no one has read. Perhaps precisely for that reason it was meritorious of Archibugi to apply her directorial skills to such an untrendy work as Goethe's *Wilhelm Meister's Apprenticeship*. After almost two centuries since Goethe-bashing was invented in Germany (to say nothing of recent North American efforts, which, in comparison, pale into insignificance),[4] Archibugi bravely and successfully set out to make once again topical what no longer seemed to be so.

In *Mignon Has Left*, her re-creation of Mignon's misadventures, Archibugi took a series of drastic measures to that effect. First, she adopted only limited segments of the original narrative material (the characters Giorgio/Wilhelm, Mignon/Mignon, and their general attitudes). Second, she assimilated such elements into a situation of her own times, filling in, where necessary, with conditions and circumstances that appropriately suited their new cultural-historical surroundings. Third, she inverted the sign of much of her borrowings in order to make them suitable for her own cultural context: her Mignon is, by most standards, the obverse of Goethe's, and thus looks as close to her as mirror images do to one another.

Granted, Archibugi's course of action arguably produced the very type of 'adaptation' for which Mitry reserved his most vitriolic attacks. On re-creations involving temporal and cultural updating, the critic wrote: 'That other kind of salad [*cette autre salade*] carried out by adapters ... borders on lunacy or imbecility. In either case, it shows a profound contempt for the original work which it exploits, or else a complete lack of understanding of its characteristic qualities.'[5] However, Mitry's fulminations notwithstanding, it takes no Galileian genius to say of *Mignon Has Left*: '*eppur si muove*' ('yet move it does').[6] The external features of the world we see around us may be apparently different from the ones in *Wilhelm Meister*, but their underlying structures are not, and having the two series interact in the film leads to a mutual illumination that enriches our comprehension of both. Archibugi's pendulum movement between the early nineteenth and the late twentieth century is a brilliant testimony to the fact that, to sharp-eyed observers of Western postmodern societies, Mignon may have left – but Goethe hasn't.

The greatest difficulty to be overcome by Fellini in his re-creation of Kafka's American novel probably was to bridge the gap between his own open-ended perception of life and Kafka's pessimistically deterministic one. Kafka's narrator tells us a story about bonded will, and – whether explicitly or not – the report of even the most minute incident in it goes to show that our fate is both inescapable and inescapably tragic. Fellini's *Intervista*, by contrast, tells many stories on free will, in which, good or bad, we all have a say in our own destinies; indeed, within certain bounds, we are allowed to play with them at leisure.

How, then, does Fellini act to accommodate Kafka in what is a truly new world and alien for him? He acts selectively on certain situations he finds in the original, without allowing himself to be encumbered by the plot that surrounds them. Karl, Brunelda, Delamarche, and Robinson all come to *Intervista* with their own Kafkaesque identity; yet, by the time the film is edited and we get to view it, Fellini has naturalized them into his own world for his own purposes. Kafka's actual plot has been left behind in the process; but what matters is that in Fellini the 'lost' components have been made up for by other significant artistic elements. Indeed, that very loss was functional to a richly independent artistic statement.

Part Two: Coextensive Re-creations

Anyone dealing with Gogol will inevitably find his narrator to be the greatest challenge to any resettlement of our Ukrainian-in-St Petersburg under more forgiving skies. What could be called the non-sequitur of the human condition constantly pierces through the fabric of Gogol's prose – in particular, of *Shinel'* – by means of an obsessively rehearsed stylization in the storytelling voice. Does Lattuada 'solve' this problem? Yes and no. Yes, because in *Il cappotto* much of the sense of absurdity flashing through the mind of Gogol's narrator is repositioned and attributed to the empirically verifiable behaviour of his small clerk. No, because Lattuada to a large extent recasts Gogol: the small clerk's alogism is not the main issue – the alogism of society is.

While Gogol is more interested in existential generalizations, Lattuada considers the social ones primal. This change in approach can be rationalized by the fact that, while Lattuada acted within the chronological bounds of Italian neorealism, Gogol wrote well before the tradition of Russian nineteenth-century realism became established. What matters most for our purposes is that Lattuada's approach offers us a self-consistent system with which to replace the Gogolian one. In *Il cappotto*, nothing impossible is attempted; and the possible is brilliantly delivered.

Unlike Kafka's narrator, Tolstoy's does not hide the meaning of the world beyond screens so thick that they make Brunelda's seem like open curtains by comparison; and he does not agonize over the attendant aimlessness that consistently haunts the human beings' journey through their lives. Unlike Gogol's narrator, Tolstoy's does not stray, spin, stop, digress, deride, or denounce; he neither suddenly forgets nor blabbers on with a self-important grimace. Like Gogol's narrator, Tolstoy's too can see the devil on the wall; unlike Gogol's, however, he sees him not because he feels that the devil was put in charge of running the universe, but because he knows that it is human beings who paint him there. Unlike Sade's narrator – and where *is* the like of Sade's narrator? – Tolstoy's approaches the representation of pleasure not as a pyrotechnic experience, but in a sober, shy manner almost akin to mourning: a mourning derived from the awareness that, far from unleashing human beings' potential and liberating their minds, hedonism in fact represents the most painful enslavement to which a mind can become subjected. Unlike Mérimée's narrator, Tolstoy's narrator creates no ironic distance between himself and the characters whose vicissitudes he details; quite the contrary, his words are uttered from the viewpoint of compassion, indeed of a deep-seated sense of brotherhood with them. Unlike Stendhal's narrator, Tolstoy's narrator does not race through southern lands in quest of an uncorrupted vitality, authentic in the directness with which it practises passion, and 'virtuous' even in the simplicity with which it embraces crime. *Politesse*, Tolstoy's narrator would certainly agree with Stendhal's, is a bane of self-righteous civilized society; but crime with effrontery lies no closer to true freedom than does crime with hypocrisy. And finally, unlike Thomas Mann's narrator, who counts his every syllable with the aim punctiliously to counterbalance the tidal forces that threaten to tear his decency-loving Aschenbach apart, Tolstoy's insouciant narrator allows repetitions and plain language into his text. Tolstoy's narrator, in sum, can be described as telling stories calmly, simply, unaffectedly. Why? Because anything short of self-effacement would be sure to get in the way of the *message* Tolstoy wishes to convey.[7] The specific message varies with each of his texts; but the general one hardly does. In his last works, in particular, Tolstoy's altogether transparent message is that humanity needs to regenerate itself morally, ridding itself of corrupt social, political, and spiritual institutions, not by espousing some pseudo-answer in their stead (scientism, a politicized materialism, decadentism) but by going back in a literal manner to a fully evangelical set of principles. In fact, what seems truly miraculous about Tolstoy's art is that someone who so obviously had an axe to grind in the direction taken by his plots, and so uncompromisingly steered them onto a didactic path, could nonetheless succeed in endowing them with impressive artistic qualities. A frequently quoted empirical observation holds that good intentions make for bad literature; but Tolstoy offers ample proof that this rule can have remarkable exceptions.

Does this leave Paolo and Vittorio Taviani, in *The Night Sun*, with a simpler task than that of their fellow *auteurs*, or a more complex one? The issue can be argued both ways. The Tavianis' task in re-creating Tolstoy is simpler than it could otherwise have been, because of the absence of eccentric peculiarities in Tolstoy's narrator. On the other hand, one also needs to deal with a conceptual core that *is* present in Tolstoy and could only be avoided at the cost of sovereign artistic and ethical indifference. Hence the Tavianis' strategy, in re-creating Tolstoy, of transcoding the religious onto the non-confessional plane. Their Tolstoy is still recognizably a voice that comes from the past, a past in which almost universal practice made religious discourse the dominant one in conveying moral imperatives; but the Tavianis make him relevant to our times by re-creating his concerns in a lay manner compatible with our times' almost universal practice of world-immanent ethics. Formulating the confessional and the non-confessional in such a way that either reading will be equally possible and equally seamless: this is the Tavianis' greatest accomplishment in their Tolstoyan film. It is to serve this purpose of moral update that they so painstakingly strive for the re-creation of literary features by way of a narration based on visual and auditive ones.

Pasolini's Salò: *The Re-creation to End All Creation*

The challenge faced by Pasolini's *Salò* in tackling Sade's *Les 120 journées de Sodome* was unrelated to converting into image any irregularities in the narrative voice: Sade's narrator (including his four sub-narrators) is comparatively straightforward, as deviance is heaped by Sade in the plot line rather than applied to diction. To be sure, as a consequence Sade's plot lines are subversive indeed – but that is exactly what attracted Pasolini to Sade to begin with.

To re-create *Les 120 journées* in film presents two distinct hurdles: first, to implement visually Sade's superhuman narrative perversions; second – if, that is, one seriously intends to go beyond the bounds of a narrow historical illustration – to re-motivate Sade's plot in such a way as to justify anew its obsessively elaborate ritual of violence.[8] First, it is hardly doubtful that there can be no way to settle the scores with Sade's text in a literal manner; if nothing else, the sheer numbers of victims and tortures involved make that impossible. Second, it is difficult for a director of our time to articulate convincingly the motives behind the cruelty to be re-presented; who is torturing whom, and why, are hardly matters of little import in lending credibility to the re-created film. In taking up both challenges, Pasolini displayed, to say the least, great daring.

Two circumstances went into making Pasolini's efforts effective – technical circumstances, in the first case, and philosophical in the other. On the first count, Pasolini could dispense with a literal visualization of Sade's text because of the nature of the medium itself: due to its greater directness, cinema can use one murder as a synecdoche for many, and still cause in the viewer, everything else being equal, an impact no smaller than that experienced by someone who reads about one hundred similar deaths in sequence. On the second subject, Pasolini managed to square the circles of his Hell by inverting the moral sign he wished to see attached to the tortures portrayed. As an act of rebellion against the repressive regime under which he lives, Sade sides with *Les 120 journées*' torturers; in Pasolini, however, the torturers *are* the obscurantist regime – and this (with the qualifications I put forward in the relevant chapter) allows the director to espouse what, by all standards, strikes as a humanitarian, indeed utopian, viewpoint. It was the symbolic identification of today's consumeristic capitalist regime with that of the Fascist one of the Salò republic that allowed Pasolini to inject powerful new meaning into Sade's solipsistic delirium.[9] If we accept that this is *not* Sade – and it isn't – we can argue both that it is impossible to reproduce Sade successfully and that *Salò* is a successfully re-created film.

Part Three: Mediated Re-creations

According to statistics, *Carmen* is the opera most frequently performed in today's theatres. That alone identifies for us the concern that must top the list of those on the mind of a director wishing to re-create it: originality. Only, which kind of originality? Ironically, the proliferation of Carmens in recent times has been such that even – indeed, especially – the path of personalized reformulations of the theme has been heavily trodden.

Rosi's *Carmen* responds to these circumstances by an intelligent conservatism. On the one hand, the director chooses to preserve the letter of Bizet's opera, with its beauty and its constraints, its melodrama and its mesmerizing music, its intrinsic ideological prejudices and its Meridionalist *limpidezza*. Rosi's *Carmen* is the *Carmen* we know, the *Carmen* that Nietzsche knew and had excellent reasons to appreciate. On the other hand, Rosi decides to do away with the romanticized, aseptic Carmen most current in theatre productions. He puts her back where she belongs, against the backdrop of the alternately rugged and baroque natural and human landscape of the Mediterranean; and he puts that natural and human landscape right back where it belongs – all around Carmen. Unquestionably, in Rosi's *Carmen* the Mediterranean *is* the real-life Mediterranean we know from Rosi's life work.

Not the least of the reasons why Rosi can afford to do all this is, of course, that he is a film director, not a theatre director, and that he can thus exploit the possibilities of his medium to the full extent of his inclinations. This permits him to reach back to certain features of the literary text in pursuit of its diegetic rejuvenation. Rosi's Carmen sings like the Carmen of Bizet, but she is certainly like Mérimée's in the way she dresses, thinks, and acts – and, probably, smells. Literature and cinema may well (to apply to them the motto of Lessing's *Laokoon*) 'differ in the object and manner of their imitation' of reality;[10] but they can, and in Rosi's *Carmen* certainly do, imitate it in strikingly convergent ways.

By contrast, dealing with literary narrators is a problem Moretti can happily dispense with in *Palombella rossa*: David Lean's *Doctor Zhivago* has already done (and bungled) the job for him. The most important task Moretti faces in re-creating Pasternak is, rather, how to make Pasternak relevant to a new context that is specifically political. This Moretti does, persuasively, by using an off-the-shelf *Zhivago* to highlight the dilemmas that arise when a historically identified political movement becomes permanently magnetized in any one direction and thus loses the ability to question, critically and intelligently, established commonplaces of language and thought. Although this particular effect was only partially planned by the director, it is entirely appropriate that the specific magnet used by Moretti to illustrate his thesis should, on analysis, prove to be Lean's uncritical and unintelligent film: this merely reinforces Moretti's point that commonplaces inevitably lead to defeat. *Palombella rossa* could have been even more cogent, had it somehow verbalized the fact that the David Lean footage it contains suffers from the very same ills that *Palombella rossa* denounces. On the other hand, given that its focus *are* Michele Apicella's shortcomings, *Palombella rossa* proves its point even more solidly via a second-degree process of sorts.

Part Four: Hypertextual Re-creations

In considering Rossellini's re-creation of Stendhal's *Vanina Vanini*, the first and foremost lesson we learn about the relationship between film and literature is that it is imperative for *auteurs* re-creating authors of literature to be well informed about the text they intend to bring to the screen. It can prove disastrous for them, as it did for Rossellini, to approach a Renaissance-loving atheist writer for the single purpose of extracting from him the subject matter for a docudrama on the ubiquitousness of Catholicism in the Italy of the *Risorgimento*. This was disastrous, not because it is wrong to have an interest in Catholicism, but because trying to force stories to convey the exact opposite of what they were conceived to 'say' is a strategy that seems likely to fail every time. When the existential gap between partners in the re-creative dialogue is so considerable, it might be advisable to re-create (if at all) selectively, with circumspection, on a small scale. Such an ideal may appear to be minimalist and purely technical, but it is indeed a wise one. Yet human beings clearly never act in a purely technical sphere; they act in almost endlessly interrelated objective and subjective contexts.

This leads us to the broader sense in which we need to understand *Vanina Vanini*'s lesson on cinema and literature – or perhaps on cinema *tout court*. In a broader sense, Rossellini's experience teaches us the following four things, in order of increasing importance. First, *Vanina Vanini* teaches us that scriptwriters need to be cohesive among themselves and with the director as to the film's intent; without a shared aim, there will never be a viable script. Second, there must be an appropriate cast for the script so devised; without actors able to deliver their lines with credibility, even the most exalted exchanges can fall flat. Third, there must be a producer who feels he or she has a commitment, however self-interested, to director, scriptwriters, and cast; without a supportive producer, or worse still, in the hands of a capricious, self-serving one, even the best director, script, and cast will likely see the seeds of discord flourish. Fourth, and most depressingly, it is extremely difficult even for well-meaning intellectuals, aware of the need for art to be a tool of elevation rather than stultification, to obtain from the institutions within which they act the autonomy they yearn for. As a rule, these institutions will only by oversight allow the pursuit of any priority that is not in their own interest, narrowly defined.

Vanina Vanini taught Rossellini – and teaches us – that, however passionately one may be attracted to the theoretical issue of just what to substitute for Stendhal's fast-paced, energy-loving narrator, in practice such issues are rarely permitted to score much better than last among a filmmaker's concerns. That is, indeed, the reason why soon after *Vanina Vanini* Rossellini turned to television to pursue his encyclopaedic project of mass education; however imperfect, this other institution at least gave him a chance to practise what he believed to be just and necessary.

Thomas Mann's *Der Tod in Venedig* seems a work unique in Western literatures for the unsurpassable concentration with which it asks an endlessly embarrassing question: how can human beings decently deal with that most indecent denizen of their souls, desire? And what are they to do if *it* threatens to win out over *them*? But in fact, *Der Tod in Venedig* is less a unique specimen than a member of a very ancient club: at the latest since Sappho's poetry, humanity has had a reasonably clear perception that desire can be not only a devastating host inside our minds, but worse, our most dangerous landlord. After Mann came Visconti, and we saw with how much artistry he set about replacing Mann's quasi-hexameters with image and sound. What better occasion than this for us to build on this basis a contrastive theory of what literature can do that film cannot, and vice versa? There surely would be material enough for arguing and counter-arguing, since some of Aschenbach's chimaeras (a few of the Italian petty devils that surround him) are ferried over by Visconti fairly safely from the book to the film, while others (for example, his nightmare of the orgy) are, after initial hesitation, thrown overboard.

Nonetheless, I believe that, here as elsewhere, framing the issue in the polarized terms 'literature versus cinema' would merely scratch the surface of the problem; it would certainly create a conceptual opposition where there is none. Why is there none? Because, at any rate at this level of abstraction, Mann's quasi-hexameters are themselves 're-creations' of something inexpressible, something that radically defies representation – desire in its pure, uncontrollable state.[11] Thus, *pace* literal-minded philologists bent on endowing literature with an ontological (as opposed to merely chronological) priority it does not have, re-created cinema is not there/here to convert a pre-existing literary text already perfectly accomplished in all its levels of expressiveness. At the same time, *pace* concerned theorists who in querying the small fry of conversion omit to question (i.e., passively accept) the much larger ontological prejudice just mentioned, in this sense at least literature and cinema are not on opposite sides of a watershed: they are *on the same one*.

In this fundamental sense, Aschenbach's story is only apparently about Venice, Polish boys, and Italian cholera; rather, it is about the 'forces of the abyss' alluded to by the Eleusinian mysteries in *Der Tod in Venedig* and by music in *Morte a Venezia*. *Der Tod in Venedig* uses the conventions proper to a millenary tradition, steeped in forms made familiar to us by ancient Greece; but these, too, are in turn mere epiphenomenal conventions intended to approximate the ἀπείρων, the Infinite. In fact, how very appropriate – but also, at the same time, inane – that language should resort to the rhythmically controlled form of hexameters in order to attempt keeping that Infinite in check.

If I were a director, in these circumstances I would feel that seeking one-on-one equivalents for words of literature could be in some sense the least of my concerns. I would, indeed, feel that this pseudo-problem would distract me from the one true problem at hand: how to establish contact with the dark world to express which both images *and* words are inadequate.[12] It is to that common source, to that *indecent* world jointly shared by all arts that I would try to reach.

Lectio difficilior: Seeking the Less Obvious Meaning

I hope *Masters of Two Arts* has been able to argue persuasively for the need for any meaningful debate on the filmic re-creation of literature to take into account the cultural continuum in which all literature, all cinema, and even all theory is immersed at each moment in our history. Intellectual, technical, artistic possibilities exist not on a two-dimensional surface, but in a three-dimensional space where our past, our present, and our future are dialectically interdependent. Nothing can arise out of itself; in the realm of the mind no less than in that of nature, the present is but a metamorphic moment that shapes a future state we do not yet know out of countless preceding ones, the latest few of which we do. In his essay on Dostoevsky's indebtedness to Gogol, Tynianov wrote sharply: 'Every literary inheritance is primarily a struggle, the destruction of an old unity and a new edification of old elements.'[13] A *new* edification of *old* elements: continuity, in other words, by way of reversals; gradual transformation by way of discrete revolutions.

Not coincidentally, a person with reliable professional qualifications in both Italian cinema and European literatures, Luchino Visconti, explained at some length why what could be called an 'independently arising' filmmaking is in any case a theoretically impossible hypothesis:

> If I wrote a book, exactly as is the case when I make a film, I would be writing on the basis of all the input I have received from my readings and from

my artistic predilections. And there is little doubt that what I would then say would already have been said by someone else. I would be at liberty not to indicate my sources. They would exist nonetheless.

A man who had never read a book, never looked at a painting, never heard any music? His glance, his sense of hearing absolutely virgin? And who would be using a camera to look at the world and translate it into images? Yes, that person could certainly practise pure cinema. But ... [there can be no such thing].[14]

By one of those striking coincidences that sometimes cause us to suspect that the meeting of certain masters may well, in the end, be no coincidence at all, decades earlier Èizenshtein had already formulated his own answer to the dilemma in almost identical terms:

When we try to express in artistic form the social needs of our times, when we try to give shape to the solution required by those needs, we rely on the experience we collected in the observations of all our personal past. This material is complemented by whatever we specifically seek out, for each given concrete solution, by turning to what has already been done and resolved in this same sense by someone else in the context of a different task, in different times and places ...

By relying on the framework of an intelligently accumulated experience one can build one's own 'original,' 'different,' and, above all, 'appropriate' building – that is to say, a building that is suitable [*tselesoobraznoe*] with respect to a concrete task. And this is the most important and decisive thing.[15]

True to the same principle, Èizenshtein adduces further argument from the works of another author to whom he feels indebted. This is Goethe, quoted and commented by Èizenshtein as follows:

'What is [artistic] invention, and who can say he has invented this or that? It is, in the first place, foolish to boast about one's priority. And not to acknowledge that one is, after all, a plagiarist, is just unconscionable braggery ...'

How many unconfessed associations, how many prototypes, which often we ourselves do not want to confess, actually steer us! ...

And once again it is Goethe who gives the key to an explanation ...: 'What I wrote is mine! Whether I took it from life or from books is immaterial; it was up to me to use it appropriately!'[16]

Visconti, for his part, raises the critical stakes further by adding a new and original dimension to the debate. This he does in the conclusion to his own argument:

> To read a book is already a creative work. Loyalty does not imply a lack in creative powers. Whatever one does, one always builds upon a myth or a story that has more or less already been told. The only thing that matters is the new glance cast on it. When I choose a specific literary work, it is so that I can give it a new dimension; or rather, a dimension which it already possesses implicitly, but which only 'another' glance is able to give it – precisely the glance called for by the creator, a glance that is creative in and of itself.
>
> *My purpose is to strive for the most difficult reading among those that the author would have chosen, the secret meaning which he wished his most attentive readers to uncover.* It seems to me that doing this, too, means being an author.[17]

It is that 'most difficult reading,' which an established philological tradition calls the *lectio difficilior* of a text, that Visconti encourages us to seek when we peruse a work composed by a master of literature. Fortunately, during the last half-century many masters of Italian cinema have been able to set an example for us in the way they sought 'the most difficult readings' contained in the works of their great predecessors, enriching us – *and* cinema, *and* literature – in the process.

Notes

Opening Epigraphs

1 'La contraffazione (*poddelka*) è ripugnante. La ri-costruzione (*vossozdanie*) è magnifica.' From 'Diderot Wrote about Cinema,' in *Stili di regia. Narrazione e messa in scena: Leskov, Dumas, Zola, Dostoevskij, Gogol'*, ed. Pietro Montani and Alberto Cioni (Venice: Marsilio, 1993), 385.

2 'Jamais, moi vivant, on ne m'illustrera, parce que la plus belle description littéraire est dévorée par le plus piètre dessin. Du moment qu'un type est fixé par le crayon, il perd ce caractère de généralité, cette concordance avec mille objets connus qui font dire au lecteur: "J'ai vu cela" ou "Cela doit être." Une femme dessinée ressemble à une femme, voilà tout.' Gustave Flaubert, letter to Ernest Duplan, 12 June 1862, in vol. 3 of *Correspondance*, ed. Jean Bruneau (Paris: Gallimard Pléiade, 1991), 221–2.

3 'Le illustrazioni di un'opera letteraria hanno valore artistico nella misura in cui non sono illustrazioni. Così è per il cinema.' Michelangelo Antonioni, in an open letter to Italo Calvino, on his own re-creation from Pavese, *The Girlfriends* (*Le amiche*, 1955), in *Cinema Nuovo* 76 (10 Feb. 1956); repr. in Franca Faldini and Goffredo Fofi, eds, *L'avventurosa storia del cinema italiano raccontata dai suoi protagonisti, 1935–1959* (Milan: Feltrinelli, 1979), 323, as well as in M. A., 'Loyalty to Pavese,' in his *The Architecture of Vision: Writings and Interviews on Cinema*, ed. Carlo di Carlo and Giorgio Tinazzi, trans. M. Cottino-Jones (New York: Marsilio Publishers, 1996), 76; 'Fedeltà a Pavese,' in his *Fare un film è per me vivere*, ed. Carlo di Carlo and Giorgio Tinazzi (Venice: Marsilio, 1994), 72.

Introduction

1 For readers wishing to obtain coverage of the entire field of Italian cinema, the obvious works in English that come to mind are Peter Bondanella's *Italian Cinema from Neorealism to the Present* (New York: Continuum, 1991 [1983]); Marcia Landy, *Italian Film* (Cambridge: Cambridge University Press, 2000); and Pierre Sorlin's *Italian National Cinema 1896–1996* (London and New York: Routledge, 1996). These can be usefully complemented by Mira Liehm, *Passion and Defiance: Film in Italy from 1942 to the Present* (Berkeley: University of California Press, 1984); Millicent Marcus, *Italian Film in the Light of Neorealism* (Princeton, NJ: Princeton University Press, 1986); and, particularly for the latest developments, Manuela Gieri, *Contemporary Italian Filmmaking: Strategies of Subversion* (Toronto: University of Toronto Press, 1995).

As for works in Italian, the most detailed coverage to date can be found in Gian Piero Brunetta's monumental four-volume *Storia del cinema italiano* (Rome: Editori Riuniti, 1993 [1982]). One must also mention Fernaldo Di Giammatteo's *The Restless Glance* (*Lo sguardo inquieto: Storia del cinema italiano 1940–1990* [Florence: La nuova Italia, 1994]) – a book that, in almost 500 dense pages, covers topics ranging from Fascist cultural policy since the inauguration of Cinecittà in 1937 to the early years of the *nuovo cinema italiano* toward the end of the 1980s, interspersed where appropriate with significant statistics on the economic trends affecting Italian studios at each given time.

2 Cristina Bragaglia, *Il piacere del racconto: Narrativa italiana e cinema (1895–1990)* (Florence: La nuova Italia, 1993).

3 Giuliana Nuvoli, with Maurizio Regosa, *Storie ricreate: Dall'opera letteraria al film* (Turin: UTET, 1998).

4 Nuvoli, *Storie ricreate*, 4.

5 Ibid., 56.

6 Further works that, though useful in their own right, seem not to grasp the sheer magnitude of the issue are Sara Cortellazzo and Dario Tomasi, *Letteratura e cinema* (Rome: Laterza, 1998); and Filippo La Porta, 'Cinema e narrativa: Una possibile alleanza?' in Mario Sesti, ed., *La 'scuola' italiana: Storia, strutture e immaginario di un altro cinema (1988–1996)* (Venice: Marsilio, 1996), 275–80. Thorough and well-conceived books, by contrast, are Vito Attolini's *Storia del cinema letterario in cento film* (Recco: Le Mani, 1998) and Angelo Moscariello, *Cinema e/o letteratura* (Bologna: Pitagora editrice, 1981). Both however, devote only a very brief space to Italian cinema, and hardly any to the Italo-European connection we are examining here.

7 A less polarized, more open-ended approach to the dialogism between literature and film has been developed by the Soviet school of semioticians in

Tartu clustered around Yurii Lotman and inspired by Mikhail Mikhailovich Bakhtin's previous work. I will return to Lotman both below and in the Conclusion.

Further books that, in different theoretical areas, I have found no less stimulating on the subject of re-creation, inter-media and otherwise, are the following: Umberto Eco, *Experiences in Translation*, trans. Alastair McEwen (Toronto: University of Toronto Press, 2001); Umberto Eco, *Interpretation and Overinterpretation*, ed. Stefan Collini (Cambridge: Cambridge University Press, 1992); *Interpretazione e sovrainterpretazione*, ed. Stefan Collini, trans. Sandra Cavicchioli (Milan: Bompiani, 1995); and André Gaudreault, *Du littéraire au filmique: Système du récit* (Montréal: Presses de l'Université Laval; Paris: Klincksieck, 1988).

8 See Sandro Bernardi, ed., *Storie dislocate* (San Miniato: Edizioni ETS, 1999).

9 'Sure, one can give a man a trombone and then tell him: "Now play the Kazan cathedral"; but this will be either jest or ignorance.' 'Конечно, можно дать человеку тромбон и сказать "сыграйте на нем Казанский собор," но это будет или шутка или невежество.' Viktor Shklovskii, *Literatura i kinematograf* (Berlin: Russkoe universal'noe izdatel'stvo, 1923), 21.

   I have been unable to locate an English edition of this text; an Italian translation was published as V. S., 'Letteratura e cinema,' in *I formalisti russi nel cinema*, ed. and trans. Giorgio Kraiski (Milan: Garzanti, 1987 [1971]) (quote in ibid., 115). Shklovskii's trenchant, sometimes scathing style testifies to the broadly speaking revolutionary and Futurist atmosphere of the times when he was writing – a style that we often find, *inter alios*, in Èizenshtein too. (Some of Shklovskii's later readers picked up from him not only the points he made but – out of context – also the stylistic register he used to convey them.)

   The best-known postwar reformulation of Shklovskii's early position is probably the one, whether by accident or by design, adopted/'adapted' in Jean Mitry's work: '[A]daptations of the great works of fiction ... never in fact happened, for the simple reason that it is *just not possible*' (*The Aesthetics and Psychology of the Cinema*, trans. C. King [Bloomington: Indiana University Press, 1997], 326; emphasis added). '[E]xaminant ici le strict problème de l'adaptation, nous allons voir qu'il n'en fut rien parce que la chose est *impossible*' (Mitry, *Esthétique et psychologie du cinéma*, vol. 1 [Paris: Éditions universitaires, 1963], 346; emphasis added).

10 This is, not least, a consequence of the fact that little by Lotman and his collaborators is available in English; unless things work the other way around – little is available in English because few outside the field of Slavic semiotics care to know.

11 Bazin's and Andrew's contributions are included in the following recent collection of essays: James Naremore, ed., *Film Adaptation* (New Brunswick, NJ: Rutgers University Press, 2000), respectively 19–27 and 28–37.

12 Millicent Marcus, *Filmmaking By the Book: Italian Cinema and Literary Adaptation* (Baltimore, Md.: Johns Hopkins University Press, 1993), 15.

13 Marcus is not even quoted in any of the following recent books on 'adaptation': Deborah Cartmell and Imelda Whelehan, eds, *Adaptations: From Text to Screen, Screen to Text* (London: Routledge, 1999); James Griffith, *Adaptations as Imitations: Films from Novels* (Newark: University of Delaware Press, 1997); Greg Jenkins, *Stanley Kubrick and the Art of Adaptation: Three Novels, Three Films* (Jefferson, NC: McFarland, 1997); Brian McFarlane, *Novel to Film: An Introduction to the Theory of Adaptation* (Oxford: Clarendon Press, 1996); and Naremore, ed., *Film Adaptation*. An identical tolerance of F-parameters and even the F-word itself can also be found in the slightly earlier collection by John Orr and Colin Nicholson, eds, *Cinema and Fiction: New Modes of Adapting, 1950–1990* (Edinburgh: Edinburgh University Press, 1992).

14 More on this subject can be found in Carlo Testa, 'Dalla letteratura al cinema: Adattamento o ri-creazione?' *Bianco & Nero* 62:1–2 (April 2001), 37–51.

15 On Visconti's reception in America, see Peter Bondanella, 'La (s)fortuna critica del cinema viscontiano in USA,' in David Bruni and Veronica Pravadelli, eds, *Studi viscontiani* (Venice: Marsilio, 1997), 277–86.

16 I in no way imply that working within the Italian context automatically guarantees greater sophistication in matters re-creational. A case in point is Nuvoli and Regosa's book, whose title (*Storie ricreate*) seems, after all, to indicate that this and nothing else is the authors' focus. However, contrary to all expectations, in their text they have systematic (and tediously frequent) recourse to the expressions *trasposizione, riduzione, materia, riduzione, tratto da, trasposizione, portato sullo schermo,* and the like – *exclusively.* Not even their opening theoretical section mentions re-creation; it is, in fact, titled 'La trasposizione' (!) and refers to Èizenshtein's notion of 'visual imagery,' asserting its indispensable status for *a successful transposition* ('una trasposizione riuscita'; Nuvoli and Regosa, 25). How the two authors can, on this basis, arrive at the 're-creation' mentioned in their title thus remains something of a mystery.

17 Robert Stam, 'Beyond Fidelity: The Dialogics of Adaptation,' in Naremore, ed., *Film Adaptation*, 68–9; emphasis added.

18 The Gramscian-Viscontian connection I am referring to, which I describe as tendentially characterizing the Italian tradition in opposition to the North American one, has been explored most explicitly, in English, by Marcus herself (*Italian Film in the Light of Neorealism, Filmmaking By the Book*) and Marcia Landy (*Italian Film*, as well as *Film, Politics, and Gramsci* [Minneapolis: Univer-

sity of Minnesota Press, 1994]). For relevant publications in Italian, see the appropriate bibliographies in Landy and Marcus.

19 The present-day convergence between film history and film theory has been scrutinized – and welcomed – in at least the following works: David Bordwell, *Making Meaning: Inference and Rhetoric in the Interpretation of Cinema* (Cambridge, Mass.: Harvard University Press, 1989), esp. 266ff.; Francesco Casetti, *Theories of Cinema: 1945–1995*, trans. F. Chiostri et al. (Austin: University of Texas Press, 1999), 289–313; *Teorie del cinema 1945–1990* (Milan: Bompiani, 1994), 332–8; Francesco Casetti, 'Lo sguardo novecentesco,' in Bernardi, ed., *Storie dislocate*, 17–26; and Robert Stam, *Film Theory: An Introduction* (Oxford: Blackwell, 2000), esp. 328–30.

20 On Bakhtin and film in general see Robert Stam's useful *Subversive Pleasures: Bakhtin, Cultural Criticism, and Film* (Baltimore, Md.: Johns Hopkins University Press, 1989); and, in more condensed form, by the same author, 'Russian Formalism and the Bakhtin School,' in his *Film Theory*, 47–55.

21 Iurii M. Lotman, *Lektsii po struktural'noi poètike: Vvedenie, teoriia stikha* (Providence, RI: Brown University Press, 1968), 16.

22 Among the authors with whose names Western readers will be familiar, Èizenshtein's favourites included Dickens, Balzac, Zola, Joyce, and Dreiser. The theme 'Èizenshtein and literature' would be a worthy subject for a substantial monograph; and even its subset, 'Èizenshtein and the cinematic re-creation of literature,' could well call for an only slightly less sizeable volume. My treatment of the subject here is therefore necessarily cursory and incomplete. To be sure, what strikes one most immediately about the issue is how fragmentary the publication and the translation of Èizenshtein's writings on the subject have been. Many of the most interesting ones appeared, in post-Soviet times, outside the six volumes of the *Izbrannye proizvedenia* (*Selected Works*); many items in *IP* were anyway never translated; even if they were, the anthologies put out in different languages include texts that vary widely and show only accidental overlaps; translations are abridged, often seemingly at random. It is a true jungle, which Èizenshtein did nothing to deserve.

23 For example, a monumental reputation for inadequacy in the practice of *les équivalences* surrounds the cinema of the French Fourth Republic (1945–58). For perhaps the most effective contextualization of those circumstances, see René Prédal, *Le cinéma français depuis 1945* (Paris: Nathan Université, 1991), 78–81.

24 S.M. Èizenshtein, 'Literature and Cinema: Reply to a Questionnaire,' in *Writings, 1922–1934*, ed. and trans. Richard Taylor, vol. 1 of *Selected Works* (London: British Film Institute and Bloomington: Indiana University Press, 1988), 97–8.

'О "взаимоотношениях" могу сказать, что сейчас пройден последовательный путь очищения кинематографии от:

1) литературы (примитивной, оперирующей только сюжетом: авантюризм чистый – *Рокамбол, 813, Нибелунги* или авантюризм психологический, например *Парижанка*);

2) театра (игровой жанр) ...

В сегодняшних тенденциях по отысканию форм, действительно ей присущих, кинематография лучшую *опору* находит в том, что происходит в области обновления форм литературных.

Это помогает лучше разобраться в ряде проблем, возникших совершенно самостоятельно из киноматериала, пользуясь опытом и аналогиями из "соседней" сферы.'

'Literatura i kino,' in *Izbrannye proizvedeniia v shesti tomakh* (Moskva: Iskusstvo, 1968), 5: 527.

25 *Selected Works*, 1: 98; emphasis in the original.

'(Р)ежиссеров следует заставлять находить *киноэквиваленты* этим произведениям. (Когда это требуется).

Таким путем мыслимо и обновление и оплодотворение также и формальной стороны и возможностей кино, а не только тематически-сюжетной, что, в конце концов, с успехом выполняется и другими родами литературы.'

Izbrannye proizvedeniia, 5: 528; emphasis in the original.

26 And woe befell him for that – but for reasons that had little or nought to do with the relation between film and literature. Quite simply, the film fell afoul of Stalin's ideas about admissible aesthetic practices. Accused of Formalist deviationism, Èizenshtein had to stop work on the film and recant. See S.M. Èizenshtein, 'The [Errors] of Bezhin Meadow,' in *Writings, 1934–1947*, ed. Richard Taylor, trans. W. Powell, vol. 3 of *Selected Works* (London: British Film Institute, 1996), 100–5 (not included in *Izbrannye proizvedeniia*).

27 Depending on the context, the technical meaning of *oformlenie* ranges from 'mise-en-scène' to 'typesetting.'

28 To be precise, Èizenshtein's *Selected Works* in English include a *Torito* in which the theoretical part is dropped and only the autobiographical one retained. However, a generally accurate full version in Italian appears in Èizenshtein, *Stili di regia*, 329.

'Сколько было в советской кинематографии неудачных попыток втиснуть элементы американского кино "как они есть," например типичную ситуацию финалов ранних ковбойских фильмов ... Но американская ситуация никак не лезла в фильмы, отражающие наши социальные и идеологические условия. Не лезла, по тому что ее принцип проявлялся в частном специфически американском чтении.

Между тем ее принцип, но только облаченный в наше чтение, совершенно благополучно освоился в нашей кинематографии. Правда, его надо было узнать сквозь это наше оформление. Узнать в том новом качестве, в котором, отражая нашу социальную действительность, он появился у нас ...

(Ф)инал *Броненосца "Потемкин"* построен по принципу последних актов ковбойских картин.'

Torito, in *Izbrannye proizvedeniia,* 4: 648.

29 Cf. Èizenshtein, *Stili di regia,* 330, 332.

'Чтобы лишний раз подчеркнуть всеобщность, а отнюдь не исключительность изложенного здесь явления, будет не вредно, быть может, сослаться еще на одну опорную аналогию.

Пусть напоминанием о заимствовании принципа ... останется в вашей памяти аэроплан ... Настоящая победа человека над воздухом, несомненно, началась с того момента, когда от подражания внешней форме летающих прообразов аэроплана – птиц – он перешел к осознанию *формы как закона строения явлений.*

Другими словами, попытки человека взлететь были обречены на неудачу до тех пор, пока на первом месте у него оставалось внешнее подражание полету птиц ...

(Образ этот) поможет вам запомнить, что "заимствованные" элементы будут живительно входить в состав вашего изобретения лишь тогда, когда они будут не случайными фрагментами другого частного случая, а результатом мудрого освоения принципа, уместно примененного в других или аналогичных условиях.'

Izbrannye proizvedeniia, 4: 649, 650; emphasis added.

30 It seems to be one of the best-kept secrets in the field that De Sica's *Bicycle Thieves* (*Ladri di biciclette,* 1948) – a film often considered to belong to the ten best of all time – was also re-created from a book, the homonymous novel by Luigi Bartolini. Again, though, the film was studied so extensively in every other respect that it seems only fair to give some other item a chance.

Ironically, Bartolini in fact hated the film – because, to him, it was not 'faithful' enough to his book. Within the vast secondary literature on *Bicycle Thieves,* the liveliest version of this particular anecdote can be found in Vittorio De Sica and Cesare Zavattini, *Parliamo tanto di noi,* ed. Ottavio Iemma and Paolo Nuzzi (Rome: Editori Riuniti, 1997), 93–104.

31 Henry James, 'Gustave Flaubert,' in his *Notes on Novelists: With Some Other Notes* (London: J.M. Dent, 1914), 65. *Sentimental Education* (*L'Éducation senti-*

mentale, 1869) is indeed devoted to the dubious glory of a provincial youth whose sole claim to excellence is the dedication with which he pursues his own superfluousness in the bourgeois society of Paris. For the record, I have three possible, mutually exclusive, answers to James's 'why him?' complaint: (1) Because most of the others are considerably worse; (2) Frédéric is not the book's true protagonist; and (3) The quintessence of mediocrity is, as such, quintessentially revealing.

32 David Bordwell and Kristin Thompson, *Film History: An Introduction* (New York: McGraw-Hill, 1994), xxxix–xl.

33 The reference is to Eco's double entendre in the title of his thriller novel *The Name of the Rose.* Eco's pun is based on the ambiguity between *rosa,* the flower, and *rosa,* 'gamut of choices, or list of people, among which one is to be picked' – the latter alluding to the sought-for culprit in the book.

34 The terms 'intrinsic excellence' and 'masterliness' problematize the notion of authorship. On auteur theory, see at least John Caughie, ed., *Theories of Authorship* (London: Routledge, 1981) and Susan Hayward, *Cinema Studies* (London: Routledge, 2000), 19–27 (with further bibliography).

35 In one substantial aspect I must avow dissatisfaction with my very subject matter. There are fewer women filmmakers in Italy than I wish there were; and even fewer have produced re-creations from a work of modern literature in the French, German, or Russian traditions. (For a more detailed account on this subject, see my *Italian Cinema and Modern European Literatures.*) This will no doubt change in the future, in parallel with the changes continuously taking place in Italian society.

36 Iurii Tynianov, 'On Literary Evolution (1927),' in Ladislav Matejka and Krystyna Pomorska, eds, *Readings in Russian Poetics: Formalist and Structuralist Views* (Ann Arbor, Mich.: Michigan Slavic Publications, 1978), 77. 'Изучение эволюции литературы возможно только при отношении к литературе как к ряду, системе, соотнесенной с другими рядами, системами, ими обусловленной.' 'O literaturnoi èvoliutsii,' in Iurii Striedter, ed., *Texte der russischen Formalisten* (Munich: Wilhelm Fink Verlag, 1969), 1: 458–60.

37 As limit cases we could consider, among others, Olmi's *The Job / The Sound of Trumpets,* Comencini's *The Traffic Jam,* and Antonioni's *Beyond the Clouds,* where Kafka, Beckett, and Ionesco, respectively, appear indirectly. It is the three situations, not their surface-level plots, that show Kafka-esque, Beckett-esque, and Ionesco-esque traits.

38 Analogous situations that come to mind are the use of a cluster of well-established personal or place names ('Parma,' 'Fabrizio,' 'Gina,' all from Stendhal, in Bertolucci's *Before the Revolution*); the quoting of literary passages (Beckett's *Waiting for Godot* in Martone's *Death of a Neapolitan Mathema-*

tician); the display of a book or reading of a short text as interpretive keys to the film (Broch's *The Sleepwalkers* in Antonioni's *La notte*, Rimbaud's poems and Tolstoy's stories in Pasolini's *Teorema*).

39 A few among the best partially coextensive re-creations are Bellocchio's *The Butterfly's Dream* (one scene visually quoted from Kleist's *Prince Friedrich von Homburg*), Rosi's *Three Brothers* (the *incipit* and plot structure from Platonov's *The Third Son*), Scola's *What Time Is It* (discussion of one episode from Stendhal's *The Charterhouse of Parma*), the Tavianis' *Saint Michael Had a Rooster* (part of the plot line reworked from Tolstoy's *The Divine and the Human*), and Scola's *The Terrace* (one scene – fictionally – aired on TV: Matamore's death from Gautier's *Captain Fracassa*). In each such case, at least one episode or occurrence from the prior text that is of particular symbolic significance is absorbed into the cinematic text, becoming part and parcel of it.

40 Other worthy candidates would have been Camerini's *The Captain's Daughter*, from Pushkin; Olmi's *The Legend of the Holy Drinker*, from Roth; Scola's *The Voyage of Captain Fracassa*, from Gautier; and the Tavianis' *Elective Affinities*, from Goethe. On my excluding from this group films such as Rosi's *Carmen* and Visconti's *Death in Venice*, see below. (On the alternative options – and more – mentioned in this note and the preceding ones, cf. my *Italian Cinema and Modern European Literatures*.)

41 In this context, one should note that adjustments undergone in the re-creative process by the film's time frame tend to strike the viewer as less intrusive than other modifications. Except for extreme cases, in other words, spectators seem to pay little heed to anachronism. With respect to the films in Part Two, it takes some critical effort to remember that, as compared to their prior texts, *The Overcoat* is delayed, and *The Night Sun* brought forward, by about a century. To be sure, this could well say more about our empirical historical sensitivity – or lack thereof – than about a general characteristic of cinematography as such.

42 It goes without saying that some films can be placed in different locations in the classification I have just sketched, according to which of their aspects and which frame of reference we choose to privilege. The Tavianis' *Saint Michael Had a Rooster*, for example, re-creates about two-thirds of the 'hero's zone' – *zona geroia* – in *The Divine and the Human*, but practically none of Tolstoy's soteriological message. How is this situation to be exactly and univocally quantified?

43 Yet things are not so straightforward. As I will explain in the relevant chapter, the hypertextual connotations in *Carmen* relate to Rosi's own *oeuvre* rather than to Mérimée's. It definitely seems as though reality was too messy a business for taxonomy ever to become an exact science – unless, that is, we

declare ourselves ready to accept the existence of very large numbers of sets containing only one element.

44 For other possible categories, see those listed and described in the useful survey in McFarlane, *Novel to Film*, 10–11. I am – reluctantly – leaving to one side an endlessly stimulating book, Gérard Genette's *Palimpsests: Literature in the Second Degree*, trans. C. Newman and C. Doubinsky (Lincoln: University of Nebraska Press, 1997); *Palimpsestes: La littérature au second degré* (Paris: Seuil, 1982). This is because it includes no reference to the inter-media literature-to-cinema issue. It seems to me that I might be demanding too much of my readers if, as guidance for a book on literature-to-cinema re-creation, I were to take concepts so obviously developed for literature-to-literature processes.

45 In Naremore, ed., *Film Adaptation*, 35.

46 A very good and full technical account of the issues faced by transliterators from Russian can be found, most conveniently for our purposes, at the beginning of vol. 3 of Èizenshtein's works in English: *Selected Works*, 3: xii.

47 Paul Verlaine, *Selected Verse*, ed. and trans. Doris-Jeanne Gourévitch (Waltham, Mass.: Blaisdell, 1970), 137.

48 Paul Verlaine, *Oeuvres poétiques complètes*, ed. Y.-G. Le Dantec (Paris: Gallimard Pléiade, 1954), 206.

Chapter 1: Goethe and Archibugi

1 Goethe, *Wilhelm Meister's Apprenticeship*, vol. 7 of *Works*, ed. and trans. Thomas Carlyle (London: Anthological Society, [1901?]), 134 (book 3, chap. 1); repr. under same title, ed. William Allan Neilson (New York: P.F. Collier, 1917), 142–3. This particular version of Mignon's lines has seemed to me the poetically most satisfactory one among those available in English.

'Kennst du das Land? wo die Zitronen blühn,/ Im dunkeln Laub die Gold-Orangen glühn,/ Ein sanfter Wind vom blauen Himmel weht,/ Die Myrte still und hoch der Lorbeer steht./ Kennst du es wohl?/ Dahin! Dahin!/ Mögt' ich mir dir, o mein Geliebter, ziehn ...

Nachdem sie das Lied zum zweitenmal geendigt hatte, hielt sie einen Augenblick inne, sah Wilhelmen scharf an und fragte: kennst du das Land? – Es muß wohl Italien gemeint sein, versetzte Wilhelm, woher hast du das Liedchen? – Italien! sagte Mignon bedeutend: gehst du nach Italien, so nimm mich mit, es friert mich hier. – Bist du schon dort gewesen, liebe Kleine? fragte Wilhelm. – Das Kind war still und nichts weiter aus ihm zu bringen.'

Wilhelm Meisters Lehrjahre, ed. Hans-Jürgen Schings, vol. 5 of *Sämtliche Werke nach Epochen seines Schaffens. Münchner Ausgabe*, ed. Karl Richter et al. (Munich: Carl Hanser, 1987), 142 (book 3, chap. 1).

Mignon, as represented in *Wilhelm Meister*, is an archetypally – indeed, stereotypically – Italian character *as perceived by the northern glance*. For an introductory approach to the cultural and historical dimension of the subject, see Giulio Bollati, 'L'italiano,' in *I caratteri originali*, vol. 1 of *Storia d'Italia* (Turin: Einaudi, 1972), 949–1022; Franco Venturi, 'L'Italia fuori d'Italia,' in *Dal primo Settecento all'Unità*, vol. 3 of *Storia d'Italia* (Turin: Einaudi, 1973), 985–1481; and Robert Paris, 'Dopo il '45: Miti e immagini nuove,' in *Dall'Unità a oggi*, vol. 4/1 of *Storia d'Italia* (Turin: Einaudi, 1975), 769–818. Different aspects of the topic are recurrent in *Masters of Two Arts* (see the chapters on Pasolini, Rosi, Rossellini, and Visconti).

2 Virtually any monograph on the *Bildungsroman*, in Germany or outside it, is certain to include a chapter on, or reference to, the *Lehrjahre*. Among such works see Mikhail Mikhailovich Bakhtin, 'The *Bildungsroman* and Its Significance in the History of Realism (Toward a Historical Typology of the Novel),' in his *Speech Genres and Other Late Essays*, ed. Caryl Emerson and Michael Holquist, trans. V.W. McGee (Austin: University of Texas Press, 1986), 10–59; 'Roman vospitaniia i ego znachenie v istorii realizma,' in his *Èstetika slovesnogo tvorchestva* (Moscow: Iskusstvo, 1979), 188–236; W.H. Bruford, *The German Tradition of Self-Cultivation: Bildung from Humboldt to Thomas Mann* (Cambridge: Cambridge University Press, 1975); Melitta Gerhard, *Der deutsche Entwicklungsroman bis zu Goethes* Wilhelm Meister, Halle a. d. Saale: Max Niemeyer, 1926; Jürgen Jacobs and Marcus Krause, *Der deutsche Bildungsroman: Gattungsgeschichte vom 18. bis zum 20. Jahrhundert* (Munich: C.H. Beck, 1989); Lothar Köhn, 'Entwicklungs- und Bildungsroman: Ein Forschungsbericht,' *Deutsche Vierteljahresschrift für Literaturwissenschaft und Geistesgeschichte* 42:3 (1968), 427–73, expanded and published separately under same title (Stuttgart: J.B. Metzler, 1969); Todd Kontje, *Private Lives in the Public Sphere: The German* Bildungsroman *as Metafiction* (University Park: Pennsylvania State University Press, 1992); Todd Kontje, *The German* Bildungsroman: *History of a National Genre* (Columbia, SC: Camden House, 1993); Fritz Martini, 'Der Bildungsroman: Zur Geschichte des Wortes und der Theorie,' *Deutsche Vierteljahresschrift für Literaturwissenschaft und Geistesgeschichte* 35:1 (1961), 44–63; Gerhart Mayer, *Der deutsche Bildungsroman: Von der Aufklärung bis zur Gegenwart* (Stuttgart: J.B. Metzler, 1992); Michael Minden, *The German* Bildungsroman: *Incest and Inheritance* (Cambridge: Cambridge University Press, 1997); Franco Moretti, *The Way of the World: The* Bildungsroman *in European Culture* (London: Verso, 1987); Marc Redfield, *Aesthetic Ideology and the* Bildungsroman (Ithaca, NY: Cornell University Press, 1996); Rolf Selbmann, *Der deutsche Bildungsroman* (Stuttgart: Metzler, 1984); Rolf Selbmann, ed., *Zur Geschichte des deutschen Bildungsromans* (Darmstadt: Wissen-

schaftliche Buchgesellschaft, 1988); and Martin Swales, *The German Bildungsroman from Wieland to Hesse* (Princeton, NJ: Princeton University Press, 1978).

3 Johann Wolfgang Goethe, *Wilhelm Meister's Apprenticeship*, vol. 9 of *Collected Works*, ed. Eric Albert Blackall and Victor Lange (New York: Suhrkamp, 1989), 304 (book 7, chap. 9). 'Der echte Schüler lernt aus dem Bekanntem das Unbekannte entwickeln, und nähert sich dem Meister.' *Wilhelm Meisters Lehrjahre*, vol. 5 of *Sämtliche Werke. Münchner Ausgabe*, 498 (book 7, chap. 9).

4 This is precisely the point on which Novalis took exception to Goethe's narrative 'efficiency.' Novalis, *Schriften. Die Werke Friedrich von Hardenbergs*, ed. Paul Kluckhohn and Richard Samuel (Stuttgart: Kohlhammer, 1960–75), 2: 640–2, and 3: 646.

5 Book 8, chap. 8.

6 Goethe, *Wilhelm Meister's Apprenticeship*, 303 (book 7, chap. 9). 'Wer bloß mit Zeichen wirkt, ist ein Pedant, ein Heuchler oder ein Pfuscher. Es sind ihrer viel, und es wird ihnen wohl zusammen.' *Wilhelm Meisters Lehrjahre*, 498 (book 7, chap. 9).

7 The director, aged twenty-eight when she made *Mignon Has Left*, was familiar with Goethe's name: she had played Ottilie in *Elective Affinities* for RAI-TV at the age of sixteen. While we are inadequately informed about the extent to which Archibugi cultivated the German author between 1976 and 1988, it seems reasonable to assume that Goethe was part and parcel of what in her published interviews she describes as her almost exclusive pastimes: reading and writing.

   On Archibugi and her films, see Áine O'Healy, 'Are the Children Watching Us? The Roman Films of Francesca Archibugi,' in G. Marrone, ed., *New Landscapes in Contemporary Italian Cinema*, thematic issue of *Annali d'Italianistica* 17 (1999), 121–36; Carola Proto, ed., *Francesca Archibugi* (Rome: Dino Audino Editore, [1995?]) (22–30 on *Mignon*), and Sesti, *Nuovo cinema italiano*, 44–7 and 115–16.

8 Mikhail Mikhailovich Bakhtin, *The Dialogic Imagination: Four Essays*, ed. Michael Holquist, trans. C. Emerson and M. Holquist (Austin: University of Texas Press, 1981), 404.

9 Jonathan Culler, *Flaubert: The Uses of Uncertainty* (Ithaca: Cornell University Press, 1985), 151.

10 Gustave Flaubert, *Sentimental Education*, trans. R. Baldick (Harmondsworth: Penguin, 1980), 419. 'C'est là ce que nous avons eu de meilleur!' *L'Éducation sentimentale*, in *Oeuvres complètes*, ed. Bernard Masson (Paris: Seuil Intégrale, 1964), 2: 163.

11 Mignon's comprehension of sexual intercourse is only inadequate in a linguistic sense: what she is uninformed about is the particular Italian verb that

expresses the action. Giorgio's blindness is, by contrast, a much more far-reaching one: he fails to 'understand' sex because he opts to remove unacceptable facts from his horizon of the events. Typically enough, he understands and uses words – the *tokens* of meaning – with perfect accuracy so long as their *referents* lie outside his own sphere; that is to say, so long as they do not threaten to visit upon him a painful confrontation with reality.

12 In the same vein, 'Chekhov' is misspelled in the bookstore on a sign advertising a sale. This is probably a deliberately ironic choice on Archibugi's part, since the film's late-romantic, crepuscular atmosphere is in many respects Chekhovian.

13 '[E]in *Candide* gegen die Poësie.' Novalis, *Schriften*, 4: 323. Novalis conceived his own *Heinrich von Ofterdingen* (which he never completed) to counter *Wilhelm Meister*.

14 Goethe, *Wilhelm Meister's Apprenticeship*, 373 (book 8, chap. 10). 'Saul ging [aus], seines Vaters Eselinnen zu suchen, und [fand] ein Königreich.' *Wilhelm Meisters Lehrjahre*, 610 (book 8, chap. 10).

15 'Le piante grasse vivono felici, perché si accontentano di poco.'

Chapter 2: Kafka and Fellini

1 Franz Kafka, *The Man Who Disappeared* (*Amerika*), trans. Michael Hofmann (London: Penguin, 1996), 3; emphasis added. This translation, based on the German critical edition of the novel published in the 1980s, is freer and more colloquial, and closer to the original manuscript, than the earlier and still routinely encountered one by Edwin Muir: *Amerika* (New York: New Directions, 1946). Unless otherwise indicated, I will quote from *The Man Who Disappeared* but also give the corresponding page reference to the older, established translation (henceforth *America*, with a *c*).
   'Als ... Karl Roßmann ... in den Hafen von Newyork [*sic*] einfuhr, erblickte er die schon längst beobachtete Statue der Freiheitsgöttin .... Ihr Arm *mit dem Schwert* ragte wie neuerdings empor und um ihre Gestalt wehten die freien Lüfte.' Kafka, *Der Verschollene*, ed. Jost Schillemeit, vol. 1 of *Schriften Tagebücher Briefe. Kritische Ausgabe*, ed. Jürgen Born et al. (Frankfurt am Main: S. Fischer, 1983), 7; emphasis added.

2 Federico Fellini, *Comments on Film*, ed. Giovanni Grazzini, trans. Joseph Henry (Fresno: The Press at California State University Fresno, 1988), 53–4.
   'Un giorno, Marcello Marchesi arrivò da Milano con un libro, *La metamorfosi* ... L'inconscio, che era stato territorio d'indagine e di diagnosi ... in Dostoevskij, qui diventava la materia stessa della rappresentazione ... [Q]ui era l'inconscio individuale, la zona d'ombra, il sottosuolo privato che veniva improvvisamente rischiarato ...

Kafka mi emozionò profondamente. Rimasi colpito da quel suo modo di affrontare l'aspetto misterioso delle cose, la loro indecifrabilità, il senso del labirinto, del quotidiano che diventa magico.'
Intervista sul cinema, ed. Giovanni Grazzini (Bari: Laterza, 1983), 45–6.

3   *The Man Who Disappeared,* 3; *America,* 1.
'Als der siebzehnjährige Karl Roßmann,
    der von seinen armen Eltern nach Amerika geschickt worden war,
        weil ihn ein Dienstmädchen verführt
        und ein Kind von ihm bekommen hatte,
in ... den Hafen von Newyork einfuhr ...'
Der Verschollene, 7.

4   *America,* 120. Muir's 'free' is here more eloquent than Hofmann's 'at liberty' (*The Man Who Disappeared,* 88).

'Dann sind Sie also frei?' fragte sie.
'Ja frei bin ich,' sagte Karl und nichts schien ihm wertloser.

Der Verschollene, 171.

5   For critical references to the *Bildungsroman,* see the previous chapter, note 2.

6   In 1912, at a time when he was working on his American novel (and, among other things, *The Metamorphosis* itself), Kafka wrote to Felice Bauer: '*Sentimental Education* ... is a book that for many years has been as dear to me as are only two or three people; whenever and wherever I open it, I am startled and succumb to it completely, and I always feel as though I were the author's spiritual son, albeit a weak and awkward one. Tell me at once whether you read French.' Letter to Bauer, 15 Nov. 1912, in *Letters to Felice,* ed. Erich Heller and Jürgen Born (New York: Schocken Books, 1973), 42. 'Die *Éducation sentimentale* ... ist ein Buch, das mir durch viele Jahre nahegestanden ist, wie kaum zwei oder drei Menschen; wann und wo ich es aufgeschlagen habe, hat es mich aufgeschreckt und völlig hingenommen, und ich habe mich dann immer als ein geistiges Kind dieses Schriftstellers gefühlt, wenn auch als ein armes und unbeholfenes. Schreib mir sofort, ob Du französisch liest.' *Briefe an Felice,* ed. Erich Heller and Jürgen Born, in *Gesammelte Werke,* ed. Max Brod (Frankfurt am Main: Fischer, 1967), 95–6.

7   For a refreshingly polemical reading of Flaubert's novel – as a means, that is, to question the ideological presuppositions of the entire *Bildungsroman* genre – see Redfield, *Aesthetic Ideology and the* Bildungsroman, 171–200.

8   To Kafka, *Sentimental Education* was a book so admirable that 'it should not have other people's writing in it.' 24 Nov. 1912, in *Letters to Felice,* 63. 'Es ist ein Buch, in das keine fremde Schrift hineingehört.' *Briefe an Felice,* 124.
As a child, Franz confesses to Felice, 'I used to enjoy dreaming of reading aloud to a large, crowded hall ... the whole of the *Sentimental Education* at one

sitting [!], for as many days and nights as it required, in French of course (oh dear, my accent!), and making the walls reverberate.' 4–5 Dec. 1912, *Letters to Felice*, 86. 'Als Kind ... träumte ich gern davon, in einem großen mit Menschen angefüllten Saal ... die ganze *Éducation sentimentale* ohne Unterbrechung so viel Tage und Nächte lang, als sich für notwendig ergeben würde, natürlich französisch (o du meine liebe Aussprache!) vorzulesen und die Wände sollten widerhallen.' *Briefe an Felice*, 155.

9 Kafka and Fellini have been so successful in the creation of what could be termed own-brand types of universe that the two artists share the curiously rare characteristic of having had adjectives – to be sure, of very different meanings – fashioned after their last names and adopted by common parlance.

10 'Optimism' or 'pessimism'? Kafka's intimate friend and first editor, Max Brod, emphasizes that Franz's intention was to lead Karl to final 'redemption' ('Erlösung'), albeit 'not a complete one' ('nicht ganz vollgültig'), due to 'certain contingent circumstances' ('gewisse Nebenumstände'). Franz Kafka, *Amerika. Roman*, ed. Max Brod (Frankfurt am Main: S. Fischer, 1953), 358. On Brod's reading, see more *infra* (note 23).

11 *The Man Who Disappeared*, 154; *America*, 212. 'Karl, der aufstand, sah nun zu, wie Robinson, ohne aufzustehen, sich auf den Bauch herüberwälzte und mit ausgestreckten Händen unter dem Sessel eine versilberte Schale hervorzog, wie sie etwa zum Aufbewahren von Visitkarten dient. Auf dieser Schale lag[en] aber eine halbe ganz schwarze Wurst, einige dünne Cigaretten, eine geöffnete aber noch gut gefüllte und von Öl überfließende Sardinenbüchse und eine Menge meist zerdrückter und zu einem Ballen gewordener Bonbons. Dann erschien noch ein großes Stück Brot und eine Art Parfümflasche, die aber etwas anderes als Parfüm zu enthalten schien.' *Der Verschollene*, 297–8.

12 Some forty years later, a similar effect was specifically thematized by Ionesco's drama *The New Tenant* (*Le nouveau locataire*, 1953).

13 While apparently heterogeneous, the two episodes are in fact not unrelated to the main body of Kafka's narration. First, the street becomes the stage for a political rally that is peculiarly reminiscent of the description of a circus parade. At a minimum a *schadenfroh* dig at democracy, this episode makes a general mockery of the notion of free will as it applies to the human polis. Later, we are informed about a conversation between Karl and his next-balcony neighbour, a student who acts as the sole potential Mentor in the young man's fast imploding *Bildungsroman*. On account of the difficulty of finding jobs of any sort, the student advises Karl to retain the 'position' that he currently holds. This Karl does – again reinforcing a world view permeated by the notion of bondage of the will.

14 *America*, 252 (*The Man Who Disappeared*, 183). 'scheinbar von schweren Träumen geplagt.' *Der Verschollene*, 354.

15 *The Man Who Disappeared*, 184. These sections were not included in Muir's earlier translation. '"Auf! Auf!" rief Robinson, kaum daß Karl früh die Augen öffnete.' *Der Verschollene*, 355.

16 *The Man Who Disappeared*, 199. 'zehn Kartoffelsäcke ... eine ganze Ernte Äpfel.' *Der Verschollene*, 380, 382.

17 *The Man Who Disappeared*, 200–1. 'Wohl ... erschreckte ihn, als er jetzt den Wagen in den Flur schob, der Schmutz, der hier herrschte und den er allerdings erwartet hatte. Es war, wenn man näher zusah, kein faßbarer Schmutz. Der Steinboden des Flurs war fast rein gekehrt, die Malerei der Wände nicht alt, die künstlichen Palmen nur wenig verstaubt, und doch war alles fettig und abstoßend, es war, als wäre von allem ein schlechter Gebrauch gemacht worden und als wäre keine Reinlichkeit mehr imstande, das wieder gut zu machen.' *Der Verschollene*, 384.

18 'Das Teater von Oklahoma [*sic*]. For a useful cross-referencing of sources, see Hartmut Binder, *Kafka-Kommentar zu den Romanen, Rezensionen, Aphorismen und zum Brief an den Vater* (Munich: Winkler, 1976), 152–7.

19 *The Man Who Disappeared*, 207; *America*, 262. 'Legitimationspapiere.' *Der Verschollene*, 400.

20 *The Man Who Disappeared*, 218; *America*, 276. 'Am ersten Tag fuhren sie durch ein hohes Gebirge. Bläulichschwarze Steinmassen giengen in spitzen Keilen bis an den Zug heran, man beugte sich aus dem Fenster und suchte vergebens ihre Gipfel, dunkle schmale zerrissene Täler öffneten sich, man beschrieb mit dem Finger die Richtung, in der sie sich verloren, breite Bergströme kamen eilend als große Wellen auf dem hügeligen Untergrund und in sich tausend kleine Schaumwellen treibend, sie stürzten sich unter die Brücken über die der Zug fuhr und sie waren so nah daß der Hauch ihrer Kühle das Gesicht erschauern machte.' *Der Verschollene*, 418–19.

21 Among the innumerable works that make up the critical corpus on Kafka, I have found the following ones particularly useful: Chris Bezzel, *Kafka-Chronik* (Munich and Vienna: Carl Hanser Verlag, 1975); Wilhelm Emrich, *Franz Kafka* (Bonn: Athenäum Verlag, 1958); Ralf R. Nicolai, *Kafkas Amerika-Roman Der Verschollene: Motive und Gestalten* (Würzburg: Königshausen u. Neumann, 1981); and Jürgen Pütz, *Kafkas Verschollener – ein Bildungsroman?* (Frankfurt am Main: Peter Lang, 1983).

22 Kafka's novel belongs to a long-standing literary tradition depicting the 'journey of salvation,' i.e., an allegorical voyage through the canonical sequence Hell–Purgatory–Paradise, among whose specimens Dante's *Comedy* and Gogol's *Dead Souls* rank foremost. The project of *The Lost One* is peculiarly reminiscent of Chichikov's travels through Russia, if only in consider-

ation of the fact that, while both Gogol and Kafka were entirely successful in tackling 'Hell,' both gave up on trying to complete the paradisian part of their work.

23 Brod characteristically writes: 'It is clear that the novel [*The Man Who Disappeared*] is deeply intertwined with *The Trial* and *The Castle* ... What Kafka has left behind is a *trilogy of solitude*. Estrangement and isolation among human beings are its fundamental themes ... In the three novels the issue is the insertion of the individual into the human community ... What is shown are the dreadful obstacles that, in the process, block the path of precisely that human being who takes care to be good and just. In *The Trial* and in *The Castle* the obstacles take the upper hand ... In the American novel, by contrast, we [can feel] that this good lad, Karl Rossmann, who quickly gains all our sympathy, will, despite all false friendships and perfidious enmities, achieve his goal of proving himself a respectable [*anständig*] human being and of reconciling his parents.'

'Es ist klar, daß der Roman [*Der Verschollene*] mit dem *Prozeß* und *Schloß* ... innig zusammenhängt. Es ist eine *Trilogie der Einsamkeit*, die Kafka hinterlassen hat. Fremdheit, Isoliertheit mitten unter den Menschen sind das Grundthema ... In allen drei Romanen geht es um die Einordnung des Einzelnen in die menschliche Gemeinschaft ... Die ungeheuren Widerstände, die sich gerade dem sorgsam guten und rechtlichen Menschen hierbei entgegensetzen, werden gezeigt. Im *Prozeß* und im *Schloß* überwiegen die Widerstände ... Im Amerika-Roman dagegen [fühlen wir], wie dieser gute Junge Karl Roßmann, der schnell unsere ganze Liebe gewinnt, allen falschen Freundschaften und perfiden Feindschaften zum Trotz, sein Ziel, sich im Leben als anständiger Mensch zu bewähren und die Eltern zu versöhnen, erreichen wird.' Postface to Kafka, *Amerika: Roman*, 357–8.

24 'In each culture of the past lie immense semantic possibilities that have remained undisclosed, unrecognized, and unutilized throughout the entire historical life of a culture. Antiquity itself did not know the antiquity that we know now. There used to be a school joke: the ancient Greeks did not know the main thing about themselves, that they were *ancient* Greeks, and they never called themselves that.' Bakhtin, 'Response to a Question from *Novy Mir*,' in his *Speech Genres and Other Late Essays*, 6.

'В каждой культуре прошлого заложены огромные смысловые возможности, которые остались не раскрытыми, не осознанными и не использованными на протяжении всей исторической жизни данной культуры. Античность сама не знала той античности, которую мы теперь знаем. Существовала школьная шутка: древние греки не знали о себе самого главного, они не знали, что они *древние* греки, и никогда себя так не называли.' 'Otvet na vopros redaktsii "Novogo mira,"' in his *Èstetika slovesnogo tvorcestva*, 333; emphasis in the original.

At the same time, I acknowledge that some critics have chosen to stress the continuity between Kafka and his great European predecessors. See, e.g., Mark Spilka, *Dickens and Kafka: A Mutual Interpretation* (Bloomington: Indiana University Press, 1963).

25 The four options are, I suspect, ultimately equivalent; it is difficult to discern how human language could, at a certain level of abstraction, select among parallel and mutually exclusive ontological notions. It seems to me that what we perceive as different *hypotheses* (the religious, the psychoanalytical, the semiotic, the socio-philosophical) are, in the last analysis, but different *metaphors*, each of which – because there is no supreme arbitration within human language able to rule definitively over any of its parts – should be allowed to stand on an equal footing, with the understanding that none of them is 'really' true, but rather, only figuratively such.

A view all critics would probably agree to about Kafka's American novel is that Karl's emigration indicates an urge for a decent life among decent people in a decent world; that at first only Nothingness responds to his quest; and that, when there finally is a response, the novel suddenly breaks off. Individual readers may prefer to understand and reformulate such emptiness in terms that are most germane to the existential vocabulary each of them cultivates; but the actual wording of their respective formulations is, to my mind, a translation (*meta-phor*) of sorts, not the 'ultimate meaning' of Kafka's original.

26 'Sì, yo creo que, en definitiva, todo lo que uno escribe es autobiográfico. Sólo que eso puede ser dicho: "Nací en tal año, en tal lugar" o "Había un rey que tenía tres hijos."' Jorge Luis Borges, *Borges, el palabrista*, ed. Esteban Peicovich (Madrid: Letra viva, 1980), 21 (1).

27 I am far from proposing a dismissive or reductive critical approach to the complex topic of autobiography. Good texts on the subject include: Michel Beaujour, *Poetics of the Literary Self-Portrait*, trans. Y. Milos (New York: New York University Press, 1991); *Miroirs d'encre: Rhétorique de l'autoportrait* (Paris: Seuil, 1980); Susanna Egan, *Patterns of Experience in Autobiography* (Chapel Hill: University of North Carolina Press, 1984); Robert Elbaz, *The Changing Nature of the Self: A Critical Study of the Autobiographic Discourse* (London: Croom Helm, 1988); Robert Folkenflik, ed., *The Culture of Autobiography: Constructions of Self-Representation* (Stanford, Calif.: Stanford University Press, 1993); Reimar Klein and Rossana Bonadei, eds, *Il testo autobiografico nel Novecento* (Milan: Guerini Studio, 1993); Jacques Lacan, 'The Mirror Stage as Formative of the Function of the I,' in *Ecrits*, trans. A. Sheridan (New York:

Norton, 1977, 1–7; 'Le stade du miroir comme formateur de la fonction du
Je,' in *Écrits I* (Paris: Seuil, 1981 [1966]), 89–97; Philippe Lejeune, *On Autobi-
ography*, ed. Paul John Eakin, trans. K. Leary (Minneapolis: University of
Minnesota Press, 1989; *Le pacte autobiographique* (Paris: Seuil, 1975); Georges
May, *L'autobiographie* (Paris: Presses Universitaires de France, 1984 [1979]);
Günter Niggl, ed., *Die Autobiographie: Zu Form und Geschichte einer literarischen
Gattung* (Darmstadt: Wissenschaftliche Buchgesellschaft, 1989); James
Olney, ed., *Autobiography: Essays Theoretical and Critical* (Princeton, NJ: Prince-
ton University Press, 1980); Roy Pascal, *Design and Truth in Autobiography*
(Cambridge, Mass.: Harvard University Press, 1960); and Jean Starobinski,
L'oeil vivant (Paris: Gallimard, 1970).

28 Fellini anyway deliberately questions the notion of a unified self. See his
comments to Kezich in Tullio Kezich, *Fellini* (Milan: Rizzoli, 1988), 5.

29 Peter Bondanella, 'Dreams and Metacinema,' chapter 4 of his *The Cinema of
Federico Fellini* (Princeton, NJ: Princeton University Press, 1992), 205–13, esp.
211. While the copious, and ever-expanding, critical literature on Fellini
offers titles for all tastes and preferences, I would like to single out here, over
and above those directly quoted in the present chapter, at least the following
(particularly with respect to Fellini's metanarrative practice): Marco Bertozzi, '*Intervista* di F. Fellini: Il Signor Cinema,' in Lino Micciché, ed., *Schermi
opachi: Il cinema italiano degli anni '80* (Venice: Marsilio, 1998), 296–308; Peter
Bondanella, ed., *Federico Fellini: Essays in Criticism* (New York: Oxford University Press, 1978); P. Bondanella and Cristina Degli-Esposti, eds, *Perspectives on
Federico Fellini* (New York: Hall, 1993); Frank Burke, 'Fellini's *Intervista* as
Postcolonial Text,' *Romance Languages Annual* 7 (1995), 212–17; F. Burke,
'*Intervista*,' in his *Fellini's Films: From Postwar to Postmodern* (New York: Prentice
Hall–Twayne, 1996), 274–89; Gilles Ciment, ed., *Federico Fellini* (Paris: Édi-
tions Rivages, 1988); Claudio Giorgio Fava and Aldo Viganò, *I film di Federico
Fellini* (Rome: Gremese, 1995 [1981]), esp. 181–6; Gieri, *Contemporary Italian
Filmmaking*; Tullio Kezich, *Fellini del giorno dopo: Con un alfabetiere felliniano*
(Rimini: Guaraldi–Associazione Fellini, 1996); Ben Lawton, 'Fellini and the
Literary Tradition,' *Italian Journal* 4:3–4 (Sept. 1990), 32–40; Christian Metz,
'*Intervista*,' in his *L'énonciation impersonnelle, ou le site du film* (Paris: Méridiens
Klincksieck, 1991), 105–7; and Mario Verdone, *Federico Fellini* (Florence: La
nuova Italia, 1996).

    A wealth of statements by the director is also contained in the three
volumes of Franca Faldini and Goffredo Fofi (eds): *L'avventurosa storia ...
1935–1959* and *L'avventurosa storia ... 1960–1969* (Milan: Feltrinelli, 1979,
1981); and *Il cinema italiano d'oggi 1970–1984 raccontato dai suoi protagonisti*
(Milan: Mondadori, 1984). Contrary to pattern, only an essay on Fellini, with-

out an interview, is contained in Aldo Tassone, *Parla il cinema italiano* (Milan: Il Formichiere, 1980), 1: 117–36. On the subject of metafiction, see also note 33 below.

30 As alluded to in chapter 1, we owe the concept to Bakhtin (*The Dialogic Imagination*, 404ff.).

31 This is suggested by Fellini as 'competing with God the Father.' *Comments on Film*, 101. 'far concorrenza al Padreterno.' *Intervista sul cinema*, 83.

32 Peculiarly, he bears the same (real) last name as does the (fictional) protagonist of *La dolce vita*, the journalist Marcello Rubini (there played by Marcello Mastroianni).

33 Schlegel defines irony (romantic irony, that is) as 'a permanent digression' ('eine permanente Parekbase'). Friedrich Schlegel, *Philosophische Lehrjahre 1796–1806*, vol. 18 of *Kritische F.-S.-Ausgabe*, ed. Ernst Behler (Munich: Schöningh, 1963), 85 (668).

Fellini's postmodernism and Friedrich Schlegel's ironic (philosophical) romanticism join hands as milestones in a long tradition of self-reflexive textuality, or metafiction. Bondanella's richly informative chapter in *The Cinema of Federico Fellini* should be complemented on the literary watershed by at least the two following items: Robert Alter, *Partial Magic: The Novel as Self-Conscious Genre* (Berkeley: University of California Press, 1975); and Jorge Luis Borges, 'Magías parciales del Quijote,' in *Obras completas* (Barcelona: Emecé, 1989), 2: 45–7. Among the many general publications on metafiction well worth reading are Mark Currie, ed., *Metafiction* (London: Longman, 1995); Lucien Dällenbach, *The Mirror in the Text*, trans. J. Whiteley and E. Hughes (Chicago: University of Chicago Press and Cambridge: Polity Press, 1989); *Le récit spéculaire: Essai sur la mise en abyme* (Paris: Seuil, 1977); Linda Hutcheon, *Narcissistic Narrative: The Metafictional Paradox* (Waterloo, Ont.: Wilfrid Laurier University Press, 1980); Robert Stam, *Reflexivity in Film and Literature: From Don Quixote to Jean-Luc Godard* (Ann Arbor, Mich.: UMI Research Press, 1985); Patricia Waugh, *Metafiction: The Theory and Practice of Self-Conscious Fiction* (London and New York: Methuen, 1984); and Ulrich Wicks, 'Borges, Bertolucci, and Metafiction,' in Syndy M. Conger and Janice R. Welsch, eds, *Narrative Strategies* ([Macomb, Ill.]: Western Illinois University, 1980), 19–35.

34 Translation mine (corresponds to 116 of Fellini, *Comments on film*). 'Davanti all'obbiettivo uno mette solo se stesso.' *Intervista sul cinema*, 94.

35 Fellini, *Comments on Film*, 28. 'Un'opera d'arte nasce in una sua unica espressione; trovo mostruose, ridicole, aberranti [certe] trasposizioni. Le mie preferenze vanno in genere a soggetti originali scritti per il cinema. Io credo che il cinema non abbia bisogno di letteratura, ma ha bisogno soltanto di

autori cinematografici, cioè di gente che si esprima attraverso i ritmi, le cadenze, che sono particolari del cinema. Il cinema è un'arte autonoma che non ha bisogno di trasposizioni su un piano che, nel migliore dei casi, sarà sempre e soltanto illustrativo. Ogni opera d'arte vive nella dimensione in cui è stata concepita e nella quale si è espressa. Che cosa si prende da un libro? Delle situazioni. Ma le situazioni, di per sé, non hanno alcun significato. E' il sentimento con cui queste vengono espresse che conta, la fantasia, l'atmosfera, la luce: in definitiva l'interpretazione di quei fatti. Ora l'interpretazione letteraria di quei fatti non ha nulla a che fare con l'interpretazione cinematografica di quegli stessi fatti. Sono due modi di esprimersi completamente diversi.' *Intervista sul cinema*, 23–4.

36 Fellini makes no bones about his infatuation for Kafka's subject. Kafka's *America* was 'a film [he had] always wanted to make' ('un film che volev[a] fare da sempre'). See Federico Fellini, *Il mestiere di regista: Intervista con F. F.*, ed. Rita Cirio (Milan: Garzanti, 1994), 57. *America* fascinated him ever since he had read the book. See Fellini, *Raccontando di me* (Rome: Editori Riuniti, 1996 [1995]), 206. (As is frequently and sadly the case in the field, the English translation cuts off the original just when the ship starts sailing – here, just before Kafka is mentioned. See *Fellini on Fellini*, ed. Costanzo Costantini, trans. S. Sorooshian [London and Boston: Faber and Faber, 1995], 154.)

Elsewhere, after confirming at length the reasons why directors had better stay clear of literary sources, Fellini goes on to confess that literature, 'who knows why,' *was* on occasion inspirational for him – as in the case of Petronius's *Satyricon*. Fellini, *Fare un film* (Turin: Einaudi, 1980), 100–1.

37 Federico Fellini, *Block-notes di un regista* (Milano: Longanesi, 1988), 83.

38 'due giovanetti aggraziati e rispettosi.' Fellini, *Block-notes*, 121.

39 'Sono andata dappertutto: conservatori, biblioteche, istituti religiosi; ambasciata polacca, ungherese, cecoslovacca, tutte le ho girate, beh se fra questi non c'è ancora il vostro personaggio allora non ho mica capito cosa vuole!' Ibid., 153.

40 'Maurì, Brunelda è bionda però.' Ibid., 92. (As her name suggests, however, this is unlikely to have been Kafka's original perception.)

41 'Sì, ho capito, dev' essere bionda, ma mo' vo' vedé pure le more.' Ibid., 143.

42 'Mangia, dorme, e fa sempre l'amore, non c'ha mica torto!' Ibid., 144.

43 'Io il nudo non lo faccio! Lo dico con tutto il rispetto per il signor Fellini ma io il nudo non lo faccio! Non perché non lo potrei fare eh, perché ancora ...' Ibid., 145.

44 *Maurizio*. 'Guarda me! Una maschera impressionante: di perversità, di ferocia, ma anche di dolcezza.'

Mostra l'espressione a una magnifica ragazza in blazer bianco generosamente aperto sui seni e gli occhiali da sole alzati sulla fronte.

'Ascoltami, devi essere animalesca, belluina ... Ah ecco, la narice che palpita: *fondamentale.* Fídati; la narice che palpita può risolvere tutto.'

La ragazza annuisce con buona volontà. Ibid., 146.

45 Other slight differences worth mentioning are the following: (1) Unlike Fellini's, Kafka's Robinson shows no particular self-complacency in eating sardines; he eats them just as any brute such as himself spontaneously would. (2) In the novel, Brunelda's transportation in the early hours of the day happens through the streets of a city; in the film, it occurs in a deserted countryside.

46 As is characteristic of editions preceding the critical one of 1983, the Italian text used by Fellini is seriously problematic. It includes all events in Delamarche's apartment as 'Chapter Seven'; it leaps, without a transition, to the Theatre of Oklahoma, which it numbers as 'Chapter Eight'; and it closes with the train-ride episode, *only then* proceeding to give the bath drama and Brunelda's departure as appended fragments – *i.e., out of sequence.* In other words, this particular edition discourages, or even defeats, all attempts at a diachronic reading of Karl's psychological situation as it evolves in the (admittedly unfinished) novel. Cf. Franz Kafka, *America*, trans. Alberto Spaini, in *Romanzi*, ed. Ervino Pocar (Milan: Mondadori, 1969). In Italy, too, a new translation was recently published: Franz Kafka, *America o Il disperso*, ed. and trans. Umberto Gandini (Milan: Feltrinelli, 1996).

47 'una ferrovia sopraelevata di una città americana.' *Block-notes*, 155.

48 *Ora il paesaggio cambia. Nel rombo dell'acqua che precipita, vediamo il vapore luminoso di una grandiosa cascata diffondersi sul verde intenso della vegetazione. Sergio Rubini si sposta per ammirarla dal finestrino di Antonella ... Un velo di acqua polverizzata arriva ad appannare il vetro dietro al quale scompare il volto della ragazza ...*

Notarianni/Gerarca. 'Niagara, Niagara! Come vedete, caro giovanotto, l'Italia non ha niente da invidiare a nessuno! Neanche in fatto di cascate!' Ibid., 103–4.

49 *Il paesaggio è ancora cambiato. Le coste* [creste?] *frastagliate di una catena di monti sfilano oltre i finestrini.*

Il tranvetto entra in una specie di forra, un passaggio angusto tra due pareti di roccia nuda ...

Manovratore (ai passeggeri). 'Signori, guardate lassù! Gli indiani!' Ibid., 104.

A subject of inquiry that is adjacent to the Kafka connection, though not identical with it, is Fellini's verifiable biographical interaction with 'America'

(= the USA). Readers interested in evidence about Fellini's relationship with the real country – as opposed to Kafka's symbolic one – will find the director's own statements on the topic in Fellini, *Comments on Film*, 113–20; *Intervista sul cinema*, 92–8; also rpt. as a separate chapter in *Block-notes*, 61–5.

50 This can be confirmed by verifying Fellini's appropriate source in Italian: 'Il primo giorno [di viaggio] passarono in mezzo ad alte montagne. Cumuli di pietre nero-azzurrognole scendevano a cono appuntito fino al treno, chi si sporgeva dal finestrino cercava invano le cime; valli scure, strette, frastagliate si aprivano e si perdevano in direzioni che i viaggiatori seguivano col dito, larghi torrenti scendevano dai monti, correvano sul fondo accidentato con le onde gonfie, sormontate da mille creste di schiuma, si infilavano sotto i ponti sui quali passava il treno, ed erano così vicini che il soffio della loro frescura faceva rabbrividire.' Kafka, *America*, in *Romanzi*, 293.

51 'una mangia-uomini.' *Block-notes*, 144. Nowhere is she so defined by Kafka, however.

52 *'The beautiful, opulent lady is entirely wrapped in a large orange-coloured bathrobe and wears on her head, turban-style, a towel of the same colour.'* 'La bella opulenta signora è tutta avvolta in un grande accappatoio arancione, con in testa a mo' di turbante un asciugamano dello stesso colore.' Ibid., 162.

   The film is powerfully colour-coded: the precise shade of Anita Ekberg's orange attire refers us back not to Kafka's Brunelda (who wears red), but *to the FID's many would-be ones* (who all wear bright orange dresses for their screen tests).

53 'E' mitica!' Ibid., 165.

54 In his real-life interview with Grazzini, Fellini speaks at length about his involvement with Jungian philosophy. Fellini, *Comments on Film*, 162–7; *Intervista sul cinema*, 129–32.

55 Friedrich Nietzsche, *Beyond Good and Evil: Prelude to a Philosophy of the Future*, trans. H. Zimmern, vol. 12 of *Complete Works*, ed. Oscar Levy (New York: Russell and Russell, 1964 [1909–11]), 100 (Apophthegms and Interludes 4, 169). 'Viel von sich reden kann auch ein Mittel sein, sich zu verbergen.' *Jenseits von Gut und Böse*, vol. 5 of *Sämtliche Werke. Kritische Studienausgabe in fünfzehn Einzelbänden*, ed. Giorgio Colli and Mazzino Montinari (Munich: dtv and Berlin: de Gruyter, 1988), 102 (Sprüche und Zwischenspiele 4, 169).

56 My use of the Möbius strip as an icon by which to conceptualize Fellini's artistic method is but a cognitive metaphor – and I do not, of course, claim for metaphors the status of mathematical proofs. I do, however, believe (see note 25 above) that they are useful, indeed indispensable tools for human beings' existential self-reflection. Not coincidentally perhaps, it is, at the

latest, since Immanuel Kant that Western thought has abandoned previous attempts to handle the existential realm of experience by means of axiom-based argumentation. The field is, at any rate, vast (metaphor by all means intended), and for an effective survey of its most recent implications I refer interested readers to Michael Hanne, 'Getting to Know the Neighbors: When Plot Meets Knot,' *Narrative Chunnels*, special issue of *Canadian Review of Comparative Literature/ Revue Canadienne de Littérature Comparée* 26:1 (March 1999), 35–50.

57 *O mi ya ge* (Jap.) = souvenir brought back from afar.

58 We are informed about this incident by Fellini's own voice-over; the voice does not, however, specify just which producer it is alluding to. Rizzoli, it turns out, was the culprit – on the eve of the shooting of *La dolce vita*, according to one version (Kezich, *Fellini*, 276), or after *8½*, according to Fellini himself (*Il mestiere di regista*, 95). On the other hand, Gianfranco Angelucci, who co-authored with Fellini the script of *Intervista*, unhesitatingly asserts that on Fellini's mind were the producers of *La strada*, Ponti and De Laurentiis (private communication to the author, October 1995). A definitive solution to this peculiarly Fellinian riddle may well be beyond our reach – and beside the point. In the last analysis, our inability to pin down the anecdote to any single context seems to be entirely consistent with the *sui generis* concept of veracity that we see dominate the Fellinian universe.

59 'Selbsterkenntnis hat nur das Böse.' Kafka, 21 November 1917, in *Hochzeits-vorbereitungen auf dem Lande und andere Prosa aus dem Nachlaß*, ed. Max Brod (New York: Schocken Books, 1953), 84.

60 *Comments on Film*, 19. I am approximating the Italian *ascesi* (gr. *askêsis*, 'training') with 'a long process of self-discipline,' instead of using the translator's (incorrect) 'ascent.' 'In quella favoletta orientale sull'apprendista stregone, il libro della sapienza, al quale [l'apprendista] arriva al termine di una lunga ascesi, è composto di fogli che sono specchi; cioè, l'unica possibilità di conoscere è conoscersi.' *Intervista sul cinema*, 17.

61 I am not referring to *all* conceptions of art, but only to a particular, dualist one. From a theoretical background partially different from mine, Leo Bersani makes a persuasive and thought-provoking point on this subject: 'I want to show that ... apparently acceptable views of art's beneficently reconstructive function in culture depend on a devaluation of historical experience and of art [itself]. The catastrophes of history matter much less if they are somehow compensated for in art, and art itself gets reduced to a kind of superior patching function, [if] enslaved to those very materials to which it presumably imparts value.' *The Culture of Redemption* (Cambridge, Mass.: Harvard University Press, 1990), 1.

Chapter 3: Gogol and Lattuada

1 'C'est horrible et ce n'est pas sérieux.' Eugène Ionesco (1960), *Notes et contrenotes* (Paris: Gallimard, 1966), 166.

2 Gr. ἄ-κακος = 'innocent,' 'harmless'; hence *Akakii,* the (admittedly rare) name of a saint in the Russian Orthodox tradition. Gogol's penchant for the grotesque seized upon the less than spiritual associations phonetically suggested by the name.

A good start-up bibliography on *Shinel'* could be the following: Boris Eichenbaum, 'How Gogol's Overcoat Is Made' [1918–24], in Robert A. Maguire, ed. and trans., *Gogol from the Twentieth Century: Eleven Essays* (Princeton, NJ: Princeton University Press, 1974), 267–91, and 'How Gogol's Overcoat Is Made' (a different translation), in Elizabeth Trahan, ed., *Gogol's Overcoat: An Anthology of Critical Essays* (Ann Arbor, Mich.: Ardis, 1982), 21–36; Victor Erlich, 'Gogol and Kafka: Note on "Realism" and "Surrealism,"' in Morris Halle et al., eds, *For Roman Jakobson. Essays on the Occasion of His Sixtieth Birthday* (The Hague: Mouton, 1956), 100–8; Victor Erlich, *Gogol* (New Haven, Conn.: Yale University Press, 1969); Vasilii Vasil'evich Gippius, *Gogol,* ed. and trans. Robert A. Maguire (Ann Arbor, Mich.: Ardis, 1981); *Gogol'* (Leningrad: Mysl', 1924; anastatic repr.: Providence, RI: Brown University Press, 1963); Simon Karlinsky, *The Sexual Labyrinth of Nikolai Gogol* (Cambridge, Mass.: Harvard University Press, 1976); and Vsevolod Setschkareff, *N. V. Gogol: Leben und Schaffen* (Berlin and Wiesbaden: Harrassowitz, 1953). Alphabetically last, but certainly far from least, one can recommend the short and sharp article 'Gogol'' by Tolstoy, in Lēv Nikolaevich Tolstoi, *Polnoe sobranie sochinenii* (Moscow and Leningrad: Khudozhestvennaia literatura, 1936), 38: 50–1. For further titles on specific subjects, see below.

3 *Puppet* would be a more precise word. After all, European romanticism – Brentano (*Gockel, Hinkel and Gackeleia*), E.T.A. Hoffmann (*The Sandman / Der Sandmann*) and Kleist (*On the Puppet Theater / Über das Marionettentheater*) are the first names that come to mind – was generally mesmerized by models of a quasi-human shape unencumbered by the factory defects of the Adamitic race. Some time later, Collodi's Pinocchio was, of course, the most successful 'puppet' to come along in modern times.

4 For a comprehensive overview of 'humane' vs. 'formal' interpretations of the novella, see F.C. Driessen, *Gogol as a Short-Story Writer: A Study of His Technique of Composition,* trans. Ian F. Finlay (The Hague: Mouton, 1965); and Trahan, ed., *Gogol's Overcoat.*

5 The critical work best highlighting Gogol's tormented personality is Abram Terts / Andrei Siniavsky, *V teni Gogolia* (London: Collins, Overseas Publica-

tions Interchange, 1975), of which there exists a French translation (though, so far, not an English one): *Dans l'ombre de Gogol,* trans. G. Nivat (Paris: Seuil, 1978).

6 On the larger frame of conservative romantic Utopia, see Carlo Testa, 'Being Outside Time: Gogol, Brentano, and Literary Utopia,' *Germano-Slavica* 9: 1–2 (1995–6), 103–24.

7 The suggestion was put forward by Konstantin Vasil'evich Mochul'skii, *Dukhovnyi put' Gogolia* (Paris: YMCA Press, 1976 [1934]), 59.

8 This is not what Gogol *believed*; this is the perception that he *expressed* in his art. He was, at any rate, deeply religious – so deeply, in fact, that he took the ontological view of the Evil One altogether literally.

9 Persian Zoroastrianism, in fact, preceded Gnostic-Manichaean doctrines in this path. Priscillian, an early Christian mystic, bishop in Spain (Galicia), seems to have been influenced – for all his official rejection of it – by the dualism of Manichaean thought. He was put on trial, found guilty of heresy, and executed at Trier in AD 385, the first Christian martyr to become one at the hands of his own hierarchy. On Priscillian's life and works, see Virginia Burrus, *The Making of a Heretic: Gender, Authority, and the Priscillianist Controversy* (Berkeley: University of California Press, 1995); Henry Chadwick, *Priscillian of Avila: The Occult and the Charismatic in the Early Church* (Oxford: Clarendon Press, 1976); and Benedikt Vollmann, *Studien zum Priszillianismus: Die Forschung, die Quellen, der fünfzehnte Brief Papst Leos des Großen* (St Ottilien: Eos Verlag, 1965).

10 This suggestion can and should, I believe, be usefully complemented by the insights of psychoanalysis, which have revealed a wealth of primal subconscious components under the devil's deceptively unified appearance. While books on demonology are legion, the best psychoanalytic reading of Gogol in this connection is without contest Daniel Rancour-Laferrière's *Out From Under Gogol's Overcoat: A Psychoanalytic Study* (Ann Arbor, Mich.: Ardis, 1982). See also, by the same author, a comprehensive account of the uses of puppetification in Gogol: 'All the World's a *Vertep*: The Personification/Depersonification Complex in Gogol's *Sorochinskaia iarmarka*,' *Harvard Ukrainian Studies* 6:3 (Sept. 1982), 339–71.

11 The most important introduction to the subject in English is Marcus, *Italian Cinema in the Light of Neorealism.* In Italian, see the indispensable, many times updated and reissued comprehensive anthology edited by Lino Micciché, *Il neorealismo cinematografico italiano* (Venice: Marsilio, 1999 [1978, 1974]).

12 Good biographical accounts on Lattuada can be found in Edoardo Bruno, *Alberto Lattuada* (Rome: Edizioni Cinecittà International, 1993); Claudio

Camerini, *Alberto Lattuada* (Florence: La nuova Italia, 1982); Faldini and Fofi, eds, *1935–1959*, 48–9; and Tassone, *Parla il cinema italiano*, 1: 141–51.

13 In the first years of Lattuada's career, the adjective 'calligraphic' (hence, aestheticizing and therefore decadent) was brandished against him by some critics. The epithet unwittingly uncovers real reason for praise: most of the director's films can indeed count on exquisite photography – not surprisingly, since Lattuada made his debut as a photographer before turning to motion pictures. For Lattuada's own position toward this (and some later) critical labels, see the interviews contained in Camerini, *Alberto Lattuada*, 10–11, and Tassone, 1: 154–5ff.

14 *Giacomo the Idealist* (*Giacomo l'idealista*, 1943), from Emilio De Marchi (1897); *The Arrow in the Flesh* (*La freccia nel fianco*, 1945), from Luciano Zuccoli (1913); *Giovanni Episcopo's Crime* (*Il delitto di Giovanni Episcopo*, 1947), from Gabriele D'Annunzio (1891); *The Mill on the River Po* (*Il mulino del Po*, 1949), from Riccardo Bacchelli (1938–40); and *The She-Wolf* (*La lupa*, 1952), from Giovanni Verga (1880).

15 *Anna* (1951); *White, Red and …* (*Bianco, rosso e …*, 1972).

16 *The Bandit* (*Il bandito*, 1946); *Merciless* (*Senza pietà*, 1948); *Variety Lights* (*Luci del varietà*, with Fellini, 1950); *Elementary School* (*Scuola elementare*, 1955).

17 *Italian Men Turn Their Heads* (*Gli italiani si voltano*, 1953), an episode in *Love in the City* (*L'amore in città*), a film collectively authored by Lattuada with Antonioni, Fellini, Risi, Lizzani, Maselli, and Zavattini.

18 *The Beach* (*La spiaggia*, 1954); *Don Juan in Sicily* (*Don Giovanni in Sicilia*, 1967), from Vitaliano Brancati; *The Girlfriend* (*L'amica*, 1969); *Come Have Coffee … with Us* (*Venga a prendere il caffè … da noi*, 1970), from Piero Chiara's *La spartizione*; and *Oh Serafina!* (1976), from Giuseppe Berto.

19 *Letters by a Novice* (*Lettere di una novizia*, 1960), from Guido Piovene; *The Mishap* (*L'imprevisto*, 1961); *Mafioso* (1962); and *It Was I Who Did It* (*Sono stato io*, 1973).

20 *Matchless* (1967) and *Fräulein Doktor* (1969).

21 *The Mandrake* (*La mandragola*, 1965), from Machiavelli.

22 Along with *Il cappotto*, from Gogol, also *The Storm* (*La tempesta*, 1958), from Pushkin; *The Steppe* (*La steppa*, 1962), from Chekhov; and *Heart of a Dog* (*Cuore di cane*, 1976), from Bulgakov. On all these, see the corresponding sections in my *Italian Cinema and Modern European Literatures*.

23 *Gwendalin* (*Guendalina*, 1957); *Sweet Illusions* (*I dolci inganni*, 1960); *I'll Act as Her Father* (*Le farò da padre*, 1974); *As You Are* (*Così come sei*, 1978); and *Cicada* (*La cicala*, 1980).

24 Two anthologies of Lattuada's writings (with some overlaps in their choice of texts) bear out this aspect with particular clarity. Leopardi inspires Lattuada

to look at the many delusions – in particular, the ideology of scientific progress – perennially misleading humans into pursuing false objectives; Gogol guides him in his exploration of the path by which evil can transform the world into a monstrous zoo; and Kafka offers him the model for a sober depiction of the plight of small human cogs in a faceless and nameless social machine. Lattuada, *L'occhio di Dioniso: Racconti, ricordi, lettere d'amore* (Florence: La casa Usher, 1990); and *Il mio Set: Qualche sogno, qualche verità, una curiosità illimitata*, ed. Vito Zagarrio (Ragusa: Libroitaliano, 1995).

25 By what seems – but perhaps is not – a coincidence, Gogol was himself a Southerner (a Ukraininan) who had emigrated to the northern city of St Petersburg, and never quite felt at home there.

26 Cesare Zavattini, *Sequences from a Cinematic Life*, trans. W. Weaver (Englewood Cliffs, NJ: Prentice-Hall, 1970), 15–16.

Soprabito Nuovo, febbraio 1947 – E' il primo capo di vestiario che mi sono fatto dopo la guerra, indossato una mattina di marzo, felice, o quasi perché avevo un paio di scarpe indegne di questo soprabito. Sul giornale non c'erano fatti gravi quel giorno, potevo godere in pace la inaugurazione ...

A un tratto incontrai Giuseppe Ungaretti. Veniva avanti calmo, col suo assistente Barlozzini. Bello, disse. Barlozzini convenne che il soprabito era bello. Ungaretti aggiunse che era soffice e con calma dolcissima: 'Io non ce l'ho.' Lo disse senza invidia. Risposi che lui mi toglieva il piacere di possederlo, cercai di svalutare la qualità del soprabito, e che lo avevo comperato a rate. Intanto continuava a passare la mano sulla stoffa come accarezzasse un agnello. Ci salutammo, dovrei forse mandargliene a casa una manica cristianamente? Quanti poeti sono vissuti in miseria. Vogliono la gloria? Abbiano la gloria, gloria e soprabito è troppo.

Cesare Zavattini, *Straparole*, in *Opere. 1931–1986*, ed. Silvana Cirillo, intro. Luigi Malerba (Milan: Bompiani, 1991), 423–4.

The fact that Zavattini writes in February 1947 about a garment he 'inaugurated' almost a year before ('March') – is in itself further proof of the epoch-making relevance of such an event in that historical context. (For the record, the diary entry *also* testifies in lively fashion to the divergence in political ideas between Zavattini and Ungaretti.)

27 On the vexed question of the actual extent of Zavattini's contribution to the script, see Lattuada's account in Faldini and Fofi, eds, *1935–1959*, 261, versus Micciché in Alberto Lattuada, *Il cappotto: La storia, lo stile, il senso*, ed. Lino Micciché (Turin: Ass. Philip Morris Progetto Cinema – Museo Nazionale del Cinema – Lindau, [1995]), 34. Henceforward quoted as Lattuada, ed. Micciché.

28 Lattuada discusses at some length his own understanding of *Shinel'* (which can be squarely placed among the 'humane' readings carried out by the Russian nineteenth-century populists), along with details of the film's production, in Faldini and Fofi, eds, *1935–1959*, 261–2, and Tassone, 1: 161–2.

29 See, most explicitly, Vito Zagarrio, 'Il tessuto del *Cappotto*: Idee sulla regia di Lattuada,' in Lattuada, ed. Miccichè, 74. The article is identically reprinted in V.Z., *Messi in scena: Analisi filmologiche di autori eccellenti* (Ragusa: Libroitaliano, 1996).

30 Even in the latest publication on *Il cappotto*, just quoted, the critics who analyse the film do not analyse the novella, and the one Slavist who analyses *Shinel'* does not analyse the film. Inevitably, the differences between the two are overlooked; but that ought to be, to a large extent, the very point of the exercise.

31 Nikolai Gogol, *The Overcoat*, in *The Complete Tales*, trans. C. Garnett, ed. and rev. Leonard Kent (Chicago: The University of Chicago Press, 1985), 304–5.

В департаменте ... но лучше не называть в каком департаменте. Ничего нет сердитее всякого рода департаментов, полков, канцелярий и, словом, всякого рода должностных сословий. Теперь уже всякой частный человек считает в лице своем оскорбленным всё общество. Говорят, весьма недавно поступила просьба от одного капитана-исправника, не помню какого-то города, в которой он излагает ясно, что гибнут государственные постановления и что священное имя его произносится решительно всуе. А в доказательство приложил к просьбе преогромнейший том какого-то романтического сочинения, где, чрез каждые десять страниц, является капитан-исправник, местами даже совершенно в пьяном виде. Итак, во избежание всяких неприятностей, лучше департамент, о котором идет дело, мы назовем *одним департаментом*. Итак, *в одном департаменте* служил *один чиновник* ...

Gogol', *Shinel'*, in *Povesti*, vol. 3 of *Polnoe sobranie sochinenii* [hereafter *PSS*] (Moscow and Leningrad: Izdatel'stvo Akademii Nauk SSSR, 1938), 141; emphasis in the original.

It would seem that Gogol's narrative voice would be *the* impregnable linguistic feature par excellence. Perhaps so; but Gogol challenged Èizenshtein immensely, and the director had a lot to say about his great predecessor. Thus, the good news is that there exists the transcript of a seminar that Èizenshtein taught on *The Overcoat* in 1936, as well as the first draft of an article he was planning to write in 1941. The bad news is that (to my knowledge) both items are so far only available in the post-Soviet journal that originally published them, or in an Italian translation from the 1990s: 'Le straordinarie avventure del *Cappotto*' ('O *Shineli* N. V. Gogolia'), in Èizenshtein, *Stili di regia*, 119–44, and 'Gogol' e il linguaggio cinematografico' ('Gogol' i kinoiazyk'), ibid., 145–64 (all these are editorial titles).

32 On nonsense and comic alogism in Gogol, see Aleksander Slonimsky, 'The Technique of the Comic in Gogol,' in Maguire, ed., *Gogol from the Twentieth Century*, 323–73; Aleksandr Slonimskii, *Tekhnika komicheskogo u Gogolia* (Petrograd: Academia, 1923; anastatic repr., Providence, RI: Brown University Press, 1963).

33 On the cultural ambiguities of the Western-style capital city imposed by Peter I upon Russia in an utterly unfavourable geographical setting, see Iurii M. Lotman, 'The Symbolism of St Petersburg,' in his *Universe of the Mind: A Semiotic Theory of Culture*, trans. A. Shukman, intro. Umberto Eco (London and New York: I.B. Tauris, 1990), 191–202; 'Simvolika Peterburga,' in his *Vnutri mysliashchikh mirov: Chelovek – Tekst – Semiosfera – Istoriia* (Moscow: Yazyki russkoi kul'tury, 1996), 275–95. Robert A. Maguire portrays Gogol's uneasy relation to St Petersburg in *Exploring Gogol* (Stanford, Calif.: Stanford University Press, 1994), 74–80. Rancour-Laferrière does likewise in *Out From Under Gogol's Overcoat* (54ff.), then proceeds to show how the tailor Petrovich's own demonism reflects on the city where he lives (and, indeed, vice versa). For Petrovich as a devil, see note 47 below.

34 The 'warm steam' scene has no *direct* equivalent in Gogol, though it does indirectly transpose Gogol's recurrent rantings about St Petersburg's foul weather. It should be noted, however, that from the very start of our parallel narrations we can find a considerable hiatus between a grotesque original and a compassionate reinterpretation of it.

The original idea for the scene in the film has been claimed by Luigi Malerba, who defines it as 'more Zavattinian than Zavattini.' 'Memorie di uno sceneggiatore e assistente alla regia,' in Lattuada, ed. Miccichè, 21.

35 It is, however, incongruous of the film to make Carmine look as though he were able to influence the outcome of their applications for old-age pensions: in Italy, these could never have been (mis)handled locally. Neorealism, yes, but of the fantastic sort.

36 While the use of an unequivocally southern name and last name stresses the protagonist's status as an immigrant and a stranger, there is a further and more complex reason to the mix of backgrounds in *Il cappotto* (northern city, southern clerk, Tuscan tailor): namely, the intention to avoid a regionalist aesthetic. See Mino Argentieri, 'Uno dalle "mezze maniche" da Pietroburgo a Pavia,' in Lattuada, ed. Miccichè, 58.

37 This is the so-called first 'humane passage' in the short story. *The Overcoat*, 307; *PSS* 3: 143–4.

38 *The Overcoat*, 308. 'переменить заглавный титул, да переменить кое-где глаголы из первого лица в третье.' *PSS* 3: 144.

39 *The Overcoat*, 307. 'свой разнообразный и приятный мир.' *PSS* 3: 144.

40 *The Overcoat*, 308. 'ел всё это с мухами и со всем тем, что ни посылал Бог на ту пору.' *PSS* 3: 145.

41 *The Overcoat*, 309–10. 'сильный враг всех, получающих четыреста рублей в год жалованья, или около того: наш северный мороз.' *PSS* 3: 147.

42 *The Overcoat*, 310; emphasis added. '*Подумал* ... не заключается ли каких грехов в его шинели ... *рассмотрел* ее хорошенько ... *открыл*, что ... она сделалась точная сепянка ... *решил*, что шинеь нужно будет снести к Петровичу.' *PSS* 3: 147–8; emphasis added.

Gogol uses here the word *grekh* ('sin') in the sense of 'defect.' This usage is entirely metonymical; by mixing the religious and the ridiculous, he creates a grotesquely allusive ambiguity.

43 To the end of the film, Lattuada's Mayor remains nameless and frozen in his office, defined solely by his social function. It has been astutely pointed out that this is entirely in keeping with the director's roots in German expressionism (on which see Argentieri, in Lattuada, ed. Micciché, 58; and Callisto Cosulich, '"Occhio quadrato" puntato in direzione Nord,' in Lattuada, ed. Micciché, 49–56). If I thus spell 'Mayor' with a capital M, this is less to honour the character's hardly majuscule moral stature than, by adopting one of the defining stylemes of expressionism, to formalize an important cultural heritage in the film.

44 The EUR area was developed by the regime in view of the world exhibition to be held on its twentieth anniversary in 1942 (hence the acronym, *Esposizione Universale Roma*). Given his training as an architect, Lattuada was particularly well placed to elaborate on the matter.

While, for today's viewers, a heavy rhetorical imprint positions the Mayor's speeches somewhere between the unwittingly comic and the pathetic, this was not the case in 1952 – barely seven years after the fall of Fascism (and still very much in the age of cold war propaganda).

45 The numbers do add up: in 1911–12 Italy was at war with Turkey over Libya, and the film was made in 1952.

46 As is proper in literature and film as distinct media, Akaky had arrived at the momentous decision by interior self-examination; Carmine is led to it by the dynamics of a visible process.

47 As of Akaky's very arrival, there are a number of symbolic signposts in Gogol's text which show that all is not according to the cosmic order in and around Petrovich's home. Akaky arrives not by way of the main entrance, but from the back stairs; and these stairs, the narrator keenly observes, 'to do

them justice, were all soaked with water and slops and saturated through and through with that smell of ammonia which [bites] the eyes, and is, as is well known, inseparable from the backstairs of St Petersburg houses.' *The Overcoat*, 311. 'надобно отдать справедливость, была вся умащена водой, помоями и проникнута насквозь тем спиртуозным запахом, который ест глаза и, как известно, присутствует неотлучно на всех черных лестницах петербургских домов.' *PSS* 3: 148.

In a similar fashion, everything seems demonically aberrant about Petrovich: his deformed toenail, his pierced snuffbox, his recurrent cursing, his inflexible pride, and so forth. With respect to his origin, he is a freed serf – a status that, if consulted, the devil (particularly the Promethean devil of romanticism) would likely embrace as an appropriate self-description. Furthermore, he has a habit of getting drunk on each and every Sunday or religious festivity. An earlier version of the short story (which does not appear in the Kent edition) is even more sarcastically explicit on Petrovich's blasphemous habit of pulling out the bottle at the slightest hint of a cross in the calendar: 'From this side, Petrovich was strongly tied to religion' ('С этой стороны Петрович был сильно привязан к религии.' *PSS* 3: 449).

For Petrovich as a devil, see Dmitry Chizhevsky, 'About Gogol's *Overcoat*,' in Maguire, ed., *Gogol from the Twentieth Century*, 319–21; and, more extensively, Rancour-Laferrière, *Out From Under Gogol's Overcoat*, 58–77 (Petrovich as devil, alien, related to things done *backwards*); 165–77 (Petrovich as phallic, castrating); 181–7 (Petrovich as a 'paternal trickster'). In Gogol, in other words, Petrovich is surrounded by demonic allusions copiously scattered about by the narrator, whereas in Lattuada, *pace* Andrea's persuasion to stand at an incomparably higher creative level than his customer, clerk and tailor are portrayed as two equally poor devils.

48 That said, *both* Akaky and Carmine peculiarly combine elements of the puppet, the clown, and the holy fool (*iuródivyi*). They can perhaps best be described by the category of *social outsiders* in literature, of whom Bakhtin writes that it is their privilege 'to be "other" in this world' (*The Dialogic Imagination*, 159–61). At this particular juncture, the Bakhtinian outsider once again applies an uncomprehending glance that relativizes and 'makes strange' the certainties ossified (automatized) by habit.

49 *The Overcoat*, 317. 'куницы не купили, потому что была точно дорогà, а вместо ее выбрали кошку лучшую, какая только нашлась в лавке, кошку, которую издали можно было всегда принять за куницу.' *PSS* 3: 155.

50 'Всё не так и не то – тут-то и скрывается чорт.' Terts/Siniavsky, *V teni Gogolia*, 530.

51 *The Overcoat*, 319. 'внутреннее удовольствие.' *PSS* 3: 157.

52 *The Overcoat*, 318. 'обогнувши кривым переулком.' *PSS* 3: 157. Demonically enough, the adjective *krivoi* – with its entire gamut of connotations: 'curved,' 'slanted,' 'one-eyed,' and hence figuratively also 'crooked' – is dropped in the Kent edition. (To be sure, a 'twisting shortcut' strikes one as a spasmodically Gogolian oxymoron, necessitated by the devil's constitutive inability to travel straight paths.)

53 'He absolutely must have a glass of champagne in honor of the new coat ... They made Akaky Akakievich drink two glasses.' *The Overcoat*, 321. 'Непременно надо выпить, в честь обновки, по бокалу шампанского ... Акакия Акакиевича заставили выпить два бокала.' *PSS* 3: 160.

54 *The Overcoat*, 321. 'что уже двенадцать часов и что давно пора домой.' *PSS* 3: 160.

55 'Ci sono 295 bolli nella supplica ... Ecco, qui ci sono un sacco di cose che non vanno bene. E fuori nevica, e hanno freddo, e si bagnano. I pensionati coi bambini piccoli, i disoccupati ... Ecco, qui c'è la supplica. La legga [signor Sindaco]. Perché se non le legge nessuno le suppliche ...' Scenes 340–4.

56 By far the most comprehensive treatment of the carnivalesque time when social barriers are momentarily suspended is to be found in Bakhtin's seminal work on Rabelais: *Rabelais and His World*, trans. H. Iswolsky (Bloomington: Indiana University Press, 1984 [1968]); *Tvorcestvo Fransua Rable i narodnaia kul' tura srednevekov'ia i Renessansa* (Moscow: Khudozhestvennaia literatura, 1990 [1965]).

57 On the scandalous impropriety of juxtaposing Akaky's Passion with Christ's, suffice it to remember – *Diabolus simia Dei* – that demonic imitations are always, by definition, imperfect parodies of their model (and to that extent also self-parodies). In Terts/Siniavsky's terms, they are inevitably 'wrong and out of place'; that is the very essence of their demonic nature.

58 *Carmine*. 'Guardia, guardia, aiuto, al ladro! Se gli corre appresso lo prende.' / *Guardia*. 'Eh ma ... io smonto adesso. E' sette ore che pedalo, caro mio. E poi ho i reumatismi.' / *Carmine*. 'Ma scusi, che guardia è lei'? / *Guardia*. 'Ah, forse lei non è pratico, ma io sono un vigile notturno. Vada lì al commissariato, in fondo a destra.' / *Carmine* (*piangendo*). 'Il mio cappotto!' Sc. 376.

59 In *Bicycle Thieves*, the police are too busy repressing anti-government political rallies.

The bicycle and the overcoat have been seen as emblems of two distinct and successive phases in the history of Italian reconstruction after the Second World War. Miccichè comments: 'The *metaphor of the bicycle* and the *metaphor of the overcoat* correspond to two different phases in postwar life and reconstruction. In the former, toward the end of the 40s, the country, and in particular the proletarian social strata (to whom the protagonist of *Bicycle*

Thieves belongs), are going through a primary phase in postwar reconstruction and in overcoming the conditions of an economico-industrial crisis, and hence of poverty, in which five years of war have plunged the country. In the latter, we are well into the 50s, and the country, in particular the petty-bourgeois social strata (of whom the protagonist of *Il cappotto* is a member), are overcoming their condition of poverty, though still very far from reaching a condition of dignity and of an established social position.'

'La *metafora della bicicletta* e *la metafora del cappotto* corrispondono a due diverse fasi della vita e della ricostruzione postbelliche: quella, fine anni '40, dove il Paese, e in particolare i ceti proletari (cui appartiene il protagonista di *Ladri di biciclette*), attraversano una fase ancora primaria della ricostruzione postbellica e dell'uscita dalle condizioni di crisi economico-industriale e conseguentemente di indigenza in cui cinque anni di guerra hanno lasciato il Paese; e quella degli avviati anni '50, dove il Paese, e in particolare i ceti piccolo-borghesi (cui appartiene il protagonista de *Il cappotto*) stanno superando la condizione di indigenza ma sono ancora molto lontani dal pervenire a una condizione di dignità e di riconosciuta identità sociale.' Lino Micciché, 'Un cappotto per dieci inverni,' in Lattuada, ed. Micciché, 35.

60 The fact that an object of demonic origin would eventually vanish reproduces a pattern richly documented in literatures and folklores from the Urals to the Atlantic. For an episode that is, in this perspective, readily comparable to Gogol's, cf. the incident of Voland's evening at the Moscow Variety Theatre in Bulgakov's novel *The Master and Margarita* (*Master i Margarita*, 1966 [1940]).

61 *The Tale of How Ivan Ivanovich Quarreled with Ivan Nikiforovich*, in *The Complete Tales*, 2: 214. 'Скучно на этом свете, господа!' *Povest' o tom, kak possorilsia Ivan Ivanovich s Ivanom Nikiforovichem*, in *Mirgorod*, vol. 2 of *PSS* (1937), 276.

62 *The Overcoat*, 324–5; *PSS* 3: 164.

63 *The Overcoat*, 325. 'Впрочем он был в душе добрый человек, хорош с товарищами, услужлив; но генеральский чин совершенно сбил его с толку. Получивши генеральский чин, он как-то спутался, сбился с пути и совершенно не знал, как ему быть.' *PSS* 3: 165.

64 'The wind, as its way is in Petersburg, blew upon [Akaky Akakievich] from all points of the compass and from every side street.' *The Overcoat*, 328. 'Ветер, по петербургскому обычаю, дул на него со всех четырех сторон, из всех переулков.' *PSS* 3: 167.

65 A further subtextual historical link to the Fascist era is pursued in *Il cappotto*, on the one hand, by casting the Mayor's friend as a look-alike of the regime's high dignitary Italo Balbo and, on the other, by including shots of para-Fascist slogans on the walls. The latter are the cinematic equivalent of the

Person of Consequence's favourite maxim: 'Strictness, strictness, strictness!' *The Overcoat*, 325. 'Строгость, строгость, и–строгость!' *PSS* 3: 164.

66 Scenes 427–9. He mentions, in particular, putting mousetraps inside the overcoat – an exact duplication of a delirious wish of Akaky's (*The Overcoat*, 328; *PSS* 3: 168).

67 *The Overcoat*, 328–9. 'наконец, даже сквернохульничал, произнося самые страшные слова, так что старушка хозяйка даже крестилась, отроду не слыхав от него ничего подобного.' *PSS* 3: 168.

68 *The Overcoat*, 329, is where the sentence ought to appear – but does not, probably due to oversight. 'Акакия Акакиевича свезли и похоронили.' *PSS* 3: 169.

69 It is entirely in keeping with demonic tradition – *vide* Auerbach's cellar in Goethe's *Faust* – for the evil principle to sow disarray among unsuspecting (though hardly innocent) humans. By contrast, *Il cappotto* is self-consistent in refraining from making Carmine responsible for human beings' divisions among themselves.

70 In Gogol's story, the mention of a bridge occurs here for the first time.

71 *The Overcoat*, 330. 'в полиции сделано было распоряжение поймать мертвеца, во что бы то ни стало, живого или мертвого, и наказать его, в пример другим, жесточайшим образом, и в том едва было даже не успели.' *PSS* 3: 170.

72 *The Overcoat*, 331. 'Фантастическо(е) направлени(е) впрочем сове ршенно истинной истории.' *PSS* 3: 170.

73 *The Overcoat*, 331. 'что-то вроде сожаления.' *PSS* 3: 171.

74 'His conscience reproached him, and he was depressed all day.' *The Overcoat*, 331. 'Слышал упреки совести и весь день был не в духе.' *PSS* 3: 171.

75 *The Overcoat*, 332. 'Вдруг почувствовал значительное лицо, что его ухватил кто-то весьма крепко за воротник. Обернувшись, он заметил человека небольшого роста в старом поношенном вицмундире, и не без ужаса узнал в нем Акакия Акакиевича. Лицо чиновника было бледно, как снег, и глядело совершенным мертвецом. Но ужас значительного лица превзошел все границы, когда он увидел, что рот мертвеца покривился и, пахнувши на него страшно могилою, произнес такие речи: "А! так вот ты наконец! наконец я тебя того, поймал за воротник! твоей-то шинели мне и нужно! не похлопотал об моей, да еще и распек–отдавай же теперь свою!" Бедное значительное лицо чуть не умер.' *PSS* 3: 172.

76 *The Overcoat*, 332–3. 'Он сам даже скинул поскорее с плеч шинель свою и закричал кучеру не своим голосом: "пошел во весь дух домой!"' *PSS* 3: 172–3.

77 The analogy between *Il cappotto* and De Sica's *Miracle in Milan* (*Miracolo a Milano*, 1951) has been particularly pursued by Argentieri, in Lattuada, ed. Micciché, 57.

78 One notices here how much more compressed the film's time frame is than the story's.

79 *The Overcoat*, 333. 'Впрочем многие деятельные и заботливые люди никак не хотели успокоиться и поговаривали, что в дацьних частях города всё еще показывался чиновник-мертвец. И точно, один коломенский будочник видел собственными глазами, как показалось из-за одного дома привидение ... Один раз обыкновенный взрослый поросенок, кинувшись из какого-то частного дома, сшиб его с ног, к величайшему смеху стоявших вокруг извозчиков, с которых он вытребовал за такую издевку по грошу на табак.' *PSS* 3: 173–4.

Vladimir Nabokov wrote in a famous essay on his predecessor that 'Gogol's *Shinel'* is a grotesque and grim nightmare making black holes in the dim pattern of life.' Nabokov, '*The Overcoat* (1842),' in his *Lectures on Russian Literature*, ed. Fredson Bowers (New York: Harcourt Brace Jovanovich, 1981 [1944]), 54.

80 That seems to be the end of the story. But in case we think, complacently, that the times of cold winters are forever gone and all is now for the best in the cleanest of all possible worlds, let us think again. It is so entirely Gogolian that the restoration of the film about the little man's helplessness against abuse by the anonymous machinery of power should have been sponsored by a multinational company with innumerable affiliates and cross-shareholders, at least some of which sell products that can cause – and doubtless have caused – little persons' premature deaths. Gogol's corpse is alive and kicking, and playing practical jokes on us. What are we laughing about?

81 Fredric Jameson, *The Political Unconscious: Narrative as a Socially Symbolic Act* (Ithaca, NY: Cornell University Press, 1981), 31.

82 Lattuada's criticism of Italian society, while mild, was as sharp as could be tolerated by the economic and financial system within whose constraints Lattuada operated. On political discrimination against more openly critical, 'un-Italian' filmmaking during the cold war, see Lorenzo Quaglietti, *Storia economico-politica del cinema italiano 1945–1980* (Rome: Editori Riuniti, 1980); and Vito Zagarrio, 'La generazione del neorealismo di fronte agli anni Cinquanta,' in Giorgio Tinazzi, ed., *Il cinema degli anni '50* (Venice: Marsilio, 1979), 99–116. On the particular situation in 1952, see Callisto Cosulich, *I film di Alberto Lattuada* (Rome: Gremese, 1985), 57.

83 On the 'end-tail' nature of *Il cappotto*'s neorealism, see Attolini, *Storia del*

cinema letterario, 143–5. The *Senso/La strada* diatribe was a telling tale of what could happen when the critical struggle did boil over. See the relevant polemical articles collected in Federico Fellini, La strada: *Federico Fellini, Director,* ed. Peter Bondanella and Manuela Gieri (New Brunswick, NJ: Rutgers University Press, 1987), 197–220.

84 Neorealism's third soul I mentioned, the comical one, lived on – just – by being residually absorbed into the *commedia all'italiana.*

85 For an ethically different point of view, cf. theft in Pasolini (*Accattone, Mamma Roma*); on which see Maurizio Viano, *A Certain Realism: Making Use of Pasolini's Film Theory and Practice* (Berkeley: University of California Press, 1993), esp. 88 and 96–7.

Chapter 4: Tolstoy and the Tavianis

1 'C'est un film russe, *Le Père Serge,* qui m'a, pendant la guerre, laissé entrevoir les possibilités de cet art jeune: le Rêve, le Souvenir, l'Hallucination, la Folie, le Dédoublement de la personnalité. Si les cinématographistes voulaient, il y aurait là de si grandes choses à faire!' French quote from Antonio Costa, *Immagine di un'immagine: Cinema e letteratura* (Turin: UTET, 1993), 108; and Gieri, *Contemporary Italian Filmmaking,* 77. The source is an interview by René Jeanne originally published in *Les nouvelles littéraires* (Costa: 'Cinq minuits [?] avec Pirandello,' 19 Nov. 1924; Gieri: 'Cinq minutes avec Pirandello,' 15 Nov. 1924, 8).

2 The interaction between Nanni Moretti and the Tavianis makes for one of the most absorbing chapters in the history of intergenerational rapports in Italian cinema. See Faldini and Fofi, eds, *1970–1984,* 540–1.

3 Viktor Shklovskii, *Lëv Tolstoy,* trans. Olga Shartse (Moscow: Progress Publishers, 1978), 701–10; *Lëv Tolstoi* (Moscow: Izdatel'stvo Molodaia Gvardiia, 1963), 644–52.

4 Pasternak *Sr* worked on illustrating *Resurrection* in 1898, when Boris was eight years old. On the close relationship between Tolstoy and the Pasternaks, see Christopher Barnes, *Boris Pasternak: A Literary Biography. Vol. 1: 1890–1928* (Cambridge: Cambridge University Press, 1989), 11, 19, 21–3, 96; and Guy de Mallac, *Boris Pasternak: His Life and Art* (Norman: University of Oklahoma Press, 1981), 3–4, 11, 27, 53.

5 According to Tolstoy, who follows Matthew verbatim, man should: (a) not kill (21–6); (b) not commit adultery (27–32); (c) never bind himself by oath (33–7); (d) not demand an eye for an eye, but, when struck on one cheek, offer the other (38–42); (e) neither hate his enemies nor fight them, but love them instead (43–8). Lëv Tolstoi, *Resurrection,* vol. 19 of *The Works of*

L. T. / *Tolstoy Centenary Edition*, trans. A. Maude (London: Tolstoy Society and Oxford University Press, 1929), 459–60.

'1. (Ч)еловек не только не должен убивать ... 2. не только не должен прелюбодействовать ... 3. не должен обещаться в чём-нибудь с клятвою ... 4. не только не должен воздавать око за око, но должен подставлять другую щеку, когда ударят по одной ... 5. не только не должен ненавидеть врагов, не воевать с ними, но должен любить их.' *Voskresenie*, vol. 32 of *Polnoe sobranie sochinenii*, 1933, 443.

The work on Tolstoy's faith that I have found most useful is unquestionably Pier Cesare Bori, *L'altro Tolstoj* (Bologna: Il Mulino, 1995), esp. 79–114.

6 The amount of space devoted to *Father Sergius* in both Soviet and Western scholarship is more often to be measured in sentences than in chapters or even pages. Within a Tolstoyan critical body of gigantic dimensions, some information about the novella can be gleaned – in unequal proportions – from the following works: Bori, *L'altro Tolstoj*, 104; R.F. Christian, *Tolstoy: A Critical Introduction* (Cambridge: Cambridge University Press, 1969), 234–6; Martin Doerne, *Tolstoj und Dostojewskij: Zwei christliche Utopien* (Göttingen: Vandenhoeck und Ruprecht, 1969), esp. 48–61; Richard F. Gustafson, *Leo Tolstoy, Resident and Stranger: A Study in Fiction and Theology* (Princeton, NJ: Princeton University Press, 1986), 415–20; G.W. Spence, *Tolstoy the Ascetic* (Edinburgh and London: Oliver and Boyd, 1967); and Nicolas Weisbein, *L'évolution religieuse de Tolstoï* (Paris: Librairie des cinq continents, 1960), 349–50.

A recent welcome addition to such a small critical corpus is Robert L. Jackson, 'Father Sergius and the Paradox of the Fortunate Fall,' *Russian Literature* 40:4 (Nov. 1996), 463–80.

7 Lěv Tolstoi, *Father Sergius*, in *The Devil and Cognate Tales*, vol. 16 of *Tolstoy Centenary Edition* (henceforth *TCE*), 299.

'В Петербурге в 40-х годах случилось удивившее всех событие: красавец, князь, командир лейб-эскадрона кирасирского полка ... за месяц до свадьбы с красавицей фрейлиной, пользовавшейся особой милостью императрицы, попал в отставку, разорвал свою связь с невестой ... и уехал в монастырь, с намерением поступить в него монахом.' *Otets Sergii*, in vol. 31 of *Polnoe sobranie sochinenii*, 1954, 5.

8 'Mèri' is a direct transliteration of the original (Мэри), which, in the first place, transliterates the English 'Mary' into Russian. The name strikes as an affected Westernization – a Westernization that Tolstoy's context negatively associates with loose morals.

9 Tolstoy indicts not only her but her whole milieu when, somewhat sardonically, he suggests that 'apart from the Imperial dignity [she] would not have

preferred [the emperor] to [Kasatskii].' *TCE* 16: 306. 'Если бы не императорство, не променяла бы этого на того.' *PSS* 31: 10.

10 An association between Carnival (*maslenitsa*) and the buttery quality of the road (*maslenaia doroga*) slips through Tolstoy's text (*PSS* 31: 17, 18). Thus, while Russian winter weather bears out without effort the idea of comfortable travel by sled, the smoothness of this particular itinerary also seems to act as a metaphorical connection with the proverbially easy road to Hell.

11 Russ. *mak* = 'poppy' (*papaver*) and esp. 'opium poppy' (*papaver somniferum*). The allusion, however, is richer than that. See Jackson, 'Father Sergius and the Paradox of the Fortunate Fall,' 467–8.

12 Matt. 5: 29–30. Alexander Jones, ed., *The Jerusalem Bible* (Garden City, NY: Doubleday, 1968). '[S]i dextra manus tua scandalizat te, abscinde eam et proice abs te.' Augustinus Merk, ed., *Novum testamentum* (Rome: Pontificium Institutum Biblicum, 1964), 13. Appropriately, the passage is one of those in Matthew to which *Resurrection* makes explicit reference.

13 *TCE* 16: 332. '(Д)ьявол подменил всю его деятельность для Бога деятельностью для людей.' *PSS* 31: 29.

14 *TCE* 16: 331–2. 'точно его выворачивали наружу ... Он чувствовал, как внутреннее переходило во внешнее.' *PSS* 31: 28–9.

15 *TCE* 16: 339; *PSS* 31: 34. That is to say, his surrender would not have been possible without his prior commercial de-moral-ization.

16 The narrator introduces here an episode that speaks volumes as to the real target of Tolstoy's salvoes: in his frenzy to have Father Sergius all to himself, *the merchant ejects the believers from the temple.* However ill-conceived or superstitious the religious perceptions of many visitors at Father Sergius's (something the novella is far from trying to conceal), the fact remains that the tradesman turns the Gospel of Matthew inside out – just as the monastery did to Sergius's motivation. *TCE* 16: 336–7; *PSS* 31: 32.

   The availability of this passage for allegorical reference to merchants in the temple of art is confirmed by Tolstoy's explicit usage of the expression, in exactly those terms, in *What Is Art?* (*TCE* 18: 271; *PSS* 30: 182). Clearly, Tolstoy's goal is less to indict sex per se than to denounce the blasphemy of an arrangement in the religious establishment that allows for sexual temptations of just this kind to occur.

17 *TCE* 16: 344. 'Да, надо покончить. Нет Бога. Как покончить? Броситься? Умею плавать. Не утонешь. Повеситься? Да, вот кушак, на суку.' *PSS* 31: 37.

18 While the episode was not taken up by the Tavianis for *The Night Sun*, it was by no means lost on them. It appears, in a different context, in their *Floréal*

(*Fiorile*, 1993), where a semi-demented Renzo Benedetti demonstrates dry-land swimming for the benefit of his sister Elisa.

The anecdote seems to have been introduced into modern literature by Goethe's *Faust II* (vv. 10, 734–10, 741). Mephisto revels in befuddling soldiers' senses in battle – and then mocks them to boot: 'Nothing I see of all this moist illusion:/ To human eyes alone it brings confusion,/ And in the wondrous chance I take delight./ They fly in headlong, hurried masses;/ That they are drowning, think the asses:/ Though on the solid land, they see an ocean,/ And run absurdly with a swimming motion./ It is a most bewildering plight.' Goethe, *Faust. A Tragedy*, trans. B. Taylor, intro V. Lange (New York: Modern Library, 1967 [1870]), 211.

'Ich sehe nichts von diesen Wasserlügen,/ Nur Menschen Augen lassen sich betrügen/ Und mich ergötzt der wunderliche Fall./ Sie stürzen fort zu ganzen hellen Haufen,/ Die Narren wähnen zu ersaufen,/ Indem sie frey auf festem Lande schnaufen,/ Und lächerlich mit Schwimmgebärden laufen./ Nun ist Verwirrung überall.' Goethe, *Faust II*, in *Letzte Jahre. 1827–1832*, ed. Gisela Henckmann et al., vol. 18/1 of *Sämtliche Werke nach Epochen seines Schaffens. Münchner Ausgabe*, 306. For Goethe's own possible sources, see Hans Arens, *Kommentar zu Goethes* Faust II (Heidelberg: Carl Winter Universitätsverlag, 1989), 805.

19 *TCE* 16: 345. 'Иди к Пашеньке и узнай от нее, что тебе надо делать, и в чем твой грех, и в чем твое спасение.' *PSS* 31: 38.

20 *TCE* 16: 354. 'Я жил для людей под предлогом Бога, (Пашенька) живет для Бога, воображая, что она живет для людей ... (Н)ет Бога для того, кто жил, как я, для славы людской. Буду искать Его.' *PSS* 31: 44.

21 *TCE* 16: 315. 'Меня показывают, как зверя.' *PSS* 31: 16.

22 *TCE* 16: 356–7. 'В Сибири он поселился на заимке у богатого мужика и теперь живет там. Он работает у хозяина в огороде, и учит детей, и ходит за больными.' *PSS* 31: 46.

23 Among these are *A Man to Be Burned* (*Un uomo da bruciare*, 1962); *The Subversives* (*I sovversivi*, 1967); *Saint Michael Had a Rooster* (*San Michele aveva un gallo*, 1971), from Tolstoy; *Allons enfants* (*Allonsanfán*, 1974); *Padre padrone* (1977); *The Meadow* (*Il prato*, 1978), inspired by Goethe's *The Sorrows of Young Werther*; *The Night of the Shooting Stars* (*La notte di S. Lorenzo*, 1982); *Kaos* (1984); *Floréal* and *Elective Affinities* (*Le affinità elettive*, 1996), from Goethe. See my *Italian Cinema and Modern European Literatures* for the three among these films that were re-created from European national traditions.

24 Private communication to the author, 21 Dec. 1995. On the Tavianis' films, see Fulvio Accialini and Lucia Coluccelli, *Paolo e Vittorio Taviani* (Florence: La nuova Italia, 1979); Guido Aristarco, *Sotto il segno dello scorpione: Il cinema dei fratelli Taviani* (Messina and Florence: G. D'Anna, 1978); Bondanella,

Italian Cinema, 175–8, 341–5, and 392–8; Pier Marco De Santi, *I film di Paolo e Vittorio Taviani* (Rome: Gremese, 1988); Faldini and Fofi, eds, *1970–1984;* Riccardo Ferrucci and Patrizia Turini, *Paolo e Vittorio Taviani: La poesia del paesaggio* (Rome: Gremese Editore, 1995); also in parallel English edition *Paolo and Vittorio Taviani: Poetry of the Italian Landscape);* Landy, *Italian Film,* 164–8; Piero Spila, 'La fine delle "utopie" nel cinema dei Taviani,' in Lino Micciché, ed., *Il cinema del riflusso: Film e cineasti italiani degli anni '70* (Venice: Marsilio, 1997), 154–62; Tassone, *Parla il cinema italiano,* 2: 325–80; and Bruno Torri, ed., *Il cinema dei Taviani* (Roma: Ministero degli affari esteri, Direzione generale relazioni culturali, 1989). With respect, in particular, to Gramsci's influence on the Tavianis, see Landy, *Film, Politics, and Gramsci,* 155–84.

25 Repositioning the events so as to cover the middle of the eighteenth century allows the Tavianis to turn away from the *Risorgimento* (anyway already the object of their earlier *Allonsanfán*), whose historical uniqueness in Italian culture would have been sure to eclipse the focus on individualism that characterizes Father Sergius's story.

Carlo di Borbone (1716–88), eldest son of Philip V of Spain and Elisabetta Farnese, successfully asserted his claim to the throne of Naples against the Habsburgs'. He was *Re delle due Sicilie* from 1734 to 1759. Thereafter, the death of the king of Spain (a relative) allowed him to ascend to the throne in Madrid, which he did under the name Carlos III. The relevance to the film of Carlo's dynastic origin is discussed below.

26 Carlo Levi's book of memoirs *Christ Stopped at Eboli* (*Cristo si è fermato a Eboli,* 1945) is also set in Lucania, and also pays particular homage to the pictorial beauty of the land.

27 In the Tavianis: 'il suo sconfinato orgoglio.'

28 *TCE* 16: 300; *PSS* 31: 6.

29 'L'ho studiato con amore, per essere più vicino al popolo.'

It would be anachronistic to assume that, just because of their rank, preunification Italian rulers were more likely to speak the literary language than their respective local populations. In fact, the usage of a language shared with its subjects could convey the strength of a monarchy's sense of belonging to the *nation* over which it ruled. Hence the linguistic efforts of a first-generation foreigner, such as Carlo di Borbone certainly was.

To be sure, the situation as depicted by the Tavianis is counterfactual: the king's German accent in the film has no historical basis (see note 25 above). The theoretical justification for this is that the Tavianis' usage of dialect is part and parcel of their *anti-naturalistic poetics:* characters' accents (Neapolitan, Lucanian, Sicilian) and accent-free Italian alternate in the film with scant relation to geographical necessity. It is not for the sake of reproducing

reality more faithfully, but in order to introduce incisiveness and expressiv-
ity, that the Tavianis broaden the film's vernacular register.

It was for the very same reason, the two brothers lucidly point out, that in
Saint Michael Had a Rooster and *Allonsanfán* they took great historical liberties
with the costumes (in particular with the red shirts of the latter). See Faldini
and Fofi, eds, *1970–1984*, 130; and Jean A. Gili, ed., *Paolo et Vittorio Taviani:
Entretien au pluriel* (Arles: Institut Lumière–Éditions Actes Sud, 1993), 173–4
and 176–7. In view of this, Bertelli's remarks on certain inadequacies in the
directors' historical reconstruction seem, in the case of *The Night Sun*, to be
true enough but beside the point. Sergio Bertelli, *I corsari del tempo: Gli errori e
gli orrori dei film storici* (Florence: Ponte alle Grazie, 1995), 157–8 and 189–90.

For a perceptive general analysis of the Tavianis' post-neorealist poetics,
see Marcus, *Italian Film*, 362–6.

30 *TCE* 16: 301; *PSS* 31: 6.

31 'L'aggio imparato dalla balia mia.'

32 'Viene dalle campagne della Basilicata! Sotto questo aspetto, la maggior
parte degli altri cadetti è più degna.'

33 *TCE* 16: 302–3; *PSS* 31: 8.

34 'I vostri ministri e la corte erano scettici ... Io allora avevo otto anni e non
potevo saperlo, ma capii che Vostra Maestà era solo. Quando tornammo a
casa, non volli prendere la carrozza, ma feci tutto il tragitto a piedi.'

35 This shows through in the genesis of the film. In the 1980s, the Tavianis had
begun work on two separate screenplays whose protagonists rejected their
world and its dominant ideals – 'the artificial myths of success and glory' –
and, having removed themselves from society, joined groups of political ter-
rorists. When the directors could not come to any formulation of either
project that would ultimately satisfy them, Giuliani De Negri, their producer,
noticed the analogy between those two tentative scripts and one the Tavianis
had drafted and then put aside in the 1970s – the story of Father Sergius.
The producer suggested going back to the older *sui generis* revolutionist,
whom the Tavianis thus rediscovered and enthusiastically re-embraced.
(Needless to say, this perspective did not coincide with Tolstoy's indeed religious view of Father Sergius.) See the Tavianis' account in Gili, ed., *Paolo et
Vittorio Taviani*, 151–78, esp. 152 and 155.

36 *Madre.* 'Che cos'è questo sasso?'
Sergio. 'Ho fatto un voto ... Da grande voglio essere io a stare accanto al re,
per aiutarlo.'

37 For full Italian titles and dates, see note 23 above. On the Tavianis' view of the
– broadly understood – utopian dimension in their protagonists, see Vittorio's
comments in Faldini and Fofi, eds, *1970–1984*, 131. Similarities among many
of them are further stressed in Gili, ed., *Paolo et Vittorio Taviani*, 155.

38 Since the Tavianis' re-creation of the story neutralizes Tolstoy's critique of 'Westernized' mores, there is no reason for them to retain her original name, Mèri.

39 The presents also act as foreshadowings of Sergio's connection with pigeons, on which more below.

40 *TCE* 16: 306. 'Если бы вы не были женщины!' *PSS* 31: 10.

41 'Tutti lo sapevano ... e solo per questo la mia famiglia ti ha accettato.' The well-known autocratic tradition of the southern kingdom certainly qualified it as an ideal Italian proxy for the czar's absolutism (*samoderzhavie*). It also seems that the cultural stereotype of the southern Italian conception of (male) 'honour' overdetermined the Tavianis' choice at this particular narrative juncture.

42 *TCE* 16: 306. 'Не трогайте, не трогайте меня. О, как больно!' *PSS* 31: 10.

43 'Io lo so perché lo fa: perché vuole trovarsi più in alto di chi l'ha umiliato.'
   In Tolstoy, it is the sister (Varvara, or Varenka) who supports Stiva's decision, while his mother advises against it: 'By becoming a monk he ... ascended a height from which he could look down on those he had formerly envied.' *TCE* 16: 307. 'Поступая в монахи, он ... становился на новую такую высоту, с которой он мог сверху вниз смотреть на тех людей, которым он прежде завидовал.' *PSS* 31: 11.

44 'Non mi affogherei mai nell'acqua dove da bambini abbiamo imparato a nuotare.' The implications of this statement become clear only later on in the film, after Sergio has collapsed in the face of temptation.

45 'Prendimi, Signore, prendimi!'
   Tolstoy had written: 'But it was not this [feeling] alone, as his sister Varvara supposed, that influenced him.' *TCE* 16: 307. 'Но не одно это чувство, как думала сестра его Варенька, руководило им.' *PSS* 31: 11. That is to say, Kasatskii was not motivated by ambition alone, but by a component of sincere religiosity as well.

46 'Io ho rinunciato al mondo; perché voi mi volete ancora mettere in mostra?'
   There are some differences in presentation between the novella and the film. In Tolstoy, Father Sergius uses the terms *podvergat'*, 'to subject,' and *soblazn*, 'seduction' (of the world) (*TCE* 16: 314; *PSS* 31: 16); Mèri and her husband do not attend the Mass; and the abbott offers no refreshments to the visiting dignitaries.
   Aside from editing Sergius's lines, taking Cristina to church, and introducing the drinks, a further (remarkable) cinematic innovation devised by the Tavianis is the *crescendo* of gossipy whispers that at one point takes over the soundtrack – a non-verbal rendering of Sergio's sense that, as he helps serve Mass, he is being observed and commented upon by the crowd of believers behind his shoulders.

The prototype of the 'gossip device' (also employed to striking effects in *Padre padrone* apropos the village of Siligo) is to be found in the aria 'Slander is a gentle breeze' ('La calunnia è un venticello') from Act I, scene 2 of Rossini's *The Barber of Seville*. 'Let us talk, if anything, about cinema and *music*' ('Semmai parliamo di cinema e *musica*'), Vittorio replies to Tassone when asked to comment on the relationship between cinema and *literature* (Tassone, *Parla il cinema italiano*, 2: 359). The directors further stress the paramount importance of the soundtrack in the very process of structuring their work (Faldini and Fofi, eds, *1970–1984*, 132–3).

47　For the relevance in particular of Italian landscapes to *The Night Sun*, see Ferrucci and Turini, *Paolo e Vittorio Taviani: La poesia del paesaggio*, 159–65. The distances between the Basento valley and the province of L'Aquila, where the Tavianis place our recluse, are such as to rule out the relatively prompt communication on foot between them that we see occur in the film. This infringement on the realist code is a further sign of the directors' espousal of an anti-naturalistic poetic program.

48　*Inferno* III, 60. For a sympathetic book-length dramatic reconstruction of Pietro da Morrone–Celestino V's plight, see Ignazio Silone, *L'avventura di un povero cristiano* (Milan: Mondadori, 1968).

49　Eugenio and Concetta are not the only elderly couple that the Tavianis depict with touching sympathy. Another case that comes to mind is that of the two long-time acquaintances Concetta [!] and Galvano, who are miraculously (though fleetingly) reunited by war in *The Night of the Shooting Stars*. See Marcus, *Italian Film*, 380–2.

50　'Tante giornate buone!' 'Col sole pure la notte.' Private communication to the author, 21 Dec. 1995.

51　She complains to her travel mates that she did not like the excursion at all because the two of them could, being men, take the liberty of going fishing and swimming, while she, as a woman, was not permitted by custom to do either.

52　Although Tolstoy mentions three times Makovkina walking barefoot about the room (*TCE* 16: 325–6; *PSS* 31: 24), in the story there is no reference to the sounds caused by Aurelia brushing her hair or removing her clothes. These were added by the Tavianis. Conversely, the directors excise a circumstance they would have been hard put to convey tactfully: the fact that Makovkina is favourably disposed by the manly, wild smell that lingers in the passionate hermit's hut.

53　*TCE* 16: 329; *PSS* 31: 26.

54　The feat is physically possible because in the film the episode occurs not in a snow-covered mountain forest, but amidst verdant, rain-soaked summer pastures. It seems probable that the Tavianis intended to apply to Aurelia a form of *contrappasso* of the kind systematically inflicted on the damned by Dante – an author already on their minds anyway because of the historico-cultural link to Celestino V alluded to above.

55 *Sergio.* 'Da quando siete entrata, ho dimenticato le ragioni per cui sono quassù ...'
Aurelia. 'Io non riesco a vederne nemmeno una.'
Sergio. 'Mi viene in mente solo lo stupore che avevo da ragazzo, meravigliandomi dell'indifferenza della gente ... E' possibile, mi sono sempre chiesto, che nessuno pensi a nessun altro, e che nessuno se ne chieda il perché? Questa è la ragione per cui mi sono detto che se almeno un uomo, un solo uomo, si isolasse da tutto il mondo, per pensare a tutti gli altri e per tutti gli altri, potremmo forse ancora sperare.'

56 'la più alta perfezione, sia quella esterna che quella interiore.'

57 The high visibility of the surplus that the monastery, via Sergio, extracts from the people makes it altogether reasonable to suspect that *The Night Sun* – no less so than the Tavianis' earlier, openly political films – is *also* about the liberation of humanity from exploitation.

58 While it is true that *The Night Sun* takes place in the century preceding the political unification of Italy in 1861, its reference to the phenomenon of brigandism is only relatively anachronistic; one should consider that lawlessness – whatever the circumstances – remained long endemic in the South of the peninsula. The standard reference works on the subject date from about one generation ago: Renzo Del Carria, *Proletari senza rivoluzione: Storia delle classi subalterne italiane dal 1860 al 1950* (Rome: Savelli, 1975); Eric J. Hobsbawm, *Primitive Rebels: Studies in Archaic Forms of Social Movement in the 19th and 20th Centuries* (Manchester: Manchester University Press, 1959); Hobsbawm, *Bandits* (London: Weidenfeld and Nicolson, 1969); and Franco Molfese, *Storia del brigantaggio dopo l'Unità* (Milan: Feltrinelli, 1964). More recently, the subject has been effectively broached by Giovanni De Matteo in *Brigantaggio e Risorgimento: Legittimisti e briganti tra i Borbone e i Savoia* (Naples: Alfredo Guida, 2000); and by Paolo Pezzino in 'Risorgimento e guerra civile,' in Gabriele Ranzato, ed., *Guerre fratricide* (Turin: Bollati Boringhieri, 1994), 56–85.
  Peculiarly, Italian cinematography shows a similar distribution over time: many titles on banditry, past and present, turn up around the first centennial of the unification in 1961 (Castellani's *Il brigante*, Camerini's *I briganti italiani*, De Seta's *Banditi a Orgosolo*, and Rosi's *Salvatore Giuliano*; in 1957, Germi had released his analogous *Il brigante di Tacca del Lupo*); then nothing until Pasquale Squitieri's *And They Called Them Brigands* (*E li chiamarono briganti*) in 1999.

59 They have taken these coats from their victims among the military. The Tavianis seem to be symbolically conveying the message that the criminals themselves only subsist by usurping a legitimacy whose source lies elsewhere. On the anachronistic red shirts of *Allonsanfán*, see n. 29 above.

60 Tolstoy implies as much, but never says so explicitly. He only writes: 'At first [Sergius] was in doubt, but afterwards this indecision passed. He [became used to it] and yielded to the devil.' *TCE* 16: 333. 'Сначала (Сергий) был в нерешительности, потом нерешительность прошла, он привык и покорился дьяволу.' *PSS* 31: 29.

61 'Tu non puoi più aiutarmi, Egidio; ti hanno trasformato nell'albero della cuccagna.'

The Land of Cockaigne (Paese di cuccagna), re-created by Collodi as a fool's paradise reserved for lazy schoolchildren (Land of Toys / Paese dei balocchi), features in *Pinocchio* in chapter 31. For its part, the tree effortlessly multiplying seed money into fabulous fortunes that tinkle in the wind is allegedly located in the Field of Miracles (Campo dei miracoli), near the town of Sillybillytrap (Acchiappacitrulli), and is peddled to Pinocchio by the two archetypal fraudsters, the Fox and the Cat, in chapters 12 and 18. Both the Tavianis and Collodi draw on the same Tuscan folk tradition, which they re-create differently for different purposes. See Carlo Collodi, *The Adventures of Pinocchio,* trans. Ann Lawson Lucas (Oxford: Oxford University Press, 1996), 122–9, 33–7, and 58–63; *Le avventure di Pinocchio,* ed. Cesare Zavattini (Turin: Einaudi, 1961), 135–41, 40–5, and 67–71.

62 In Tolstoy, he arrives from 1400 miles away (*TCE* 16: 337; *PSS* 31: 32). In the Tavianis, he travels from Calabria – almost as far as possible within the kingdom.

63 'Maiali per i tuoi poveri, e prigionieri liberati per te!'

64 *Sergio.* 'Il mio non è un mestiere, è una missione ... solo che adesso sta *diventando* un mestiere.'
Santobuono. 'Eppure qui dovrebbe essere meno difficile cercare Dio.'
Sergio. 'Ho paura che chi cerca Dio non Lo trovi. Chi cerca la verità forse incontra Dio.'

The device allows the directors to render through dialogue states of mind that in the novella are described by the omniscient narrator (beginning section of chapter 7). (*TCE* 16: 331–3; *PSS* 31: 28–30.)

65 So, for example, Sergio's fainting is accompanied by rapidly spinning shots of bell towers and churches in Rome – an allusion to his increasing yearning for fame and glory. Furthermore, a portable organ accompanied by three *castrati* singers is shown as being presented to the monastery by the merchant.

66 'E' maiale, sì, ma è il maiale del miracolo. Vi dà forza.' The pig was donated because of the 'miracle' performed on the brigand's son. Shortening the concept to 'the pig of the miracle' is, of course, an ideal example of a demonic perversion of language.

67 The original, which is Mar'ia, seems to allude to the archetypal sinner Mary (Mèri?) Magdalene.

68 *TCE* 16: 338; *PSS* 31: 33. In the father's uneducated speech, the term is a comical *nerastenikha*, a non-word that – given his daughter's defective development – Tolstoy's merchant is sure to intend, folk-etymologically, as a combination of the prefix *ne –* ('not') with the root *rost* ('growth').

69 *TCE* 16: 343; *PSS* 31: 36. '*Se tu non fossi malata, direi che* sei il diavolo.'

70 *TCE* 16: 343. 'что он побежден, что похоть ушла уже из-под руководства.' *PSS* 31: 36.

Paradoxically, the mad girl's irruption into Father Sergius's / Sergio's life plays a providential role of sorts. After all, it is her peculiar intercession that shocks the hermit out of his self-complacent connivance with the devil and on to the path of his ultimate self-discovery. (See also Jackson's article on Father Sergius's *felix culpa*.)

71 *TCE* 16: 344; *PSS* 31: 37.

72 Far from representing suicide in a generic form, this episode is firmly anchored in the Tavianis' artistic history. It triplicates Giulio Manieri's self-inflicted death in *Saint Michael Had a Rooster* and what could be called Lionello's 'accidental suicide' by drowning on Lake Orta in *Allonsanfán*. (The Tavianis' family was painfully marked by a similar experience shortly after the First World War – see Faldini and Fofi, eds, *1970–1984*, 129.) It must have seemed to the Tavianis a suggestive coincidence that in *Father Sergius* Tolstoy created a context so appropriate for development in *The Night Sun*.

73 'Avevate bisogno dello sterco dei piccioni?' (Part of the dialogue occurs in dialect.)

74 'Sono morti benissimo, sono morti insieme! ... Sono morti alla stessa ora – proprio là dietro a voi, mentre raccoglievano lo sterco, uno un minuto dopo l'altro. Angela, ti ricordi? Come se si fossero messi d'accordo!' (Part of the dialogue occurs in dialect.)

75 The first page number I am quoting is that of the Max Hayward and Manya Harari translation: Boris Leonidovich Pasternak, *Doctor Zhivago* (New York: Ballantine Books, 1981; henceforward NY). As for the original, I am giving the page numbers of three of the most commonly used editions: *Doktor Zhivago. Roman* (Paris: Société d'Édition et d'Impression Mondiale, 1959; henceforward P); *Doktor Zhivago* (Ann Arbor: University of Michigan Press, 1959 [1958]; henceforward AA); *Doktor Zhivago. Roman*, vol. 3 of *Sobranie*

sochinenii v piati tomakh (Moscow: Khudozhestvennaia literatura, 1990; henceforward M).

Pasternak, *Doctor Zhivago*, NY 10. 'А что такое история? Это установление вековых работ по последовательной разгадке смерти и ее будущему преодолению ... Человек умирает не на улице под забором, а у себя в истории, в разгаре работ, посвященных преодолению смерти, умирает, сам посвященный этой теме.' *Doktor Zhivago*, P' 17; AA 10; M 14 (book 1, part I, sect. 5).

76 Pasternak, *Doctor Zhivago*, NY 13. 'Все движения на свете в отдельности были рассчитанно-трезвы, а в общей сложности безотчетно пьяны общим потоком жизни, который объединял их. Люди трудились и хлопотали, приводимые в движение механизмом собственных забот. Но механизмы не действовали бы, если бы главным их регулятором не было чувство высшей и краеугольной беззаботности. Эту беззаботность придавало ощущение связности человеческих существований, уверенность в их переходе одного в другое, чувство счастья по поводу того, что всё происходящее совершается не тоъко на земле, в которую закапывают мертвых, а еще в чем-то другом, в том, что одни называют царством Божиим, а другие историей, а третьи еще как-нибудь.' *Doktor Zhivago*, P 20; AA 12–13; M 16–17 (book 1, pt. I, sect. 7).

77 *Paolo.* Se i nostri film hanno un senso, l'hanno in corrispondenza ai momenti diversi che hanno contrassegnato questi anni di storia, dal 1960 in poi. Vivendo appassionatamente, fino in fondo, questi venti anni di storia, questi venti anni della nostra vita, bisognava in qualche modo riuscire a esprimerli ...
Vittorio. Le idee ... non nascono a caso, né tanto meno dal cervello di Giove. Sono il patrimonio comune di un certo momento, e volta a volta possono concretizzarsi, magari in forme impensabili, attraverso certi individui, che sono poi gli autori.

Tassone, *Parla il cinema italiano*, 2: 349, 355.

78 However, it would be simplistic and reductive to identify in the rise of commercial TV the single cause for the loss on Italian cinema's part of the ability to shape the collective unconscious of the nation. The author and scriptwriter Ugo Pirro puts the matter in the simplest and crispest terms when he argues: 'Anyway when, just to use a cinematographic term, society as a whole has no theme, cinema can have none either. In a society as splintered as ours is, there is no way for cinema to be any different – to be unifying, representative.' 'Del resto, quando una società non ha un tema, tanto per usare un termine cinematografico, non ce l'ha nemmeno il cinema. In una società tanto disgregata quanto la nostra non può esserci un cinema diverso – unificante,

rappresentativo.' Faldini and Fofi, eds, *1970–1984*, 692; the entire section 'Le ragioni della crisi' (639–73) is devoted to this subject.

79 It is not television *tout court* that I have in mind here, but a certain mercantile variant of it. Brilliant examples of synergy between cinema and television have come from, among many, Rossellini, Olmi, Fellini, Archibugi – and, of course, the Tavianis themselves, who cooperated with RAI for the production of a number of their films. *The Night Sun* was, indeed, produced by Giuliani G. De Negri for Filmtre, with the cooperation of, *inter alia*, RAI 1. Ever more often, as of the 1990s a new modus vivendi is being struck: cinema aims at reaching its intended audiences through both the small and the large screen as complementary commercial circuits, and from the outset productions are planned accordingly.

The best available English-language discussion of the present relationship between cinema and television in Italy is to be found in Sorlin, *Italian National Cinema*, 144–64. In Italian, see Aldo Bernardini, 'La collaborazione internazionale nell'era della televisione,' in Gian Piero Brunetta, ed., *L'Europa: Miti, luoghi, divi*, vol. 1/1 of his *Storia del cinema mondiale* (Turin: Einaudi, 1999), 1043–8; Giuseppe Cereda, 'Piccoli schermi e grandi antenne: Cinema e televisione, ieri oggi e domani,' in Sesti, ed., *La 'scuola' italiana*, 239–48; Ivano Cipriani, 'Il cinema della/nella televisione,' in Micciché, ed., *Schermi opachi*, 61–77; and Enrico Menduni, 'I contesti mediologici: Cinema e tv anni Novanta,' in Vito Zagarrio, ed., *Il cinema della transizione: Scenari italiani degli anni Novanta* (Venice: Marsilio, 2000), 82–90.

Sade and Pasolini

1 In conformity with a trend current in utopian studies, I am specifically using the spelling *eutopia* (as a variant of utopia) to indicate the desirable land opposed to *dystopia – utopia* being, per se, neither good nor bad in meaning, but simply 'nowhere.' See, among others, L.E. Hough, 'Disaffected from Utopia,' in *Utopian Studies III*, ed. Michael S. Cummings and Nicholas D. Smith (Lanham, Md.: University Press of America, 1991), 118–27.

2 Roland Barthes, *Sade Fourier Loyola*, trans. R. Miller (Berkeley: University of California Press, 1989 [1976]), 170. 'Le sadisme ne serait que le *contenu* grossier (vulgaire) du texte sadien.' *Sade Fourier Loyola* (Paris: Seuil, 1971), 174.

3 Pierre Klossowski, *Sade My Neighbor*, trans. A. Lingis (Evanston, Ill.: Northwestern University Press, 1991), 51. 'homme intégral.' *Sade mon prochain* précédé de *Le philosophe scélérat* (Paris: Seuil, 1967), 64–5.

4 Klossowski, *Sade My Neighbor*, 52. 'corruption ... portée à son comble.' *Sade mon prochain*, 65.

5 Klossowski, *Sade My Neighbor*, 140n. 'insurrection permanente.' *Sade mon prochain*, 84n.

6 I am alluding to *Philosophy in the Dressing Room* (*La philosophie dans le boudoir*, 1795) – in English a.k.a. *Philosophy in the Bedroom*. On Sade and eutopia/utopia, see Barthes, *Sade Fourier Loyola*, esp. 17 (English); 23 (French). What interests Barthes in these three authors is less their emphasis on (clearly, mutually incompatible) values than the text itself as a source of pleasure, 'the pleasure of the Text' (7) – '*le plaisir du Texte*' (12).

7 On the concept of eutopia/utopia in Sade, Barthes's essay mentioned above – rich in insights but sparing in footnotes – can be usefully complemented by Timo Airaksinen, 'The Parody of the Civil Contract,' in his *The Philosophy of the Marquis de Sade* (London: Routledge, 1995 [1991]), 117–39; Pierre Favre, *Sade utopiste: Sexualité, pouvoir et état dans le roman* Aline et Valcour (Paris: Presses Universitaires de France, 1967); and A.M. Laborde, 'La sémiosis sadienne,' in his *Sade romancier* (Neuchâtel: Éditions de la Baconnière, 1974), 29–40. *Mutatis mutandis*, the epoch's obsession with contracts turned up in another area as well: the sphere of *individual* Good and Evil – an issue poignantly crystallized in the literary theme of the pact with the devil. The social and the individual examine the same coin, only from opposite sides.

8 The expression – in a different, but again, not-so-different – context is Rimbaud's. See Arthur Rimbaud, *Oeuvres*, ed. Suzanne Bernard and André Guyaux (Paris: Garnier, 1987), 346–8.

Having already mentioned Restif de la Bretonne as a literary legislator, it seems appropriate to refer to him again in his capacity as a writer of fiction. Restif is a telling example of how even a person inclined to side with the Revolution, and certainly keen on sharing Sade's rejection of repressive constraints on personal behaviour, could nonetheless perceive Sade's radicalism as little short of monstrous. Restif directly and vehemently attacks Sade in the preface to a work of his that he never brought to completion, *L'anti-Justine*. See Nicolas-Edmé Restif de la Bretonne, *Oeuvres érotiques* (Paris: Fayard, 1985), 287. This is a symptom of how isolated Sade was even in his own time and country. Not surprisingly perhaps, Sade held no higher an opinion of Restif than Restif did of him. See Gilbert Lely, *Vie du Marquis de Sade 1778–1814*, vol. 2 of Donatien-Alphonse de Sade, *Oeuvres complètes*, ed. Gilbert Lely (Paris: Cercle du Livre Précieux, 1967), 485–7.

9 A prime element of differentiation can be detected in the text's inchoateness, which in part obviously relates to the circumstances of its drafting in the Bastille. While Airaksinen argues that, regardless of those conditions,

'the sketchy line-drawings' at the end of *Les 120 Journées* 'cannot be completed' (*The Philosophy of the Marquis de Sade*, 132), Barthes sees such devices as peculiarly Sadean stylemes, classifying them as 'pornograms' (158–9) – *pornogrammes* (162).

10 The ten days of Boccaccio's *Decameron* narrate, respectively, (1) whatever pleases the ten storytellers, (2) success beyond one's hope, (3) acquisition of the object of one's desire, or recovery of it when lost, (4) loves with an unhappy ending, (5) loves with a tormented but happy ending, (6) sharp-witted ripostes, (7) tricks (*beffe*) played by wives on their husbands, (8) tricks played by women on men, by men on women, or by men on men, (9) whatever pleases the ten storytellers, and (10) grand or magnificent deeds revolving around love or other subjects. Giovanni Boccaccio, *Decameron*, ed. Vittore Branca (Turin: Einaudi, 1992), 2 vols.

11 'Imagine-toi que toute jouissance honnête ou prescrite par cette bête dont tu parles sans cesse sans la connaître et que tu appelles nature, que ces jouissances, dis-je, seront expressément exclues de ce recueil.' Sade, *Les 120 journées de Sodome ou L'école du libertinage*, vol. 13 of *Oeuvres complètes* (henceforth *OC*), 60–1.

12 *OC* 13: 432.

13 *OC* 13: 50–60 (*Règlements*).

14 To the best of my knowledge, this direction of research has been neglected in major recent books dealing with Sade. I am advancing the hypothesis as a possibility for further development.

An exposition of C.G. Jung's views on the quaternary distribution of psychic realities can be found in vols. 9 and 14 of his works. See in particular two sections: 'The Structure and Dynamics of the Self,' chap. 14 of *Aion: Researches into the Phenomenology of the Self*, vol. 9/2 of *The Collected Works*, ed. Herbert Read et al., trans. R.F.C. Hull (Princeton, NJ: Princeton University Press, 1968), 222–65; 'Die Struktur und Dynamik des Selbst,' chap. 14 of *Aion: Beiträge zur Symbolik des Selbst*, vol. 9/2 of *Gesammelte Werke* (Olten and Freiburg i. B.: Walter-Verlag, 1966), 238–80; 'The Components of the Coniunctio,' chap. 1 of *Mysterium Coniunctionis: An Inquiry into the Separation and Synthesis of Psychic Opposites in Alchemy*, vol. 14 of *The Collected Works* (1977), 1–41; 'Die Komponenten der Coniunctio,' chap. 1 of *Mysterium Coniunctionis: Untersuchungen über die Trennung und Zusammensetzung der seelischen Gegensätze in der Alchemie*, vol. 14/1 of *Gesammelte Werke* (Zürich and Stuttgart: Rascher Verlag, 1968), 1–42.

15 The most important statements by Sade on the subject are collected in Sade, *Discours contre Dieu*, ed. and intro. Gilbert Lely (Paris: Union Générale d'Édi-

tions, 1980). Further pertinent samples could be added – so, for example, Léonore's 'philosophical reflections' in *Aline and Valcour, OC* 5: 220.

16 '[N]ous devons répondre à la perpetuelle objection de quelques esprits atra-biliaires qui ... ne cessent de vous dire: *A quoi servent les romans?* A quoi il servent, hommes hypocrites et pervers? car vous seules faites cette ridicule question: ils servent à vous peindre tels que vous êtes.' Sade, *Idée sur les romans*, in *Les crimes de l'amour. Nouvelles héroïques et tragiques, OC* 10: 15.

17 'Soffocato da tutta la *vita* che c'è nel mio corpo, io sono preso dalla deci-sione *di dar morte per morire*.' Pier Paolo Pasolini, *Orgia*, in *Teatro* (Milan: Garzanti, 1988), 535; emphasis in the original.

18 The macabre joke was, of course, on Pasolini himself, given his status as the widely acclaimed author of the films in the 'Trilogy of Life': *Decameron, The Canterbury Tales, The Arabian Nights*. Success was clearly not something for which Pasolini was about to forgive himself.

19 Viano is the critic who most emphatically (perhaps even too emphatically) stresses the enigmatic quality of the episode. See *A Certain Realism*, 308–11.

20 The most thought-provoking comment I have found on the two dancing boys within the huge critical corpus on *Salò* (they are the future fathers of stultified future consumers) is put forward in Gary Indiana, *Salò or The 120 Days of Sodom* (London: British Film Institute, 2000), 89.

21 Paul Celan, 'Death Fugue,' in *Poems*, trans. M. Hamburger (London: Anvil Press Poetry 1995 [1988]), 63; emphasis added. 'Schwarze Milch der Frühe wir trinken sie abends/ wir trinken sie mittags und morgens wir trinken sie nachts/ wir trinken und trinken/ wir schaufeln ein Grab in den Lüften da liegt man nicht eng/ Ein Mann wohnt im Haus der spielt mit den Schlangen der schreibt/ der schreibt wenn es dunkelt nach Deutschland dein goldenes Haar Margarete/ er schreibt es und tritt vor das Haus und es blitzen die Sterne er pfeift seine Rüden herbei/ er pfeift seine Juden hervor läßt schaufeln ein Grab in der Erde/ er befiehlt uns *spielt auf nun zum Tanz*.' 'Todesfuge,' in *Gedichte I*, vol. 1 of *Gesammelte Werke in fünf Bänden* (Frankfurt am Main: Suhrkamp, 1983), 41; emphasis added.

22 For detailed presentations and interpretations of the poem, see John Fel-stiner, *Paul Celan: Poet, Survivor, Jew* (New Haven: Yale University Press, 1995), 26–41; Jerry Glenn, *Paul Celan* (New York: Twayne, 1973), 67–76; and Heinz Michael Krämer, *Eine Sprache des Leidens: Zur Lyrik von Paul Celan* (Munich: Kaiser and Mainz: Grünewald, 1979), 87–96.

23 In *Faust II*, v. 12,068–9, she is characterized as 'Una poenitentium, *formerly named* [Gretchen]' (emphasis mine). Johann Wolfgang von Goethe, *Faust. A Tragedy*, trans. Taylor, 256. 'Una poenitentium, sonst Gretchen genannt.' *Faust II*, in *Letzte Jahre. 1827–1832*, 18/1: 350.

24 See 'Ragazzi, com'erano alla fine degli anni '50,' in Pier Paolo Pasolini, *La divina mimesis* (Turin: Einaudi, 1975 [1973]), 76–7 (photo 10).

25 After the opening credits, *Salò* immediately cites a bibliography of no less than five major items (Barthes, *Sade Fourier Loyola*; Simone de Beauvoir, *Faut-il brûler Sade?* [Paris: Gallimard, 1955]; Maurice Blanchot, 'La raison de Sade,' in his *Lautréamont et Sade* [Paris: Les Éditions de Minuit, 1963]; Pierre Klossowski, *Sade My Neighbor / Sade mon prochain*; Philippe Sollers, 'Sade dans le texte,' in his *L'écriture et l'expérience des limites* [Paris: Seuil, 1968]. 'Some excerpts from Barthes and Klossowski are quoted in the film,' Pasolini goes as far as announcing.

In my view, this serves a double purpose. In the first place, Pasolini subtly reinforces the Dantean connection by a mimetic re-creation of the ominous lines found at the entrance of Hell, 'Leave all hope behind, ye who enter' ('Lasciate ogni speranza o voi ch'entrate'). This acts as a preventive disclaimer, warning would-be viewers that advancing farther is not for the faint-hearted. Second, the director thereby not-so-subtly warns the general public that he has done his homework – and that he intends to accept no criticism of the film articulated at anything but the impressive intellectual level required to discuss *Salò* in the light of the French *nouvelle critique*. Since film-goers are likely to be gravely at fault on this score (so Pasolini's reasoning seems to run), it is they who 'sin' first, and so deserve to burn in the Hell that *Salò* promptly proceeds to inaugurate for them.

26 A critical persuasion widespread in Sade scholarship is that, whether tolerable or intolerable, Sade is in the first place *impossible* to convert into image. The notion can be found in general terms in Philippe Sollers, 'Sade dans le Temps,' in his *Sade contre l'Être suprême* (Paris: Gallimard, 1996), 28–9. The principle is castigatorily applied to Pasolini in the particular instance of *Salò* by, among others, the following authors: Roland Barthes, 'Sade–Pasolini' [orig. pub. 1976], in his *Oeuvres complètes*, ed. Éric Marty (Paris: Seuil, 1995), 3: 391–2; Maurizio De Benedictis, *Pasolini, la croce alla rovescia: I temi della vita e del sacrificio* (Anzio: De Rubeis, 1995), 89–92; Lino Micciché, 'L'ideologia della morte nell'ultimo Pasolini,' in *Storia del cinema: Autori e tendenze negli anni Cinquanta e Sessanta*, ed. Adelio Ferrero (Venice: Marsilio, 1978), 3: 49–55; and Leonardo Sciascia, 'Dio dietro Sade,' in Gian Piero Brunetta, ed., *Spari nel buio. La letteratura contro il cinema italiano: Settant'anni di stroncature memorabili* (Venice: Marsilio, 1994), 261–5.

The idea that Sade cannot be 'faithfully' reproduced in images seems to me true but beside the point: Pasolini is not out to reproduce Sade in a phil-ologically satisfactory manner, but to re-create him in order to transform a pre-existing text into a statement about the new socio-historical context in which the director operates. I comment on analogous critical positions below, when broaching philologists' objections to Visconti's *La morte a Venezia*, and then again in the Conclusion.

27 Despite Pasolini's fairly explicit statements on the matter, the concept that flaunting a total aesthetic and commercial irrecuperability *was the whole point* of *Salò* dawned on the critics at a relatively late time. (See also note 43 below.) Of course, I do not here mean to suggest that Pasolini viewed the political systems of the West *anno* 1975 as in fact liberal – on the contrary.

28 Pasolini proceeded deliberately in this matter: 'Among other things, I realized that Sade, as he wrote, was certainly thinking of Dante. So I began to restructure the book in three Dantean circles.' 'Mi sono accorto tra l'altro che Sade, scrivendo[,] pensava sicuramente a Dante. Così ho cominciato a ristrutturare il libro in tre bolge dantesche.' Nico Naldini, *Pasolini, una vita* (Turin: Einaudi, 1989), 388.

29 *OC* 13: 406.

30 The mistake was undoubtedly Sade's; Lely, the general editor, even indicates it as recurring repeatedly. *OC* 13: cx.

31 *Faust I*, v. 1765. Goethe, *Faust. A Tragedy*, trans. B. Taylor, 60. 'Du hörest ja, von Freud' ist nicht die Rede.' *Faust I* in *Weimarer Klassik. 1798–1806*, ed. Victor Lange, *Sämtliche Werke nach Epochen seines Schaffens*, 6/1: 582.

32 This point is well taken by, among others, Naomi Greene, '*Salò*: The Refusal to Consume,' in *Pier Paolo Pasolini: Contemporary Perspectives*, ed. Patrick Rumble and Bart Testa (Toronto: University of Toronto Press, 1994), 235 (the contribution reworks and condenses parts of her *Pier Paolo Pasolini: Cinema as Heresy* [Princeton, NJ: Princeton University Press, 1990], 196–217); and Indiana, *Salò*, 53 and 71.

33 What I mean is that no pleasure is acted out *in the film* (diegetically). It is true, as some observers have pointed out, that one might see homosexual pleasure *in the director* as certain scenes unfold: when, for example, the Communist youth is shot in spite of his clenched fist (more below on the episode). But why kill him to obtain that pleasure? My point, in other words, is that earlier works by Pasolini show no trace of authorial pleasure – homosexual or otherwise – in raging against victims. Thus, the fact that the older Pasolini is at variance with his earlier self must be explained by some diachronic process that is due to something other than his (unchanged) sexual preference and is specifically characteristic of his later years.

Using Pasolini's homosexuality to account for the intensity of his pleasure in torturing *Salò*'s victims would imply assuming that violence and/or outright S/M-ism are essential components of gay pleasure – indeed, possibly, of pleasure *tout court*. On this broader subject, see the important discussions by

Leo Bersani in his *A Future for Astyanax: Character and Desire in Literature* (Boston: Little, Brown and Co., 1975), esp. 12–14; *Théorie et violence: Freud et l'art* (Paris: Seuil, 1984), esp. 72–97; and, most recently, *Homos* (Cambridge, Mass.: Harvard University Press, 1995), esp. chap. 3, 'The Gay Daddy' [Foucault], 77–112. However, while a conceptual move of this kind could help us better account for works of art by intellectuals, homosexual or not, who are S/M-istically inclined, it would also, I believe, create correspondingly greater difficulties in approaching the large number of them that are not.

To return to Pasolini: my position on this issue being a historical one, I have difficulty accepting that one and the same non-diachronic theoretical blanket could cover such diverse works as *Salò* and, say, *La ricotta / Rogopag*, or *Accattone*. It seems arduous to argue away the *real historical causes* for the *real affective transformation* suffered by Pasolini over the period 1960–75 – a transformation on which, after all, the director himself elaborates at length in *Scritti corsari* and *Lutheran Letters*. On the subject, see also Ben Lawton, 'The Evolving Rejection of Homosexuality, the Sub-Proletariat, and the Third World in the Films of Pier Paolo Pasolini,' *Italian Quarterly* 82–3 (Fall 1980–Winter 1981), 167–73. On Pasolini's relation to 'homosexualiti(es),' an interesting recent contribution can be found in Patrick Rumble, *Allegories of Contamination: Pier Paolo Pasolini's Trilogy of Life* (Toronto: University of Toronto Press, 1996), esp. 135–9.

34 'I [Sergio Citti] was the one who had written *Salò*, I was the one who was supposed to make it, but I would have made it differently ... I wanted to take the torturers' side ... [Pasolini] argued that I should do the opposite ... Then he ended up making the film himself ... He made the film so tragic because he loved these people.' '*Salò* l'avevo scritto io, dovevo farlo io, ma l'avrei fatto in un altro modo ... Io volevo stare dalla parte dei carnefici ... [Pasolini] sosteneva che io dovevo fare il contrario ... Poi il film l'ha fatto lui ... Lui ha fatto il film così tragico perché amava 'sta gente.' Sergio Citti, in Faldini and Fofi, eds, *1970–1984*, 12–13.

35 The girl is a black African; she hails from Pasolini's beloved Third World. She, too, is killed by 'modern capitalism' – just like the Third World, as Pasolini many times argued.

36 *In cauda venenum*. The generosity of the girl's father, as depicted by Pasolini, is not an uninterested one: he senses a commercial advantage in allying himself to Riccardo's wealthy family.

37 Yukio Mishima, *Madame de Sade*, trans. D. Keene (New York: Grove Press, 1967), 28.

38 Pier Paolo Pasolini, *Heretical Empiricism*, ed. Louise K. Barnett, trans. B. Lawton and L.K.B. (Bloomington: Indiana University Press, 1988), 288 and 296;

Empirismo eretico, intro. Guido Fink (Milan: Garzanti 1991 [1972]), 290 and 296.

39 While it is certain that Pasolini read, e.g., Tanizaki's *The Makioka Sisters* (published in Italy as *Neve sottile*), which he reviewed for *Tempo* in March 1974 (now repr. in his *Descrizioni di descrizioni* [Turin: Einaudi, 1979], 278–82), there is no evidence of his knowing Mishima. Acquaintance could nonetheless have occurred via the Parisian intellectual milieu; there, Mishima was well known, as shown by the (somewhat later) publication of a perceptive book on his life and work by Marguerite Yourcenar – who, revealingly, in her concluding chapter describes Mishima by means of an image drawn from Pasolini's cinema. See Marguerite Yourcenar, *Mishima: A Vision of the Void*, trans. A. Manguel and M.Y. (New York: Farrar, Straus and Giroux, 1986), 139; *Mishima ou la vision du vide* (Paris: Gallimard, 1980), 118. On the other hand, Mishima's extreme right-wing reputation may just possibly have discouraged even as omnivorous a reader as Pasolini.

40 In the post-Napoleonic era, this cultural phenomenon swept through European ruling classes from France (Bonald, De Maistre) to Germany (Fichte, Görres, most of the romantic writers and poets) and Russia (Gogol, the Slavophiles, and later on, Dostoevsky, all the way to Solzhenitsyn).

In major Western languages at least, there does not seem to be a comparative study that positions Mishima against the historically recurrent supranational pattern of *rejection of modernization in the name of traditional ethical values*, although precisely this is likely to be the most fruitful way of making sense of his *arrière-garde* struggle. Peter Wolfe justly – but, also, tantalizingly – writes: 'Dostoevsky championed an ideal [that combined religious worship and government] ... Yet his theocratic ideal is usually admired, whereas Mishima's is mocked. It might surprise us to know how many of Mishima's detractors admire Dostoevsky, who endorsed some of the same principles.' *Yukio Mishima* (New York: Frederick Ungar – Continuum, 1989), 31–2.

For an authoritative, albeit brief, statement on the issue, see also the article by the recent Nobel Prize winner, Kenzaburo Ôe, 'The Centre and the Periphery,' in *Writers in East-West Encounter: New Cultural Bearings*, ed. Guy Amirthanayagam (London: Macmillan Press, 1982), 46–50.

41 The analogy I would personally be inclined to pursue as closest would be that between Pasolini and Gogol. For both, militarism remained in the background; for both, the major existential factors were instead religion, commun(itarian)ism, homosexuality, and last but not least, an unresolved emotional relationship to the South (the city of Rome in particular).

42 'You are talking about facts, not truth. People are all alike – as soon as something suspicious occurs, they suck out the facts, like flies swarming over a

corpse. When they've finished with the corpse, they record what has happened in their diaries and give it a name. Dishonor, shame, whatever you please. I am not talking about that kind of knowledge. I have confronted something that cannot be given a name.' Mishima, *Madame de Sade*, 28–9. The voice we overhear in these words is obviously Mishima's own (as is the characteristic imagery).

43 Pasolini's comments are collected in Faldini and Fofi, eds, *1970–1984* (10, 12–15, 16–17, and 18). A number of critics have been able to carry out a shrewd reading of Pasolini's pendulum movement between the literal and the figurative – to the precise extent, I would argue, that they succeeded in accurately positioning *Salò* within its Pasolinian (and Italian societal) context. See esp. Bondanella, *Italian Cinema*, 293–6; Luciano De Giusti, *I film di Pier Paolo Pasolini* (Rome: Gremese, 1983), 146; Greene, '*Salò*: The Refusal to Consume,' 236–7 and 240–1; Greene, *Pier Paolo Pasolini: Cinema as Heresy*, 207–9 and 215–17; Indiana, *Salò*, 90; Serafino Murri, *Pier Paolo Pasolini* (Milan: Il Castoro, 1994), 144–55; Murri, *Pier Paolo Pasolini: Salò o le 120 giornate di Sodoma* (Turin: Lindau, 2001); Piero Spila, *Pier Paolo Pasolini* (Rome: Gremese, 1999, 114–19); and Viano, *A Certain Realism*, 294–302.

44 Pasolini uses the reference to the 'death of the fireflies' to allude metonymically to the passing away of the Italy of old. See 'L'articolo delle lucciole' (1 Feb. 1975) in his *Scritti corsari* (Milan: Garzanti, 1977), 156–64; repr. ibid., 1990, 128–34.

45 Pier Paolo Pasolini, *Trasumanar e organizzar* (Milano: Garzanti, 1976 [1971]).

46 Pasolini, *San Paolo* (Turin: Einaudi, 1977).

47 His long-time companion, Ninetto, married in 1973 – a decision which seems to have precipitated a crisis in Pasolini's interaction with his social environment that had been in the making at the latest since 1968 (the year he identified as a turning point in the rise of a materialistically minded modern Italy). See Nico Naldini, *Pasolini, una vita*, 374; and Enzo Siciliano, *Pasolini: A Biography*, trans. J. Shepley (New York: Random House, 1982), 364; *Vita di Pasolini* (Florence: Giunti, 1995 [1978]), 473.

48 Pier Paolo Pasolini, '*Trilogy of Life* Rejected,' in *Lutheran Letters*, trans. S. Hood (Manchester: Carcanet and Dublin: Raven Arts Press, 1983), 49–52; 'Abiura dalla *Trilogia della vita*,' in *Lettere luterane* (Turin: Einaudi, 1976), 71–6.

Among the most recent relevant literature, one should note the disagreement in interpretation between Rumble's *Allegories of Contamination* (according to which Pasolini's rejection ought to be viewed ironically) and Indiana's *Salò* ('One needs to take it seriously' – 30).

49 This shows through, among other things, in the fact that Pasolini – unlike Sade – understands blasphemy as being directed not toward God, but toward

society, an 'indirect discourse' of sorts. See 'The Bad Mimesis,' in *Heretical Empiricism*, 119; 'La mala mimesi,' in *Empirismo eretico*, 120.

50 The altogether appropriate term 'filicide' is used in Sam Rohdie, *The Passion of Pier Paolo Pasolini* (Bloomington: Indiana University Press and London: British Film Institute, 1995), 179.

51 The analogy between the scenes of Ettore's death and depictions of the crucifixion of Christ is dealt with in detail by Alberto Marchesini, *Citazioni pittoriche nel cinema di Pasolini da* Accattone *al* Decameron (Florence: La nuova Italia, 1994), 30–4. Elsewhere, too, Pasolini expresses the (by any current standard) 'heretical' view that the humble and meek he prefers are the ones who *remain* humble and meek: 'The most adorable people are those who do not know they have any rights.' *Lutheran Letters*, 120. 'Le persone più adorabili sono quelle che non sanno di avere dei diritti.' *Lettere luterane*, 186.

52 Preparatory papers to *Petrolio*, now reproduced in facsimile opposite the title page. Pasolini, *Petrolio*, trans. A. Goldstein (New York: Pantheon, 1997); *Petrolio* (Turin: Einaudi, 1992).

53 While this is not the appropriate context in which to rehearse once more the countless occasions – at almost every page in *The Antichrist*, and in countless variations in *Thus Spake Zarathustra* – on which Nietzsche assures his readers that 'God is dead' and announces the liberating potential of this discovery, it may be useful to mention at least two passages no less emphatic in pointing out the difficulty of braving the transition from the God-fearing era to the unknown one.

One persona articulating the conflicts of the new times is the Madman. See 'The Madman,' *The Joyful Wisdom*, trans. Thomas Common, in *Complete Works* 10: 167–9 (Book 3, 125); 'Der tolle Mensch,' *Die fröhliche Wissenschaft*, in vol. 3 of *Sämtliche Werke. Kritische Studienausgabe* [henceforth *SW-KSA*], 480–2 (Book 3, 125).

The other voice expressing the complexity of the necessary metamorphosis is Zarathustra's own: 'Creating – that is the great salvation from suffering, and life's alleviation. But for the creator to appear, suffering itself is needed, and much transformation. Yea, much bitter dying must there be in your life, ye creators! Thus are ye advocates and justifiers of all perishableness. For the creator himself to be the new-born child, he must also be willing to be the child-bearer, and endure the pangs of the child-bearer.' 'In the Happy Isles,' *Thus Spake Zarathustra*, trans. T. Common, in *CW* 11: 100 (Part 2, XXIV). 'Schaffen – das ist die grosse Erlösung vom Leiden, und des Lebens Leichtwerden. Aber dass der Schaffende sei, dazu selber thut Leid noth und viel Verwandelung. Ja, viel bitteres Sterben muss in eurem Leben sein, ihr

Schaffenden! Also seid ihr Fürsprecher und Rechtfertiger aller Vergänglich-keit. Dass der Schaffende selber das Kind sei, das neu geboren werde, dazu muss er auch die Gebärerin sein wollen und der Schmerz der Gebärerin.' 'Auf den glückseligen Inseln,' *Also sprach Zarathustra*, in *SW-KSA* 4: 110–11 (Part 2, 2).

54 'Io rimpiangere l' "Italietta"? Ma allora tu non hai letto un solo verso delle *Ceneri di Gramsci* o di *Calderón*, non hai letto una sola riga dei miei romanzi, non hai mai visto una sola inquadratura dei miei films, non sai niente di me! Perché tutto ciò che io ho fatto e sono *esclude* per sua natura che io possa rimpiangere l'Italietta.

'E' questo illimitato mondo contadino prenazionale e preindustriale, sopravvissuto fino a solo pochi anni fa, che io rimpiango. (Non per nulla dimoro il più a lungo possibile nei paesi del Terzo Mondo, dove esso soprav-vive ancora, benché il Terzo Mondo stia anch'esso entrando nell'orbita del cosiddetto Sviluppo.)

'Gli uomini di questo universo non vivevano un'*età dell'oro*, come non erano coinvolti, se non formalmente, con l'Italietta. Essi vivevano ... *l'età del pane*. Erano cioè consumatori di beni estremamente necessari. Ed era questo, forse, che rendeva estremamente necessaria la loro povera e precaria vita. Mentre è chiaro che *i beni superflui rendono superflua la vita* (tanto per essere estremamente elementari, e concludere con questo argomento).'

'Lettera aperta a Italo Calvino. Pasolini: quello che rimpiango,' *Paese Sera*, 8 July 1974; repr. in Pasolini, *Scritti corsari*, 60–3 (1977); 51–3 (1990); empha-sis added in last clause.

55 Friedrich Nietzsche, 'The Animal with Good Conscience,' *The Joyful Wisdom*, in *CW* 10: 108–9 (Book 2, 77). 'Das Gemeine in Alledem, was im Süden Europa's gefällt – sei diess nun die italiänische Oper ... oder der spanische Abenteuer-Roman ... – bleibt mir nicht verborgen, aber es beleidigt mich nicht, ebensowenig als die Gemeinheit, der man bei einer Wanderung durch Pompeji und im Grunde selbst beim Lesen jedes antiken Buches begegnet: woher kommt diess? Ist es, dass hier die Scham fehlt und dass alles Gemeine so sicher und seiner gewiss auftritt, wie irgend etwas Edles, Lieb-liches und Leidenschaftliches in der selben Art Musik oder Roman? "Das Thier hat sein Recht wie der Mensch: so mag es frei herumlaufen, und du, mein lieber Mitmensch, bist auch diess Thier noch, trotz Alledem!" – das scheint mir die Moral der Sache und die Eigenheit der südländischen Humanität zu sein.' 'Das Thier mit gutem Gewissen,' *Die fröhliche Wissen-schaft*, in *SW-KSA* 3: 432–3 (Book 2, 77).

56 His exact wording differs from mine only in the form, not in the substance: '*Decameron* represents my nostalgia for an ideal people, with its poverty, its

lack of a political consciousness (it's terrible to have to say that, but it's true), for a people that I knew when I was a child. It may still exist, deep down in the underbelly of Naples. Meanwhile, in just six–seven years Italy has witnessed the rise of an industrial society. But this has happened so quickly that we weren't able to realize it right away.' 'Il *Decameron* rappresenta la mia nostalgia di un popolo ideale, con la sua miseria, la sua assenza di coscienza politica (è terribile dirlo, ma è vero), di un popolo che ho conosciuto quando ero bambino. Forse esiste ancora nel ventre di Napoli. Nel frattempo si è avuto in Italia, in sei–sette anni, l'insediamento di una società industriale. Ma ciò è stato così rapido che non abbiamo potuto rendercene conto nell'immediato.' Faldini and Fofi, eds, *1970–1984*, 1.

57 For a perhaps only apparently facetious appraisal of the phenomenon, see its cinematic illustration in Dino Risi's *The Monsters* (*I mostri*, 1963) and Risi-Monicelli-Scola's *The New Monsters* (*I nuovi mostri*, 1978).

58 For more details (and bibliography) on 1968 in Italy, see chap. 8, on Thomas Mann and Visconti.

59 Vittorio De Seta, epigraph to Faldini and Fofi, eds, *1960–1969*, vii.

Chapter 5: Mérimée, Bizet, and Rosi

1 Friedrich Nietzsche, *The Joyful Wisdom*, in *CW* 10: 14 (Prelude, 4B). 'Denn gesund ist, wer vergass.' *Die fröhliche Wissenschaft*, in *SW-KSA* 3: 354 (Vorspiel, 4B).

2 The classic work on the subject is Edward Saïd's *Orientalism: Western Conceptions of the Orient* (Harmondsworth: Penguin, 1991 [1978]). The idea is tested with reference to the mediterranean area in my 'Meridionalism: Northern European Conceptions of the South in Pushkin, Eichendorff, Mérimée,' *I Quaderni di Gaia* 8 (1997), 83–104 (with further bibliography).

3 This is why, although I argue on the basis of the same culturological assumptions as many critics who wrote important works on the repressive 'sexual politics' of orientalist-meridionalist literature, I cannot entirely share some of their conclusions on the matter. Among these, and with particular emphasis on the *Carmen* case, I have found most useful Catherine Clément, *Opera: Or, the Undoing of Women*, trans. B. Wing (Minneapolis: University of Minnesota Press, 1988); *L'opéra, ou la défaite des femmes* (Paris: Bernard Grasset, 1979) (thanks to Geoffrey Nowell-Smith for recommending this title); Linda and Michael Hutcheon, *Opera: Desire, Disease, Death* (Lincoln: University of Nebraska Press, 1996); Susan McClary, *Feminine Endings: Music, Gender, and Sexuality* (Minneapolis: University of Minnesota Press, 1991); McClary, *Georges Bizet:* Carmen (Cambridge: Cambridge University Press, 1992); and

Jeremy Tambling, *Opera, Ideology and Film* (Manchester: Manchester University Press, 1987).

4 Even the intent to anthologize only visitors from one nation (France) to one other one (Italy) for only two centuries (the eighteenth and the nineteenth) has produced a large volume of over 1000 pages: Yves Hersant, ed., *Italies: Anthologie des voyageurs français aux XVIIIe et XIXe siècles* (Paris: Laffont, 1988).

5 For bibliographical references to both the translation and its original, see chapter 1, on Goethe and Archibugi's *Mignon Has Left*.

6 Byron, 'The Bride of Abydos,' in vol. 3 of *Poetry, The Works of Lord Byron*, ed. Ernest Hartley Coleridge (London: Murray and New York: Scribner, 1900), 157.

7 'Кто знает край, где небо блещет': 'Кто знает край, где небо блещет/ Неизъяснимой синевой,/ Где море теплою волной/ Вокруг развалин тихо плещет;/ Где вечный лавр и кипарис/ На воле гордо разрослись;/ Где пел Торквато величавый;/ Где и тепер во мгле ночной/ Адриатической волной/ Повторены его октавы;/ Где Рафаэль живописал ...' Aleksandr Sergeevich Pushkin, *Polnoe sobranie sochinenii* (Moscow and Leningrad: Izdatel'stvo Akademii Nauk SSSR, 1948), vol. 3/1: 96.

8 A curious variant of the lemon-tree topos can be found in Flaubert, who, in Egypt, admitted to being charmed exactly by something that so revolted his fellow countrypersons: the juxtaposition of, as he puts it, 'lemon trees and corpses' ('l'odeur des citronniers et celle des cadavres'). Letter to Louise Colet, 27 March 1853, in vol. 2 of *Correspondance*, ed. Jean Bruneau (Paris: Gallimard Pléiade, 1980), 283.

9 Sexuality was (inevitably) more ostensibly *acted out* in the opera version than in Mérimée's work. Gone was the narrator, the multi-layered voice that presented the story 'as if in quotation marks' – to use an expression made popular in Bakhtin's treatment of dialogism. What remained seemed too heady a story to be appreciated at face value by *comme-il-faut* bourgeois (in public and with their families, anyway).

A useful guide to the complexities of the narrating voice in Mérimée's text can be found in P.W.M. Cogman's 'The Narrators of Mérimée's *Carmen*,' *Nottingham French Studies* 27:2 (Nov. 1988), 1–12.

10 For today's reader, some of the contemporaneous fault-finding verges on incomprehensibility; so, for example, the charge that Bizet practised 'Wagnerism' – an argument presumably based on the fact that the bullfight theme and the torero one recur, in *Leitmotif*-style, at particular junctures in his score. Imitating a German musician such a short time after a crushing national defeat was, of course, the deepest abomination of which a French

composer could be accused in 1875. Being conveniently vague, the charge was, at the same time, difficult to disprove. On the limited impact Wagner in fact had on Bizet's music, see Horst Menzel, Carmen *von Georges Bizet* (Berlin, Lichterfelde: Lienau, 1972), 25–6 and 31.

11 For fuller details on the circumstances surrounding *Carmen*'s premiere, see Ellen H. Bleiler, ed. and trans., Carmen *by Georges Bizet* (New York: Dover Publications, 1970), 18–20, and Kurt Pahlen, ed., *Georges Bizet*. Carmen *in der Originalsprache* (Munich: Goldmann-Schott, 1979), 285–99.

Since both French and German culture had long been receptive toward meridionalist themes, it makes sense to argue that 'such a completely opposite welcome [in Vienna] belongs to those phenomena that simply allow for no logical explanation' (Pahlen, ed., *Carmen*, 293).

12 In a German context, innocence and seduction combined in a pre-moral state were embodied to the fullest in Frank Wedekind's quasi-Nana – the equally alliterative Lulu, heroine of *The Spirit of the Earth* (*Der Erdgeist*, 1898) and *Pandora's Vase* (*Die Büchse der Pandora*, 1902), later merged as *Lulu* (1913). (Alban Berg's opera by this last title premiered, albeit in incomplete form, in 1937.) Lulu's animal quality would have been unthinkable outside the Carmen-Nana line.

13 Friedrich Nietzsche, *The Case of Wagner*, trans. O. Levy, in *CW* 8: 1. 'Ich hörte gestern – werden Sie es glauben? – zum zwanzigsten Male *Bizet*'s Meisterstück. Ich harrte wieder mit einer sanften Andacht aus, ich lief wieder nicht davon. Dieser Sieg über meine Ungeduld überrascht mich. Wie ein solches Werk vervollkommnet! Man wird selbst dabei zum "Meisterstück."' Friedrich Nietzsche, *Der Fall Wagner*, SW-KSA 6: 13.

14 Nietzsche, *The Case of Wagner*, in *CW* 8: 3–5. 'Auch dies Werk erlöst; nicht Wagner allein ist ein "Erlöser." Mit ihm nimmt man Abschied vom *feuchten* Norden, von allem Wasserdampf des Wagnerischen Ideals. Schon die Handlung erlöst davon. Sie hat von Mérimée noch die Logik in der Passion, die kürzeste Linie, die *harte* Nothwendigkeit; sie hat vor Allem, was zur heissen Zone gehört, die Trockenheit der Luft, die *limpidezza* in der Luft. Hier ist in jedem Betracht das Klima verändert. Hier redet eine andre Sinnlichkeit, eine andre Sensibilität, eine andre Heiterkeit. Diese Musik ist heiter; aber nicht von einer französischen oder deutschen Heiterkeit. Ihre Heiterkeit ist afrikanisch; sie hat das Verhängniss über sich, ihr Glück ist kurz, plötzlich, ohne Pardon. Ich beneide Bizet darum, dass er den Muth zu dieser Sensibilität gehabt hat, die in der gebildeten Musik Europa's bisher noch keine Sprache hatte, – zu dieser südlicheren, bräuneren, verbrannteren Sensibilität ... Sie sehen bereits, wie sehr mich diese Musik *verbessert*? – *Il faut méditerran[é]iser la musique.*' *Der Fall Wagner*, SW-KSA 6: 15–16.

15 On other re-creations of *Carmen* and certain contrasts (or parallels) between them and Rosi's work, see Denis Bertrand, 'Les migrations de Carmen,' *Le français dans le monde* 23:181 (Nov.–Dec. 1983), 103–8; Freddy Buache, *Le cinéma italien 1945–1990* (Lausanne: L'Âge d'homme, 1992), 453–5; Gwynne Edwards, '*Carmen*,' in *Catholic Tastes and Times: Essays in Honour of Michael E. Williams*, ed. Margaret A. Rees (University of Leeds: Trinity and All Saints' College, 1987), 127–55; and Robert Wangermée, 'L'opéra sur la scène et à l'écran: À propos de *Carmen*,' in *Approches de l'opéra: Actes du colloque AISS (Royaumont, sept. 1984)*, ed. André Helbo (Paris: Didier Erudition, 1986), 251–8.

16 Howard Thompson, '*Hands Over the City; Salvatore Giuliano*,' *New York Times* (28 Sept. 1964, 28). Repr. in *NYT Film Reviews* (1959–68): 3490.

17 Somewhat schematically, it could be said that most of the recent cinematic interpretations pull Bizet's *Carmen* toward intellectualization; Rosi's moves toward historicization.

18 Such scenes are, in fact, so numerous that during the shooting, in Carmona, Rosi facetiously confessed to Michel Ciment who was interviewing him, 'It's unbearable! One hundred and seventy-five extras one day, seven hundred the next, eighty the following, three hundred on the fourth day! Sometimes there are only two characters; then I am happy!' 'C'est insupportable! Cent soixante-quinze figurants un jour, sept cents le lendemain, quatre-vingts le jour suivant, trois cents le quatrième! Parfois, il y a deux personnages: alors, je suis heureux!' In Michel Ciment, *Le dossier Rosi* (Paris: Ramsay, 1987 [1976]), 267.

19 Bizet, *Carmen*, ed. Bleiler, 148 (Act III, scene 5); all further references are to this edition.

20 Micaëla can pose problems for two interrelated reasons. First, she does not appear in Mérimée's original novella, having been introduced by the librettists as a counter-influence to Carmen's dangerous charms. Second, she has a very 'pale' narrative role. However, convincing arguments in favour of her functionality within the opera have been put forward in Dominique Maingueneau, *Carmen: Les racines d'un mythe* (Paris: Éditions du Sorbier, 1984), 37–46.

21 'I took my inspiration from the drawings by Gustave Doré that illustrated *Voyage to Spain* by baron Davillier, of which I am positive that they influenced Bizet and his librettists.' 'Je me suis inspiré des dessins de Gustave Doré qui illustrèrent le *Voyage en Espagne* du baron Davillier et dont je suis sûr qu'ils ont influencé Bizet et ses librettistes.' Rosi, in Ciment, *Le dossier Rosi*, 261.

22 For a detailed treatment of a well-known filmic prototype of this scene, Èizenshtein's Odessa Steps sequence in *Battleship Potëmkin*, see David Bord-

well, *The Cinema of Eisenstein* (Cambridge, Mass.: Harvard University Press, 1993), 73–9.

23 The street urchins meanwhile scream: 'First now comes, walking along,/ the ugly-faced *alguazil.*/ Down with him! Down with him! Down with him!' 'Voici d'abord, marchant au pas,/ L'*alguazil* à vilaine face,/ À bas! à bas! à bas! à bas!' *Carmen*, 162–3 (Act IV, scene 1). The especially self-satisfied demeanour of this dignitary suggests that he be identified as the one the children are mocking.

24 In 1875 the female singers were instructed to smoke on stage, also as a naturalistic device. This caused many eyebrows to be raised – and not because of the fire hazard. See *Carmen*, 18.

25 Rosi's *Carmen* responds to what could be called an implicit hypertextual attitude – hypertextual, that is, vis-à-vis *the director*'s own work. The next section of this volume is devoted to examples of films re-created on a hypertextual basis with respect to the original *literary author*.

26 The film was re-created from Carlo Levi's *Christ Stopped at Eboli.* By coincidence, the village where Levi was exiled appears in the book under the name 'Gagliano' (the real name was Aliano).

27 For more information on Rosi's titles mentioned here and elsewhere in the chapter, see also Francesco Bolzoni, *I film di Francesco Rosi* (Rome: Gremese Editore, 1986); Jean Gili, *Francesco Rosi: Cinéma et pouvoir* (Paris: Éditions du Cerf, 1977); Anton Giulio Mancino and Sandro Zambetti, *Francesco Rosi* (Milan: Il Castoro, 1998 [1977]); and Carlo Testa, ed., *Poet of Civic Courage: The Films of Francesco Rosi* (Trowbridge, Wiltsh.: Flicks Books, 1996).

28 The sympathetic treatment of smugglers seems to fit the same narrative intention. Because in large tracts of southern Italy smugglers are a universally accepted presence on the economic scene, Rosi, as a Neapolitan, had the insight necessary to deal with the subject from the inside, rather than with the awkward external (damning and/or aestheticizing) view typical of the foreigner.

The smuggler issue happens to remain very much a social one to this day – both in Naples and in Andalusia. For a sense of the urgency of the problem in Italy, see Bocca's interview with Judge Agostino Cordova in Giorgio Bocca, *Il sottosopra* (Milan: Mondadori, 1994), esp. 131. As for Gibraltar, its status as a magnet for illegal trade is no less strong today than it was over a century ago. See 'Rocky Relations,' *The Economist*, 17 June 1995, 58.

29 One can find shrewd observations on the coincidence between 'lower parts' of the body and 'lower parts' of the map as observed from the North (here, France) in Maingueneau, *Carmen*, 17–24.

30 This is true to the point that in Rosi Lt. Zuñiga uses *a pair of binoculars* to
observe Carmen. The incident, not to be found in Bizet's opera, reaches
back directly to an episode of voyeurism mentioned in Mérimée's novella.
This is reported in a narratorial aside at the beginning of the second
chapter – an aside, it must be stressed, unrelated to Carmen's story. What
makes Rosi's innovativeness clear beyond all doubt is that at any rate no
binoculars are involved *chez* Mérimée.

Doré's engravings show no indication of the relative positioning of the
fortress vis-à-vis the tobacco factory. While I have insufficient information
for a topographic comparison of historical Seville with its filmic proxy, the
essential point is that verticality was not merely exaggerated but deliberately
exploited by Rosi as a non-verbal equivalent of certain literary effects.

31 Pushkin's *The Captive of the Caucasus* (*Kavkazskii plennik*, 1822), an eminent
specimen of meridionalist literature within Russian culture – in fact, the very
prototype of it – shows an identical usage of the military metaphor. For a
projection of *The Captive of the Caucasus* against the cultural backdrop of
meridionalism, see Katya Hokanson, 'Literary Imperialism, *Narodnost'* and
Pushkin's Invention of the Caucasus,' *The Russian Review* 53:3 (July 1994),
336–52.

32 While this is particularly clear in Rosi's *Carmen*, the possibility to interpret
the events in precisely this light is encouraged in no uncertain terms in the
libretto itself.

33 'Je repensais à tout, je m'abîmais de tristesses et de rêveries – je m'amusais à
tuer sur le mur les punaises qui marchaient et ça faisait sur cette muraille
blanchie de longues arabesques rouge-noir.' Gustave Flaubert, *Voyage en
Égypte. Édition intégrale du manuscrit original*, ed. Pierre-Marc de Biasi (Paris:
Bernard Grasset, 1991), 287. To the best of my knowledge, there is no complete English translation of Flaubert's manuscript. The closest approximation is *Flaubert in Egypt, A Sensibility On Tour: A Narrative Drawn from G. F.'s
Travel Notes and Letters*, ed. and trans. F. Steegmuller (Chicago: Academy
Chicago Ltd., 1979).

34 Mérimée's novella is considerably more direct than the opera on this subject. For a fuller discussion of Nietzsche's concept of the 'animal with a good
conscience,' see above (Pasolini chapter, n. 55).

35 Less theatrically, but with greater verisimilitude, the novella places the final
confrontation in a mountain gorge near the smugglers' abode.

The inescapability of Carmen's and Don José's situation is conveyed by
Rosi not just by the high walls that surround them, but also by a locked door
appearing in the background, with which the camera repeatedly aligns the
two lovers during their duet. The connection between closed doors and tri-

angular relationships is intuitive, but reinforced and arguably overdetermined here by the association existing in the French context since Sartre's existentialist one-act drama *No Exit* (*Huis clos*, 1944).

36 'Je t'aime, Escamillo, et que je meure/ Si j'ai jamais aimé quelqu'un autant que toi.' *Carmen*, 166 (Act IV, scene 1).

37 C'est l'*espada*, la fine lame,/ Celui qui vient terminer tout,/ Qui paraît à la fin du drame/ Et qui frappe le dernier coup. Ibid., 164 (Act IV, scene 1).

38 Carmen spills a negligible amount of blood, compared to that which we see flow inside the bullring – yet another semiotic displacement in the film.

39 The epistemological cards come down, in fact, as early as the film's first sequence: Rosi illustrates the instrumental prelude to the opera with images, shot inside the arena, that culminate in the bull's ritual sacrifice.

40 Bolzoni, *I film di Francesco Rosi*, 134 and 136. On the overwhelming impact of television on Italian cinema during the 1980s, see, among others, the essays by Micciché, Gallo, Maselli, Petraglia and Rulli, and Piscicelli in Lino Micciché, ed., *Schermi opachi*.

41 For more details on the southern heritage in Rosi's *oeuvre*, see Jean Gili, 'A Man of the South,' in Vittorio Giacci, ed., *Francesco Rosi* (Rome: Cinecittà International, 1994), 25–33; 'Un uomo del Sud,' in Sebastiano Gesù, ed., *Francesco Rosi* (Acicatena: Incontri con il cinema, 1991), 23–31.

42 To be precise, despite her living in Egypt Kuchuk Hanem was neither Egyptian nor a 'gypsy,' but a Syrian with a Turkish name. For more details, see Di Biasi's introduction to Flaubert's *Voyage en Égypte*, as well as Gustave Flaubert, *Les lettres d'Égypte de G. F. d'après les manuscrits autographes. Édition critique*, ed. Antoine Youssef Naaman (Paris: Nizet, 1965).

43 With a highly parodic diction, one of de Musset's characters exclaims: 'Romanticism – that's the star that weeps, the wind that cries, the night that shivers, the flower that flies and the bird that gives out a fragrance; it's the unexpected gush, the languid ecstasy, the water tank under the palms, and ruby-red hope and its thousand loves, the angel and the pearl, the white dress of the willows, oh what a beautiful thing, sir!' 'Le romantisme, c'est l'étoile qui pleure, c'est le vent qui vagit, c'est la nuit qui frissonne, la fleur qui vole et l'oiseau qui embaume; c'est le jet inespéré, l'extase alanguie, la citerne sous les palmiers, et l'espoir vermeil et ses mille amours, l'ange et la perle, la robe blanche des saules, ô la belle chose, monsieur!' Alfred de Musset, *Lettres de Dupuis et Cotonet* [1836–7], in *Oeuvres complètes*, ed. Philippe van Tieghem (Paris: Seuil Intégrale, 1963), 877.

44 At the turn of the new century, the phenomenon of immigration – along with the cinema inspired by it – is rapidly growing. See Carlo Durante, 'Extracomunitari,' in Mario Sesti, ed., *La 'scuola' italiana*, 343–8; Monica

Rossi, 'Apologia della differenza: Uno sguardo dall'esterno alla condizione degli immigrati africani in Italia ...' *Canadian/American Journal of Italian Studies* (ed. Antonio Vitti) 54 (1997), 91–110; and Sesti, *Nuovo cinema italiano*, passim.

Chapter 6: Pasternak, Lean, and Moretti

1 Fëdor Dostoevskii, *Notes from Underground,* ed. and trans. M.R. Katz (New York: Norton, 1989), 22. 'Я, может быть, скрыпя зубами шучу.' *Zapiski iz podpol'ia,* in *Povesti i rasskazy 1862–1866,* vol. 5 of *Polnoe sobranie sochinenii v tridsati tomakh* (Leningrad: Nauka, 1972), 117.

2 So entrenched was the cake-eating pattern that Morettiphiles were struck as though by an epoch-making abjuration when, in the autobiographical-looking *Dear Diary* (*Caro diario,* 1994), episode *Islands* (*Isole*), 'Moretti' walked into a bar and, after a moment's hesitation, ordered – *a sandwich and an orange juice.* Would this herald a new political line? Quite possibly; after all, the Berlin wall had collapsed only shortly before. That said, 'Sacher' is, to this day, the name of Moretti's own production house, as well as that of the yearly prizes it assigns (for shorts made by young filmmakers), and 'Nuovo Sacher' the name of his theatre in Rome.

3 I deliberately use the adjectives 'uncommon,' 'unusual' and 'rare' to echo ideas that were on Nanni Moretti's mind as he was making the film: '[*Palombella rossa*] is above all a film on my inability, as a spectator, to trust any longer the usual scripts, the usual dialogues, the usual settings, the usual dining rooms, the usual acting. I didn't want to make a realistic movie about the usual crisis of the usual Communist militant, the usual debates in a remote cell of the party, the usual return to Rome during the usual night which sees the driver, half-asleep, drink the usual espresso in the usual small countryside café.' '[*Palombella rossa*] è soprattutto un film sull'impossibilità di credere ancora io (come spettatore) alle solite sceneggiature, ai soliti dialoghi, ai soliti ambienti, alle solite stanze da pranzo, alla solita recitazione. Non volevo fare un film realistico sulla solita crisi del solito militante comunista, i soliti dibattiti in una sezione lontana, il solito ritorno a Roma nella solita notte che vede il guidatore mezzo addormentato, il solito caffè nel solito piccolo bar di campagna.' Interview with Mario Sesti, in Sesti, *Nuovo cinema italiano* (Rome: Theoria, 1994), 80.

For a further useful bibliography on Moretti and/or *Palombella rossa* in particular see the following: Flavio De Bernardinis, *Nanni Moretti* (Milan: Il Castoro, 1998), esp. 88–101; Faldini and Fofi, eds, *1960–1969,* 439; *1970–1984,* 540, 541, 574, 580, 582–6, 610–13, 629–32, 636, and 692; Gieri, *Contemporary*

Italian Filmmaking, 229–30 (where the film is referred to as *Red Lob*); Giulio Martini and Guglielmina Morelli, eds, *Patchwork Due: Geografia del nuovo cinema italiano* (Milan: Il Castoro, 1997), 175–80; Stefania Parigi, '*Palombella rossa* di N. Moretti: La partita del cinema,' in Micciché, ed., *Schermi opachi*, 309–19; Georgette Ranucci and Stefanella Ughi, eds, *Nanni Moretti* (Rome: Dino Audino Editore, [1995?]), esp. 52–9; and Federica Villa, '*Palombella rossa*,' in Sandro Bernardi et al., *Nanni Moretti* (Turin: Paravia Scriptorium, 1999), 60–2.

4 Michele was also the first name of another Morettian protagonist, that of his earliest release *I Am an Autarkist* (*Io sono un autarchico*, 1976).

5 'Siamo uguali!' Because the smooth-talking, glib fundamentalist is named Simon, one is immediately led to suspect that the choice of just that name may hide a directorial allusion to Simon the Magus – a hypothesis in turn reinforcing the cultural homology between Michele and Flaubert's Saint Antony that I will propose in greater detail shortly.

6 Having qualified the professorial labor-union leader as imposingly paternalistic, I must hasten to add that an altogether ironic 'paternalistic' feature does indeed characterize him: he is played by Nanni Moretti's real father, Professor Luigi Moretti. For an account of Luigi's roles in Nanni's films, see Ranucci and Ughi, eds, *Nanni Moretti*, 68.

7 I stress that *strategy* is the key concept here. The consistency with which the Monteverde team is defeated by its opponents could well, I believe, be ascribed to its coach's garrulous obsession with *tactics* before, during, and after each game. Political parties cannot survive on tactical battles alone; it is a broad strategy they need in order to win – and this, the film implies, the Italian Communist Party has historically lacked.

8 '... fare come un eremita/ che rinuncia a sé ...' The lyrics, by the *cantautore* Franco Battiato ('E ti vengo a cercare,' EMI Publishing Italia), are true to Battiato's characteristic style in shifting from socially critical passages to others of a quasi-theosophical nature. By the process of reaccentuation they undergo in a new context, they become an ideal vehicle for Moretti to poke fun at the apparently little short of 'mystical' motivation required of PCI supporters in the 1980s.

9 Good editions of Flaubert's closet drama are Gustave Flaubert, *The Temptation of Saint Antony*, trans. K. Mrosovsky (Harmondsworth: Penguin, 1980); *La Tentation de Saint Antoine*, in *Oeuvres complètes*, ed. Bernard Masson (Paris: Seuil Intégrale, 1964), vol. 1.

10 A detailed analysis of how the concept of metaphor can be applied to cinema would require a book of its own – a book that, in fact, already exists: Trevor Whittock, *Metaphor and Film* (Cambridge: Cambridge University Press, 1990).

11 Significantly, the title of the super-8 production was *The Defeat* (*La sconfitta*, 1973). See Faldini and Fofi, eds, *1970–1984*, 583; and Ranucci and Ughi, eds, *Nanni Moretti*, 18. Whatever it may have been in the original context, in *Palombella rossa* the point of mentioning defeat in this conjunction is that nothing can be gained by insisting on nostalgically invoking the 'good old times' of purity and ... failure.

12 One of Michele's many obsessions – a perfectly Flaubertian one, it should be noted – is to expose and pillory the penchant in his contemporaries for expressing themselves through worn-out metaphors. 'To speak miserably means to think miserably; and to think miserably means to live miserably,' he correctly argues. 'One must find *the right word!*' ('Parlare male vuol dire pensare male; e pensare male vuol dire vivere male ... Bisogna trovare *la parola giusta!*') The parallelism with Flaubert's *mot juste* hardly needs pointing out.

It is easy to imagine Michele compiling a present-day *Dictionary of Received Ideas* (*Dictionnaire des idées reçues*) in order to lambast the stupidity (*bêtise*) of his decade, the 1980s. In *Palombella rossa*, he certainly gives us several possible entries. On this matter, see also Alberto Arbasino, anthologized in Ranucci and Ughi, eds, *Nanni Moretti*, 58.

13 I am, of course, alluding not to any one particular work of Dostoevsky's, but to his biographical experience.

14 'Su, continuiamo così, facciamoci del male.' In *Bianca*, these words were uttered by Michele at a dinner *chez* a bourgeois family from Roman well-to-do circles. (No prizes for guessing what type of dessert was being served as Michele spoke.)

15 The actor who plays the giant-sized Hungarian professional athlete named Imre happens to be a giant-sized Hungarian professional athlete named Imre Budavari. The choice of an Aci club as the allegorical enemy of the 'Communist team' seems ironic. Since the times of Verga's *I Malavoglia* and Visconti's *The Earth Trembles*, Aci had become something of an emblem for the plight of the Italian working classes, and a rallying cry for the urgency of an Italian revolution.

16 Of course, the autobiographical fallacy is an ever-present danger for the critics in the case of Moretti's films – one similar to that we would be facing if, for the sake of a comparable hypothesis, Fellini himself and not Mastroianni had starred in *La dolce vita* or *8½*.

The question of autobiography in Moretti is quite complex. See Moretti's own statements in Faldini and Fofi, eds, *1970–1984*, 586, 611, 632; and Sesti, *Nuovo cinema italiano*, 79. (For an essential bibliography on autobiography, see the Fellini chapter *supra* n. 27.) In my view, the point is not to ascertain at a biographical level whether – for example – Nanni Moretti ever played water polo against a Hungarian called Imre, but to analyse how the presence of a Hungarian called Imre in the team that defeats the 'Communist' players of *Palombella rossa* affects the structure of the film.

17 Private communication to the author, Rome, 18 December 1995.

18 In *Ecce Bombo*, too, the revolution-minded intellectuals of Michele's group had missed the dawn they were eagerly expecting. To that end, they had installed themselves on the beach at Ostia, without considering that the Tyrrhenian coast looks out to the West. With an entirely intended comic effect in the film, the sunrise thus took them by surprise from behind their backs.

19 On the issue of cinematic quotes within a film, see Viacheslav Vs. Ivanov, 'Fil'm v fil'me,' in *Tekst v tekste: Trudy po znakovym sistemam* 14 (1981), 19–32; and Christian Metz, 'Film(s) dans le film,' in his *L'énonciation impersonnelle*, 93–112.

20 To avoid confusion, I am referring to the English-language film as *'Doctor' Zhivago*, with a *c*, and to the Russian-language novel as *'Doktor' Zhivago*, with a *k*. *'Doctor' Zhivago* is, of course, also the title of the English translation of the novel. My (slightly abridged) quotes from Lean are translated back into English from the Italian-dubbed version actually watched by Michele Apicella and his crowd.

21 More accurately, from another *circle* ('девочка из другого круга' – Book 1, part II).

22 Pasternak, *Doctor Zhivago*, NY 25. 'Забыть думать о танцах. В них всё зло ... Какая безумная вещь вальс!' *Doktor Zhivago*, P 34–5; AA 26; M 29 (Book 1, part II, sect. 4). The novel is rife with references to Komarovsky as a cheap Mephisto. Waltzing (1, II, 4) was held to be 'the devil's dance' in the nineteenth century; Komarovsky walks about Moscow with a small, angry dog (an allusion to Mephisto in Goethe's *Faust*); his only friend of sorts is called 'Satanidi' (both 1, II, 13); and Lara thinks of her own weakness toward the *viveur* as due to 'black magic' (1, III, 5).

23 *Doctor Zhivago*, NY 44–5; emphasis added. 'Как это случилось? Как могло это случиться?' *Doktor Zhivago*, P 56; AA 45; M 47 (Book 1, part II, sect. 12).

24 Russ. *komar* = 'mosquito.'

25 On the cultural shift in European nineteenth-century culture from the focus on the Evil One to that on a myriad petty 'evil ones,' see my *Desire and the Devil* (New York: Peter Lang, 1991), 129–59.

26 *Doctor Zhivago*, NY 146. 'Ведь только раз в вечность случается такая небывальщина ... Что-то евангельское, не правда ли?' *Doktor Zhivago*, P 169; AA 147–8; M 145 (Book 1, part V, sect. 8).

27 *Doctor Zhivago*, NY 148. 'Больше таких объяснений между ними не

повторялось. Через неделю Лариса Федоровна уехала.' *Doktor Zhivago*, P 171; AA 149; M 147 (Book 1, part V, sect. 8).

28 On the move to the countryside of the populist-revolutionary *narodnik* groups, see especially Franco Venturi's detailed history of the movement: *Dall'andata nel popolo al terrorismo*, vol. 3 of his *Il populismo russo* (Turin: Einaudi, 1972 [1952]).

29 Pasternak, *Doctor Zhivago*, NY 53. 'О, как задорно щелкают выстрелы ... Блаженны поруганные, блаженны оплетенные. Дай вам Бог здоровья, выстрелы! Выстрелы, выстрелы, вы того же мнения!' *Doktor Zhivago*, P 65; AA 54; M 56 (Book 1, part II, sect. 19).

30 The true atmosphere of the lovers' final thirteen days is unambiguously described in sections 4 through 9 of Book 2, part XIV. Lara cooks, washes, starches, and has 'endless chores' (sect. 9); first and foremost among these is heating the house (sect. 6). She does talk about an 'instinct for domesticity' (sect. 6), but that is meant by her as an antidote to the systematic homelessness inflicted on the nation by a tiny group of fumbling 'professional revolutionists' – i.e., party bureaucrats. It should also be noted that Lara and Yurii live in a very plain house vacated by the Mikulitsyn family, not in a fancy pseudo-Andalusian marriage cake such as the one whipped up in Lean's film.

31 The word is used three times. The translation has, respectively, *gully, gully, ravine* (NY 439, 440, 441); Pasternak writes three times *ovrag* ('ravine,' 'gorge') (P 508, 509, 511; AA 449, 449, 451; M 432, 432, 434).

32 Pasternak, *Doctor Zhivago*, NY 492. 'Юрий Андреевич уже несколько раз терял ее из виду, когда починенный трамвай трогался с места и обгонял ее. И она несколько раз возвращалась в поле его зрения, когда новая поломка останавливала трамвай и дама нагоняла его.' *Doktor Zhivago*, P 568; AA 502; M 483 (Book 2, part XV, sect. 12).

33 'постоянное криводушие.' For more on this issue, see my '*Doktor Zhivago*: Values versus Voodoo,' *The Russian Review* 56:3 (July 1997), 383–401, esp. 389–90.

34 Marina who? The Marina with whom Yurii lives in the 1920s, and with whom he has two daughters. She is herself the daughter of Markel, the Zhivagos' concierge from pre-revolutionary times, who has risen to a position of power under the new regime. Her presence covers sections 6 through 12 of Book 2, part XV (the Conclusion).

35 Khrushchёv, it will be remembered, renewed this promise after Stalin's death; and Pasternak was writing under Khrushchёv.

36 Book 2, part XV, sect. 12. The stuffiness of air *after* the revolution (Bertolucci, where are you?) is also sharply thematized in another important epi-

sode occurring toward the end of Zhivago's life: the dinner he has with Gordon and his other friends. It is on that very occasion that the subject of 'twisted souls' is mentioned (Book 2, part XV, sect. 7).

37 My point on Lean's re-creation might bear some explicit summary and reiteration here. Moretti's importing literature *en abyme* into *Palombella rossa* via Lean's film forces us to face the fact that, *when it comes to certain particularly tragic subject matters*, some re-creations can be – and are – far, far less equal than others. This is not to say that a book as averse as *Masters of Two Arts* to fidelity-based evaluative categories for cinematic re-creation is now suddenly having second thoughts. Rather, there seems to be every reason to argue, for reasons that should now be self-evident, that Lean's *Zhivago* is not abominable *as a re-creation*, it is abominable *as a film* – whether or not any specific book came before it. Distorting and aestheticizing real, recent, well-known historical bloodshed for the purpose of lucre is, to me, not an inadequate artistic procedure, but simply an unethical one.

38 The exact wording of Enrico Berlinguer's statement (*Tribuna politica*, 15 Dec. 1981) was as follows: 'Ciò che è avvenuto in Polonia ci induce a considerare che effettivamente la capacità propulsiva di rinnovamento delle società che si sono create nell'est europeo è andata esaurendosi ... spinta propulsiva la cui data di inizio è nella rivoluzione socialista d'ottobre.' Chiara Ottaviano and Peppino Ortoleva, eds, *I giorni della storia d'Italia dal Risorgimento a oggi* (Novara: Istituto Geografico De Agostini, 1997 [1991]), 717.

39 'Crisi, peggioramento, scompenso, accesso, parossismo, modificazione, perturbazione, difficoltà, dissesto, recessione, depressione, rovina, squilibrio, turbamento, smarrimento, inquietudine, *scon-cer-to!*'

40 Appropriately, it was Moretti who was given the responsibility to make a documentary about the nation-wide process (*La Cosa*, 1990). See Ranucci and Ughi, eds, *Nanni Moretti*, 60–1. In the symbol eventually chosen, the newly born PDS was represented by an oak tree *supported by* the old PCI logo, which appeared under it (i.e., as its 'root').

41 Peter Handke, *The Goalie's Anxiety at the Penalty Kick*, trans. M. Roloff (New York: Farrar, Straus and Giroux, 1972), 133.

'Der Tormann überlegt, in welche Ecke der andere schießen wird,' sagte Bloch. 'Wenn er den Schützen kennt, weiß er, welche Ecke er sich in der Regel aussucht. Möglicherweise rechnet aber auch der Elfmeterschütze damit, daß der Tormann sich das überlegt. Also überlegt sich der Tormann weiter, daß der Ball heute einmal in die andere Ecke kommt. Wie aber, wenn der Schütze noch immer mit dem Tormann mitdenkt und nun doch in die übliche Ecke schießen will? Und so weiter, und so weiter.'

Bloch sah, wie nach und nach alle Spieler aus dem Strafraum gingen. Der Elfmeterschütze legte sich den Ball zurecht. Dann ging er auch rückwärts aus dem Strafraum heraus.

'Wenn der Schütze anläuft, deutet unwillkürlich der Tormann, kurz bevor der Ball abgeschossen wird, schon mit dem Körper die Richtung an, in die er sich werfen wird, und der Schütze kann ruhig in die andere Richtung schießen,' sagte Bloch. 'Ebensogut könnte der Tormann versuchen, mit einem Strohhalm eine Tür aufzusperren.'

Der Schütze lief plötzlich an. Der Tormann, der einen grellgelben Pullover anhatte, blieb völlig unbeweglich stehen, und der Elfmeterschütze schoß ihm den Ball in die Hände.

Die Angst des Tormanns beim Elfmeter (Frankfurt am Main: Suhrkamp, 1970), 112. Alberto Arbasino alludes in passing to the same episode, but somewhat reductively understands it as conveying only 'la solitudine dell'attaccante (*à la* Peter Handke).' Anthologized in Ranucci and Ughi, eds, *Nanni Moretti*, 57.

42 'Non bisogna leggere! Non bisogna nemmeno scrivere! ... Perché un concetto ecco che subito diventa menzogna ... Io *odio* la parola scritta!'

The theme is recurrent in Nanni Moretti, and it has been broached again by the director in *The Son's Room* (*La stanza del figlio*, 2001).

Chapter 7: Stendhal and Rossellini

1 'Les Romains que l'on peint n'ont pas l'honneur d'être Français.' Stendhal, *Vanina Vanini*, in *Romans et nouvelles*, ed. Ernest Abravanel, vol. 38 of *Oeuvres complètes*, ed. Victor Del Litto (Geneva: Cercle du Bibliophile, 1970), 70n.

2 '[Trastevere est] un mauvais quartier, dit-on; superbe à mes yeux; il y a de l'*énergie*, c'est-à-dire, la qualité qui manque le plus au dix-neuvième siècle.' *OC* 7: 23–4 (*Promenades dans Rome* vol. 2; 27 Jan. 1828); emphasis in original.

3 'Erhabene Tollheiten. Stendhal,' is the wording in one of the paralipomena of late 1880. Friedrich Nietzsche, *Nachlaß 1880–1882*, *SW-KSA* 9: 342 (7 [120]). The love affair between Nietzsche and Stendhal was a passionate one. Nietzsche cites Stendhal many times in his work, always praising him with enthusiasm, and in particular linking him to the post-Christian philosophy of '[his] son Zarathustra' ('mein Sohn Zarathustra'). *Nachlaß Sommer-Herbst 1884*, *SW-KSA* 11: 254 (26 [394]). He wonders: 'Could it be that I am myself envious of Stendhal?' ('Vielleicht bin ich selbst auf Stendhal neidisch?') *Ecce homo*, *SW-KSA* 6: 285–6 (*Warum ich so klug bin* 3).

4 'mit einem Napoleonischen Tempo.' *Jenseits von Gut und Böse, SW-KSA* 5: 199 (VIII, 254).

5 'et le journal annonce qu'elle vient d'épouser le prince don Livio Savelli.' *OC* 38: 77.

6 For more details on the dictum attributed to D'Azeglio, see Alberto Banti, *La nazione del Risorgimento* (Turin: Einaudi, 2000), 203–5.

7 One can find a useful survey of the (highly uneven) indices of the 'modernization' of Italy under the Republic in Martin Clark, *Modern Italy 1871–1995*, (London: Longman, 1996 [1984]), 348–73.

8 For a thorough discussion of the political issues contained in the two original narratives, and developed in detail by Visconti's filmic re-creations of them, see, respectively, Millicent Marcus, 'Visconti's *Senso:* The *Risorgimento* according to Gramsci,' in her *Italian Film in the Light of Neorealism,* 164–87; and 'Visconti's *Leopard:* The Politics of Adaptation,' in her *Filmmaking By the Book,* 45–66. As for Marcia Landy, while her *Italian Film* has an excellent section on Gramsci (149–80), *Senso* is barely mentioned there, and *Vanina Vanini* not at all. Her other book on the subject, *Film, Politics, and Gramsci,* deals with Italian cinema via the films of the Taviani brothers.

9 In Italian cinema, this thesis was brought to its extreme consequences in Florestano Vancini's *The Events at Bronte: Chronicle of a Massacre Glossed Over in History Books (I fatti di Bronte: Cronaca di un massacro che i libri di storia non hanno raccontato,* 1972). The film was inspired by Verga's novella *Libertà* (first published in 1882).

After the passing away of Liberal and Fascist Italy, the 'disenchanted' or 'Gramscian' view has become so established that, rather than questioning it, 'anti-revisionist' (i.e., conservative) scholars prefer to argue past it: for all its internal contradictions, they point out, unification happened the way it did because it could never have worked out any other way. (Among others, see Luciano Cafagna, *Cavour* [Bologna: Il Mulino, 1999]; and Alfonso Scirocco, *In difesa del Risorgimento* [Bologna: Il Mulino, 1998]). This obviously misses the point raised by the critics in the first place: given its cost, was unification indeed worth having? Not coincidentally, scholars who are both conservatives *and foreigners* can afford to be much more casually open-minded than their Italian counterparts about the unification taboo – *vide* Denis Mack Smith's massive *Modern Italy: A Political History* (New Haven, Conn.: Yale University Press, 1997 [1969]).

And in case anyone thought historiography a dull exercise, here is the latest twist to the story. In the last few years of the twentieth century, left-leaning liberals have tended to renounce their historical preference for regional decentralization, swinging instead toward the centralism previously typical of conservatives. Meanwhile, the very ideal of unification has come under increasing attack from traditionally arch-unitarian conservatives (including Catholics). New contexts, different rereadings of an identical past.

10 The unreal, literary quality of the wished-for image of Italy among the Thousand, and their subsequent sense of estrangement in discovering a land utterly foreign to them, stand out with great clarity in Abba's diary. See Giuseppe Cesare Abba, *The Diary of One of Garibaldi's Thousand*, intro., trans. E.R. Vincent (London: Oxford University Press, 1962); *Da Quarto al Volturno: Noterelle d'uno dei Mille* (Bologna: Zanichelli, 1909).

On the disproportion between the 'classical' reputation of the South as a garden of the Hesperides and its true economic condition, as well as on the policy errors that were incurred after the unification on the basis of this mistaken assumption, see especially Valerio Castronovo, 'La storia economica,' in *Storia d'Italia* vol. 4/1 (Turin: Einaudi, 1976); Denis Mack Smith, 'Regionalismo e patriottismo nel Risorgimento,' *Bollettino della Società di Studi Politici* 3 (July 1970), 9–32; Emilio Sereni, *Il capitalismo nelle campagne (1860–1900)* (Turin: Einaudi, 1968 [1947]), esp. 72ff.; and Rosario Villari, ed., *Il Sud nella storia d'Italia: Antologia della questione meridionale*, 2 vols. (Bari: Laterza, 1974). For a recent, detailed analysis of other discourses that, alongside the literary one, left a deep (and mutually reinforcing) imprint on the ideological birth of the idea of Italy in the nineteenth century, see Banti, *La nazione del Risorgimento*, in its entirety. The rude awakening that awaited northern Italian patriots in and after 1860 is treated in Banti's Conclusion.

By the 1990s, with the rise in the North of autonomist or independentist political Leagues, the issue gained widespread acknowledgment, generating, in the process, phalanxes of books. See, among other no less valuable ones, Giorgio Bocca, *La disunità d'Italia* (Milan: Garzanti, 1990) and Luciano Cafagna, *Nord e Sud: Non fare a pezzi l'unità d'Italia* (Venice: Marsilio, 1994).

11 The last work by an 'Italian' that had been successful in the task – exemplarily so, in fact – was arguably Virgil's *Aeneid*.

On the subject, today's obligatory referral is to Homi K. Bhabha, ed., *Nation and Narration* (London: Routledge, 1990), where Timothy Brennan writes: 'Nations ... are imaginary constructs that depend for their existence on an apparatus of cultural fictions in which imaginative literature plays a decisive role' ('The National Longing for Form,' 49). (Nations are not, of course, *imaginary* constructs; they are thoroughly ideological historical, i.e. *real*, constructs.)

12 The film was made in 1960 and released in 1961. On the socio-cultural context from which *Viva l'Italia!* arose, on the circumstances of the film itself, and in particular on Rossellini's anti-rhetorical approach to Garibaldi, see the appropriate chapters or sections in Roberto Rossellini, *Il mio metodo*, ed.

Adriano Aprà (Venice: Marsilio, 1987), 231–5, 318–19, 341 (only the last of which found its way into the strongly reduced English edition, *My Method*, trans. A. Cancogni [New York: Marsilio, 1992], 160–1); Pio Baldelli, *Roberto Rossellini* (Rome: Samonà e Savelli, 1972) (including a long interview with Rossellini, 247–51); Peter Brunette, *Roberto Rossellini* (New York: Oxford University Press, 1987); Angela Dalle Vacche, *The Body in the Mirror: Shapes of History in Italian Cinema* (Princeton, NJ: Princeton University Press, 1992); Faldini and Fofi, eds, *1960–1969*; José Luis Guarner, *Roberto Rossellini* (New York: Praeger, 1970); Stefano Masi and Enrico Lancia, *I film di Roberto Rossellini* (Rome: Gremese, 1987); Pietro Pintus, *Storia e film: Trent'anni di cinema italiano (1945–1975)* (Rome: Bulzoni, 1980), 73–4; Gianni Rondolino, *Roberto Rossellini* (Turin: UTET, 1989), 267–70; and Pierre Sorlin, *The Film in History: Restaging the Past* (Oxford: Basil Blackwell, 1980), 133–8.

Baldelli is entirely correct in arguing that by slashing the rhetorical emphasis traditionally placed on Garibaldi by Italian nationalisms of all stripes Rossellini is far from precluding another mythicization of the character: Garibaldi *redivivus* will merely conform to a new myth, that of the hardworking simple hero (Baldelli, *Roberto Rossellini*, 157). I would, in fact, go as far as saying that the position of the new Garibaldi is altogether in keeping with the ideologically low-profile, labour-loving image sought by the Republic at a time when armies of its emigrants were replacing the hoped-for victorious Italic armies that Fascism would gladly have stationed across Europe.

13 *Late* romanticism, that is – not the romanticism of Novalis or Senancour. The very concept of romanticism is, of course, mercurial, and can generally be useful only if applied with qualifications.

14 During the late 1950s to early 1960s, the main purpose of espousing technological sophistication was clearly to claw back audiences from the advancing screens of television.

15 The director's son Renzo described this long and complex process of artistic abjuration in what seem to me the most succinct terms available to us in the vast field of Rosselliniana:

'He used to say that we were going through an exceptional historical period, because we were experiencing a phase of great technological explosion; that never in the previous millennia had there been such a development of technology; that unheard-of contradictions were challenging humanity, such as the demographic explosion, the ecological clean-up, the energy crisis [and the conquest of outer space], all phenomena of historical magnitude that were changing the face of our planet ...

To him, the problem was how to relate to this reality. In order to confront this new historical phase, one had to be aware of it and be knowledgeable about the world and its history. Since this task was carried out in a clumsy manner by the dominant culture, large sections of the masses were cut off from knowledge. He used to say that humanity is endowed with an enormous patrimony, intelligence; the question was how to use the mass media (he, for one, greatly appreciated the invention of television) so that this immense potential would receive the appropriate tools for history to make a leap forward. He entertained a gigantic and to a large extent utopian project, whose scale went far beyond his own possibilities. But, as he used to say, someone had to get it started; and therefore he plunged in, although he was aware that he would be accused of no longer being an artist, of having abandoned his creativity. Thus it was that he began to do didactic work and to narrate history.'

'Diceva che stavamo attraversando un periodo eccezionale dal punto di vista storico perché vivevamo la fase della grande esplosione tecnologica; che mai nei millenni precedenti c'era stato un tale sviluppo della tecnica; che nuovissime contraddizioni si presentavano all'uomo, come l'esplosione demografica, il riassetto ecologico, la crisi energetica [e la conquista dello spazio], fenomeni di portata storica che stavano modificando l'assetto del pianeta ...

Il problema per lui era come rapportarsi a questa realtà. Per poterlo fare e affrontare questa nuova fase storica bisognava esserne coscienti e conoscere il mondo e la sua storia. Poiché questo compito era assolto in maniera maldestra dalla cultura dominante, c'erano larghissimi settori di massa esclusi dalla conoscenza. Diceva che l'uomo è portatore di un patrimonio enorme: l'intelligenza. Si poneva il problema di utilizzare i mezzi di comunicazione di massa – proprio per questo apprezzava molto l'invenzione della televisione, per esempio – per dare strumenti a questa potenzialità immensa e aiutare a far compiere un salto in avanti nella storia dell'uomo. Aveva questo progetto gigantesco, largamente utopico, con dimensioni nettamente al di là delle sue possibilità. Ma, come diceva lui, qualcuno doveva pure iniziare; e quindi si era buttato, anche essendo conscio che sarebbe stato accusato di non essere più un artista, di avere abbandonato la sua creatività. Fu così che cominciò a fare un lavoro didattico e a raccontare la storia.'

Renzo Rossellini, in Faldini and Fofi, eds, *1960–1969*, 228.

Less condensed expositions of the director's approach can be found in Roberto Rossellini, *Quasi un'autobiografia*, ed. Stefano Roncoroni (Milan: Mondadori, 1987) (chaps. 1–2), as well as Roberto Rossellini, *Un esprit libre ne doit rien apprendre en esclave* (Paris: Fayard, 1977) (in its entirety).

16 For *Un esprit libre*, see the previous note. On the broader Rossellinian context, see Adriano Aprà, 'Rossellini's Historical Encyclopedia,' in David Forgacs et al., eds, *Roberto Rossellini: Magician of the Real* (London: British Film Institute, 2000), 126–48. The book contains other useful essays on Rossellini's political tribulations alluded to here.

An excellent recent introduction to the work of the Czech humanist Comenius (1592–1670) is offered by *Jan Amos Comenius. Philosophisches und dichterisches Werk*, special issue of *Russian Literature* 39:4 (May 1996), 419–546.

17 This period led to the TV-sponsored production of, among others, *The Iron Age* (1964), *The Struggle of Humanity for Its Survival* (1964–70), *The Acts of the Apostles* (1969), *Socrates* (1970), *Pascal* (1972), *Augustine of Hippo* (1972), *The Age of the Medicis* (1972), and *Cartesius* (1974). *The Messiah* (1975) had a different, more complicated birth.

18 I am thinking, in particular, of Tolstoy's last artistic phase – that of *Resurrection, What Is Art?*, and *Father Sergius.*

To the best of my knowledge, Rossellini refers to Tolstoy only twice in his books and in the course of his many interviews. The two quotes are virtually identical; in fact, they refer back to one single, unidentified (and not particularly enlightening) point. According to Rossellini, Tolstoy wrote that for every artistic expression an 'emotional impulse' ('impulso emotivo') is indispensable. Edoardo Bruno, ed., *Roberto Rossellini* (Rome: Bulzoni, 1979), 50, 55–6 (the latter repr. in *Il mio metodo*, 355–6; not in the English version).

19 'Mi sono accorto che seguitavo a dibattere il dramma di una formica, mentre nell'universo stava esplodendo una galassia; e il dramma della formica ha cessato allora di interessarmi.' *Il mio metodo*, 317; not in the English edition.

20 'E' sorto l'Himalaia e noi stiamo ancora a guardare la polvere della vallata!' Bruno, ed., *Roberto Rossellini*, 30.

21 It is hardly surprising that Third World countries would not partake in the perception of an existential crisis which was not, after all, of their making. Having, as former colonies, never had a hand in shaping the world around them, they clearly had no reason to feel affected by its shortcomings. Quite the contrary: the enormous practical problems with which they were (and are) grappling made them *yearn* for the technological prowess they lacked, not blame it for a global malaise that it had not caused. To simplify Rossellini's position somewhat, it could be said that after his voyage to India in 1957 the director applied to the whole issue of scientific progress a distinctly 'Indian' viewpoint.

22 The notion of hypertext is a rapidly evolving theoretical area, stressing non-linear interlinkages among texts. For an introduction see Edward Barrett,

ed., *The Society of Text: Hypertext, Hypermedia, and the Social Construction of Information* (Cambridge, Mass.: MIT Press, 1989); J. David Bolter, *Writing Space: The Computer, Hypertext, and the History of Writing* (Hillsdale, NJ: Lawrence Erlbaum, 1991); Paul Delany and George P. Landow, eds, *Hypermedia and Literary Studies* (Cambridge, Mass.: MIT Press, 1991); David Kolb, *Hypertext, Argument, Philosophy: Socrates in the Labyrinth* (Cambridge, Mass.: Eastgate Systems, 1994); George P. Landow, *Hypertext: The Convergences of Contemporary Critical Theory and Technology* (Baltimore: Johns Hopkins University Press, 1992); George P. Landow, ed., *Hyper / Text / Theory* (Baltimore: Johns Hopkins University Press, 1994); Cliff McKnight et al., eds, *Hypertext in Context* (New York: Cambridge University Press, 1991); and Jakob Nielsen, *Hypertext and Hypermedia* (Boston: Academic Press, 1990).

23 On the relation between the film and a number of Stendhalian works – *Le rouge et le noir, The Charterhouse of Parma, Rome, Naples and Florence*, and *On Love* – see Carlo Testa, 'Rossellini Reader of Stendhal: *Vanina Vanini*,' *Romance Languages Annual* 10 (1998), 380–6. *The Charterhouse of Parma* is briefly alluded to in Attolini, *Storia del cinema letterario*, 172.

24 'Beeella ... la cocca di papassuo!' For Rossellini's own facetious usage of the term 'cocca,' see Faldini and Fofi, eds, *1960–1969*, 226–7.

25 'Eh, se ciavessi vent'anni pure io! Daje cocco, daje!' Don Asdrubale's 'cocca' recurs here once more, in masculine variant.

26 Vanina seems to have entirely forgotten that just a few hours earlier she was extremely excited about a similarly enigmatic story regarding a *carbonaro* in a woman's dress.

27 One of the immaculately dressed shepherds is, predictably, Pietro in disguise. Marcella De Marchis reports the following anecdote about the shooting of the episode: 'In *Vanina Vanini* ... Danilo Donati [the costume designer] had dressed the *carbonari* in light colours: light green, light blue. Their footwear, too, was light-coloured and clean, and they had to take great care not to soil it. The scene being shot required them to descend into a sort of hidden cellar that was very dark and dirty. The stagehand came back up: "The Doctor [i.e., Rossellini] said like this: why don't you also put spangle on the shepherds' leggings?" Roberto wanted them to be black and dusty, and so Donati lost his temper and quit.' 'In *Vanina Vanini* ... Danilo Donati [il costumista] aveva vestito i carbonari con dei colori chiari, dei verdini, dei celesti. Anche le loro ciabatte [= ciocie] erano chiare, pulite e dovevano stare bene attenti a che non si sporcassero. La scena prevedeva che scendessero giù in una specie di cantina nascosta, molto buia e sporca. Tornò su il macchinista: "Ha detto così il dottore: perché non je mettete anche le paillettes sulle ciocie"

Roberto li voleva neri, impolverati e così Donati perse la pazienza e se ne andò.' Marcella De Marchis Rossellini, *Un matrimonio riuscito: Autobiografia* (Milano: Il Castoro, 1996), 86–7.

28 'Come vorrei essere libero, ricco e potente! ... Sento che potrei essere molto più utile alla causa della libertà ... E quando l'Italia fosse libera dai suoi oppressori ... resterei sempre con te!'

29 To Viscontists, the entire scene – not just Pietro's allusion to apocalyptic times ahead for the aristocracy – has the added interest of a sui generis re-creation of the famous showdown in *Senso* between Livia Serpieri and Mahler at the lieutenant's apartment in Venice.

30 'turbamenti ... creature amate ... al posto del Creatore ... amicizia, amore, parole audaci ... giovane corpo ... impulsi impuri.'

31 Brunette asserts that Pietro spurns 'America' (the USA) because of that country's capitalistic obsession (*Roberto Rossellini*, 391, n. 6). The video version I used, with Italian dialogue and English subtitles, has not enabled me to identify any comment by Pietro to that effect.

32 'Noi due! E gli altri? Perché quella notte non ero al mio posto? Non c'ero, perché non amavo soltanto l'Italia. Adesso, per fortuna, potrò morire anch'io per la mia patria.'

33 'Andrò io dai tuoi compagni, andrò a umiliarmi davanti a loro, a dire che ero folle d'amore per te ... e che sono stata io a denunciarli ...'

34 If Ergas, the much-vituperated producer, did in fact – as Rossellini asserts – expunge some fifteen minutes from the early part of the film, eliminating a large part of Vitelleschi's and Missirilli's conversation in the stagecoach as well as an abortive attempt at further erotic fraternization in Rome, I am inclined to feel that he must have been miraculously inspired to do so by the Muses as much as he probably was by Mammon.

35 '[Vanina] parut prendre plus de plaisir à tourmenter le jeune Livio Savelli ...
'Ce jeune *carbonaro* qui vient de s'échapper ... au moins celui-là a fait quelque chose de plus que de se donner la peine de naître.' *OC* 38: 46.

36 '*Monsieur le comte* ... what have you done to deserve so much wealth? you took upon yourself the trouble of being born, and nothing more.' 'Monsieur le comte ... qu'avez-vous fait pour tant de biens? vous vous êtes donné la peine de naître, et rien de plus.' Beaumarchais, *Le mariage de Figaro*, in *Oeuvres*, ed. Pierre and Jacqueline Larthomas (Paris: Gallimard Pléiade, 1988), 469 (Act V, scene 3).

37 Essentially identical concerns preoccupy Mathilde de La Mole in *Le rouge* – on which Stendhal worked immediately after *Vanina Vanini*, and which expands on many of the novella's themes. See Testa, 'Rossellini Reader of Stendhal,' 380–1.

38 In the Stendhalian universe the name *Clélia* is a hallowed one, associated not with a maid but with the heroine of *The Charterhouse of Parma*.

When Stendhal's Vanina decides to reconnoiter the *palazzo* to her satisfaction, she deliberately *gets rid* of her lady's companion: 'Elle se débarrassa de sa dame de compagnie.' *OC* 38: 47.

39 For the record, while Pietro has raven-black hair in the film, in Stendhal 'la personne' is blonde. *OC* 38: 48.

40 'Il faut que cette pauvre femme ait des ennemis bien terribles, se dit Vanina.' *OC* 38: 49.

41 For an analysis of Stendhal's procedure, see Jean Peytard, *Voix et traces narratives chez Stendhal: Analyse sémiotique de* Vanina Vanini (Paris: Éditeurs Français Réunis, 1980), esp. 33–6.

42 'Si je le vois, c'est pour moi, c'est pour me faire plaisir.' *OC* 38: 54.

43 'Un soir, après avoir passé la journée à le détester et à se bien promettre d'être avec lui encore plus froide et plus sévère qu'à l'ordinaire, elle lui dit qu'elle l'aimait. Bientôt elle n'eut plus rien à lui refuser.' *OC* 38: 54.

44 'Si sa folie fut grande, il faut avouer que Vanina fut parfaitement heureuse. Missirilli ne songea plus à ce qu'il croyait devoir à sa dignité d'homme: il aima comme on aime pour la première fois à dix-neuf ans et en Italie. Il eut tous les scrupules de l'amour-passion, jusqu'au point *d'avouer à cette jeune princesse si fière la politique dont il avait fait usage pour s'en faire aimer.* Il était étonné de l'excès de son bonheur.' *OC* 38: 54; emphasis added.

45 'une fille déshonorée.' *OC* 38: 57.

While in the film it is Clelia who prompts the sobbing princess into seeking a treatment of sorts at Porretta in the Apennines, in Stendhal the idea is autonomously mooted by Vanina.

46 *OC* 38: 56. What Stendhal's Pietro means is that he is interested *in Vanina*, not in the wealth and connections she can offer him in Italy. He is in favour of going abroad (after Italy's freedom is secured, that is), not against it – as opposed to what the film has him say.

47 According to Brunette, '[Rossellini's Vanina] reminds us of the prostitutes encountered early in the film by Pietro.' Brunette, *Roberto Rossellini*, 238.

48 'grâce à un passeport acheté d'une ambassade étrangère.' *OC* 38; 58.

49 Stendhal's key words are here 'fierté' and 'orgueil.' *OC* 38: 60.

50 '"En vérité," lui dit-elle, "vous m'aimez comme un mari; ce n'est pas mon compte."

Bientôt ses larmes coulèrent; mais c'était *de honte de s'être abaissée jusqu'aux reproches.*' *OC* 38: 58; emphasis added.

However Rossellinophile, even the French critic Serceau must repeatedly admit that we are here 'at the antipodes of Stendhal.' Michel Serceau,

Roberto Rossellini, intro. Enrico Fulchignoni (Paris: Les Éditions du Cerf, 1986), 216 and 218.

51   *OC* 38: 65.

52   Ibid. Stendhal regularly calls him *Monsignor* Catanzara (he is not, or not yet, a cardinal; cf. *OC* 38: 69). Aside from promoting him, the film also quotes his last name as Catanzara-Savelli.

53   The egalitarianism of souls for which the two lovers aim is, it seems to me, strongly emphasized by the symmetry of their cross-dressing: Pietro disguises himself as a woman, Vanina disguises herself as a man. For an astute reading of inversions of signs of just this kind, see Iurii M. Lotman, 'Perevērnutyi obraz' ('The Reversed Image'), in his *Kul'tura i vzryv* (Moscow: Gnosis, 1992), 123–75.

54   *Vanina.* 'Someone wants the life of the *carbonaro* Missirilli to be spared; if he is executed, you won't survive him by a week.' 'On veut que le carbonaro Missirilli ait la vie sauve; s'il est exécuté, vous ne lui survivrez pas d'une semaine'. *OC* 38: 71.

55   *OC* 38: 71, 73.

56   'une époque où le sang versé aujourd'hui fera tache.' *OC* 38: 73.

57   In a little-known page in *Promenades dans Rome*, Stendhal writes about conspirators who have been arrested and jailed in Castel Sant'Angelo, and then adds wryly: 'Almost all have fallen into extreme devotion.' 'Presque tous sont tombés dans une excessive dévotion.' *OC* 7: 177 (*Promenades dans Rome*, vol. 2; 1 June 1828). Pietro fits this pattern to a T with his renunciation and his advice to Vanina to marry the nobleman destined for her by her father.

58   To shriek or not to shriek? This specific interdisciplinary issue elicited a by now quite literally classical discussion in chapters 2 through 4 of Lessing's *Laokoon: or, On the Boundaries of Painting and Poetry*. Gotthold Ephraim Lessing, *Laokoon, oder Über die Grenzen der Malerei und Poesie* (1766), vol. 5/2 of *Werke und Briefe in zwölf Bänden*, ed. Wilfried Barner (Frankfurt am Main: Deutscher Klassiker Verlag, 1990).

59   'un chef d'oeuvre mutilé.' Jean-André Fieschi, 'Les deux flammes,' *Cahiers du cinéma* 135 (Sept. 1962), 40.

60   'caso esemplare del capo d'opera sviato.' Baldelli, *Roberto Rossellini*, 161.

61   Ibid., 168–70.

62   In 1959, the Venice film festival awarded Rossellini the Golden Lion, *ex-aequo* with Monicelli's *The Great War* (*La grande guerra*), for *General Della Rovere* (*Il generale Della Rovere*). For social, political, and cultural reasons, public and critics alike were then in the mood for good, healthy, realist-looking 'neo-realist' stuff some ten years after Rossellini had grown out of it – and unanimously rewarded him for (cynically) humouring them.

On *General Della Rovere*, see the appropriate chapters or sections in Rossellini, *Il mio metodo*, 226–8 (not in the English edition); Baldelli (including Rossellini's own comments during the interview), *Roberto Rossellini*, 231–2; Peter Bondanella, *The Films of Roberto Rossellini* (Cambridge: Cambridge University Press, 1993); Brunette, *Roberto Rossellini*; Faldini and Fofi, eds, *1935–1959* and *1960–1969*; Guarner, *Roberto Rossellini*; Masi and Lancia, *I film di Roberto Rossellini*; Pintus, *Storia e film*, 33–5 and 47–50; and Rondolino, *Roberto Rossellini*, 261–3.

63 Milo, mercilessly re-baptized by the critics 'Canina Canini' for her sorry performance in the film, ruefully reports the events from her vantage point in Faldini and Fofi, eds, *1935–1959*, 277 and 398–9; and *1960–1969*, 226, 276–7, and 329.

64 Even without considering doubtfully orthodox films such as *Stromboli* (*Stromboli, terra di Dio*, 1949), Rossellini had many wives and children to his debit. His marriages (whether valid, invalid, or common-law) were, in chronological order, to Assia Noris, Marcella De Marchis, Anna Magnani, Ingrid Bergman, and Sonali Das Gupta. His last companion was Silvia D'Amico, the daughter of the well-known scriptwriter Suso Cecchi D'Amico.

The best sources on the director's biography are De Marchis Rossellini, *Un matrimonio riuscito*; Fernaldo Di Giammatteo, *Roberto Rossellini* (Florence: La nuova Italia, 1990) (richly illustrated); Faldini and Fofi, eds (*1935–1959*, *1960–1969*, and *1970–1984*); Tag Gallagher, *The Adventures of Roberto Rossellini* (New York: Da Capo Press, 1998); Rossellini, *Il mio metodo*, passim; and Rossellini, *Quasi un'autobiografia* (chaps. 5–7).

65 Many critics refer, albeit only in passing, to the *Senso–Vanina Vanini* parallel, a subject worthy of systematic study. Serceau, who alone makes a sustained effort in this direction, unfortunately confuses the first war of independence against Austria-Hungary in 1848–9 with the third one in 1866. This critic wonders (*Roberto Rossellini*, 131) why Visconti does not show King Carlo Alberto di Savoia; the reason for this is simple – Carlo Alberto had died seventeen years earlier, in 1849.

66 Rossellini, *My Method*, 161. 'Io sono romano, dunque potevo capire benissimo cos'è questo personaggio in quest'epoca dove il romanticismo prendeva piede, questa ragazza pesante, che bastava desse la mano a uno per sentirsi svenire ... Il personaggio di Stendhal è di un cinismo ... cioè, è una nobile romana che non crede assolutamente a niente, soddisfa degli istinti precisi, ecco dov'è il cambiamento, mi pare proprio sostanziale, del personaggio. Con un'altra attrice poi si sarebbe fatto un altro personaggio.' *Il mio metodo*, 341–2. (The interview, originally published in *Filmcritica* in 1965, is also anthologized in Faldini and Fofi, eds, *1960–1969*, 223–4, with negligible editorial variants.)

67 'Il pretesto è la *Vanina Vanini* dello scrittore.' Rossellini in Baldelli, *Roberto Rossellini*, 241.

68 It is peculiar that at the height of the ideology-conscious 1970s Rossellini could defend with brilliance the cause of *evolution* (by enlightenment, controlled by understanding) over that of *revolution* (by force, driven by fear) – and yet remain entirely blind to the fact that the ownership of the very means whose use he was advocating for the task was (is) itself historically positioned, and anything but ideologically neutral.

   For a good catalogue of objections to Rossellini's hoped-for neutrality, technological and otherwise, see Baldelli, *Roberto Rossellini*, 173–80 and 189–96.

69 'Il faut démocratiser la connaissance.' Rossellini, *Un esprit libre*, 200.

70 Lěv Tolstoi, 'The Author's Preface,' in *What Is Art?* and *Essays on Art*, vol. 18 of *Tolstoy Centenary Edition*, 68. 'Я так подробно рассказал всю эту историю потому, что она поразительно иллюстрирует ту несомненную истину, что всякий компромисс с учреждением, не согласным с вашей совестью – компромисс, который делается обыкновенно в виду общей пользы – неизбежно затягивает вас, вместо пользы, не только в признание законности отвергаемого вами учреждения, но и в участие в том вреде, который производит это учреждение.' *Chto takoe iskusstvo?* (1897–8), vol. 30 of *Polnoe sobranie sochinenii*, 1951, 206.

Chapter 8: Mann and Visconti

1 Thomas Mann, *Death in Venice*, ed. and trans. Clayton Koelb (New York: Norton, 1994), 63. 'Und noch desselben Tages empfing eine respektvoll erschütterte Welt die Nachricht von seinem Tode.' *Der Tod in Venedig*, in *Erzählungen. Fiorenza. Dichtungen*, vol. 8 of *Gesammelte Werke in dreizehn Bänden* (Frankfurt am Main: S. Fischer, 1974), 525.

2 On the Orient and in particular what could be called the nosological/demonological tradition in European literature on Venice, see, among many, Bernard Dieterle, *Die versunkene Stadt: Sechs Kapitel zum literarischen Venedig-Mythos* (Frankfurt am Main: Peter Lang, 1995); and Walter Pabst, 'Satan und die alten Götter Venedigs: Entwicklung einer literarhistorischen Variante,' in *Euphorion* 49 (Fall 1955), 325–59. Poland may not seem particularly Oriental to Italians, but within German culture it certainly acts as a synechdoche for the Slavic (and thus by implication Asian) sphere.

3 Ilsedore B. Jonas, in her *Thomas Mann and Italy*, trans. B. Crouse (Tuscaloosa: University of Alabama Press, 1979; *Thomas Mann und Italien* [Heidelberg: Carl Winter, 1969]), seems altogether unaware that there may be

structural Italophobia in *Der Tod in Venedig* (as opposed to Aschenbach's conscious opinion of the peninsula).

Works on *Der Tod in Venedig* that I found useful are the following: Ehrhard Bahr, ed., *Thomas Mann. Der Tod in Venedig. Erläuterungen und Dokumente* (Stuttgart: Philipp Reclam jun., 1991); Erich Heller, *Thomas Mann: The Ironic German* (Cambridge: Cambridge University Press, 1981 [1958]); *Thomas Mann: Der ironische Deutsche* (Frankfurt am Main: Suhrkamp, 1970); Hans Mayer, *Thomas Mann* (Frankfurt am Main: Suhrkamp, 1980); Hans W. Nicklas, *Thomas Manns Novelle* Der Tod in Venedig: *Analyse des Motivzusammenhangs und der Erzählstruktur* (Marburg: N.G. Elwert, 1968); Terence James Reed, *Thomas Mann. Der Tod in Venedig: Text, Materialien, Kommentar mit den bisher unveröffentlichten Arbeitsnotizen T. M.s* (Munich: Carl Hanser, 1983); Hans Rudolf Vaget, *Thomas-Mann-Kommentar zu sämtlichen Erzählungen* (München: Winkler, 1984); and Rudolf Wolff, ed., *Thomas Mann. Erzählungen und Novellen* (Bonn: Bouvier, 1984). For a comprehensive collection of Mann's comments on his own work, see the *Der Tod in Venedig* chapter in Thomas Mann, *Dichter über ihre Dichtungen*, eds Hans Wysling and Marianne Fischer, vol. 1 (Frankfurt am Main: Ernst Heimeran and S. Fischer, 1975), 393–449.

4   The expression is Visconti's: 'To my mind, from the old man on the ship to the gondolier and to the hotel director, these are all *petty devils* who conspire in determining Aschenbach's fate and guide him ... to meet the angel of death who will lead him to the accomplishment of his destiny.' 'Per me, dal vecchio della nave, al gondoliere, al direttore dell'albergo, sono tutti dei *piccoli diavoli* che concorrono a determinare la sorte di Aschenbach e lo conducono ... a trovare quell'angelo della morte che lo condurrà al compimento del suo destino.' Visconti, *Morte a Venezia*, ed. Lino Miccichè (Bologna: Cappelli, 1971), 122. (Includes Visconti's script as well as interviews with Lino Miccichè.) Henceforward cited as Visconti or Visconti-Miccichè according to the section quoted.

5   *Death in Venice*, 5–8. 'die Abkehr von jeder Sympathie mit dem Abgrund ... Aufstieg zur Würde ... Durchhalten.' *Der Tod in Venedig*, 446–51.

6   *Kaiserlich-Königlich* = 'Imperial-Royal,' i.e., related to the Austro-Hungarian Empire – and thus, almost by definition, affected by an imperialistic bias vis-à-vis the subordinate ethnic groups or nations.

7   *Death in Venice*, 13. 'Es war ein betagtes Fahrzeug italienischer Nationalität, veraltet, rußig und düster. In einer höhlenartigen, künstlich erleuchteten Koje des inneren Raumes, wohin Aschenbach sofort nach Betreten des Schiffes von einem buckligen und unreinlichen Matrosen mit grinsender Höflichkeit genötigt wurde, saß hinter einem Tische, den Hut schief in der

Stirn und ein Zigarettenstummel im Mundwinkel, ein ziegenbärtiger Mann von der Physiognomie eines altmodischen Zirkusdirektors.' *Der Tod in Venedig*, 458.

8 *Death in Venice*, 15. 'Die Mahlzeit war armselig.' *Der Tod in Venedig*, 461.

9 The manager is characterized as 'a quiet, flatteringly polite little man with a black mustache and a French-style frock-coat.' *Death in Venice*, 20. 'ein kleiner, leiser, schmeichelnd höflicher Mann mit schwarzem Schnurrbart und in französisch geschnittenem Gehrock.' *Der Tod in Venedig*, 467–8. The decadent cultural connotations of the 'French style' referred to in the German context of 1912 can easily be surmised.

10 *Death in Venice*, 21. 'Der Knabe [war] vollkommen schön.' *Der Tod in Venedig*, 469.

11 *Death in Venice*, 28. 'vollreife Erdbeeren.' *Der Tod in Venedig*, 477.

12 *Death in Venice*, 28. '[die] Geburt der Götter.' *Der Tod in Venedig*, 478.

13 *Death in Venice*, 30. 'Ausharren erschien vernunftwidrig.' *Der Tod in Venedig*, 480.

14 'vollkommen zur Abreise fertig.' *Der Tod in Venedig*, 481. The published translation excises (30) this 'perfect' wink by the narrator.

15 Munich = München = MOnaCO (di Baviera) becomes CO MO. The mention of Como may simply reflect Thomas Mann's actual experience in Italy; nothing in the story is invented, he claims. See Mann, *Dichter über ihre Dichtungen*, 1: 434 and 439. On the other hand, the inversion could well be a symbolic indicator that, from a German's perspective, Italians systematically practise the traditional demonic art of going about things: backwards.

16 So, for example, in paraphrases from the *Odyssey* (IV: 563ff. and VIII: 249). See Roberto Fertonani, intro. to Thomas Mann, *La morte a Venezia. Tristano. Tonio Kröger* (Milan: Mondadori, 1970), 33–5; and, by the same author, 'Echi classici in *Der Tod in Venedig* di Thomas Mann,' *ACME* 28:1–2 (Jan.–Aug. 1975), 17–26. A fuller bibliography on the subject is given in H.R. Vaget, *Thomas-Mann-Kommentar*.

17 The obvious textual proximity to Schiller's *On the Aesthetic Education of Man in a Series of Letters* (*Über die ästhetische Erziehung des Menschen, in einer Reihe von Briefen*, 1793; pub. 1795) that can here be detected is not surprising, given that from the outset Aschenbach is said to have produced works that ranked 'alongside' what could be called Schiller's companion work to the *Letters* – *On Naïve and Sentimental Poetry* (*Über naïve und sentimentalische Dichtung*, 1795–96; pub. 1800). (*Death in Venice*, 7; *Der Tod in Venedig*, 450.)

18 *Death in Venice*, 34. 'Der Gott mit den hitzigen Wangen.' *Der Tod in Venedig*, 486.

19 *Death in Venice*, 43–4. '[Die] stehende Formel der Sehnsucht, – unmöglich

hier, absurd, verworfen, lächerlich und heilig doch, ehrwürdig auch hier noch: "Ich liebe dich!"' *Der Tod in Venedig*, 498.

20 *Death in Venice*, 44. 'der Abgott.' *Der Tod in Venedig*, 499.

21 *Der Tod in Venedig* is constructed in the manner of a (neo)-classical tragedy, with its five sections fulfilling functions equivalent to those of the traditional five acts: Act I, exposition (Aschenbach in Munich); Act II, complication (his state of mind interfering with his past); Act III, peripeteia (encounter with Tadzio and failed attempt to escape); Act IV, retardation (bliss on the beach); Act V, denouement (cholera in Venice and death).

22 The mountebank is not from Venice, but from Naples – the South of the South, Italy to the second power. Accordingly, peninsular uncanniness reaches in him a paroxysm: the seedy *virtuoso* is 'half pimp, half actor, brutal and daring, dangerous and entertaining' – over and above his lasciviousness, that is. *QED. Death in Venice*, 51. 'halb Zuhälter halb Komödiant, brutal und verwegen, gefährlich und unterhaltend.' *Der Tod in Venedig*, 507–8.

23 *Death in Venice*, 51. 'eine vorbeugende Maßregel.' *Der Tod in Venedig*, 509.

24 *Death in Venice*, 53. 'Der Brite [war] von jener gesetzten Loyalität des Wesens, die im spitzbübisch behenden Süden so fremd, so merkwürdig anmutet ... Und dann sagte er in seiner redlichen und bequemen Sprache die Wahr-heit.' *Der Tod in Venedig*, 511–12.

25 There is no evidence of Aschenbach's oral Italian being anything more than limited at the start of his stay; yet, by the end of the novella, he seems to be able to absorb quite well the meaning of the barber's astute *éloge du maquil-lage*.

26 Significantly, the narrator makes repeated usage of participles to substitute for Aschenbach's name ('the enamored one'/'der Verliebte'; 'the lonely one'/'der Einsame'; 'the charmed, enchanted one'/'der Berückte'; 'the age-ing one'/'der Alternde'; etc.), as if to drive home the point that loss of dig-nity and loss of identity go hand in hand.

27 'His entire being was bent on fame.' *Death in Venice*, 7. 'Sein ganzes Wesen [war] auf Ruhm gestellt.' *Der Tod in Venedig*, 450.

28 *Death in Venice*, 60. 'überreife und weiche Ware.' *Der Tod in Venedig*, 520.

29 *Death in Venice*, 60. 'Ein kleiner Platz, verlassen, verwunschen anmutend, öffnete sich vor ihm, er erkannte ihn, es war hier gewesen, wo er vor Wochen den verzweifelten Fluchtplan gefaßt hatte. Auf den Stufen der Zisterne, inmitten des Ortes, ließ er sich niedersinken und lehnte den Kopf an das steinerne Rund.' *Der Tod in Venedig*, 521.

30 The idea is central to *Doctor Faustus*, where the musician Leverkühn explicitly introduces – and the novel's fictional narrator Serenus Zeitblom discusses at some length – an interpretation of the *Lamentation of Doctor Faustus* as a

counter-composition ('Gegenstück') meant to 'take back' ('zurückneh-men') Beethoven's Ninth Symphony: that is to say, to cancel out Schiller's *Ode to Joy* in which Germany's humanistic classicism had culminated. Thomas Mann, *Doktor Faustus. Das Leben des deutschen Tonsetzers Adrian Leverkühn erzählt von einem Freunde,* vol. 6 of *Gesammelte Werke in dreizehn Bänden* (Frankfurt am Main: S. Fischer, 1974), 634, 645, and 649–50.

31 Friedrich Nietzsche, *The Birth of Tragedy, or Hellenism and Pessimism,* trans. W.A. Haussmann, in *CW* 1: 41 (4). 'Und siehe! Apollo konnte nicht ohne Dionysos leben!' *Die Geburt der Tragödie, SW-KSA* 1: 40 (4).

32 This is not to say that in Venice there was at the time no disease susceptible to dispatch foreign tourists; the Venice cholera outbreak was, in its own way, both 'natural' and most real. However, Mann's realism in *Der Tod in Venedig* is not a naturalistic but an ironic one – perhaps rarely more so than on the occasion of Aschenbach's death.

33 If (as a pure and simple 'go-for-Tadzio' interpretation would have it) the appropriate answer to the German writer's desire for transcendence were for him to associate with self-aware and slightly coquettish sensuous youths on Italian beaches, there would simply be no dilemma in Aschenbach, no feverish illness in him, and thus ultimately no death in Venice either; he could discard his bourgeois inhibitions and act upon his feelings. (The hurdles de facto arising in the way of such fulfilment in a homophobic society are, of course, a very real issue, but also one that seems to lie outside the direct sphere of interest of *Der Tod in Venedig*. In the novella, homosexual attraction is a subset of the general question of love for Beauty, rather than the other way around). A 'physical' behaviour would be wide of the mark for Mann's Aschenbach; it is the unattainable Apollo/Hyacinth/Narcissus, *not* the possibly attainable Tadzio, that he really desires – and Aschenbach knows that. The narrator reiterates as much in the exquisitely sensitive, almost aphoristically dense paragraph on the relationship between two persons who 'only know each other through the eyes': 'People tend to love and honor other people so long as they are not in a position to pass judgment on them; and *longing is the result of insufficient knowledge.' Death in Venice,* 42; emphasis added. 'Der Mensch liebt und ehrt den Menschen, solange er ihn nicht zu beurteilen vermag, und *die Sehnsucht ist ein Erzeugnis mangelhafter Erkenntnis.' Der Tod in Venedig,* 496–7; emphasis added.

34 To put it another way, Aschenbach's death is a trace in the text of his pained awareness that it is *beside the point* (as opposed to merely unacceptable in society) to espouse without reserve any one particular incarnation of the orgiastic. Years later, Mann was to stress, in a letter to a moralizing reader, that *Der Tod in Venedig* 'is far from being irresponsible; it is, in fact, consciously

responsible, to the point of asceticism.' '"Verantwortungslos" ist *Der Tod in Venedig* nicht. Er ist sogar bis zur Askese verantwortungsbewußt.' *Dichter über ihre Dichtungen*, 1: 448. A similar point is also put forward in E.L. Marson, *The Ascetic Artist: Prefigurations in Thomas Mann's* Der Tod in Venedig (Bern: Peter Lang, 1979), 14 and 25.

35 To, that is, an exquisitely defined 'immensity full of promise.' *Death in Venice*, 63. 'ins Verheißungsvoll-Ungeheure.' *Der Tod in Venedig*, 525. It should be noted that Tadzio's descent into the waters is constructed to match symmetrically his emerging from them in section 3 (*Death in Venice*, 28; *Der Tod in Venedig*, 478).

36 Even more remarkable is the narrator's rendering of what is perhaps the most direct occurrence of unbridled sensuality in the novella, the 'Dionysian nightmare' Aschenbach experiences on one of his last nights. Various features in its subject matter and style provide a classical framework into which to inscribe one of the most regulated and gradual releases of orgiastic desire that ever was. *Inter alia*, the scene devoted to 'the foreign God' (*der fremde Gott*) is a bit of erudition on the part of the Aschenbach-like Thomas Mann, who perused the fourth edition of Rohde's nineteenth-century classic scholarly work for the purpose. See Erwin Rohde, *Psyche: Seelencult und Unsterblichkeitsglaube der Griechen* (Tübingen: Mohr, 1907 [1890–94]).

37 My wording here alludes to another theoretical work by Schiller which had a resonance comparable to that of *On Naïve and Sentimental Poetry*, namely *On Grace and Dignity* (*Über Anmut und Würde*, 1793).

38 In the evil Cipolla of his novella *Mario and the Magician* (*Mario und der Zauberer*, 1930) Thomas Mann adumbrated the personality, and metaphorized the methods, of the *Cavaliere* (Knight) Benito Mussolini. Frate Cipolla is the prestidigitatorial liar of Boccaccio's *Decameron* (VI, 10).

39 This need not have meant adopting a mediterranean (let alone 'Italian') world view. A third alternative was persuasively suggested by Hermann Hesse's *The Steppenwolf* (*Der Steppenwolf*, 1927), a book that can in fact strike the reader as a direct response to Aschenbach's dilemma: how to integrate the Other within the Self and the Self within the Other. Hesse writes: 'When the dimensions of the bourgeois parlor are too cramping [for the spiritual, art-sensitive person], he lays it at the "wolf"'s door and refuses to see that the wolf is as often as not the best part of him. All that is wild in himself he calls wolf and considers it wicked and dangerous and the specter of all [bourgeois] life. Even though he thinks himself an artist and possessed of delicate perceptions, he cannot see that a great deal else exists in him besides and behind the wolf. He cannot see that not all that bites is wolf; and that fox, dragon, tiger, ape and bird of paradise are there also. Yet he allows this

whole world, a Garden of Eden ... of beauty and terror, of greatness and meanness, of strength and tenderness, to be huddled together and shut away by the wolf legend, just as is the real man in him by the shams and pretenses of a bourgeois existence.' Hermann Hesse, *Steppenwolf* (New York: Holt, Rinehart and Winston, 1963), 67–8.

'Wenn [ihm] die enge Bürgerstube ... zu eng wird, dann schiebt er es dem "Wolf" in die Schuhe und will nicht wissen, daß der Wolf zuzeiten sein bestes Teil ist. Er nennt alles Wilde in sich Wolf und empfindet es als böse, als gefährlich, als Bürgerschreck – aber er, der doch ein Künstler zu sein und zarte Sinne zu haben glaubt, vermag nicht zu sehen, daß außer dem Wolf, hinter dem Wolf, noch viel andres in ihm lebt, daß nicht alles Wolf ist, was beißt, daß da auch noch Fuchs, Drache, Tiger, Affe und Paradiesvogel wohnen. Und daß diese ganze Welt, dieser ganze Paradiesgarten von holden und schrecklichen, großen und kleinen, starken und zarten Gestaltungen erdrückt und gefangengehalten wird von dem Wolfmärchen, ebenso wie der wahre Mensch in ihm vom Scheinmenschen, vom Bürger, erdrückt und gefangengehalten wird.' *Der Steppenwolf*, in *Gesammelte Werke in zwölf Bänden*, vol. 7 (Frankfurt am Main: Suhrkamp, 1970), 249.

Mann and Hesse corresponded with each other for many years (though unfrequently before 1933). While their letters show no record of Hesse's thoughts on *Der Tod in Venedig*, they indicate that Mann held *Der Steppenwolf* in high esteem. See the entry of 3 January 1928 in *The Hesse / Mann Letters*, trans. R. Manheim (New York: Harper and Row, 1975), 4; Anni Carlsson and Volker Michels, eds, *Hermann Hesse–Thomas Mann: Briefwechsel* (Frankfurt am Main: Suhrkamp, 1975), 15.

40 Hypertextuality was referred to above in the Rossellini chapter, n. 22.

41 On this view, Visconti's disregarding of section 1 of the original novella (Aschenbach in Munich) responds not only to the 'negative' rationale he adduces (Visconti-Micciché, 120) but, importantly, to a positive artistic logic as well.

42 Visconti's own biography was, in fact, uniquely cosmopolitan. See Renzo Renzi, *Visconti segreto* (Bari: Laterza, 1994); Gianni Rondolino, *Luchino Visconti* (Turin: UTET, 1981); and Monica Stirling, *A Screen of Time: A Study of Luchino Visconti* (New York: Harcourt Brace Jovanovich, 1979).

43 I.e., the content of section 2 of *Der Tod in Venedig.*

44 Despite the existence of important differences between national traditions, the musical culture of modern Europe has historically been characterized by a supra-national circulation of forms unknown to the literary sphere. (I emphasize 'supra-national' over the concept of 'universal' – music being certainly no less *cultural* than literature.)

45 Visconti-Micciché, 114–15. Repr. in Faldini and Fofi, eds, *1970–1984*, 221.

46 Of the other three noticeably shady figures in the novella, one is eliminated by Visconti (the mysterious stranger in front of the cemetery in Munich); one is expanded and transcoded onto the comic register (the manager of the Hôtel des Bains); and the third undergoes no substantive touch-up (the barber). The issue of the change in Tadzio's age is raised, with varying degrees of approval, by many critics, among whom see at least Joachim Günther, '*Der Tod in Venedig*: Randbemerkungen zu Film und Buch,' *Neue Deutsche Hefte* 18:4 (Fall 1971), 89–99; and Reed, *Thomas Mann*: Der Tod in Venedig, 174.

47 For a complete list of the flashbacks in *Morte a Venezia*, see Micciché, 84.

48 'L'arte è ambigua, sempre ... E la musica è la più ambigua di tutte le arti ... Sì, Gustav, è l'ambiguità elevata a sistema.

   Aspetta ... Ascolta ... Prendi questo accordo ... oppure questo ... Lo puoi interpretare come più ti piace ... Hai davanti a te una infinita serie di combinazioni matematiche, imprevedibili, inesauribili ... Un paradiso di doppi sensi nel quale tu stesso sguazzi più di chiunque altro, come ... come ... una foca nel suo acquario ...

   La senti, no? La riconosci, vero? ... E' tua ... la tua musica.' Visconti, sc. 104.

   Augusto Sainati argues for a similarity between art in general and Visconti's use of the zoom – both are 'loci ... of a plurality of meanings' – in '*Morte a Venezia*: Lo zoom e la bellezza,' in Veronica Pravadelli, ed., *Il cinema di Luchino Visconti* (Rome: Fondazione Scuola Nazionale di Cinema, 2000), 271–80.

49 Even assuming contagion as the actual (as opposed to nominal) cause for Aschenbach's death, *Morte a Venezia* seems to take the licence of being ironically non-committal about the number – and relative importance – of his illnesses: possibly one (syphilis? cholera?), possibly two (syphilis *and* cholera?).

50 The intention was directly confirmed by Visconti in an interview. See below.

51 Paradoxically, Visconti has been accused by several critics of being unable to *reproduce* cinematically Thomas Mann's verbal irony. He did better: he *recreated* it. The difference is, of course, that here for once the joke is not on Aschenbach.

52 The concept is perhaps most effectively illustrated by a passage in Hermann Hesse's *Steppenwolf* that describes the distorting effects of canonization as they apply not only to the moral traits but indeed to the physical lineaments of the archetypal canonic artist in German culture – Johann Wolfgang 'von' Goethe. Reporting on an afternoon courtesy visit he was paying to a middle-class petty-bourgeois couple in their apartment, Hesse's first-person narrator

recounts how, having seen with repulsion a self-important-looking portrait of the poet embellish the drawing room, he could not help exclaiming:

'Let us hope ... that Goethe did not really look like this! This conceited air of nobility, the great man ogling the distinguished company, and beneath a manly exterior what a world of charming sentimentality! Certainly, there is much to be said against him. I have a good deal against his venerable pomposity myself. But to represent him like this – no, that is going too far.' Hesse, *Steppenwolf*, 86. 'Hoffen wir ... daß Goethe nicht wirklich so ausgesehen hat! Diese Eitelkeit und edle Pose, diese mit den verehrten Anwesenden liebäugelnde Würde und unter der männlichen Oberfläche diese Welt von holdester Sentimentalität! Man kann ja gewiß viel gegen ihn haben, auch habe ich oft viel gegen den alten Wichtigtuer, aber ihn so darzustellen, nein, das geht doch zu weit.' *Gesammelte Werke* 7: 267.

53 *Death in Venice*, 10. 'der Dichter all derer, die am Rande der Erschöpfung arbeiten.' *Der Tod in Venedig*, 453–4.

54 *Death in Venice*, 9. 'daß beinahe alles Große, was dastehe, als ein Trotzdem dastehe, trotz Kummer und Qual, Armut, Verlassenheit, Körperschwäche, Laster, Leidenschaft und tausend Hemmnissen zustande gekommen sei.' *Der Tod in Venedig*, 452–3.

55 At an empirical level, 'Für Elise' was used in the film because it was the first piece that occurred to the young actor impersonating Tadzio (Visconti-Micciché, 117). That, however, is only one half of the artistic truth; the other half is that Visconti chose to retain 'Für Elise' in the film. Anyway, far from undermining the notion of artistic banalization through *kitsch*, the episode seems to reinforce it.

It will be clear, on this basis, in what sense I disagree with Fletcher's otherwise accurate analysis of the Esmeralda connection in *Morte a Venezia*: there is, indeed, 'a special place for music in the thought of Visconti and his progenitors' – but I doubt that Esmeralda's chromatic performance is 'a special place' to look for it. Angus Fletcher, 'Music, Visconti, Mann, Nietzsche: *Death in Venice*,' in Thomas Harrison, ed., *Nietzsche in Italy* (Stanford, Calif.: ANMA Libri, 1988), 312.

56 We do not, in fact, know how 'unregulated' these rites truly were. On the subject see, among many, Joseph Campbell, ed., *The Mysteries: Papers from the Eranos Yearbooks* (Princeton, NJ: Princeton University Press, 1978 [1955]); Karl Kerényi, *Die Mysterien von Eleusis* (Zürich: Rhein Verlag, 1962); and R. Gordon Wasson et al., *The Road to Eleusis: Unveiling the Secret of the Mysteries* (New York: Harcourt Brace Jovanovich, 1978).

57 'Imbroglione! Mio caro imbroglione! La pura bellezza ... il rigore assoluto ... il moralismo della forma, la perfezione, l'astrazione dei sensi! ... Di tutto

questo che cosa è rimasto? Niente ... niente, niente! La tua musica è nata
morta! E tu sei stato smascherato! ...
　　Saggezza, verità, dignità umana ... Tutto finito! Ora, se vuoi, puoi scendere
nella fossa insieme alla tua musica. Hai raggiunto il perfetto equilibrio ...
L'uomo e l'artista sono una cosa sola ... Hanno toccato il fondo, insieme.
　　Tu non hai mai posseduto la castità. La castità è un dono della purezza,
non il penoso risultato della vecchiaia; e tu sei vecchio, Gustav ... E non c'è al
mondo impurità così impura come la vecchiaia.' Visconti, scenes 388 to 398,
passim.
　　Unlike Visconti, aged sixty-four when he made *Morte a Venezia*, Thomas
Mann was relatively young at the time of *Der Tod in Venedig*, having turned
thirty-seven on 6 June 1912. Age (Aschenbach's, Tadzio's) is doubtless a
major area of reaccentuation in the film.

58　Visconti-Micciché, 118.

59　*Death in Venice*, 17. 'die unwahrscheinlichste der Städte.' *Der Tod in Venedig*,
463. Thomas Mann echoes Dostoevsky's perception of St Petersburg as
'the most abstract and premeditated city in the whole world.' Dostoevskii,
Notes from Underground, 5. 'Петербург, сам(ый) отвлеченн(ый) и
умышленн(ый) город ... на всем земном шаре.' *Zapiski iz podpol' ia*, in
Povesti i rasskazy 1862–1866, *Polnoe sobranie sochinenii* 5: 101. For more on
St Petersburg's uncanny status, see chapter 3 (Lattuada), n. 33.

60　In name, though not in fact, that cityscape belonged to the Tuscan town of
Livorno. On the subject, see the *White Nights* section in my *Italian Cinema and
Modern European Literatures*.

61　'E' il giorno del Giudizio; i morti risorgono all'eterna gioia o all'eterno
dolore. Noi soli restiamo abbracciati e non ci curiamo di niente, né di paradiso né d'inferno.' Luchino Visconti, *Senso*, ed. G.B. Cavallaro (Bologna:
Cappelli, 1955), 123; 2nd ed. (ibid., 1997), 96.

62　In later editions, the collection was included in Heine's *Book of Songs* (*Buch
der Lieder*).

63　Heinrich Heine, *The Complete Poems*, trans. H. Draper (Boston: Suhrkamp–
Insel, 1982), 62 (*Lyrical Intermezzo, 32*). '*Mein süßes Lieb, wenn du im Grab,/ Im
dunkeln Grab wirst liegen,/ Dann will ich steigen zu dir hinab,/ Und will mich an
dich schmiegen.// Ich küsse, umschlinge und presse dich wild,/ Du Stille, du Kalte, du
Bleiche!/ Ich jauchze, ich zittre, ich weine mild,/ Ich werde selber zur Leiche.// Die
Toten stehn auf, die Mitternacht ruft,/ Sie tanzen im luftigen Schwarme;/ Wir beide
bleiben in der Gruft,/ Ich liege in deinem Arme.// Die Toten stehn auf, der Tag
des Gerichts/ Ruft sie zu Qual und Vergnügen;/ Wir beide bekümmern uns
um nichts,/ Und bleiben umschlungen liegen.' Werke und Briefe in zehn
Bänden*, ed. Hans Kaufmann, vol. 1 (Berlin and Weimar: Aufbau, 1980), 85

(*Lyrisches Intermezzo*, 32). I am italicizing the part suppressed by Visconti in his cinematic quote.

64 Cf. Sandra's visit to the underground water reservoir beneath the ancestral palace in *Sandra* (*Vaghe stelle dell'Orsa*, 1965).

65 The theme of self-deception through a subjective, uncontextualized view of events is recurrent in Thomas Mann, from *Der Tod in Venedig* to the late novella *The Deluded One* (*Die Betrogene*, 1953). See in particular Joseph Mileck, 'A Comparative Study of *Die Betrogene* and *Der Tod in Venedig*,' *Modern Language Forum* 42 (1957), 124–9.

66 There is, to my knowledge, at least a third important wellhead in Visconti's life: that in Grazzano Visconti, the Renaissance village reconstructed by the aristocratic family not far from Milan, next to which Luchino's mother posed for a photograph in the same year *Der Tod in Venedig* was begun, 1911 (Alain Sanzio and Paul-Louis Thirard, *Luchino Visconti cinéaste* [Paris: Persona, 1984], 123). The attire and expression of Carla Erba Visconti in the picture bear such a strong resemblance to those of Tadzio's mother in the film as to suggest that, along with the obvious identification with Aschenbach, Visconti must *also* have felt a secondary identification with Tadzio – at any rate with respect to the mother/wellhead archetype. If that is so, then Aschenbach, by now a *puer-senex* figure, touches both the alpha and the omega of existence as he collapses by the contaminated cistern in Venice.

67 The following is a short list of various critical positions on the spectrum that extends from the detection of homosexuality in *Morte a Venezia* to the raising of objections to its appropriateness, contextual, political, or otherwise: Guido Aristarco, *Su Visconti* (Rome: La Zattera di Babele, 1986), 97–107 and esp. 105; David Glassco, 'Films Out of Books: Bergman, Visconti and Mann,' *Mosaic* 16:1–2 (Winter–Spring 1983), 165–73; Joy Gould Boyum, '*Death in Venice*: The Seductiveness of the Sensual,' in her *Double Exposure: Fiction into Film* (New York: New American Library–Plume, 1985), 182–8; Günther, '*Der Tod in Venedig*'; Irving Singer, '*Death in Venice*: Visconti and Mann,' *Modern Language Notes* 91:2 (1976), 1348–59; and Hans Rudolf Vaget, 'Film and Literature. The Case of *Death in Venice*: Luchino Visconti and Thomas Mann,' *German Quarterly* 54:2 (March 1980), 159–75, esp. 162, 165, 167, and 171.

Neil Sinyard *in extremis* rescues *Morte a Venezia* because of its 'incomparable' treatment of homosexuality and 'voluptuousness of doom,' after having savaged it as, among much else, 'a well-nigh indigestible cultural pudding' (126); '*Death in Venice*,' in his *Filming Literature: The Art of Screen Adaptation* (London: Croom Helm, 1986), 126–30. This opinion would also qualify Sinyard for membership in the group of critics holding destructive views of the film, for which see below.

68 By no coincidence, *The Damned* happened to include one character called Aschenbach. See Visconti's comments on the subject in Visconti-Micciché, 112.

69 The expression 'a richly visual footnote' (to Mann) is used in Geoffrey Wagner, *The Novel and the Cinema* (London: Tantivy Press and Fairleigh Dickinson University Press, 1975), 345.

A number of film or literary scholars did not take kindly to Visconti's perceived unnatural attempt to tamper with/across art forms. The following are more among those who, in different areas and to various degrees, handed down damning judgments on *Morte a Venezia*: Jean Améry, 'Venezianische Zaubereien: Luchino Visconti und sein *Tod in Venedig*,' *Merkur* 25 (1971), 810 (target: Alfried); Goffredo Fofi, *Capire con il cinema: Duecento film prima e dopo il '68* (Milan: Feltrinelli, 1971), 246–9 ('has vulgarized Mann's dilemma ... the film sails along from one sumptuous slowness to the next, "beautiful" and reductive'); Goffredo Fofi, *Il cinema italiano: Servi e padroni* (Milan: Feltrinelli, 1971), 97–8 ('decorative, without a soul and without participation ... without even irony'); Glassco, 'Films Out of Books,' 172 ('trite thoughts and obvious emotions'); David I. Grossvogel, 'Visconti and the Too, Too Solid Flesh,' *Diacritics* 1:2 (Winter 1971), 52–5 ('too much of a mundane and sexual quality' for 'a statement that was to have been spiritual and speculative'); B.M. Kane, 'Thomas Mann and Visconti,' *Modern Languages* 53:1 (March 1972), 74–80 ('aestheticizing'); Geoffrey Nowell-Smith, *Luchino Visconti* (New York: Viking Press, 1973 [1967]), 203–4 ('vulgar-materialist reduction ... crassness of the adaptation ... an involution'); Mayer, *Thomas Mann*, 384 ('the amalgamation of Thomas Mann and Gustav Mahler does not take place'); and Reed, *Thomas Mann: Der Tod in Venedig*, 173–4.

More appreciative evaluations of the film can be found in Attolini, *Storia del cinema letterario*, 209–11; Henry Bacon, *Visconti: Explorations of Beauty and Decay* (Cambridge: Cambridge University Press, 1998), 155–72; Giorgio Bertellini, 'A Battle *d'arrière-garde*: Notes on Decadence in Luchino Visconti's *Death in Venice*,' *Film Quarterly* 50:4 (Summer 1997), 11–19; Bruni and Pravadelli, eds, *Studi viscontiani* (contains in particular: Guido Aristarco, 'La trilogia tedesca,' 131–43, and Gaetana Marrone Puglia, 'Metafore della visione in *Morte a Venezia*,' 145–53); Alessandro Cappabianca, *Il cinema e il sacro* (Recco: Le Mani, 1998), 122–4; Caterina D'Amico de Carvalho, *Life and Work of Luchino Visconti* (Rome: Cinecittà International, [1998]), 180–91; Roger Hillmann, 'Deaths in Venice,' *Journal of European Studies* 22:4 (Dec. 1992), 291–311; Suzanne Liandrat-Guigues, *Le couchant et l'aurore: Sur le cinéma de Luchino Visconti* (Paris: Klincksieck, 1999), 99–100; Lino Micciché, *Luchino Visconti: Un profilo critico* (Venice: Marsilio, 1996), 63–5; and Douglas Radcliff-

Umstead, 'The Journey of Fatal Longing: Mann and Visconti,' *Annali d'Italianistica* 6 (1988), 199–219.

On a final note, pertinent comments on Visconti's historical reconstruction of beach life in the 1910s are made by Bertelli, *I corsari del tempo*, 275–9.

70 Friedrich Nietzsche, *The Joyful Wisdom*, in *CW* 10: 14 (Prelude, 7). '*Vademecum-vadetecum.* // Es lockt dich meine Art und Sprach,/ Du folgest mir, du gehst mir nach?/ Geh nur dir selber treulich nach: – / So folgst du mir – gemach! gemach!' *Die fröhliche Wissenschaft*, SW-KSA 3: 354 (Vorspiel, 7).

71 The principle needs, of course, to be applied in context. Our analysis of *Vanina Vanini* makes it clear that it is one thing for a director to pursue a distinctly personal path, and quite another to take at every step a turn incompatible with the self-contained logic of an earlier artefact. Systems need to be internally consistent.

72 'E' quello che volevo. Mi premeva, infatti, unificare ed al tempo stesso sdoppiare l'elemento della "contaminazione" e dell'attrazione dei sensi e quello della purezza infantile. D'altronde la ragazza del bordello ricorda un po' Tadzio ... Insomma Aschenbach, nel collegare la presenza di Tadzio al ricordo della prostituta ... coglie pienamente l'aspetto più "peccaminoso" del proprio atteggiamento verso Tadzio. Visconti-Micciché, 117. Repr. in Faldini and Fofi, eds, *1970–1984*, 222.

73 '[N]oi abbiamo ormai dietro noi stessi un passato, ed in certo senso il discorso che dovevamo fare l'abbiamo fatto. Io l'ho fatto da *Ossessione* a *La caduta degli dèi* e quando mi sono concesso delle pause come nel caso di *Notti bianche* non si è comunque trattato di pause degradanti. Ora possiamo anche affrontare temi più particolari e più privati, ma dietro di noi sta un passato di lotta che in certo modo può giustificare questo tardivo rientro momentaneo in una 'privacy' che abbiamo sempre rifiutato per anni. Vuoi dire che anche la nostra è una crisi, uno stato di pigrizia? Mettiamo pure. Per arrivarci ci abbiamo messo però quarant'anni.' Visconti-Micciché, 125.

74 The films that followed *Morte a Venezia* were *Ludwig* (1973), *Conversation Piece* (*Gruppo di famiglia in un interno*, 1974), and *The Innocent* (*L'innocente*, 1976).

75 It is an enlightening intercultural experience, I feel, to reread certain parts of Mann's *Observations by an Unpolitical Man* in the decade of the debate about the 'Asian values' that underpin the economic success of many – hardly democratic – East Asian countries.

Publicizing one's distaste for 'politics' (i.e., democracy) is, of course, itself an intensely political statement: one of an anti-democratic kind, that is. Ominously, what did not occur to Thomas Mann at the time was that judgments such as his amounted to self-fulfilling prophecies. It is precisely when the honest and educated view politics as corrupt and corrupting that a vacuum is created which can be filled all the more easily by the dishonest and uneducated; in Germany's case, the Nazis. (For a further depiction from the 1910s of democracy as a grotesque, see Kafka's biting parody of it in his American novel.)

76 See esp. Bruford, 'The Conversion of an Unpolitical Man, in his *The German Tradition of Self-Cultivation,* 226–63.

77 Georg Lukács, *Essays on Thomas Mann,* trans. S. Mitchell (London: Merlin Press, 1964); *Thomas Mann* (Berlin: Aufbau, 1957). Repr. in his *Deutsche Literatur in zwei Jahrhunderten,* vol. 7 of *Werke* (Neuwied and Berlin: Hermann Luchterhand, 1964), as well as in his *Faust und Faustus,* vol. 2 of *Ausgewählte Schriften* (Hamburg: Rowohlt, 1967). For a detailed account of the Thomas Mann / Lukács relationship, see Judith Marcus, *Georg Lukács and Thomas Mann: A Study in the Sociology of Literature* (Amherst: University of Massachusetts Press, 1987); Judith Marcus-Tar, *Thomas Mann und Georg Lukács: Beziehung, Einfluß und 'repräsentative Gegensätzlichkeit'* (Köln: Böhlau, 1982). Cf. further Hans Rudolf Vaget, 'Georg Lukács, Thomas Mann and the Modern Novel,' in Kenneth Hughes, ed., *Thomas Mann in Context: Papers of the Clark University Centennial Colloquium* (Worcester, Mass.: Clark University Press, 1975), 38–65.

78 This is, of necessity, only a broad-brush description of Visconti's parabola. There are aspects of, for example, *Conversation Piece* that show the director's interest in the politicization of Italian youths in the 1970s. Conversely, as early as the politicized *Senso* one could already detect elements in his filmmaking that foreshadowed the later, personal themes.

More food for thought on Visconti's life work can be gleaned from Pio Baldelli, *Luchino Visconti* (Milan: Gabriele Mazzotta Editore, 1973); Alessandro Bencivenni, *Luchino Visconti* (Milan: Il Castoro, 1999 [1994; 1982]); and Luciano De Giusti, *I film di Luchino Visconti* (Rome: Gremese, 1985). For a general assessment of Visconti's political positions, one needs to consult Aristarco, *Su Visconti* – a book almost completely devoted to just that topic.

79 Leaving aside the occasional plot by nostalgic top brass, one of the few remaining subjects of cold-war-style confrontation between government and opposition was, at the time, Italy's position vis-à-vis the Vietnam war.

80 Left, right, or centre? Red, black, or green? Revolutionary, neo-capitalist, or neo-catholic? The most outlandish theories were – and occasionally still are – put forward to classify the protagonists of the 1968 unrest (and of the progressively lesser ones that followed in 1977, 1985, and so on). In historical perspective, the difficulty in assigning them to any one specific category simply signalled the beginning of the demise in Italy of traditional social groups with a well-defined class identity. Good introductions to the issue of 1968 in Italy

are Nanni Balestrini and Primo Moroni, *L'orda d'oro. 1968–1977: La grande ondata rivoluzionaria e creativa*, ed. Sergio Bianchi (Milan: Feltrinelli, 1997 [1988]); Marcello Flores and Alberto De Bernardi, *Il Sessantotto* (Bologna: Il Mulino, 1998); and Antonio Longo and Giommaria Monti, *Dizionario del '68: I luoghi, i fatti, i protagonisti, le parole e le idee* (Rome: Editori Riuniti, 1998).

81 The example set by the entirely uncanonical Pasolini, who in 1949 was expelled from the PCI because of his homosexuality, must have been clear in Visconti's mind.

82 *Morte a Venezia* seems to me to be endowed with a magnificent congruence between artist and protagonist – a congruence that Visconti's long hoped-for, but never realized, filming of Proust's *Recherche* doubtlessly would also have displayed.

83 Heine, *The Complete Poems*, 649–50 ('Enfant perdu,' *Lazarus* 20). 'Verlorener Posten in dem Freiheitskriege,/ Hielt ich seit dreißig Jahren treulich aus./ Ich kämpfe ohne Hoffnung, daß ich siege,/ Ich wußte, nie komm ich gesund nach Haus.// Ich wachte Tag und Nacht – Ich konnt' nicht schlafen,/ Wie in dem Lagerzelt der Freunde Schar' –/ (Auch hielt das laute Schnarchen dieser Braven/ Mich wach, wenn ich ein bißchen schlummrig war.) ... Ein Posten ist vakant! – Die Wunden klaffen –/ Der eine fällt, die andern rücken nach –/ Doch fall ich unbesiegt, und meine Waffen/ Sind nicht gebrochen – nur mein Herze brach.' *Werke und Briefe* 2: 124 ('Enfant perdu,' *Lazarus* 20).

Conclusion

1 A separate argument would have to apply to what in the course of time come to be perceived as antiquarian translation – for today's Italian readers, for example, Annibale Caro's Renaissance translation of the *Odyssey*, or Vincenzo Monti's neoclassic *Iliad*.

 The issues surrounding translation between natural languages have recently been debated in a sophisticated manner by theorists of the field. For good surveys, see Burton Pike, 'Literary Translation: Looking Toward the Future,' *Narrative Channels*, special issue of *Canadian Review of Comparative Literature / Revue Canadienne de Littérature Comparée* 26:1 (March 1999), 72–80; Lawrence Venuti, ed., *Rethinking Translation: Discourse, Subjectivity, Ideology* (London: Routledge, 1992); and Lawrence Venuti, *The Translator's Invisibility: A History of Translation* (London: Routledge, 1995).

2 As indicated in the text, these considerations of mine are most accurately described as a condensation of ideas originally articulated in the works of the Soviet semiotician Yurii Lotman, working in cooperation with colleagues from Tartu University (at the time Estonian SSR, today Estonia). See espe-

cially the following: Yurii M. Lotman, 'Tekst v tekste' ('The Text in the Text'), *Trudy po znakovym sistemam* 14 (1981), 3–18; 'K postroeniiu teorii vzaimodeistviia ku'tur (Semioticheskii aspekt)' ('Toward a Theory of Reciprocal Interaction between Cultures: Semiotic Aspect'), *Trudy po romano-germanskoi filologii* (1983), 92–113; 'O semiosfere' ('On the Semiosphere'), *Trudy po znakovym sistemam* 17 (1984), 5–23; *La semiosfera: L'asimmetria e il dialogo nelle strutture pensanti,* ed. Simonetta Salvestroni (Venice: Marsilio, 1992 [1985]); *Universe of the Mind: A Semiotic Theory of Culture,* Vnutri mysliashchikh mirov: Chelovek – Tekst – Semiosfera – Istoriia; and *Il girotondo delle Muse: Saggi sulla semiotica delle arti e della rappresentazione,* ed. Silvia Burini (Bergamo: Moretti e Vitali, 1998).

    If this list is short on English translations of Lotman's work, that is simply because hardly any have appeared in this area of his activity (a few of his earlier publications of a structuralist slant did).

3 A particularly synthetic, masterly criticism of the '2 + 2 = 4' (perfect convertibility) argument can be found in Lotman, 'Sistema s odnym iazykom' ('The One-Language System'), in his *Kul'tura i vzryv,* 12–16, esp. 13.

4 As a mere sample, see above (Visconti chapter) the comments made by the narrator of Hesse's *Steppenwolf.* But the sport was already over a century old by then. Nonetheless, it is probable that the ultimate Goethecide was successfully achieved not long ago by the experienced colleague who, in referring to the poet, obliterated his very name by calling him 'Johann von *Schiller'* (NN, *Xxx,* 2). Unless, that is, the pun was on the hapless *Friedrich* Schiller (usually no *von,* thank you).

5 Mitry, *Aesthetics,* 330. 'cette autre salade qui est le fait des adaptateurs [et qui consiste à transposer dans le temps une oeuvre romanesque dont on garde cependant la structure originale et dont on suit le développement] frise la démence ou le gâtisme précoce. Il atteste en tout cas d'un solide mépris de l'oeuvre dont, pourtant, on se sert, ou alors d'une totale incompréhension de ce qui la caractérise et en fait la valeur essentielle.' *Esthétique,* 350.

6 Galileo Galilei is said to have uttered the sentence in question as a comment on the Inquisition's demand that he recant his theories presupposing the earth's mobility.

7 This is not to imply that Tolstoy's demonstrative simplicity is unproblematic or, worse, banal; on the contrary, it is the result of a conscious choice. Equally deliberate is Tolstoy's predilection for *ostranenie* (estrangement), the narrator's feigned inability to understand what he is describing – a device aimed at rendering the described item absurd in the eyes of the readers.

8 There is no dearth of mainstream costume films re-created from Sade. Sex and violence: what more could the market call for? *Salò* is different, though;

unlike the former, its sex and its violence do not smugly pat viewers on the head. *Salò* does not tell a cute story. It is, from beginning to end, a statement about the world. It thinks too much – such films are dangerous.

9 It seems evident to me, at this level of discourse, that Pasolini's *inversion* of Sade came – philosophically speaking – with a price attached: that of muddying the waters with respect to the true nature of consumerism. How so? Pasolini's argument that consumerism *is* 'fascism' severely underestimates the importance of the ideology of free choice that, after all, underpins the entire consumerist tsunami of the late twentieth century. Historical Fascism was altogether restrictive not only politically but *as an economic ideology too*, and hence it strikes me as an inadequate icon to stand for the age of mandated materialism that has superseded it (or, as Pasolini forcefully indicates, *claims* to have superseded it). In the West at any rate, the exterior features of totalitarianism have indeed changed beyond recognition since 1945.

10 Ὕλῃ καὶ τρόποις μιμήσεως διαφέρουσι. In Lessing's German original, '[sie sind] sowohl in den Gegenständen als in der Art ihrer Nachahmung verschieden.' Lessing, *Laokoon*, 14.

11 In this respect it is altogether appropriate that Mann's rhythmic prose describing the Eleusinian mysteries should be a *re-creation* of scholarly texts consulted for just that purpose.

12 Sade's never-ending litanies of *jouissance* prove exactly this point: it is possible to articulate in language *the surface* of desire – but articulating its forms, however many times, will still fail to seize it.

13 'Всякая литературная преёмственность есть прежде всего борьба, разрушение старого целого и новая стройка старых элементов.' Iurii Tynianov, 'Dostoevskii i Gogol′': K teorii parodii' [1921], in *Texte der russischen Formalisten*, ed. J. Striedter, vol. 1 (Munich: Fink, 1969), 302.

14 'Si j'écrivais un livre, exactement [comme] lorsque je fais un film, j'écrirais avec tout ce que ma culture, mes prédilections artistiques m'auraient apporté. Et ce que je dirais, un autre, sans doute, l'aurait déjà dit. Je pourrais ne pas indiquer mes sources. Elles existeraient quand même.

Un homme qui n'aurait jamais lu, jamais regardé un tableau, entendu une musique? Le regard, l'oreille absolument vierges? Et qui se servirait d'une caméra pour voir le monde, le transcrire en images? Oui, celui–là sans doute pourrait faire du cinéma pur. Mais ...'

Interview with Anne Capelle in *Arts et loisirs* (Apr. 1967), collected in Sanzio and Thirard, *Luchino Visconti cinéaste*, 107. For an earlier, nuclear expression of similar views, see also Visconti's article 'Tradizione e invenzione,' originally published some 25 years earlier (1941) and now repr. in Aristarco, *Su Visconti*, 115–17.

15 For a – not always impeccable – Italian translation of this passage, see Èizen-shtein, *Stili di regia*, 313.

Пытаясь выразить в художественной форме социальное требование современности, стараясь оформить разрешение, диктуемое этими требованиями, мы опираемся на опыт, собранный в наблюдениях всего нашего личного прошлого. Это дополняется тем, чтó мы специально разыскиваем для данного конкретного разрешениа, прибегая к тому, что в этом же направлении, но применительно к другой задаче, к другому времени и месту уже разрешено и проделано кем-то другим.

Опираясь на леса разумно собранного опыта, можно возводить свое 'оригинальное,' свое 'несхожее,' а главным образом, свое 'уместное' – целесообразное с точки зрения конкретной задачи – здание. А это самое главное и самое решающее.

Torito, in *Izbrannye proizvedeniia* 4: 635.

16 As above in Èizenshtein, *Stili di regia*, 315 and 316.

'Что такое изобретение, и кто может сказать, что он изобрел то или другое? Да и вообще сущая глупость – чваниться первенством: не признать себя, в конце концов, плагиатором – только бессознательное самохвальство ...'

Сколько недосказанных ассоциаций, сколько прообразов, в которых мы сами часто не хотим сознаться, руководит нами! ...

И снова ключ к объяснению дает тот же Гёте ... 'Что мною написано, то мое! А взял ли я это из жизни или из книг – все равно; мое дело било употребить это кстати!'

Izbrannye proizvedeniia 4: 636–7.

17 'Lire un livre est déjà oeuvre créatrice. La fidélité n'est pas manque de pouvoir créateur. Quoi que l'on fasse, on s'appuie toujours sur un mythe ou une histoire plus ou moins déjà racontée. Qu'importe, sinon le nouveau regard? Mais quand je choisis une oeuvre littéraire précise, c'est pour lui donner une nouvelle dimension, ou plutôt une dimension qu'elle possède implicite-ment, mais que seul un regard "autre" peut lui donner. Ce regard que réclame justement le créateur et qui, lui-même, est créateur.

Mon ambition est d'aller dans le sens le plus difficile qu'aurait choisi l'auteur, le sens secret qu'il souhaitait être décelé par ses lecteurs les plus attentifs. Il me semble que cela aussi est faire oeuvre d'auteur.'

Sanzio and Thirard, *Luchino Visconti cinéaste*, 107–8; emphasis added.

Filmography

Note: Indications on availability are given in order of *easiest access* to North American viewers. Thus, 'North America / video (Italian with English subtitles)' does not imply that the film cannot be found in Italy on Italian video, that no videos are held in Italy in public media libraries, etc. On a less positive note, the indication that a film has been distributed on video does not – alas – necessarily mean that it will still be possible to purchase it from a commercial outlet; videos go out of print much faster than books.

Francesca Archibugi: *Mignon Has Left* (*Mignon è partita*, 1988)

Scenario: Francesca Archibugi
Screenplay: Francesca Archibugi, Gloria Malatesta, Claudia Sbarigia
Photography: Luigi Verga
Art direction: Massimo Spano
Costumes: Paola Marchesin
Music: Roberto Gatto, Battista Lena
Editing: Alfredo Muschietti
Main cast: Céline Beauvallet (Mignon), Massimo Dapporto (Aldo), Jean-Pierre
    Duriez (Federico), Leonardo Ruta (Giorgio), Stefania Sandrelli (the mother)
Producers: Leo Pescarolo and Guido De Laurentiis for Ellepi Film, RAI 3
    (Rome), and Chrysalide Film (Paris)
Availability: Italy / video (Italian)

Federico Fellini: *Intervista* (1987)

Scenario: Federico Fellini
Screenplay: Gianfranco Angelucci and Federico Fellini

Assistant director: Maurizio Mein
Photography: Tonino Delli Colli
Art direction and costumes: Danilo Donati
Music: Nicola Piovani
Editing: Nino Baragli
Main cast: Anita Ekberg (herself), Federico Fellini (himself), Paola Liguori (the
    star), Marcello Mastroianni (Mandrake/himself), Maurizio Mein (himself),
    Pietro Notarianni (the Fascist bigwig), Nadia Ottaviani (the vestal), Sergio
    Rubini (the young journalist), Lara Wendel (the bride)
Producer: Ibrahim Moussa for Aljosha Productions, Cinecittà, RAI 1 (Rome)
Availability: North America / video (Italian with English subtitles)

Alberto Lattuada: *The Overcoat* (*Il cappotto*, 1952)

Scenario: from Nikolai Vasil'evich Gogol'
Screenplay: Alberto Lattuada, Luigi Malerba, Cesare Zavattini et al.
Assistant director: Aldo Buzzi
Photography: Mario Montuori
Art direction: Gianni Polidori
Costumes: Dario Cecchi
Music: Felice Lattuada
Editing: Eraldo Da Roma
Main cast: Silvio Bagolini (the driver of the hearse), Giulio Calì (the tailor),
    Anna Carena (the landlady), Antonella Lualdi (Vittoria), Ettore G. Mattia
    (the secretary), Renato Rascel (Carmine De Carmine), Yvonne Sanson
    (Caterina), Sandro Somarè (Vittoria's fiancé), Giulio Stival (the Mayor)
Producer: Faro Film (Rome)
Availability: Italy / video (Italian)

Nanni Moretti: *Palombella rossa* (1989)

Scenario and screenplay: Nanni Moretti
Assistant director: Donatella Botti
Photography: Giuseppe Lanci
Art direction: Giancarlo Basili and Leonardo Scarpa
Costumes: Maria Rita Barbera
Music: Nicola Piovani
Editing: Mirco Garrone
Main cast: Asia Argento (Valentina, Michele's daughter), Imre Budavari (him-
    self), Eugenio Masciari (the referee), Luigi Moretti (the labor unionist),

Nanni Moretti (Michele Apicella), Claudio Morganti (the first character harassing Michele), Silvio Orlando (the coach), Mario Patanè (Simone), Alfonso Santagata (the second character harassing Michele), Fabio Traversa (the old-time friend), Mariella Valentini (the journalist)

Producers: Nanni Moretti and Angelo Barbagallo for Sacher Film, RAI 1 (Rome), Nella Banfi for Palmyre Film (Paris)

Availability: North America / video (Italian with English subtitles)

Pier Paolo Pasolini: *Salò or the 120 Days of Sodom*
(*Salò o le 120 giornate di Sodoma*, **1975**)

Scenario: from the Marquis de Sade
Screenplay: Sergio Citti and Pier Paolo Pasolini
Assistant director: Umberto Angelucci
Photography: Tonino Delli Colli
Art direction: Dante Ferretti
Costumes: Danilo Donati
Music: Ennio Morricone
Editing: Nino Baragli, Tatiana Casini Morigi
Main cast: Paolo Bonacelli (the duke), Caterina Boratto (Ms. Castelli), Giorgio Cataldi (the *monsignore*), Elsa De Giorgi (Ms. Maggi), Uberto Paolo Quintavalle (the excellency), Sonia Saviange (the pianist), Hélène Surgère (Ms. Vaccari), Aldo Valletti (the president)
Producer: Alberto Grimaldi for PEA (Rome), Les Productions Artistes Associés (Paris)
Availability: North America / video (Italian with English subtitles)

Francesco Rosi: *Carmen* (**1984**)

Scenario: from Prosper Mérimée by way of Georges Bizet's opera
Librettists: Ludovic Halévy and Henri Meilhac
Script: Ariane Adriani
Assistant director: Giovanni Arduini
Photography: Pasqualino De Santis
Choreography: Antonio Gadès
Set design and costumes: Enrico Job
Music: Georges Bizet
Editing: Ruggero Mastroianni, Colette Semprun
Main cast: John Paul Bogart (Zuñiga), Maria Campano (Manuelita), Susan Daniel (Mercédès), Accursio Di Leo (guide), Placido Domingo (Don José),

Faith Esham (Micaëla), Gérard Garino (Remendado), Julien Guiomar (Lillas Pastia), Jean-Philippe Lafont (Dancaïre), François Le Roux (Morales), Julia Migenes Johnson (Carmen), Ruggero Raimondi (Escamillo), Lilian Watson (Frasquita)

Producer: Patrice Ledoux for Gaumont, Marcel Dassault (Paris), Opera Film (Rome)

Availability: North America / video (French with English subtitles)

Roberto Rossellini: *Vanina Vanini* (1961)

Scenario: Franco Solinas and Antonello Trombadori, from Stendhal

Screenplay: Diego Fabbri, Jean Gruault, Monique Lange, Roberto Rossellini, Franco Solinas, Antonello Trombadori

Assistant directors: Renzo Rossellini (Jr), Franco Rossellini, Philippe Arthuys

Photography: Luciano Trasatti

Art direction: Luigi Scaccianoce

Costumes: Danilo Donati

Music: Renzo Rossellini (Sr)

Editing: Daniele Alabiso, Mario Serandrei

Main cast: Martine Carol (Countess Vitelleschi), Isabelle Corey (Clelia), Sandra Milo (Vanina Vanini), Antonio Pierfederici (Livio Savelli), Paolo Stoppa (Prince Asdrubale Vanini), Carlo Tamberlani (*Monsignor* Benini), Laurent Terzieff (Pietro Missirilli)

Producer: Moris Ergas for Zebra Film (Rome), Orsay Film (Paris)

Availability: North America / video (Italian with English subtitles)

Paolo and Vittorio Taviani: *The Night Sun* (*Il sole anche di notte*, 1990)

Scenario: from Lêv Tolstoi

Screenplay: Tonino Guerra, Paolo and Vittorio Taviani

Assistant director: Mimmola Girosi

Photography: Giuseppe Lanci

Art direction: Gianni Sbarra

Costumes: Lina Nerli Taviani

Music: Nicola Piovani

Editing: Roberto Perpignani

Main cast: Massimo Bonetti (Prince Santobuono), Teresa Brescianini (Concetta), Charlotte Gainsbourg (Matilda), Nastassja Kinski (Cristina), Margarita Lozano (Sergio's mother), Patricia Millardet (Aurelia), Lorenzo Perpignani (Sergio as a child), Matilde Piana (the peasant woman), Salvatore Rossi

(Eugenio), Julian Sands (Sergio Giuramondo), Pamela Villoresi (Giuseppina, Sergio's sister), Rüdiger Vogler (King Carlo)
Producer: Giuliani G. De Negri for Filmtre, RAI 1 (Rome), Capoul – Interpool – Sara Film (Paris), Direkt Film (Munich)
Availability: North America / video (Italian with English subtitles)

Luchino Visconti: *Death in Venice* (*Morte a Venezia*, **1971**)

Scenario: from Thomas Mann
Screenplay: Nicola Badalucco, Luchino Visconti
Assistant director: Albino Cocco
Photography: Pasqualino De Santis
Art direction: Ferdinando Scarfiotti
Costumes: Piero Tosi
Music: Gustav Mahler
Editing: Ruggero Mastroianni
Main cast: Carole André (Esmeralda), Björn Andresen (Tadzio), Marisa Berenson (Aschenbach's wife), Dirk Bogarde (Gustav von Aschenbach), Mark Burns (Alfried), Leslie French (the employee at Cook's), Sergio Garfagnoli (Jaschu), Silvana Mangano (Tadzio's mother), Nora Ricci (Tadzio's governess), Romolo Valli (the hotel director)
Producer: Mario Gallo for Alfa Cinematografica (Rome), Éditions Cinématographiques Françaises (Paris)
Availability: North America / video (Italian with English subtitles)

For ongoing updates, see the websites
http://www.imdb.com/   (Internet Movie Database)
http://kwcinema.play.kataweb.it/   (Kataweb Cinema)

Works Cited

Abba, Giuseppe Cesare. *Da Quarto al Volturno: Noterelle d'uno dei Mille.* Bologna: Zanichelli, 1909.

‒ *The Diary of One of Garibaldi's Thousand.* Intro. and trans. E.R. Vincent. London: Oxford University Press, 1962.

Accialini, Fulvio, and Lucia Coluccelli. *Paolo e Vittorio Taviani.* Florence: La nuova Italia, 1979. (Il Castoro cinema 65).

Airaksinen, Timo. *The Philosophy of the Marquis de Sade.* London: Routledge, 1995 [1991].

Alter, Robert. *Partial Magic: The Novel as Self-Conscious Genre.* Berkeley: University of California Press, 1975.

Améry, Jean. 'Venezianische Zaubereien: Luchino Visconti und sein *Tod in Venedig.*' *Merkur* 25 (1971), 808–12.

Antonioni, Michelangelo. *Fare un film è per me vivere.* Ed. Carlo di Carlo and Giorgio Tinazzi. Venice: Marsilio, 1994.

‒ *The Architecture of Vision: Writings and Interviews on Cinema.* Ed. Carlo di Carlo and Giorgio Tinazzi. Trans. Marga Cottino-Jones. New York: Marsilio Publishers, 1996.

Arens, Hans. *Kommentar zu Goethes* Faust II. Heidelberg: Carl Winter Universitätsverlag, 1989.

Aristarco, Guido. *Sotto il segno dello scorpione: Il cinema dei fratelli Taviani,* 101–52. Messina and Florence: G. D'Anna, 1978.

‒ *Su Visconti: Materiali per una analisi critica.* Rome: La Zattera di Babele, 1986.

Attolini, Vito. *Storia del cinema letterario in cento film.* Recco (GE): Le Mani, 1998.

Bacon, Henry. *Visconti: Explorations of Beauty and Decay.* Cambridge: Cambridge University Press, 1998.

Bahr, Ehrhard, ed. *Thomas Mann. Der Tod in Venedig. Erläuterungen und Dokumente.* Stuttgart: Philipp Reclam jun., 1991.

Bakhtin, Mikhail Mikhailovich. *Tvorchestvo Fransua Rable i narodnaia kul'tura srednevekov'ia i Renessansa.* Moscow: Khudozhestvennaia literatura, 1990 [1965].

– *Rabelais and His World.* Trans. Hélène Iswolsky. Bloomington: Indiana University Press, 1984 [1968].

– *Èstetika slovesnogo tvorcestva.* Moscow: Iskusstvo, 1979.

– *The Dialogic Imagination: Four Essays.* Ed. Michael Holquist. Trans. Caryl Emerson and Michael Holquist. Austin: University of Texas Press, 1981.

– *Speech Genres and Other Late Essays.* Ed. Caryl Emerson and Michael Holquist. Trans. Vern W. McGee. Austin: University of Texas Press, 1986.

Baldelli, Pio. *Roberto Rossellini.* Rome: Samonà e Savelli, 1972. (Saggistica 39).

– *Luchino Visconti.* Milan: Gabriele Mazzotta Editore, 1973.

Balestrini, Nanni, and Primo Moroni. *L'orda d'oro. 1968–1977: La grande ondata rivoluzionaria e creativa ...* Ed. Sergio Bianchi. Milan: Feltrinelli, 1997 [1988].

Banti, Alberto M. *La nazione del Risorgimento: Parentela, santità e onore alle origini dell'Italia unita.* Turin: Einaudi, 2000. (Biblioteca di cultura storica 225).

Barnes, Christopher. *Boris Pasternak: A Literary Biography. Vol. I: 1890–1928.* Cambridge: Cambridge University Press, 1989.

Barrett, Edward, ed. *The Society of Text: Hypertext, Hypermedia, and the Social Construction of Information.* Cambridge, Mass.: MIT Press, 1989.

Barthes, Roland. *Sade Fourier Loyola.* Paris: Seuil, 1971.

– *Sade Fourier Loyola.* Trans. Richard Miller. Berkeley: University of California Press, 1989 [1976].

– 'Sade – Pasolini' [orig. pub. 1976]. In his *Oeuvres complètes*, 3: 391–2. Ed. Éric Marty. Paris: Seuil, 1995.

Battiato, Franco. 'E ti vengo a cercare.' In his music CD *Battiato Studio Collection.* Rome: EMI Publishing Italia, 1996.

Beaujour, Michel. *Miroirs d'encre: Rhétorique de l'autoportrait.* Paris: Seuil, 1980.

– *Poetics of the Literary Self-Portrait.* Trans. Yara Milos. New York: New York University Press, 1991.

Beaumarchais, Pierre-Augustin Caron de. *Le mariage de Figaro.* In *Oeuvres.* Ed. Pierre and Jacqueline Larthomas. Paris: Gallimard Pléiade, 1988.

Beauvoir, Simone de. *Faut-il brûler Sade?* Paris: Gallimard, [1955].

Bencivenni, Alessandro. *Luchino Visconti.* Milan: Il Castoro, 1999 [1994; 1982]. (Il Castoro cinema 98).

Bernardi, Sandro, ed. *Storie dislocate.* San Miniato (PI): Edizioni ETS, 1999. (Il Prato 1).

Bernardi, Sandro, et al. *Nanni Moretti.* Turin: Paravia Scriptorium, 1999.

Bersani, Leo. *A Future for Astyanax: Character and Desire in Literature.* Boston: Little, Brown and Co., 1975.

- *Théorie et violence: Freud et l'art.* Paris: Seuil, 1984.

- *The Culture of Redemption.* Cambridge, Mass.: Harvard University Press, 1990.

- *Homos.* Cambridge, Mass.: Harvard University Press, 1995.

Bertelli, Sergio. *I corsari del tempo: Gli errori e gli orrori dei film storici.* Florence: Ponte alle Grazie, 1995.

Bertellini, Giorgio. 'A Battle *d'arrière-garde*: Notes on Decadence in Luchino Visconti's *Death in Venice.*' *Film Quarterly* 50:4 (Summer 1997), 11–19.

Bertrand, Denis. 'Les migrations de Carmen.' *Le français dans le monde* 181 (Nov.–Dec. 1983), 103–8.

Bezzel, Chris. *Kafka-Chronik.* Munich and Vienna: Carl Hanser Verlag, 1975. (Reihe Hanser 178).

Bhabha, Homi K., ed. *Nation and Narration.* London: Routledge, 1990.

Binder, Hartmut. *Kafka-Kommentar zu den Romanen, Rezensionen, Aphorismen und zum Brief an den Vater.* Munich: Winkler, 1976.

Bizet, Georges. *Carmen.* Ed. and trans. Ellen H. Bleiler. New York: Dover Publications, 1970.

Blanchot, Maurice. 'La raison de Sade.' In his *Lautréamont et Sade.* Paris: Les Éditions de Minuit, 1963.

Bocca, Giorgio. *La disunità d'Italia.* Milan: Garzanti, 1990.

- *Il sottosopra.* Milan: Mondadori, 1994.

Boccaccio, Giovanni. *Decameron.* Ed. Vittore Branca. Turin: Einaudi, 1992. 2 vols. (Einaudi Tascabili Classici 99).

Bolter, J. David. *Writing Space: The Computer, Hypertext, and the History of Writing.* Hillsdale, NJ: Lawrence Erlbaum, 1991.

Bolzoni, Francesco. *I film di Francesco Rosi.* Rome: Gremese, 1986. (Effetto Cinema 13).

Bondanella, Peter. *Italian Cinema from Neorealism to the Present.* New York: Continuum, 1991 [1983].

- *The Cinema of Federico Fellini.* Princeton, NJ: Princeton University Press, 1992.

- *The Films of Roberto Rossellini.* Cambridge: Cambridge University Press, 1993.

- 'La (s)fortuna critica del cinema viscontiano in USA.' In David Bruni and Veronica Pravadelli, eds, *Studi viscontiani*, 277–86.

Bondanella, Peter, ed. *Federico Fellini: Essays in Criticism.* New York: Oxford University Press, 1978.

Bondanella, Peter, and Cristina Degli-Esposti, eds. *Perspectives on Federico Fellini.* New York: Hall, 1993.

Bordwell, David. *Making Meaning: Inference and Rhetoric in the Interpretation of Cinema.* Cambridge, Mass.: Harvard University Press, 1989.

– *The Cinema of Eisenstein.* Cambridge, Mass.: Harvard University Press, 1993.

Bordwell, David, and Kristin Thompson. *Film History: An Introduction.* New York: McGraw-Hill, 1994.

Borges, Jorge Luis. *Borges, el palabrista.* Ed. Esteban Peicovich. Madrid: Letra viva, 1980.

– 'Magías parciales del Quijote.' In his *Obras completas,* 2:45–7. Barcelona: Emecé, 1989.

Bori, Pier Cesare. *L'altro Tolstoj.* Bologna: Il Mulino, 1995.

Bragaglia, Cristina. *Il piacere del racconto: Narrativa italiana e cinema (1895–1990).* Florence: La nuova Italia, 1993.

Bruford, W.H. *The German Tradition of Self-Cultivation: Bildung from Humboldt to Thomas Mann.* Cambridge: Cambridge University Press, 1975.

Brunetta, Gian Piero. *Storia del cinema italiano.* 4 vols. Rome: Editori Riuniti, 1993 [1982].

Brunetta, Gian Piero, ed. *Spari nel buio. La letteratura contro il cinema italiano: Settant'anni di stroncature memorabili.* Venice: Marsilio, 1994.

– *L'Europa: Miti, luoghi, divi.* Vol. 1/1 of his *Storia del cinema mondiale.* Turin: Einaudi, 1999.

Brunette, Peter. *Roberto Rossellini.* New York: Oxford University Press, 1987.

Bruni, David, and Veronica Pravadelli, eds. *Studi viscontiani.* Venice: Marsilio, 1997.

Bruno, Edoardo. *Alberto Lattuada.* Rome: Edizioni Cinecittà International, 1993. (I Quaderni 11).

Bruno, Edoardo, ed. *Roberto Rossellini.* Rome: Bulzoni, 1979.

Buache, Freddy. *Le cinéma italien 1945–1990.* Lausanne: L'Âge d'homme, 1992.

Burke, Frank. 'Fellini's *Intervista* as Postcolonial Text.' *Romance Languages Annual* 7 (1995), 212–17.

– *Fellini's Films: From Postwar to Postmodern.* New York: Prentice Hall–Twayne, 1996.

Burrus, Virginia. *The Making of a Heretic: Gender, Authority, and the Priscillianist Controversy.* Berkeley: University of California Press, 1995.

Byron, George Gordon Lord. *Poetry.* Vol. 3. *The Works of Lord Byron.* Ed. Ernest Hartley Coleridge. London: Murray and New York: Scribner, 1900.

Cafagna, Luciano. *Nord e Sud: Non fare a pezzi l'unità d'Italia.* Venice: Marsilio, 1994.

– *Cavour.* Bologna: Il Mulino, 1999. (L'identità italiana 11).

Camerini, Claudio. *Alberto Lattuada.* Florence: La nuova Italia, 1982. (Il Castoro cinema 91–92).

Campbell, Joseph, ed. *The Mysteries: Papers from the Eranos Yearbooks.* Princeton, NJ: Princeton University Press, 1978 [1955]. (Bollingen Series XXX, 2).

Cappabianca, Alessandro. *Il cinema e il sacro.* Recco (GE): Le Mani, 1998.

Cartmell, Deborah, and Imelda Whelehan, eds. *Adaptations: From Text to Screen, Screen to Text.* London: Routledge, 1999.

Casetti, Francesco. *Teorie del cinema 1945–1990.* Milan: Bompiani, 1994.

– *Theories of Cinema: 1945–1995.* Trans. Francesca Chiostri et al. Austin: University of Texas Press, 1999.

Castronovo, Valerio. 'La storia economica.' In *Storia d'Italia* 4/1. Turin: Einaudi, 1976.

Caughie, John, ed. *Theories of Authorship.* London: Routledge, 1981.

Celan, Paul. *Gedichte I.* Vol. 1 of *Gesammelte Werke in fünf Bänden.* Frankfurt am Main: Suhrkamp, 1983.

– *Poems.* Trans. Michael Hamburger. London: Anvil Press Poetry, 1995 [1988].

Chadwick, Henry. *Priscillian of Avila: The Occult and the Charismatic in the Early Church.* Oxford: Clarendon Press, 1976.

Christian, R.F. *Tolstoy: A Critical Introduction.* Cambridge: Cambridge University Press, 1969.

Ciment, Gilles, ed. *Federico Fellini.* Paris: Éditions Rivages, 1988. (Dossier Positif–Rivages).

Ciment, Michel. *Le dossier Rosi.* Paris: Ramsay, 1987 [1976].

Clark, Martin. *Modern Italy 1871–1995.* London: Longman, 1996 [1984].

Clément, Catherine. *L'opéra, ou la défaite des femmes.* Paris: Bernard Grasset, 1979.

– *Opera: Or, the Undoing of Women.* Trans. Betsy Wing. Minneapolis: University of Minnesota Press, 1988.

Cogman, P.W.M. 'The Narrators of Mérimée's *Carmen.*' *Nottingham French Studies* 27:2 (Nov. 1988), 1–12.

Collodi, Carlo. *Le avventure di Pinocchio.* Ed. Cesare Zavattini. Turin: Einaudi, 1961 [1883, 1881].

– *The Adventures of Pinocchio.* Trans. Ann Lawson Lucas. Oxford: Oxford University Press, 1996.

Comenius, Jan Amos. *Jan Amos Comenius. Philosophisches und dichterisches Werk.* Special issue of *Russian Literature* 39:4 (May 1996), 419–546.

Conger, Syndy M., and Janice R. Welsch, eds. *Narrative Strategies.* [Macomb, Ill.]: Western Illinois University, 1980.

Cortellazzo, Sara, and Dario Tomasi. *Letteratura e cinema.* Rome and Bari: Laterza, 1998. (Alfabeto Letterario 6).

Costa, Antonio. *Immagine di un'immagine: Cinema e letteratura.* Turin: UTET, 1993.

Cosulich, Callisto. *I film di Alberto Lattuada.* Rome: Gremese, 1985. (Effetto Cinema 10).

Culler, Jonathan. *Flaubert: The Uses of Uncertainty.* Ithaca: Cornell University Press, 1985.

Currie, Mark, ed. *Metafiction.* London: Longman, 1995.

Dällenbach, Lucien. *Le récit spéculaire: Essai sur la mise en abyme.* Paris: Seuil, 1977.

– *The Mirror in the Text.* Trans. Jeremy Whiteley and Emma Hughes. Chicago: University of Chicago Press and Cambridge: Polity Press, 1989.

Dalle Vacche, Angela. *The Body in the Mirror: Shapes of History in Italian Cinema.* Princeton, NJ: Princeton University Press, 1992.

D'Amico de Carvalho, Caterina. *Life and Work of Luchino Visconti.* Rome: Cinecittà International, [1998].

De Benedictis, Maurizio. *Pasolini, la croce alla rovescia: I temi della vita e del sacrificio.* Anzio (Rome): De Rubeis, 1995.

De Bernardinis, Flavio. *Nanni Moretti.* Milan: Il Castoro, 1998. (Il Castoro cinema 128).

De Giusti, Luciano. *I film di Pier Paolo Pasolini.* Rome: Gremese, 1983. (Effetto Cinema 6).

– *I film di Luchino Visconti.* Rome: Gremese, 1985. (Effetto Cinema 11).

Delany, Paul, and George P. Landow, eds. *Hypermedia and Literary Studies.* Cambridge, Mass.: MIT Press, 1991.

Del Carria, Renzo. *Proletari senza rivoluzione: Storia delle classi subalterne italiane dal 1860 al 1950.* 2 vols. Rome: Savelli, 1975. [Milan: Edizioni Oriente, 1970].

De Marchis Rossellini, Marcella. *Un matrimonio riuscito: Autobiografia.* Milano: Il Castoro, 1996.

De Matteo, Giovanni. *Brigantaggio e Risorgimento: Legittimisti e briganti tra i Borbone e i Savoia.* Naples: Alfredo Guida Editore, 2000.

De Santi, Pier Marco. *I film di Paolo e Vittorio Taviani.* Rome: Gremese Editore, 1988. (Effetto Cinema 16).

De Sica, Vittorio, and Cesare Zavattini. *Parliamo tanto di noi.* Ed. Ottavio Iemma and Paolo Nuzzi. Rome: Editori Riuniti, 1997.

Dieterle, Bernard. *Die versunkene Stadt: Sechs Kapitel zum literarischen Venedig-Mythos.* Frankfurt am Main: Peter Lang, 1995. (Schriften zur Soziosemiotik und Komparatistik 5).

Di Giammatteo, Fernaldo. *Roberto Rossellini.* Florence: La nuova Italia, 1990. (Immagini 4).

– *Lo sguardo inquieto: Storia del cinema italiano 1940–1990.* Florence: La nuova Italia, 1994.

Doerne, Martin. *Tolstoj und Dostojewskij: Zwei christliche Utopien.* Göttingen: Vandenhoeck und Ruprecht, 1969.

Dostoevskii (Dostoevsky), Fëdor (Fyodor) Mikhailovich. *Polnoe sobranie sochinenii v tridsati tomakh.* Leningrad: Nauka, 1972. (*Zapiski iz podpol'ia* in *Povesti i rasskazy 1862–1866,* vol. 5).

– *Notes from Underground*. Ed. and trans. Michael R. Katz. New York: Norton, 1989. (Norton Critical Edition).

Driessen, F.C. *Gogol as a Short-Story Writer: A Study of His Technique of Composition*. Trans. Ian F. Finlay. The Hague: Mouton, 1965. (Slavistic Printings and Reprintings 57).

Eco, Umberto. *Interpretation and Overinterpretation*. Ed. Stefan Collini. Cambridge: Cambridge University Press, 1992.

– *Interpretazione e sovrainterpretazione*. Ed. Stefan Collini. Trans. Sandra Cavicchioli. Milan: Bompiani, 1995.

– *Experiences in Translation*. Trans. Alastair McEwen. Toronto: University of Toronto Press, 2001.

Edwards, Gwynne. '*Carmen.*' In Margaret A. Rees, ed., *Catholic Tastes and Times: Essays in Honour of Michael E. Williams*, 127–55. University of Leeds: Trinity and All Saints' College, 1987.

Egan, Susanna. *Patterns of Experience in Autobiography*. Chapel Hill: University of North Carolina Press, 1984.

Èizenshtein (Eisenstein), Sergei M. *Izbrannye proizvedeniia v shesti tomakh*. Moskva: Iskusstvo, 1964–71.

– *Stili di regia. Narrazione e messa in scena: Leskov, Dumas, Zola, Dostoevskij, Gogol'*. Ed. Pietro Montani and Alberto Cioni. Venice: Marsilio, 1993.

– *Writings, 1922–1934*. Ed. and trans. Richard Taylor. Vol. 1 of *Selected Works*. London: British Film Institute and Bloomington: Indiana University Press, 1988.

– *Writings, 1934–1947*. Ed. Richard Taylor. Trans. William Powell. Vol. 3 of *Selected Works*. London: British Film Institute, 1996.

– *Beyond the Stars: The Memoirs of Sergei Eisenstein*. Ed. Richard Taylor. Trans. William Powell. Vol. 4 of *Selected Works*. London: British Film Institute and Calcutta: Seagull Books, 1995.

Elbaz, Robert. *The Changing Nature of the Self: A Critical Study of the Autobiographic Discourse*. London: Croom Helm, 1988.

Emrich, Wilhelm. *Franz Kafka*. Bonn: Athenäum Verlag, 1958.

Erlich, Victor. 'Gogol and Kafka: Note on "Realism" and "surrealism."' In Morris Halle et al., eds, *For Roman Jakobson: Essays on the Occasion of His Sixtieth Birthday*, 100–8. The Hague: Mouton, 1956.

– *Gogol*. New Haven, Conn.: Yale University Press, 1969.

Faldini, Franca, and Goffredo Fofi, eds. *L'avventurosa storia del cinema italiano raccontata dai suoi protagonisti, 1935–1959*. Milan: Feltrinelli, 1979.

– eds. *L'avventurosa storia del cinema italiano raccontata dai suoi protagonisti, 1960–1969*. Milan: Feltrinelli, 1981.

– eds. *Il cinema italiano d'oggi 1970–1984 raccontato dai suoi protagonisti*. Milan: Mondadori, 1984.

Fava, Claudio Giorgio, and Aldo Viganò. *I film di Federico Fellini*. Rome: Gremese, 1995 [1981]. (Effetto Cinema 1).

Favre, Pierre. *Sade utopiste: Sexualité, pouvoir et état dans le roman Aline et Valcour*. Paris: Presses Universitaires de France, 1967. (Série Science Politique 12).

Fellini, Federico. *Fare un film*. Turin: Einaudi, 1980.

– *Intervista sul cinema*. Ed. Giovanni Grazzini. Bari: Laterza, 1983. (Saggi Tascabili Laterza 96).

– *La strada: Federico Fellini, Director*. Ed. Peter Bondanella and Manuela Gieri. New Brunswick, NJ: Rutgers University Press, 1987.

– *Comments on Film*. Ed. Giovanni Grazzini. Trans. Joseph Henry. Fresno, Ca.: The Press at California State University Fresno, 1988.

– *Block-notes di un regista*. Milano: Longanesi, 1988.

– *Il mestiere di regista: Intervista con Federico Fellini*. Ed. Rita Cirio. Milan: Garzanti, 1994.

– *Raccontando di me: Conversazioni con Constanzo Costantini*. Ed. Costanzo Costantini. Rome: Editori Riuniti, 1996 [1995].

– *Fellini on Fellini*. Ed. Costanzo Costantini. Trans. Sohrab Sorooshian. London and Boston: Faber and Faber, 1995.

Felstiner, John. *Paul Celan: Poet, Survivor, Jew*. New Haven: Yale University Press, 1995.

Ferrero, Adelio, ed. *Storia del cinema: Autori e tendenze negli anni Cinquanta e Sessanta*. 3 vols. Venice: Marsilio, 1978.

Ferrucci, Riccardo, and Patrizia Turini. *Paolo e Vittorio Taviani: La poesia del paesaggio*. Rome: Gremese Editore, 1995. (English version: *Paolo and Vittorio Taviani: The Poetry of the Italian Landscape*).

Fertonani, Roberto. Intro. to Thomas Mann, *La morte a Venezia. Tristano. Tonio Kröger*, 33–5. Milan: Mondadori, 1970.

– 'Echi classici in *Der Tod in Venedig* di Thomas Mann.' *ACME* 28:1–2 (Jan.–Aug. 1975), 17–26.

Fieschi, Jean-André. 'Les deux flammes.' *Cahiers du cinéma* 135 (Sept. 1962), 40–4.

Flaubert, Gustave. *Oeuvres complètes*. Ed. Bernard Masson. Paris: Seuil Intégrale, 1964. (*La Tentation de Saint Antoine* in vol. 1; *L'Éducation sentimentale* in vol. 2).

– *Les lettres d'Égypte de G. F. d'après les manuscrits autographes. Édition critique*. Ed. Antoine Youssef Naaman. Paris: Nizet, 1965.

– *Flaubert in Egypt, A Sensibility On Tour: A Narrative Drawn from G. F.'s Travel Notes and Letters* ... Ed. and trans. Francis Steegmuller. Chicago: Academy Chicago Ltd., 1979.

– *Sentimental Education*. Trans. Robert Baldick. Harmondsworth: Penguin, 1980.

– *The Temptation of Saint Antony*. Trans. Kitty Mrosovsky. Harmondsworth: Penguin, 1980.

– *Correspondance.* Ed. Jean Bruneau. Paris: Gallimard Pléiade. (Vol. 2, 1980; vol. 3, 1991).

– *Voyage en Égypte. Édition intégrale du manuscrit original* ... Ed. Pierre-Marc de Biasi. Paris: Bernard Grasset, 1991.

Fletcher, Angus. 'Music, Visconti, Mann, Nietzsche: *Death in Venice.*' In Thomas Harrison, ed., *Nietzsche in Italy,* 301–12. Stanford, Calif.: ANMA Libri, 1988.

Flores, Marcello, and Alberto De Bernardi. *Il Sessantotto.* Bologna: Il Mulino, 1998.

Fofi, Goffredo. *Capire con il cinema: Duecento film prima e dopo il '68.* Milan: Feltrinelli, 1971.

– *Il cinema italiano: Servi e padroni.* Milan: Feltrinelli, 1971.

Folkenflik, Robert, ed. *The Culture of Autobiography: Constructions of Self-Representation.* Stanford, Calif.: Stanford University Press, 1993.

Forgacs, David, et al., eds. *Roberto Rossellini: Magician of the Real.* London: British Film Institute, 2000.

Gallagher, Tag. *The Adventures of Roberto Rossellini.* New York: Da Capo Press, 1998.

Gaudreault, André. *Du littéraire au filmique: Système du récit.* Montréal: Presses de l'Université Laval; Paris: Klincksieck, 1988.

Genette, Gérard. *Palimpsestes: La littérature au second degré.* Paris: Seuil, 1982.

– *Palimpsests: Literature in the Second Degree.* Trans. Claude Doubinsky and Channa Newman. Lincoln: University of Nebraska Press, 1997. (Stages 8).

Gerhard, Melitta. *Der deutsche Entwicklungsroman bis zu Goethes Wilhelm Meister.* Halle a. d. Saale: Max Niemeyer, 1926.

Gesù, Sebastiano, ed. *Francesco Rosi.* Acicatena (CT): Incontri con il cinema, 1991.

Giacci, Vittorio, ed. *Francesco Rosi.* Rome: Cinecittà International, 1994.

Gieri, Manuela. *Contemporary Italian Filmmaking: Strategies of Subversion.* Toronto: University of Toronto Press, 1995.

Gili, Jean A. *Francesco Rosi: Cinéma et pouvoir.* Paris: Éditions du Cerf, 1977.

Gili, Jean A., ed. *Paolo et Vittorio Taviani: Entretien au pluriel.* Arles: Institut Lumière–Éditions Actes Sud, 1993.

Gippius, Vasilii Vasil'evich. *Gogol'.* Leningrad: Mysl', 1924. Anastatic repr.: Providence, RI: Brown University Press, 1963.

– *Gogol.* Ed. and trans. Robert A. Maguire. Ann Arbor, Mich.: Ardis, 1981.

Glassco, David. 'Films Out of Books: Bergman, Visconti and Mann.' *Mosaic* 16:1–2 (Winter–Spring 1983), 165–73.

Glenn, Jerry. *Paul Celan.* New York: Twayne, 1973. (Twayne World Author Series 262).

Goethe, Johann Wolfgang von. *Wilhelm Meister's Apprenticeship.* Vol. 7 of *Works.* Ed. and trans. Thomas Carlyle. London: The Anthological Society, [1901?].

– *Wilhelm Meister's Apprenticeship.* Ed. Eric Albert Blackall and Victor Lange. Vol. 9 of *Collected Works.* New York: Suhrkamp, 1989.
– *Faust. A Tragedy.* Trans. Bayard Taylor. Intro. Victor Lange. New York: Modern Library, 1967 [1870].
– *Sämtliche Werke nach Epochen seines Schaffens. Münchner Ausgabe.* Ed. Karl Richter et al. Munich: Carl Hanser, 1987. (*Wilhelm Meisters Lehrjahre,* ed. Hans-Jürgen Schings, vol. 5; *Faust I* in *Weimarer Klassik. 1798–1806,* ed. Victor Lange, vol. 6/1; *Faust II* in *Letzte Jahre. 1827–1832,* ed. Gisela Henckmann et al., vol. 18/1).
Gogol' (Gogol), Nikolai Vasil'evich (Vasilevich). *Polnoe sobranie sochinenii.* Moscow and Leningrad: Izdatel'stvo Akademii Nauk SSSR. (*Povest' o tom, kak possorilsia Ivan Ivanovich s Ivanom Nikiforovichem* in *Mirgorod,* vol. 2, 1937; *Shinel'* in *Povesti,* vol. 3, 1938; *Mertvye dushi 2,* vol. 7, 1951).
– *The Complete Tales.* Trans. Constance Garnett. Ed. and rev. Leonard Kent. Vol. 2. Chicago: University of Chicago Press, 1985.
Gould Boyum, Joy. *Double Exposure: Fiction into Film.* New York: New American Library–Plume, 1985.
Greene, Naomi. *Pier Paolo Pasolini: Cinema as Heresy.* Princeton, NJ: Princeton University Press, 1990.
– 'Salò: The Refusal to Consume.' In Patrick Rumble and Bart Testa, eds, *Pier Paolo Pasolini: Contemporary Perspectives,* 232–42. Toronto: University of Toronto Press, 1994.
Griffith, James. *Adaptations as Imitations: Films from Novels.* Newark: University of Delaware Press, 1997.
Grossvogel, David I. 'Visconti and the Too, Too Solid Flesh.' *Diacritics* 1:2 (Winter 1971), 52–5.
Guarner, José Luis. *Roberto Rossellini.* New York: Praeger, 1970.
Günther, Joachim. '*Der Tod in Venedig.* Randbemerkungen zu Film und Buch.' *Neue Deutsche Hefte* 18:4 (Fall 1971), 89–99.
Gustafson, Richard F. *Leo Tolstoy, Resident and Stranger: A Study in Fiction and Theology.* Princeton, NJ: Princeton University Press, 1986.
Handke, Peter. *Die Angst des Tormanns beim Elfmeter.* Frankfurt am Main: Suhrkamp, 1970.
– *The Goalie's Anxiety at the Penalty Kick.* Trans. Michael Roloff. New York: Farrar, Straus and Giroux, 1972.
Hanne, Michael. 'Getting to Know the Neighbors: When Plot Meets Knot.' In *Narrative Chunnels,* special issue of *Canadian Review of Comparative Literature / Revue Canadienne de Littérature Comparée* 26:1 (March 1999), 35–50.
Hayward, Susan. *Cinema Studies.* London: Routledge, 2000.
Heine, Heinrich. *Werke und Briefe in zehn Bänden.* Ed. Hans Kaufmann. Vols. 1 and 2. Berlin and Weimar: Aufbau, 1980.

– *The Complete Poems*. Trans. Hal Draper. Boston: Suhrkamp–Insel, 1982.

Heller, Erich. *Thomas Mann: The Ironic German*. Cambridge: Cambridge University Press, 1981 [1958].

– *Thomas Mann: Der ironische Deutsche*. Frankfurt am Main: Suhrkamp, 1970.

Hersant, Yves, ed. *Italies: Anthologie des voyageurs français aux XVIIIe et XIXe siècles*. Paris: Laffont, 1988.

Hesse, Hermann. *Steppenwolf*. N.n. of trans. New York: Holt, Rinehart and Winston, 1963.

– *Der Steppenwolf*. In *Gesammelte Werke in zwölf Bänden*. Vol. 7. Frankfurt am Main: Suhrkamp, 1970.

Hesse, Hermann, and Thomas Mann. *Hermann Hesse–Thomas Mann: Briefwechsel*. Ed. Anni Carlsson and Volker Michels. Frankfurt am Main: Suhrkamp, 1975.

– *The Hesse / Mann Letters*. Trans. Ralph Manheim. New York: Harper and Row, 1975.

Hillmann, Roger. 'Deaths in Venice.' *Journal of European Studies* 22:4 (Dec. 1992), 291–311.

Hobsbawm, Eric J. *Primitive Rebels: Studies in Archaic Forms of Social Movement in the 19th and 20th Centuries*. Manchester: Manchester University Press, 1959.

– *Bandits*. London: Weidenfeld and Nicolson, 1969.

Hokanson, Katya. 'Literary Imperialism, *Narodnost'* and Pushkin's Invention of the Caucasus.' *Russian Review* 53:3 (July 1994), 336–52.

Hough, L.E. 'Disaffected from Utopia.' In Michael S. Cummings and Nicholas D. Smith, eds, *Utopian Studies III*, 118–27. Lanham, Md.: University Press of America, 1991.

Hutcheon, Linda. *Narcissistic Narrative: The Metafictional Paradox*. Waterloo, Ont.: Wilfrid Laurier University Press, 1980. (Library of *Canadian Review of Comparative Literature* 5).

Hutcheon, Linda, and Michael Hutcheon. *Opera: Desire, Disease, Death*. Lincoln: University of Nebraska Press, 1996.

Indiana, Gary. *Salò or The 120 Days of Sodom*. London: British Film Institute, 2000. (BFI Modern Classics).

Ionesco, Eugène. *Notes et contre-notes*. Paris: Gallimard, 1966. (Idées 107).

Ivanov, Viacheslav Vs. 'Fil'm v fil'me' ('The Film in the Film'). *Tekst v Tekste: Trudy po znakovym sistemam* 14 (1981), 19–32. (Uchĕnye zapiski tartuskogo gosudarstvennogo universiteta 567).

Jackson, Robert L. 'Father Sergius and the Paradox of the Fortunate Fall.' *Russian Literature* 40:4 (Nov. 1996), 463–80.

Jacobs, Jürgen, and Marcus Krause. *Der deutsche Bildungsroman: Gattungsgeschichte vom 18. bis zum 20. Jahrhundert*. Munich: C.H. Beck, 1989.

James, Henry. 'Gustave Flaubert.' In his *Notes on Novelists: With Some Other Notes*, 51–85. London: J.M. Dent, 1914.

Jameson, Fredric. *The Political Unconscious: Narrative as a Socially Symbolic Act.* Ithaca, NY: Cornell University Press, 1981.

Jenkins, Greg. *Stanley Kubrick and the Art of Adaptation: Three Novels, Three Films.* Jefferson, NC: McFarland, 1997.

Jonas, Ilsedore B. *Thomas Mann und Italien.* Heidelberg: Carl Winter, 1969.

– *Thomas Mann and Italy.* Trans. Betty Crouse. Tuscaloosa: University of Alabama Press, 1979.

Jones, Alexander, ed. *The Jerusalem Bible.* Garden City, NY: Doubleday, 1968.

Jung, Carl Gustav. *Gesammelte Werke.* (*Aion: Beiträge zur Symbolik des Selbst*, vol. 9/2, Olten and Freiburg i. B.: Walter-Verlag, 1966; *Mysterium Coniunctionis: Untersuchungen über die Trennung und Zusammensetzung der seelischen Gegensätze in der Alchemie*, vol. 14/1, Zürich and Stuttgart: Rascher Verlag, 1968).

– *The Collected Works.* Ed. Herbert Read et al. Trans. R.F.C. Hull. Princeton, NJ: Princeton University Press. (Bollingen Series XX). (*Aion: Researches into the Phenomenology of the Self*, vol. 9/2, 1968; *Mysterium Coniunctionis: An Inquiry into the Separation and Synthesis of Psychic Opposites in Alchemy*, vol. 14, 1977).

Kafka, Franz. *Amerika. Roman.* Ed., with afterword, Max Brod. Frankfurt am Main: S. Fischer, 1953 [1927].

– *Amerika.* Trans. Edwin Muir. Preface Klaus Mann, afterword Max Brod. New York: New Directions, 1946 [1940].

– *Hochzeitsvorbereitungen auf dem Lande und andere Prosa aus dem Nachlaß.* Ed. Max Brod. New York: Schocken Books, 1953.

– *Briefe an Felice.* Ed. Erich Heller and Jürgen Born. In *Gesammelte Werke.* Ed. Max Brod. Frankfurt am Main: Fischer, 1967.

– *America.* Trans. Alberto Spaini. In *Romanzi.* Ed. Ervino Pocar. Milano: Mondadori, 1969. (I Meridiani).

– *Letters to Felice.* Ed. Erich Heller and Jürgen Born. New York: Schocken Books, 1973.

– *Der Verschollene.* 2 vols. Ed. Jost Schillemeit. In *Schriften Tagebücher Briefe.* *Kritische Ausgabe.* Ed. Jürgen Born et al. Frankfurt am Main: S. Fischer, 1983.

– *America o Il disperso.* Ed. and trans. Umberto Gandini. Milan: Feltrinelli, 1996.

– *The Man Who Disappeared* (*Amerika*). Trans. Michael Hofmann. London: Penguin, 1996.

Kane, B.M. 'Thomas Mann and Visconti.' *Modern Languages* 53:1 (March 1972), 74–80.

Karlinsky, Simon. *The Sexual Labyrinth of Nikolai Gogol.* Cambridge, Mass.: Harvard University Press, 1976.

Kerényi, Karl. *Die Mysterien von Eleusis.* Zürich: Rhein Verlag, 1962.

Kezich, Tullio. *Fellini*. Milan: Rizzoli, 1988.

– *Fellini del giorno dopo: Con un alfabetiere felliniano*. Rimini: Guaraldi–Associazione Fellini, 1996.

Klein, Reimar, and Rossana Bonadei, eds. *Il testo autobiografico nel Novecento*. Milan: Guerini Studio, 1993.

Klossowski, Pierre. *Sade mon prochain* précédé de *Le philosophe scélérat*. Paris: Seuil, 1967.

– *Sade My Neighbor*. Trans. Alphonso Lingis. Evanston, Ill.: Northwestern University Press, 1991.

Köhn, Lothar. 'Entwicklungs- und Bildungsroman: Ein Forschungsbericht.' *Deutsche Vierteljahresschrift für Literaturwissenschaft und Geistesgeschichte* 42:3 (1968), 427–73.

– *Entwicklungs- und Bildungsroman*. Stuttgart: J.B. Metzler, 1969. (Expanded version of above item).

Kolb, David. *Hypertext, Argument, Philosophy: Socrates in the Labyrinth*. Cambridge, Mass.: Eastgate Systems, 1994.

Kontje, Todd. *Private Lives in the Public Sphere: The German* Bildungsroman *as Metafiction*. University Park: Pennsylvania State University Press, 1992.

– *The German* Bildungsroman: *History of a National Genre*. Columbia, SC: Camden House, 1993.

Krämer, Heinz Michael. *Eine Sprache des Leidens: Zur Lyrik von Paul Celan*. Munich: Kaiser and Mainz: Grünewald, 1979.

Laborde, A.M. *Sade romancier*. Neuchâtel: Éditions de la Baconnière, 1974.

Lacan, Jacques. 'Le stade du miroir comme formateur de la fonction du Je.' In his *Écrits I*, 89–97. Paris: Seuil, 1981 [1966].

– 'The Mirror Stage as Formative of the Function of the I.' In his *Ecrits*, 1–7. Trans. Alan Sheridan. New York: Norton, 1977.

Landow, George P. *Hypertext: The Convergences of Contemporary Critical Theory and Technology*. Baltimore, Md.: Johns Hopkins University Press, 1992.

Landow, George P., ed. *Hyper / Text / Theory*. Baltimore, Md.: Johns Hopkins University Press, 1994.

Landy, Marcia. *Film, Politics, and Gramsci*. Minneapolis: University of Minnesota Press, 1994.

– *Italian Film*. Cambridge: Cambridge University Press, 2000.

Lattuada, Alberto. *L'occhio di Dioniso: Racconti, ricordi, lettere d'amore*. Florence: La casa Usher, 1990.

– *Il cappotto: La storia, lo stile, il senso*. Ed. Lino Miccichè. Turin: Ass. Philip Morris Progetto Cinema – Museo Nazionale del Cinema – Lindau, [1995].

– *Il mio Set: Qualche sogno, qualche verità, una curiosità illimitata*. Ed. Vito Zagarrio. Ragusa: Libroitaliano, 1995.

Lawton, Ben. 'The Evolving Rejection of Homosexuality, the Sub-Proletariat, and the Third World in the Films of Pier Paolo Pasolini.' *Italian Quarterly* 82–3 (Fall 1980–Winter 1981), 167–73.

– 'Fellini and the Literary Tradition.' *Italian Journal* 4:3–4 (Sept. 1990), 32–40.

Lejeune, Philippe. *Le pacte autobiographique*. Paris: Seuil, 1975.

– *On Autobiography*. Ed. Paul John Eakin. Trans. Katherine Leary. Minneapolis: University of Minnesota Press, 1989.

Lely, Gilbert. *Vie du Marquis de Sade 1778–1814*. Vol. 2 of *Oeuvres complètes*.

Lessing, Gotthold Ephraim. *Laokoon, oder Über die Grenzen der Malerei und Poesie* (*Laokoon: or, On the Boundaries of Painting and Poetry*) (1766). Vol. 5/2 of *Werke und Briefe in zwölf Bänden*. Ed. Wilfried Barner. Frankfurt am Main: Deutscher Klassiker Verlag, 1990.

Levi, Carlo. *Cristo si è fermato a Eboli*. Rome: Einaudi, 1945.

Liandrat-Guigues, Suzanne. *Le couchant et l'aurore: Sur le cinéma de Luchino Visconti*. Paris: Klincksieck, 1999.

Liehm, Mira. *Passion and Defiance: Film in Italy from 1942 to the Present*. Berkeley: University of California Press, 1984.

Longo, Antonio, and Giommaria Monti. *Dizionario del '68: I luoghi, i fatti, i protagonisti, le parole e le idee*. Rome: Editori Riuniti, 1998.

Lotman, Iurii (Yuri) M. *Lektsii po struktural'noi poètike: Vvedenie, teoriia stikha*. Providence, RI: Brown University Press, 1968.

– 'Tekst v tekste' ('The Text in the Text'). *Tekst v tekste: Trudy po znakovym sistemam* 14 (1981), 3–18. (Uchënye zapiski tartuskogo gosudarstvennogo universiteta 567).

– 'K postroeniiu teorii vzaimodeistviia kul'tur (Semioticheskii aspekt)' ('Toward a Theory of Reciprocal Interaction between Cultures: Semiotic Aspect'). *Trudy po romano-germanskoi filologii* (1983), 92–113. (Uchënye zapiski tartuskogo gosudarstvennogo universiteta 646).

– 'O semiosfere' ('On the Semiosphere'). *Tekst v tekste : Trudy po znakovym sistemam* 17 (1984), 5–23. (Uchënye zapiski tartuskogo gosudarstvennogo universiteta 641).

– *La semiosfera: L'asimmetria e il dialogo nelle strutture pensanti*. Ed. Simonetta Salvestroni. Venice: Marsilio, 1992 [1985].

– *Universe of the Mind: A Semiotic Theory of Culture*. Trans. Ann Shukman. Intro. Umberto Eco. London and New York: I.B. Tauris, 1990.

– *Kul'tura i vzryv*. Moscow: Gnosis, 1992.

– *Vnutri mysliashchikh mirov: Chelovek – Tekst – Semiosfera – Istoriia*. Moscow: Yazyki russkoi kul'tury, 1996.

– *Il girotondo delle Muse: Saggi sulla semiotica delle arti e della rappresentazione*. Ed. Silvia Burini. Bergamo: Moretti e Vitali, 1998.

Lukács, Georg. *Thomas Mann*. Berlin: Aufbau, 1957. Repr. in his *Deutsche Litera-*

tur in zwei Jahrhunderten, vol. 7 of *Werke*. Neuwied and Berlin: Hermann Luchterhand, 1964. Further repr. in his *Faust und Faustus*, vol. 2 of *Ausgewählte Schriften*. Hamburg: Rowohlt, 1967.

– *Essays on Thomas Mann*. Trans. Stanley Mitchell. London: Merlin Press, 1964.

Mack Smith, Denis. *Modern Italy: A Political History*. New Haven, Conn.: Yale University Press, 1997 [1959].

– 'Regionalismo e patriottismo nel Risorgimento.' *Bollettino della Società di Studi Politici* 3 (July 1970), 9–32.

– *Storia d'Italia dal 1861 al 1997*. Bari and Rome: Laterza, 1997.

Maguire, Robert A., ed. and trans. *Gogol from the Twentieth Century: Eleven Essays*. Princeton, NJ: Princeton University Press, 1974.

– *Exploring Gogol*. Stanford, Calif.: Stanford University Press, 1994.

Maingueneau, Dominique. *Carmen: Les racines d'un mythe*. Paris: Éditions du Sorbier, 1984.

Mallac, Guy de. *Boris Pasternak: His Life and Art*. Norman: University of Oklahoma Press, 1981.

Mancino, Anton Giulio, and Sandro Zambetti. *Francesco Rosi*. Milan: Il Castoro, 1998 [1977]. (Il Castoro cinema 31–2).

Mann, Thomas. *Gesammelte Werke in dreizehn Bänden*. Frankfurt am Main: S. Fischer, 1974. (*Doktor Faustus. Das Leben des deutschen Tonsetzers Adrian Leverkühn erzählt von einem Freunde*, vol. 6; *Der Tod in Venedig* in *Erzählungen. Fiorenza. Dichtungen*, vol. 8).

– *Dichter über ihre Dichtungen*. Ed. Hans Wysling and Marianne Fischer. Vol. 1. Frankfurt am Main: Ernst Heimeran and S. Fischer, 1975. (Dichter über ihre Dichtungen 14).

– *Death in Venice*. Ed. and trans. Clayton Koelb. New York: Norton, 1994. (Norton Critical Edition).

Mann, Thomas, and Hermann Hesse. *See* Hesse.

Marchesini, Alberto. *Citazioni pittoriche nel cinema di Pasolini da* Accattone *al* Decameron. Florence: La nuova Italia, 1994.

Marcus, Judith. *Georg Lukács and Thomas Mann: A Study in the Sociology of Literature*. Amherst: University of Massachusetts Press, 1987. [*See also* Marcus-Tar, below.]

Marcus, Millicent. *Italian Film in the Light of Neorealism*. Princeton, NJ: Princeton University Press, 1986.

– *Filmmaking By the Book: Italian Cinema and Literary Adaptation*. Baltimore, Md.: Johns Hopkins University Press, 1993.

Marcus-Tar, Judith. *Thomas Mann und Georg Lukács: Beziehung, Einfluß und 'repräsentative Gegensätzlichkeit.'* Köln: Böhlau, 1982.

Marrone, Gaetana, ed. *New Landscapes in Contemporary Italian Cinema*. Thematic issue of *Annali d'Italianistica* 17 (1999).

Marson, E.L. *The Ascetic Artist: Prefigurations in Thomas Mann's* Der Tod in Venedig. Bern: Peter Lang, 1979. (Australian and New Zealand Studies in German
Language and Literature 9).

Martini, Fritz. 'Der Bildungsroman: Zur Geschichte des Wortes und der Theorie.' *Deutsche Vierteljahresschrift für Literaturwissenschaft und Geistesgeschichte* 35:1
(1961), 44–63.

Martini, Giulio, and Guglielmina Morelli, eds. *Patchwork Due: Geografia del nuovo
cinema italiano.* Milan: Il Castoro, 1997.

Masi, Stefano, and Enrico Lancia. *I film di Roberto Rossellini.* Rome: Gremese,
1987. (Effetto Cinema 15).

May, Georges. *L'autobiographie.* Paris: Presses Universitaires de France, 1984
[1979].

Mayer, Gerhart. *Der deutsche Bildungsroman: Von der Aufklärung bis zur Gegenwart.*
Stuttgart: J.B. Metzler, 1992.

Mayer, Hans. *Thomas Mann.* Frankfurt am Main: Suhrkamp, 1980.

McClary, Susan. *Feminine Endings: Music, Gender, and Sexuality.* Minneapolis:
University of Minnesota Press, 1991.

– *Georges Bizet:* Carmen. Cambridge: Cambridge University Press, 1992. (Cambridge Opera Handbooks).

McFarlane, Brian. *Novel to Film: An Introduction to the Theory of Adaptation.* Oxford:
Clarendon Press, 1996.

McKnight, Cliff, et al., eds. *Hypertext in Context.* New York: Cambridge University
Press, 1991.

Menzel, Horst. Carmen *von Georges Bizet.* Berlin, Lichterfelde: Lienau, 1972. (Die
Oper. Schriftenreihe über musikalische Bühnenwerke).

Mérimée, Prosper. *Carmen.* In *Romans et nouvelles.* Ed. Maurice Parturier. Vol. 2.
Paris: Garnier, 1967.

Merk, Augustinus, ed. *Novum testamentum.* Rome: Pontificium Institutum Biblicum, 1964.

Metz, Christian. *L'énonciation impersonnelle, ou le site du film.* Paris: Méridiens
Klincksieck, 1991.

Micciché, Lino. 'Cinema e letteratura.' In his *La ragione e lo sguardo: Saggi e note
sul cinema,* 147–77. Cosenza: Lerici, 1979.

– *Luchino Visconti: Un profilo critico.* Venice: Marsilio, 1996.

Micciché, Lino, ed. *Il neorealismo cinematografico italiano.* Venice: Marsilio, 1999
[1978, 1974].

– *Il cinema del riflusso: Film e cineasti italiani degli anni '70.* Venice: Marsilio, 1997.
(Nuovocinema Pesaro 50).

– *Schermi opachi: Il cinema italiano degli anni '80.* Venice: Marsilio, 1998. (Nuovocinema Pesaro 51).

Mileck, Joseph. 'A Comparative Study of *Die Betrogene* and *Der Tod in Venedig.*' *Modern Language Forum* 42 (1957), 124–9.

Minden, Michael. *The German* Bildungsroman: *Incest and Inheritance.* Cambridge: Cambridge University Press, 1997.

Mishima, Yukio. *Madame de Sade.* Trans. Donald Keene. New York: Grove Press, 1967.

Mitry, Jean. *Esthétique et psychologie du cinéma.* 2 vols. Paris: Éditions universitaires, 1963–5.

– *The Aesthetics and Psychology of the Cinema.* Trans. Christopher King. Bloomington: Indiana University Press, 1997.

Mochul'skii, Konstantin Vasil'evich. *Dukhovnyi put' Gogolia.* Paris: YMCA Press, 1976 [1934].

Molfese, Franco. *Storia del brigantaggio dopo l'Unità.* Milan: Feltrinelli, 1964.

Moretti, Franco. *The Way of the World: The* Bildungsroman *in European Culture.* London: Verso, 1987.

Moscariello, Angelo. *Cinema e/o letteratura.* Bologna: Pitagora editrice, 1981.

Murri, Serafino. *Pier Paolo Pasolini.* Milan: Il Castoro, 1994. (Il Castoro cinema 166).

– *Pier Paolo Pasolini:* Salò o le 120 giornate di Sodoma. Turin: Lindau, 2001. (Universale Film 22).

Musset, Alfred de. *Lettres de Dupuis et Cotonet* [1836–7]. In *Oeuvres complètes.* Ed. Philippe van Tieghem. Paris: Seuil Intégrale, 1963.

Nabokov, Vladimir. *Lectures on Russian Literature.* Ed. Fredson Bowers. New York: Harcourt Brace Jovanovich, 1981 [1944].

Naldini, Nico. *Pasolini, una vita.* Turin: Einaudi, 1989. (Gli struzzi 353).

Naremore, James. *Film Adaptation.* New Brunswick, NJ: Rutgers University Press, 2000.

Nicklas, Hans W. *Thomas Manns Novelle* Der Tod in Venedig: *Analyse des Motivzusammenhangs und der Erzählstruktur.* Marburg: N.G. Elwert, 1968. (Marburger Beiträge zur Germanistik 21).

Nicolai, Ralf R. *Kafkas Amerika-Roman* Der Verschollene: *Motive und Gestalten.* Würzburg: Königshausen und Neumann, 1981.

Nielsen, Jakob. *Hypertext and Hypermedia.* Boston: Academic Press, 1990.

Nietzsche, Friedrich. *Complete Works.* Ed. Oscar Levy. New York: Russell and Russell, 1964 [1909–11]. (*The Birth of Tragedy, or Hellenism and Pessimism,* trans. William A. Haussmann, vol. 1; *The Case of Wagner,* trans. Oscar Levy, vol. 8; *The Joyful Wisdom,* trans. Thomas Common, vol. 10; *Thus Spake Zarathustra,* trans. Thomas Common, vol. 11; *Beyond Good and Evil,* trans. Helen Zimmern, vol. 12).

– *Sämtliche Werke. Kritische Studienausgabe in fünfzehn Einzelbänden.* Ed. Giorgio Colli and Mazzino Montinari. Munich: dtv and Berlin: de Gruyter, 1988.

Niggl, Günter, ed. *Die Autobiographie: Zu Form und Geschichte einer literarischen Gattung*. Darmstadt: Wissenschaftliche Buchgesellschaft, 1989. (Wege der Forschung 565).

Novalis. *Schriften. Die Werke Friedrich von Hardenbergs*. Ed. Paul Kluckhohn and Richard Samuel. 4 vols. Stuttgart: Kohlhammer, 1960–75.

Nowell-Smith, Geoffrey. *Luchino Visconti*. New York: Viking Press, 1973 [1967].

Nuvoli, Giuliana, and Maurizio Regosa. *Storie ricreate: Dall'opera letteraria al film*. Turin: UTET, 1998.

Ôe, Kenzaburo. 'The Centre and the Periphery.' In Guy Amirthanayagam, ed., *Writers in East-West Encounter: New Cultural Bearings*, 46–50. London: Macmillan Press, 1982.

O'Healy, Áine. 'Are the Children Watching Us? The Roman Films of Francesca Archibugi.' In Gaetana Marrone, ed., *New Landscapes in Contemporary Italian Cinema*, thematic issue of *Annali d'Italianistica* 17 (1999), 121–36.

Olney, James, ed. *Autobiography: Essays Theoretical and Critical*. Princeton, NJ: Princeton University Press, 1980.

Orr, John, and Colin Nicholson, eds. *Cinema and Fiction: New Modes of Adapting, 1950–1990*. Edinburgh: Edinburgh University Press, 1992.

Ottaviano, Chiara, and Peppino Ortoleva, eds. *I giorni della storia d'Italia dal Risorgimento a oggi*. Novara: Istituto Geografico De Agostini, 1997 [1991].

Pabst, Walter. 'Satan und die alten Götter Venedigs: Entwicklung einer literar-historischen Variante.' *Euphorion* 49 (Fall 1955), 325–59.

Pahlen, Kurt, ed. *Georges Bizet. Carmen in der Originalsprache*. Munich: Goldmann-Schott, 1979.

Pascal, Roy. *Design and Truth in Autobiography*. Cambridge, Mass.: Harvard University Press, 1960.

Pasolini, Pier Paolo. *Trasumanar e organizzar*. Milano: Garzanti, 1976 [1971].

– *Empirismo eretico*. Intro. Guido Fink. Milan: Garzanti, 1991 [1972].

– *Heretical Empiricism*. Ed. Louise K. Barnett. Trans. Ben Lawton and L.K.B. Bloomington: Indiana University Press, 1988.

– *La divina mimesis*. Turin: Einaudi, 1975 [1973].

– 'Abiura dalla *Trilogia della vita*.' In *Lettere luterane*, 71–6. Turin: Einaudi, 1976.

– *San Paolo*. Turin: Einaudi, 1977.

– *Scritti corsari*. Milano: Garzanti, 1977. (Saggi). Repr. ibid., 1990. (Gli elefanti Saggi).

– *Descrizioni di descrizioni*. Turin: Einaudi, 1979. (Gli struzzi 194).

– '*Trilogy of Life* Rejected.' In *Lutheran Letters*, 49–52. Trans. Stuart Hood. Manchester: Carcanet and Dublin: Raven Arts Press, 1983.

– *Orgia*. In *Teatro*. Milan: Garzanti, 1988.

– *Petrolio*. Turin: Einaudi, 1992.

– *Petrolio.* Trans. Ann Goldstein. New York: Pantheon, 1997.

Pasternak, Boris Leonidovich. *Doktor Zhivago.* Ann Arbor: University of Michigan Press, 1959 [1958].

– *Doktor Zhivago. Roman.* Paris: Société d'Édition et d'Impression Mondiale, 1959.

– *Doctor Zhivago.* Trans. Max Hayward and Manya Harari. New York: Ballantine Books, 1981.

– *Doktor Zhivago. Roman.* Vol. 3 of *Sobranie sochinenii v piati tomakh.* Moscow: Khudozhestvennaia literatura, 1990.

Peytard, Jean. *Voix et traces narratives chez Stendhal: Analyse sémiotique de* Vanina Vanini. Paris: Éditeurs Français Réunis, 1980.

Pezzino, Paolo. 'Risorgimento e guerra civile: Alcune considerazioni preliminari.' In Gabriele Ranzato, ed., *Guerre fratricide: Le guerre civili in età contemporanea,* 56–85. Turin: Bollati Boringhieri, 1994. (Nuova Cultura 42).

Pike, Burton. 'Literary Translation: Looking Toward the Future.' In *Narrative Chunnels,* special issue of *Canadian Review of Comparative Literature / Revue Canadienne de Littérature Comparée* 26:1 (March 1999), 72–80.

Pintus, Pietro. *Storia e film: Trent' anni di cinema italiano (1945–1975).* Rome: Bulzoni, 1980.

Pravadelli, Veronica, ed. *Il cinema di Luchino Visconti.* Rome: Fondazione Scuola Nazionale di Cinema, 2000. (Biblioteca di Bianco & Nero: Quaderni 2).

Prédal, René. *Le cinéma français depuis 1945.* Paris: Nathan Université, 1991.

Proto, Carola, ed. *Francesca Archibugi.* Rome: Dino Audino Editore, [1995?].

Pushkin, Aleksandr Sergeevich. *Stikhotvoreniia* [Poetry] *1826–1836. Skazki.* Vol. 3/1 of *Polnoe sobranie sochinenii.* Moscow and Leningrad: Izdatel'stvo Akademii Nauk SSSR, 1948.

Pütz, Jürgen. *Kafkas* Verschollener – *ein Bildungsroman?* Frankfurt am Main: Peter Lang, 1983.

Quaglietti, Lorenzo. *Storia economico-politica del cinema italiano 1945–1980.* Rome: Editori Riuniti, 1980.

Radcliff-Umstead, Douglas. 'The Journey of Fatal Longing: Mann and Visconti.' *Annali d'Italianistica* 6 (1988), 199–219.

Rancour-Laferrière, Daniel. *Out From Under Gogol's Overcoat: A Psychoanalytic Study.* Ann Arbor, Mich.: Ardis, 1982.

– 'All the World's a *Vertep*: The Personification/Depersonification Complex in Gogol's *Sorochinskaia iarmarka.*' *Harvard Ukrainian Studies* 6:3 (Sept. 1982), 339–71.

Ranucci, Georgette, and Stefanella Ughi, eds. *Nanni Moretti.* Rome: Dino Audino Editore, [1995?].

Redfield, Marc. *Aesthetic Ideology and the* Bildungsroman. Ithaca, NY: Cornell University Press, 1996.

Reed, Terence James. *Thomas Mann.* Der Tod in Venedig: *Text, Materialien, Kommentar mit den bisher unveröffentlichten Arbeitsnotizen T. M.s.* Munich: Carl Hanser, 1983.

Renzi, Renzo. *Visconti segreto.* Bari: Laterza, 1994.

Restif de la Bretonne, Nicolas-Edmé. *Oeuvres érotiques.* Paris: Fayard, 1985.

Rimbaud, Arthur. *Oeuvres.* Ed. Suzanne Bernard and André Guyaux. Paris: Garnier, 1987.

'Rocky Relations' [with Gibraltar]. *The Economist,* 17 June 1995, 58.

Rohde, Erwin. *Psyche: Seelencult und Unsterblichkeitsglaube der Griechen.* Tübingen: Mohr, 1907 [1890–4].

Rohdie, Sam. *The Passion of Pier Paolo Pasolini.* Bloomington: Indiana University Press and London: British Film Institute, 1995.

Rondolino, Gianni. *Luchino Visconti.* Turin: UTET, 1981.

– *Roberto Rossellini.* Turin: UTET, 1989.

Rossellini, Roberto. *Un esprit libre ne doit rien apprendre en esclave.* Paris: Fayard, 1977.

– *Quasi un'autobiografia.* Ed. Stefano Roncoroni. Milan: Mondadori, 1987.

– *Il mio metodo.* Ed. Adriano Aprà. Venice: Marsilio, 1987.

– *My Method.* Trans. Annapaola Cancogni. New York: Marsilio, 1992.

Rossi, Monica. 'Apologia della differenza: Uno sguardo dall'esterno alla condizione degli immigrati africani in Italia in *Pummarò* di Michele Placido e *L'articolo due* di Maurizio Zaccaro.' In Antonio Vitti, ed., *Canadian/American Journal of Italian Studies* 54 (1997), 91–110.

Rumble, Patrick. *Allegories of Contamination: Pier Paolo Pasolini's* Trilogy of Life. Toronto: University of Toronto Press, 1996.

Sade, Donatien-Alphonse de. *Oeuvres complètes.* Ed. Gilbert Lely. Paris: Cercle du Livre Précieux, 1967. (*Idée sur les romans* in *Les crimes de l'amour. Nouvelles héroïques et tragiques,* vol. 10; *Les 120 journées de Sodome ou L'école du libertinage,* vol. 13).

– *Discours contre Dieu.* Ed. and intro. Gilbert Lely. Paris: Union Générale d'Éditions, 1980. (Collection *10/18* 1358).

Saïd, Edward. *Orientalism: Western Conceptions of the Orient.* Harmondsworth: Penguin, 1991 [1978].

Sanzio, Alain, and Paul-Louis Thirard. *Luchino Visconti cinéaste.* Paris: Persona, 1984.

Schlegel, Friedrich. *Philosophische Lehrjahre 1796–1806.* Vol. 18 of *Kritische Friedrich-Schlegel-Ausgabe.* Ed. Ernst Behler. Munich: Schöningh, 1963.

Sciascia, Leonardo. 'Dio dietro Sade.' In Gian Piero Brunetta, ed., *Spari nel buio,* 261–5.

Scirocco, Alfonso. *In difesa del Risorgimento.* Bologna: Il Mulino, 1998.

Selbmann, Rolf. *Der deutsche Bildungsroman*. Stuttgart: Metzler, 1984. (Sammlung Metzler M 214).

Selbmann, Rolf, ed. *Zur Geschichte des deutschen Bildungsromans*. Darmstadt: Wissenschaftliche Buchgesellschaft, 1988. (Wege der Forschung 640).

Serceau, Michel. *Roberto Rossellini*. Intro. Enrico Fulchignoni. Paris: Les Éditions du Cerf, 1986.

Sereni, Emilio. *Il capitalismo nelle campagne (1860–1900)*. Turin: Einaudi, 1968 [1947].

Sesti, Mario. *Nuovo cinema italiano*. Rome: Theoria, 1994. (Geografie 24).

– *La 'scuola' italiana. Storia, strutture e immaginario di un altro cinema (1988–1996)*. Venice: Marsilio, 1996. (Nuovocinema Pesaro 49).

Setschkareff, Vsevolod. *N. V. Gogol: Leben und Schaffen*. Berlin and Wiesbaden: Harrassowitz, 1953.

Shklovskii (Shklovsky), Viktor (Victor) Borisovich. *Literatura i kinematograf*. Berlin: Russkoe universal'noe izdatel'stvo, 1923. (Vseobshchaia biblioteka 51).

– *Lëv Tolstoi*. Moscow: Izdatel'stvo Molodaia Gvardiia, 1963.

– *Lëv Tolstoy*. Trans. Olga Shartse. Moscow: Progress Publishers, 1978.

– 'Letteratura e cinema.' In *I formalisti russi nel cinema*. Ed. and trans. Giorgio Kraiski. Milan: Garzanti, 1987 [1971].

Siciliano, Enzo. *Vita di Pasolini*. Florence: Giunti, 1995 [1978].

– *Pasolini: A Biography*. Trans. John Shepley. New York: Random House, 1982.

Silone, Ignazio. *L'avventura di un povero cristiano*. Milan: Mondadori, 1968.

Singer, Irving. '*Death in Venice*: Visconti and Mann.' *Modern Language Notes* 91:2 (1976), 1348–59.

Sinyard, Neil. *Filming Literature: The Art of Screen Adaptation*. London: Croom Helm, 1986.

Slonimskii, Aleksandr. *Tekhnika komicheskogo u Gogolia*. Petrograd: Academia, 1923. Anastatic repr.: Providence, RI: Brown University Press, 1963.

Sollers, Philippe. 'Sade dans le texte.' In his *L'écriture et l'expérience des limites*. Paris: Seuil, 1968.

– 'Sade dans le Temps.' In his *Sade contre l'Être suprême*, 1–54. Paris: Gallimard, 1996.

Sorlin, Pierre. *The Film in History: Restaging the Past*. Oxford: Basil Blackwell, 1980.

– *Italian National Cinema 1896–1996*. London and New York: Routledge, 1996.

Spence, G.W. *Tolstoy the Ascetic*. Edinburgh and London: Oliver and Boyd, 1967. (Biography and Criticism 8).

Spila, Piero. *Pier Paolo Pasolini*. Rome: Gremese, 1999.

Spilka, Mark. *Dickens and Kafka: A Mutual Interpretation*. Bloomington: Indiana University Press, 1963.

Stam, Robert. *Reflexivity in Film and Literature: From* Don Quixote *to Jean-Luc Godard.* Ann Arbor, Mich.: UMI Research Press, 1985. (Studies in Cinema 31).

– *Subversive Pleasures: Bakhtin, Cultural Criticism, and Film.* Baltimore, Md.: Johns Hopkins University Press, 1989.

– *Film Theory: An Introduction.* Oxford: Blackwell, 2000.

Starobinski, Jean. *L'oeil vivant.* Paris: Gallimard, 1970.

Stendhal [Henri Beyle]. *Oeuvres complètes.* Ed. Victor Del Litto. Geneva: Cercle du Bibliophile. (*Promenades dans Rome,* ed. Armand Caraccio, Victor Del Litto, and Ernest Abravanel, vol. 7 [6–8], 1969; *Vanina Vanini* in *Romans et nouvelles,* ed. Ernest Abravanel, vol. 38, 1970).

Stirling, Monica. *A Screen of Time: A Study of Luchino Visconti.* New York: Harcourt Brace Jovanovich, 1979.

Storia d'Italia. General editors Ruggiero Romano and Corrado Vivanti. Vols. 1, 3, 4/1. Turin: Einaudi, 1972–5.

Swales, Martin. *The German* Bildungsroman *from Wieland to Hesse.* Princeton, NJ: Princeton University Press, 1978.

Tambling, Jeremy. *Opera, Ideology and Film.* Manchester: Manchester University Press, 1987.

Tassone, Aldo. *Parla il cinema italiano.* 2 vols. Milan: Il Formichiere, 1980.

Terts, Abram [Andrei Siniavskii]. *V teni Gogolia.* London: Collins, Overseas Publications Interchange, 1975.

– *Dans l'ombre de Gogol.* Trans. Georges Nivat. Paris: Seuil, 1978.

Testa, Carlo. *Desire and the Devil: Demonic Contracts in French and European Literature.* New York: Peter Lang, 1991.

– 'Being Outside Time: Gogol, Brentano, and Literary Utopia.' *Germano-Slavica* 9:1–2 (1995–6), 103–24.

– 'Meridionalism: Northern European Conceptions of the South in Pushkin, Eichendorff, Mérimée.' *I Quaderni di Gaia* 8 (1997), 83–104.

– '*Doktor Zhivago*: Values versus Voodoo.' *Russian Review* 56:3 (July 1997), 383–401.

– 'Rossellini Reader of Stendhal: *Vanina Vanini.*' *Romance Languages Annual* 10 (1998), 380–6.

– 'Dalla letteratura al cinema: Adattamento o ri-creazione?' *Bianco & Nero* 62: 1–2 (April 2001), 37–51.

– *Italian Cinema and Modern European Literatures 1945–2000.* Westport, Ct.: Greenwood Praeger, 2002.

Testa, Carlo, ed. *Poet of Civic Courage: The Films of Francesco Rosi.* Trowbridge, Wiltsh.: Flicks Books, 1996.

Thompson, Howard. '*Hands Over the City*; *Salvatore Giuliano.*' *New York Times,* 28 Sept. 1964, 28. Repr. in *The NYT Film Reviews* (1959–68), 3490.

Tinazzi, Giorgio, ed. *Il cinema degli anni '50*. Venice: Marsilio, 1979. (Cinema Saggi 8).

Tolstoi (Tolstoy), Lëv (Leo) Nikolaevich. *Polnoe sobranie sochinenii*. Moscow and Leningrad: Khudozhestvennaia literatura. (*Chto takoe iskusstvo?*, vol. 30, 1951; *Otets Sergii*, in vol. 31, 1954; *Voskresenie*, vols. 32–3, 1933; 'Gogol',' in vol. 38, 1936).

– *The Works of Leo Tolstoy. Tolstoy Centenary Edition*. Trans. Aylmer Maude. London: Tolstoy Society and Oxford University Press, 1929. (*Father Sergius* in *The Devil and Cognate Tales*, vol. 16; *What Is Art?*, in vol. 18; *Resurrection*, vol. 19).

Torri, Bruno, ed. *Il cinema dei Taviani*. Roma: Ministero degli affari esteri, Direzione generale relazioni culturali, 1989.

Trahan, Elizabeth, ed. *Gogol's* Overcoat: *An Anthology of Critical Essays*. Ann Arbor, Mich.: Ardis, 1982.

Tynjanov (Tynianov), Jurij (Yuri). 'Dostoevskii i Gogol': K teorii parodii' (1921). In Iurii Striedter, ed., *Texte der russischen Formalisten*, 1:300–71. Munich: Wilhelm Fink Verlag, 1969.

– 'O literaturnoi èvoliutsii' (1927). In *Texte der russischen Formalisten*, 1:432–61.

– 'On Literary Evolution.' In Ladislav Matejka and Krystyna Pomorska, eds, *Readings in Russian Poetics: Formalist and Structuralist Views*, 66–78. Ann Arbor, Mich.: Michigan Slavic Publications, 1978.

Vaget, Hans Rudolf. 'Georg Lukács, Thomas Mann and the Modern Novel.' In Kenneth Hughes, ed., *Thomas Mann in Context: Papers of the Clark University Centennial Colloquium*, 38–65. Worcester, Mass.: Clark University Press, 1975.

– 'Film and Literature. The Case of *Death in Venice*: Luchino Visconti and Thomas Mann.' *German Quarterly* 54:2 (March 1980), 159–75.

– *Thomas-Mann-Kommentar zu sämtlichen Erzählungen*. München: Winkler, 1984.

Venturi, Franco. *Dall'andata nel popolo al terrorismo*. Vol. 3 of his *Il populismo russo*. Turin: Einaudi, 1972 [1952].

Venuti, Lawrence, ed. *Rethinking Translation: Discourse, Subjectivity, Ideology*. London: Routledge, 1992.

– *The Translator's Invisibility: A History of Translation*. London: Routledge, 1995.

Verdone, Mario. *Federico Fellini*. Florence: La nuova Italia, 1996. (Il Castoro cinema 165).

Verlaine, Paul. *Oeuvres poétiques complètes*. Ed. Y.-G. Le Dantec. Paris: Gallimard Pléiade, 1954.

– *Selected Verse*. Ed. and trans. Doris-Jeanne Gourévitch. Waltham, Mass.: Blaisdell, 1970.

Viano, Maurizio. *A Certain Realism: Making Use of Pasolini's Film Theory and Practice*. Berkeley: University of California Press, 1993.

Villari, Rosario, ed. *Il Sud nella storia d'Italia: Antologia della questione meridionale*. 2 vols. Bari: Laterza, 1974. (Universale Laterza 43–4).

Visconti, Luchino. *Senso*. Ed. G.B. Cavallaro. Bologna: Cappelli, 1955. (Dal soggetto al film 2). 2nd edition: ibid., 1997. (NUC Cinema 4).

– *Morte a Venezia*. Ed. Lino Micciché. Bologna: Cappelli, 1971. (Dal soggetto al film 42).

Vitti, Antonio, ed. *Italian Cinema*. Special anniversary issue, *Canadian/American Journal of Italian Studies* 54 (1997).

Vollmann, Benedikt. *Studien zum Priszillianismus: Die Forschung, die Quellen, der fünfzehnte Brief Papst Leos des Großen*. St Ottilien: Eos Verlag, 1965. (Kirchengeschichtliche Quellen und Studien 7).

Wagner, Geoffrey. *The Novel and the Cinema*. London: Tantivy Press and Fairleigh Dickinson University Press, 1975.

Wangermée, Robert. 'L'opéra sur la scène et à l'écran: À propos de *Carmen*.' In *Approches de l'opéra. Actes du colloque AISS (Royaumont, sept. 1984)*, 251–8. Ed. André Helbo. Paris: Didier Érudition, 1986.

Wasson, R. Gordon, et al. *The Road to Eleusis: Unveiling the Secret of the Mysteries*. New York: Harcourt Brace Jovanovich, 1978.

Waugh, Patricia. *Metafiction: The Theory and Practice of Self-Conscious Fiction*. London and New York: Methuen, 1984.

Weisbein, Nicolas. *L'évolution religieuse de Tolstoï*. Paris: Librairie des cinq continents, 1960.

Whittock, Trevor. *Metaphor and Film*. Cambridge: Cambridge University Press, 1990.

Wolfe, Peter. *Yukio Mishima*. New York: Frederick Ungar–Continuum, 1989.

Wolff, Rudolf, ed. *Thomas Mann. Erzählungen und Novellen*. Bonn: Bouvier, 1984. (Sammlung Profile 8).

Yourcenar, Marguerite. *Mishima ou la vision du vide*. Paris: Gallimard, 1980.

– *Mishima: A Vision of the Void*. Trans. Alberto Manguel and Marguerite Yourcenar. New York: Farrar, Straus and Giroux, 1986.

Zagarrio, Vito. 'Il tessuto del *Cappotto*. Idee sulla regia di Lattuada.' In his *Messi in scena: Analisi filmologiche di autori eccellenti*, 139–55. Ragusa: Libroitaliano, 1996. (Eppurecinema 2).

Zagarrio, Vito, ed. *Il cinema della transizione: Scenari italiani degli anni Novanta*. Venice: Marsilio, 2000. (Nuovocinema Pesaro 53).

Zavattini, Cesare. *Straparole* (1967). In *Opere. 1931–1986*. Ed. Silvana Cirillo. Intro. Luigi Malerba. Milan: Bompiani, 1991.

– *Sequences from a Cinematic Life*. Trans. William Weaver. Englewood Cliffs, NJ: Prentice-Hall, 1970.

Index

Abba, Giuseppe Cesare, 293n
Abruzzi, 87
Accialini, Fulvio, 258n
Acireale (prov. of Catania), 146
Aci Trezza (prov. of Catania), 120
Adriatic Sea, 127, 185
Afghanistan, 156
Africa, 129, 134, 141
Airaksinen, Timo, 268n
Albania, 141
Alighieri, Dante, 87, 105, 108, 109, 111, 184, 234n, 262–3n, 271n, 272n
Alps, 125, 195
Alter, Robert, 238n
Amelio, Gianni, 76, 141; *Stolen Children* (*Il ladro di bambini*, 1992), 76; *Lamerica* (1994), 141
America. *See* North America, United States of America
American Indians (First Nations), 50
Améry, Jean, 313n
Andalusia, 126, 282n
Andrew, Dudley, 6, 20, 222n
Angelucci, Gianfranco, 242n
Antonioni, Michelangelo, ix, 3, 219n, 226–7n

Apennines, 162
Apollo, 186, 188
Aprà, Adriano, 294n, 296n
Apulia, 134
Arbasino, Alberto, 287n, 291n
Archibugi, Francesca, 17, **27–32**, 207, 230n, 231n, 267n; *Mignon Has Left* (*Mignon è partita*, 1988), 17, **27–32**, 207, **230–1n**, 279n
Arens, Hans, 258n
Argentieri, Mino, 248n, 249n, 254n
Argento, Dario, 15
Aristarco, Guido, 258n, 312n, 315n, 318n
Asia Minor, 126
Attolini, Vito, 220n, 254n, 297n, 313n
Austria, Austro-Hungarian Empire, 164, 166, 195
autobiography, 43, 46, 52, 147, 236–7n, 287n

Bahr, Ehrhard, 303n
Bakhtin, Mikhail Mikhailovich, 6, 7, 8, 30, 42, 221n, 223n, 229n, 230n, 235–6n, 238n, 250n, 251n, 279n
Baldelli, Pio, 179, 294n, 300–2n, 315n

Balestrini, Nanni, 316n
Balkans, the, 141
Balzac, Honoré de, 128; *La Comédie humaine*, 135
Banti, Alberto M., 292n, 293n
Bardot, Brigitte, 150
Barnes, Christopher, 255n
Barrett, Edward, 296n
Barthes, Roland, 101, 267–9n, 271n
Bartolini, Luigi, 225n
Basento River, 86, 93
Basilicata (or Lucania), 82, 83, 134
Battiato, Franco, 286n
Bazin, André, 6, 222n
Beaujour, Michel, 236n
Beaumarchais, Pierre-Augustin Caron de, 174, 298n
Beauvoir, Simone de, 271n
Beethoven, Ludwig van, 193, 306n, 310n
Bellocchio, Marco, 227n
Bencivenni, Alessandro, 315n
Berg, Alban, 280n
Bergman, Ingrid, 167, 168
Berlinguer, Enrico, 156, 290n
Berlin Wall, 156
Bernardi, Sandro, 221n, 223n, 286n
Bernardini, Aldo, 267n
Bersani, Leo, 242n, 273n
Bertelli, Sergio, 260n, 314n
Bertellini, Giorgio, 313n
Bertolucci, Bernardo, 226n, 289n
Bertozzi, Marco, 237n
Bertrand, Denis, 281n
Bezzel, Chris, 234n
Bhabha, Homi K., 293n
Bible, 205, 257n. *See also* Gospel
Bildungsroman, 27, 29, 36, 37, 40, 41, 43, 52, 59, 229n, 232n, 233n
Binder, Hartmut, 234n

Bizet, Georges, 16, 19, **125–42**, 211, 212, **278–84n**; *Carmen* (1875), 16, 17, 19, 33, **125–42**, 211, 212, **278–84n**
Blanchot, Maurice, 271n
Bleiler, Ellen H., 280n
Bocca, Giorgio, 282n, 293n
Boccaccio, Giovanni, 103, 104, 105, 111, 118, 269n, 307n
Bollati, Giulio, 229n
Bolter, J. David, 297n
Bolzoni, Francesco, 139, 282n, 284n
Bonadei, Rossana, 236n
Bonaparte, Louis (Napoleon III), 127
Bonaparte, Napoleon, 102, 103, 162, 175, 176
Bondanella, Peter, 44, 220n, 222n, 237n, 238n, 255n, 258n, 275n, 301n
Boniface VIII, pope, 87
Bordwell, David, 15, 223n, 226n, 281–2n
Borges, Jorge Luis, 43, 236n, 238n
Bori, Pier Cesare, 256n
Bragaglia, Cristina, 3, 220n
Brahe, Tycho, 6
Brentano, Clemens, 243n
Bresson, Robert: *L'argent*, 4
brigands, brigandism, 90, 91, 165, 166, 263n, 264n, 293n
Britons, 187
Brod, Max, 42, 233n, 235n
Bruford, W.H., 229n, 315n
Brunetta, Gian Piero, 220n, 267n, 271n
Brunette, Peter, 294n, 298n, 299n, 301n
Bruni, David, 222n, 313n
Bruno, Edoardo, 244n, 296n
Buache, Freddy, 281n
Bulgakov, Mikhail Afanas'evich, 252n
Burke, Frank, 237n

Burrus, Virginia, 244n
Byron, George Gordon Lord, 118, 126, 279n

Caetani, 161
Cafagna, Luciano, 292n, 293n
California, 141
Calvino, Italo, 117, 118
Camerini, Claudio, 245n
Camerini, Mario, 227n; *The Italian Brigands* (*I briganti italiani*, 1961), 166, 263n
Campbell, Joseph, 310n
Canada, 78
canon (artistic), canonic status, canonization, 183, 184, 191, 193, 200, 309–10n
Cappabianca, Alessandro, 313n
carbonari, 162, 166, 169, 171, 172, 174, 177
Caribbean, the, 4
Carlo di Borbone, king of Naples, 82, 83, 84, 85
Carmona (Spain), 132, 134, 281n
Cartmell, Deborah, 222n
Casetti, Francesco, 223n
Castellani, Renato: *The Brigand* (*Il brigante*, 1961), 263n
Castel Sant'Angelo (Rome), 162
Castronovo, Valerio, 293n
Catholic church, Catholicism, 103, 114, 173, 178, 179, 180, 213
Caucasus, 125
Caughie, John, 226n
Celan, Paul, 109, 110, 270n
Celestino V, pope, 87
Cereda, Giuseppe, 267n
Cesena (prov. of Forlì), 162, 163, 172, 173
Chadwick, Henry, 244n

Charenton, 103
Chile, 4
Chizhevsky, Dmitry, 250n
Christ, Christianity, 34, 58, 61, 67, 70, 78, 82, 86, 87, 89, 92, 95, 102, 105, 107, 114–16, 118, 144, 145, 177, 210, 251n, 262–3n, 282n
Christian, R.F., 256n
Christian Democrats (*Democrazia Cristiana*, DC), 147
Ciment, Michel, 237n, 281n
Cinecittà (Rome), 33, 34, 38, 42, 44, 45, 47, 49, 50, 52, 53
Cipriani, Ivano, 267n
Città Castellana, 163, 178
Citti, Sergio, 273n
Clark, Martin, 292n
Clément, Catherine, 278n
Cogman, P.W.M., 279n
cold war, 74, 75, 163, 249n, 254n, 315n
Collodi, Carlo, 243n, 264n
Coluccelli, Lucia, 258n
Comencini, Luigi, 226n
Comenius, Jan Amos, 167, 296n
commedia all'italiana, 15, 59, 75
Communes, Italian, 164
Communism (in general), 113, 114, 118, 155
Communists, Italian (in particular *Partito Comunista Italiano*, PCI), 120, 143–58, 179, 180
Como, 185
Concordat, 103
Conger, Syndy M., 238n
Copernicus, 6
Cortellazzo, Sara, 220n
Costa, Antonio, 255n
Cosulich, Callisto, 249n, 254n
Craco (prov. of Matera), 134

Culler, Jonathan, 230n
Currie, Mark, 238n

Dadaism, 109
Dällenbach, Lucien, 238n
Dalle Vacche, Angela, 294n
D'Amico de Carvalho, Caterina, 313n
Dante. *See* Alighieri, Dante
D'Azeglio, 164, 292n
De Benedictis, Maurizio, 271n
De Bernardi, Alberto, 316n
De Bernardinis, Flavio, 285n
De Giusti, Luciano, 275n, 315n
Degli-Esposti, Cristina, 237n
Delany, Paul, 297n
De Laurentiis, Dino, 242n
Del Carria, Renzo, 263n
De Marchis Rossellini, Marcella, 297–
    8n, 301n
De Matteo, Giovanni, 263n
De Negri, Giuliani G., 260n, 267n
De Santi, Pier Marco, 258n
De Seta, Vittorio, 120, 278n; *Bandits
    in Orgosolo* (*Banditi a Orgosolo*,
    1961), 263n
De Sica, Vittorio, 68, 76, 225n; *Bicycle
    Thieves* (*Ladri di biciclette*, 1948), 68,
    76, 225n, 251–2n; *Miracle in Milan*
    (*Miracolo a Milano*, 1951), 254n
desire, 214
devil, demonism, demonic literature
    or art, 57, 58, 61, 62, 65–71, 90, 184,
    185, 189–94, 197, 209, 214, 244n,
    248–53n, 264n, 265n, 303n, 304n
Dickens, Charles, 42
didactic, educational, pedagogical
    role of art, 167, 168, 180, 181, 189,
    213, 214, 295n
Dieterle, Bernard, 302n
Di Giammatteo, Fernaldo, 220n, 301n

Dionysus, Dionysian art, 188, 194
Doerne, Martin, 256n
Dolcino, fra (Brother), 118
Doré, Gustave, 281n, 283n
Dostoevskii (Dostoevsky), Fëdor (Fyo-
    dor) Mikhailovich, 22, 33, 35, 143,
    146, 205, 215, 274n, 287n, 311n;
    White Nights (*Belye nochi*, 1848), 33;
    Notes from Underground (*Zapiski iz
    podpol'ia*, 1864), 146, 205, 206,
    285n, 311n
Driessen, F.C., 243n
Duce, the. *See* Mussolini, Benito
Dukhobors (Dukhobortsy), 78
dystopia, 101, 267n; in Pasolini, 107–
    21; in Sade, 101–13, 115

Eco, Umberto, 15, 221n, 226n
economic miracle (*miracolo econom-
    ico*), 75, 119, 163
Edwards, Gwynne, 281n
Egan, Susanna, 236n
Egypt, 141
Eichenbaum, Boris, 243n
Èizenshtein (Eisenstein, Eizenstejn),
    Sergei M., ix, 4, **8–12**, 18, 22, 132,
    216, 219n, 221–5n, 228n, 247–8n,
    281n
– Films: *Battleship Potëmkin* (*Bronenos-
    ets Potëmkin*, 1925), 11, 225n, 281n
– Texts: 'Literature and Cinema'
    (1928), **9–11**; 'Torito' (ca. 1933–4),
    11–12, 18, **216**, 319n; 'Diderot
    Wrote about Cinema' (ca. 1943?,
    posth.), **8–9**; *Selected Works* (*Izbran-
    nye proizvedeniia*), 12
Ekberg, Anita, 50, 51, 241n
Elbaz, Robert, 236n
Eldorado, 141
Eleusinian mysteries, 215, 310n, 318n

Emrich, Wilhelm, 234n
Ergas, Moris, 179, 298n
Erlich, Victor, 243n
EUR (Rome), 63
Europe, 4, 35, 127, 129, 135, 141, 190;
  Eastern Europe, 141; Western
  Europe, 147

Faldini, Franca, and Goffredo Fofi,
  219n, 237n, 245–7n, 255n, 259n,
  260n, 262n, 265n, 267n, 273n, 275n,
  277n, 285n, 287n, 294n, 295n, 297n,
  301n, 309n, 314n
Fascism (Italian regime, 1922–45),
  35, 59, 63, 112, 163, 164, 165, 211,
  318n
'fascism' (totalitarian social system),
  117, 318n
Fassbinder, Rainer Werner: Effi Briest,
  4
Fava, Claudio Giorgio, 237n
Favre, Pierre, 268n
Fellini, Federico, 3, 18, 20, **33–53**, 75,
  76, 148, 207, 208, **231–3n, 236–42n**,
  267n, 287n; The Road (La strada,
  1954), 75, 76, 255n; The Nights of
  Cabiria (Le notti di Cabiria, 1957),
  76; La dolce vita (1960), 20, 50, 75,
  238n, 287n; 8½ (1963), 287n; Juliet
  of the Spirits (Giulietta degli spiriti,
  1965), 34; Satyricon (1969), 33; **Inter-
  vista** (1987), 18, 20, 21, **33–53**, 208,
  236–42n
Felstiner, John, 270n
Feltrinelli bookstores, 4
Fénelon, François de Salignac de la
  Mothe: Télémaque, 36
Ferrero, Adelio, 271n
Ferrucci, Riccardo, 259n, 262n
Fertonani, Roberto, 304n

Fieschi, Jean-André, 179, 300n
film history and film theory, 8, 223n
'first' (Italian) Republic, 76, 164, 165,
  166
First World War, 151, 152, 191
Flaubert, Gustave, ix, 14, 31, 36, 41,
  128, 137, 148, 219n, 225n, 279n,
  287n; Sentimental Education (L'Édu-
  cation sentimentale, 1869), 14, 36, 41,
  225–6n, 230n, 232n, 233n; The
  Temptation of Saint Antony (La Ten-
  tation de Saint Antoine, 1849–74),
  145, 148, 286n; Voyage en Égypte
  (posth.), 283n, 284n; Les lettres
  d'Égypte (posth.), 284n; Flaubert in
  Egypt, 283n
Fleming, Victor: Gone with the Wind, 4
Fletcher, Angus, 310n
Flores, Marcello, 316n
Fofi, Goffredo, 313n. See also Faldini,
  Franca
Folkenflik, Robert, 236n
Fontane, Theodor, 42
Forgacs, David, 296n
Formalists. See Russian Formalists
Fourier, Charles, 101
France, the French, 126–8, 161, 165,
  187
French literature and culture, 13, 17.
  See also names of individual authors
Futurism, 109, 221n

Gagliano, 134
Galilei, Galileo, 6, 207, 317n
Gallagher, Tag, 301n
García Márquez, Gabriel, 33
Garibaldi, Giuseppe, 164–6, 293n,
  294n
Gaudreault, André, 221n
Genette, Gérard, 228n

Gerhard, Melitta, 229n
Germany, Germans, 110, 165, 166,
    183, 185, 188–91, 195, 199, 207;
    German literature and culture,
    13, 17, 191, 195–7. *See also* names of
    individual authors
Germi, Pietro: *The Brigand of Tacca del
    Lupo* (*Il brigante di Tacca del Lupo*,
    1957), 263n
Gesù, Sebastiano, 284n
Giacci, Vittorio, 284n
Gibraltar, 134, 282n
Gieri, Manuela, 220n, 237n, 255n,
    285n
Gili, Jean A., 260n, 282n, 284n
Gippius, Vasilii Vasil'evich, 243n
Glassco, David, 312n, 313n
Glenn, Jerry, 270n
Gnosticism, 58
Godard, Jean-Luc: *Le mépris*, 4
Goethe, Johann Wolfgang von, 16,
    17, **27–32**, 34, 36, 109, 110, 112, 118,
    126, 207, 216, 279n, 309–10n, 317n,
    319n; *Wilhelm Meister's Apprentice-
    ship* (*Wilhelm Meisters Lehrjahre*,
    1795–6), 16, 17, **27**, **28**, **32**, 36, 126,
    207, **228–31n**; *Faust I* (1808), 110,
    112, 253n, 272n, 288n; *Faust II*
    (1832), 258n, 270n
Gogol' (Gogol), Nikolai Vasil'evich
    (Vasilevich), 16, 18, 21, 22, **57–76**,
    116, 208, 209, 215, 234n, 235n, **243–
    54n**, 274n; *The Tale of How Ivan
    Ivanovich Quarreled ...* (*Povest' o tom,
    kak possorilsia ...*, in *Mirgorod*, 1835),
    252n; *The Overcoat* (*Shinel'*, 1842),
    16, 17, 18, 21, **57–76**, 208, **243–54n**;
    Dead Souls (*Mërtvye dushi*, 1842), 57,
    58, 116, 234n
Golgotha, 67

Goncourt, Edmond and Jules de, 128
'Good-bye My Beauty' ('Bella ciao')
    (folk song), 30
Gospel, Gospel of Matthew, 78, 79,
    81, 151, 255–7n. *See also* Bible
Gould Boyum, Joy, 312n
Gramsci, Antonio, 7, 8, 164, 166,
    222n, 259n, 292n
Greece, 126, 186, 197, 215
Greene, Naomi, 272n, 275n
Griffith, James, 222n
Grossvogel, David I., 313n
Guarner, José Luis, 294n, 301n
Guatemala, 4
Günther, Joachim, 309n, 312n
Gustafson, Richard F., 256n

Halle, Morris, 243n
Handke, Peter, 157, 158, 290n, 291n
Hanne, Michael, 242n
Hayward, Susan, 226n
Heine, Heinrich, 126, 195, 197, 200,
    311–12n, 316n
Heller, Erich, 303n
Hersant, Yves, 279n
Hesse, Hermann, 307–8n, 309–10n,
    310n, 317n
Hillmann, Roger, 313n
Himalaya, 168
history, 94–96
Hobsbawm, Eric J., 263n
Hoffmann, E.T.A., 243n
Hofmannsthal, Hugo von, 157
Hokanson, Katya, 283n
Hollywood, 140, 180
homophobia, 200
homosexuality, representation of,
    196, 272–3n, 312n
Hough, L.E., 267n
Hugo, Victor, 127

Hungary, 146, 153
Hutcheon, Linda, 238n, 278n
hypertext, 296–7n

Iliad, The, 316n
India, 180, 296n
Indiana, Gary, 270n, 272n, 275n
Ionesco, Eugène, 57, 144, 233n, 243n
Iron Curtain, 146
Italophobia, 184, 186, 188, 191, 197
Italy, Italians, 3, 14, 16, 20, 27, 28, 30,
   32, 45, 49, 58, 60, 63, 64, 66, 70, 74–
   6, 82, 88, 90, 118–20, 126, 127, 141,
   142, 147, 156, 161–6, 171, 173, 176,
   179, 183–91, 195–200, 213, 214. See
   also Mediterranean, Meridional-
   ism, South Italian literature and
   culture, 13
Italian Renaissance, 161, 164, 213
'Italietta,' 117
Ivanov, Viacheslav Vs., 288n

Jackson, Robert L., 256n, 257n, 265n
Jacobins, 171
Jacobs, Jürgen, 229n
James, Henry, 14, 225–6n
Jameson, Fredric, 74, 254n
Japan, the Japanese, 4, 13, 45
Jenkins, Greg, 222n
Jews, Judaism, 107, 110
John Paul II, pope, 114
Jonas, Ilsedore B., 302n
Jung, Carl Gustav, 105, 241n, 269n

Kafka, Franz, 16, 17, 18, 22, **33–53**,
   207, 208, **231–6n, 239–42n**; Amerika
   (Amerika. Roman, 1912–13) (pre-
   critical edition), 16, 17, 35, 36, 43,
   47, 233–4n; **The Man Who Disappeared** (Der Verschollene, 1912–13)

(critical edition), 16, 17, 18, **33–42**,
   43, **45–50**, 207, **231–6n**, 315n; Amer-
   ica (Italian, pre-critical), 43, 47,
   240n, 241n; America o Il disperso
   (Italian, critical), 240n; The Trial
   (Der Prozeß, 1914), 36, 235n; The
   Metamorphosis (Die Verwandlung,
   1915), 35, 232n; The Castle (Das
   Schloss, 1922), 36, 235n; Preparations
   for a Marriage in the Countryside
   (Hochzeitsvorbereitungen auf dem
   Lande, posth.) 53, 242n
Kane, B.M., 313n
Kant, Immanuel, 242n
Karlinsky, Simon, 243n
Kerényi, Karl, 310n
Kezich, Tullio, 237n, 242n
Klein, Reimar, 236n
Kleist, Heinrich von, 243n
Klossowski, Pierre, 101, 267n, 268n,
   271n
Köhn, Lothar, 229n
Kolb, David, 297n
Kontje, Todd, 229n
Korea, 74
Krämer, Heinz Michael, 270n
Krause, Marcus, 229n
Kubrick, Stanley: Eyes Wide Shut, 4
Kuchuk Hanem, 137, 141

Laborde, A.M., 268n
Lacan, Jacques, 236n
Lamartine, Alphonse de, 118
Lancia, Enrico, 294n, 301n
Landow, George P., 297n
Landy, Marcia, 220n, 222n, 223n,
   259n, 292n
La Porta, Filippo, 220n
Lattuada, Alberto, 15, 18, 21, **57–76**,
   208, **244–55n**; The Overcoat (Il cap-

potto, 1952), 15, 18, 21, 22, **57–76**, 208, **244–55n**; *The Storm* (*La tempesta*, 1958), 15, 245n; *Heart of a Dog* (*Cuore di cane*, 1976), 15, 245n; *Giacomo the Idealist* (*Giacomo l'idealista*, 1943), *The Arrow in the Flesh* (*La freccia nel fianco*, 1945), *The Bandit* (*Il bandito*, 1946), *Giovanni Episcopo's Crime* (*Il delitto di Giovanni Episcopo*, 1947), *Merciless* (*Senza pietà*, 1948), *The Mill on the River Po* (*Il mulino del Po*, 1949), *Variety Lights* (*Luci del varietà*, with Fellini, 1950), *Anna* (1951), *The She-Wolf* (*La lupa*, 1952), *Italian Men Turn Their Heads* (*Gli italiani si voltano*) in *Love in the City* (*L'amore in città*, 1953), *The Beach* (*La spiaggia*, 1954), *Elementary School* (*Scuola elementare*, 1955), *Gwendalin* (*Guendalina*, 1957), *Sweet Delusions* (*I dolci inganni*, 1960), *Letters by a Novice* (*Lettere di una novizia*, 1960), *The Mishap* (*L'imprevisto*, 1961), *Mafioso* (1962), *The Steppe* (*La steppa*, 1962), *The Mandrake* (*La mandragola*, 1965), *Matchless* (1967), *Don Juan in Sicily* (*Don Giovanni in Sicilia*, 1967), *Fräulein Doktor* (1969), *The Girlfriend* (*L'amica*, 1969), *Come Have Coffee ... with Us* (*Venga a prendere il caffè ... da noi*, 1970), *White, Red and ...* (*Bianco, rosso e ...*, 1972), *It Was I Who Did It* (*Sono stato io*, 1973), *I'll Act as Her Father* (*Le farò da padre*, 1974), *Oh Serafina!* (1976), *As You Are* (*Così come sei*, 1978), *Cicada* (*La cicala*, 1980) – all 245n

Lawton, Ben, 237n, 273n

Lean, David: *Doctor Zhivago* (1965), 16, 19, **147–58**, 212, **288–91n**

lectio difficilior, 217

Lejeune, Philippe, 237n

Lely, Gilbert, 268n, 272n

Lenin [Ul'ianov, Vladimir Il'ich], 78, 155

Leone, Sergio, 15

Lessing, Gotthold Ephraim, 212, 300n, 318n

Levi, Carlo, 259n, 282n

Liandrat-Guigues, Suzanne, 313n

Libya, 64

Lido (Venice), 183, 184, 197, 201

Liehm, Mira, 220n

Linnaeus, 104

Longo, Antonio, 316n

Loren, Sophia, 15

Lotman, Iurii (Jurij, Yuri) Mikhailovich, 6, 9, 206, 221n, 223n, 248n, 300n, 316–17n

Loyola, Ignacio de, 101

Lucania. *See* Basilicata

Lukács, Georg, 199, 315n

Machiavelli, Niccolò, 113

Mack Smith, Denis, 292n, 293n

Maguire, Robert A., 243n, 248n, 250n

Mahler, Gustav, 191, 195, 196

Maiella, Mt., 87

Maingueneau, Dominique, 281n, 282n

Malerba, Luigi, 61, 248n

Mallac, Guy de, 255n

Mancino, Anton Giulio, 282n

Manicheism, 58

Mann, Thomas, 16, 17, 19, 21, 33, 118, **183–201**, 209, 214, **302–16n**; *The Buddenbrooks* (*Buddenbrooks*, 1901), 199; *Death in Venice* (*Der Tod in Venedig*, 1912), 16, 17, 19, 21, 33, **183–201**, 214, 215, **302–16n**, 318n;

Observations by an Unpolitical Man
(*Betrachtungen eines Unpolitischen,*
1918), 199, 314n; *Mario and the
Magician* (*Mario und der Zauberer,*
1930), 189, 307n; *Doctor Faustus*
(*Doktor Faustus,* 1947), 19, 188, 189,
190, 192, 193, 305–6n; *The Deluded
One* (*Die Betrogene,* 1953), 312n
Maradona, Diego, 131
Marchesi, Marcello, 35, 231n
Marchesini, Alberto, 276n
Marcus, Millicent, 6, 7, 220n, 222n,
223n, 244n, 260n, 262n, 292n
Marcus/Marcus-Tar, Judith, 315n
Marrone, Gaetana, 230n
Marsala (prov. of Trapani), 165
Marson, E.L., 307n
Martini, Fritz, 229n
Martini, Giulio, 286n
Martone, Mario, 226n
Marxists, 180, 199
Masaniello (Aniello, Tommaso), 131
Masi, Stefano, 294n, 301n
'masterliness' of filmmakers, 14, 15
Mastroianni, Marcello, 15, 51, 238n,
287n
Matejka, Ladislav, 226n
Matera, 86, 93
Mattei, Enrico, 134
Maupassant, Guy de, 128
May, Georges, 237n
Mayer, Gerhart, 229n
Mayer, Hans, 303n, 313n
McClary, Susan, 278n
McFarlane, Brian, 222n, 228n
McKnight, Cliff, 297n
Mediterranean Sea or area, 17, 127,
129, 130, 134, 135, 137, 139, 194,
212, 278n. *See also* Italy, Meridional-
ism, South

Menduni, Enrico, 267n
Menzel, Horst, 280n
Meridionalism, 120, 125–42, 183, 185,
209, 212, 229n, 278n. *See also* Italy,
Mediterranean, South
Mérimée, Prosper: *Carmen* (1845), 16,
17, 19, 33, **125–42**, 212, **278–81n**
metafiction (self-reflexive textuality),
238n
metaphor, metaphorical expression,
236n, 241–2n, 286n, 287n
Metz, Christian, 237n, 288n
Mexico, 11
Mezzogiorno. See the South, of Italy
Micciché, Lino, 198, 237n, 244n,
246n, 251–2n, 259n, 267n, 271n,
284n, 286n, 313n
Mikhalkov, Nikita: *Oblomov* (1979),
Ochi chërnye (1987), 4
Milan (Milano), 35, 72
Mileck, Joseph, 312n
Milo, Sandra, 170, 179, 301n
Minden, Michael, 229n
miracolo economico. See economic mira-
cle
Mishima, Yukio, 113, 273–5n
Mitry, Jean, 207, 221n, 317n
Mochul'skii, Konstantin Vasil'evich,
244n
Möbius strip, 52, 241n
Molfese, Franco, 263n
Monicelli, Mario, 278n, 300n
Montelepre (prov. of Palermo), 134
Monteverde (Roma), 144, 146, 147,
157, 158
Monti, Giommaria, 316n
Morelli, Guglielmina, 286n
Moretti, Franco, 229n
Moretti, Nanni, 18, 77, **143–58**, 212,
255n, **285–91n**; *The Defeat* (*La scon-*

fitta, 1973), 145, 287n; *Ecce Bombo* (1978), 143, 288n; *Sweet Dreams* (*Sogni d'oro*, 1981), 143; *Bianca* (1984), 143, 146, 287n; **Palombella rossa** (a.k.a. *Red Lob*) (1989), 19, 20, 77, **143–58**, 212, **285–91n**; *The Thing* (*La Cosa*, 1990), 290n; *Dear Diary* (*Caro diario*, 1993), 285n; *The Son's Room* (*La stanza del figlio*, 2001), 291n

Moroni, Primo, 316n

Moscariello, Angelo, 220n

Moscow, 151, 153, 154

Munich, 17, 183–6, 191, 194

Murnau, Friedrich Wilhelm: *Faust*, 4

Murri, Serafino, 275n

music, 188, 190–2, 194, 215, 305–6n, 308n, 309n, 311n

Musset, Alfred de, 141, 284n

Mussolini, Benito, 164, 307n

Nabokov, Vladimir, 254n

Nagy, Imre, 146

Naldini, Nico, 272n, 275n

Naples (Napoli), 82, 91, 165, 278n, 282n, 305n

Napoleon. *See* Bonaparte, Napoleon

Naremore, James, 222n, 228n

narodniki, 152

NATO, 164

Nazism, 189, 197

neorealism, 7, 15, 57–60, 67, 71, 72, 119, 168, 208, 248n, 255n

New York City, 34, 35, 37

New York State, 38

Niagara Falls, 49, 50

Nicholas I, czar, 83, 84

Nicholson, Colin, 222n

Nicklas, Hans W., 303n

Nicolai, Ralf R., 234n

Nielsen, Jakob, 297n

Nietzsche, Friedrich, 51, 116, 117, 119, 121, 125, 128–30, 188, 197, 212, 291n; *The Birth of Tragedy* (*Die Geburt der Tragödie*, 1871), 188, 306n; *The Joyful Wisdom* (*Die fröhliche Wissenschaft*, 1887 [1882]), 119, 197, 276n, 277n, 278n, 283n, 314n; *Thus Spake Zarathustra* (*Also sprach Zarathustra*, 1883–5), 276–7n; *Beyond Good and Evil* (*Jenseits von Gut und Böse*, 1886), 162, 241n, 292n; *The Case of Wagner* (*Der Fall Wagner*, 1888), 129, 130, 280n

Niggl, Günter, 237n

Nobel Prize for literature, 113

North America, 7, 16, 22, 40–2, 53, 207

the North, Northerners: of Europe, 60, 126, 135, 141, 189; of Italy, 60, 65, 164

nouveau roman, 157

Novalis (Friedrich von Hardenberg), 32, 230n, 231n

novel of education. *See* Bildungsroman

Nowell-Smith, Geoffrey, 278n, 313n

Nuvoli, Giuliana, 3, 4, 220n, 222n

Ockham's razor, 157

Odyssey, The, 165, 304n, 316n

Ôe, Kenzaburo, 274n

Offenbach, Jacques, 128

O'Healy, Áine, 230n

Oklahoma, 40, 41, 49

Olmi, Ermanno, 226n, 227n, 267n

Olney, James, 237n

Opéra Comique (Paris), 128

Ophuls, Max: *La ronde*, 4

Orient, the, 137

orientalism, 125, 126, 183, 278n

Orr, John, 222n
Ortoleva, Peppino, 290n
Ottaviano, Chiara, 290n

Pabst, Walter, 302n
Pahlen, Kurt, 280n
Paris, 29, 107, 128
Paris, Robert, 229n
Parisian Commune, 127
Pascal, Roy, 237n
Pasolini, Pier Paolo, 4, 14, 19, **101–21**, 125, 210, 211, 227n, **270–8n**, 316n, 318n
– Films: *Accattone* (1961), 118, 255n, 273n; *Mamma Roma* (1962), 116, 118, 255n; *La ricotta* in *Rogopag* (1963), 118, 273n; *Oedipus Rex* (*Edipo Re*, 1967), 120; *Teorema* (1968), 120; *Porcile* (1969), 120; *Medea* (1970), 120; *Decameron* (1971), 14, 112, 115, 270n, 273n, 277–8n; *The Canterbury Tales* (*I racconti di Canterbury*, 1972), 115, 270n; *Arabian Nights* (*Il fiore delle mille e una notte*, 1974), 115, 270n; *Salò* (1975), 4, 19, **101–21**, 210, 211, **270–8n**, 317–18n
– Texts: *The Ashes of Gramsci* (*Le ceneri di Gramsci*, 1957), 117, 118, 277n; *Trasumanar e organizzar* (1971), 114, 275n; *Heretical Empiricism* (*Empirismo eretico*, 1972), 113, 273–4n, 276n; *Calderón* (1973), 117, 118, 277n; *The Divine Mimesis* (*La divina mimesis*, 1973), 111, 271n; 'Trilogy of Life rejected' ('Abiura dalla Trilogia della vita,' 1975), 115, 275n; *Scritti corsari* (1975), 273n, 275n, 277n; *Lutheran Letters* (*Lettere luterane*, posth.), 115, 273n, 275n, 276n; *San*

Paolo (posth.), 114, 115, 275n; *Orgia* (posth.), 270n; *Petrolio* (posth.), 276n
Pasternak, Boris Leonidovich, 16, 19, 22, 78, 95, **147–58**, 212, 255n, 265–6n, **288–91n**; *Doctor Zhivago* (*Doktor Zhivago*, 1957), 16, 17, 19, 78, 95, **147–58**, 212, 265–6n, **288–91n**
Pasternak, Leonid Osipovich, 78, 255n
Paul of Tarsus (St Paul), 114, 115
Pavese, Cesare, 219n
Pavia, 60, 62, 72, 75, 76
Petronius Arbiter: *Satyricon*, 33, 239n
Peytard, Jean, 299n
Pezzino, Paolo, 263n
Pietro da Morrone, 87
Pike, Burton, 316n
Pinocchio, 91, 243n, 264n
Pintus, Pietro, 294n, 301n
Pirandello, Luigi, 77, 255n
Pirro, Ugo, 266n
Pius VII, pope, 168
Placido, Michele: *Pummarò* (1990), 141
Plato, 186
Poe, Edgar Allan, 184
Pola (Istria, now Croatia), 184, 189
Poland, Poles, 156, 183, 185, 187, 214
Pomorska, Krystyna, 226n
Pompeii, 119
Ponti, Carlo, 242n
Porretta Terme, 162, 171
Poseidon, 165
poshlost', 152
Prague, 33, 36, 199
Pravadelli, Veronica, 222n, 309n, 313n
Prédal, René, 223n
Priscillian, 58, 244n

Protazanov, Iakov Aleksandrovich:
    Father Sergius (*Otets Sergii*, 1917),
    77
Proto, Carola, 230n
Proust, Marcel, 316n
Prussia, 127
Pudovkin, Vsevolod: *Mat'*, 4
Pütz, Jürgen, 234n
puppets, 57, 243n, 244n
Pushkin, Aleksandr Sergeevich, 126,
    127, 279n, 280n, 283n
Pyrenees, 125

Quaglietti, Lorenzo, 254n

Radcliff-Umstead, Douglas, 313–14n
Rancour-Laferrière, Daniel, 244n,
    248n, 250n
Ranucci, Georgette, 286n, 287n,
    290n, 291n
Ranzato, Gabriele, 263n
Raphael (Raffaello Sanzio), 127
re-creation (of literature in cinema),
    ix, **4–12**, **205–17**, 220–2n, 271–2n,
    290n
Redfield, Marc, 229n, 232n
Red Shirts (Garibaldi's Thousand),
    164, 165
Reed, Terence James, 303n, 309n,
    313n
Regosa, Maurizio, 220n, 222n
Renoir, Jean: *La bête humaine*, 4
Renzi, Renzo, 308n
Resistenza, 30, 164, 165
Restif de la Bretonne, Nicolas-Edmé,
    102, 268n
Rimbaud, Arthur, 268n
Risi, Dino, 278n
Risorgimento, 76, 163, 164, 166, 213,
    292n, 293n

Rizzoli, Angelo, 242n
Rohde, Erwin, 307n
Rohdie, Sam, 276n
Rohmer, Eric: *La Marquise d'O*, 4
Romagna, 33, 162, 169, 170
Roman Republic, 103, 161
Rome, Romans, 29, 30, 33–5, 39, 47,
    49, 63, 70, 161–4, 168–72, 174, 176–
    8, 180
Ronda (Spain), 132, 134
Rondolino, Gianni, 294n, 301n, 308n
Rosi, Francesco, 19, 33, 76, **125–42**,
    211, 212, 227n, **281–5n**; *The Chal-
    lenge* (*La sfida*, 1957), 140; *Salvatore
    Giuliano* (1961), 130, 134, 135, 140,
    263n; *Hands Over the City* (*Mani
    sulla città*, 1963), 76, 130, 140; *The
    Moment of Truth* (*Il momento della
    verità*, 1965), 140; *Just Another War*
    (*Uomini contro*, 1970), 140; *The Mat-
    tei Affair* (*Il caso Mattei*, 1972), 134;
    Illustrious Corpses (*Cadaveri eccellenti*,
    1975), 134; *Christ Stopped at Eboli*
    (*Cristo si è fermato a Eboli*, 1979), 134,
    140; *Three Brothers* (*Tre fratelli*,
    1981), 134; *Carmen* (1984), 19, 33,
    125–42, 211, 212, **281–8n**; *Chronicle
    of a Death Foretold* (*Cronaca di una
    morte annunciata*, 1987), 33, 140
Rossellini, Renzo, 294–5n
Rossellini, Roberto, 15, 19, 119, 120,
    166, **167–81**, 189, 213, 214, 267n,
    293–302n
– Films: *Rome Open City* (*Roma città
    aperta*, 1945), 168; *Paisan* (*Paisà*,
    1946), 168; *Germany Year Zero* (*Ger-
    mania anno zero*, 1948), 189; *Strom-
    boli, Land of God* (*Stromboli terra di
    Dio*, 1949), 301n; *Voyage to Italy*
    (*Viaggio in Italia*, 1953), 119; *General*

Della Rovere (*Il generale Della Rovere*, 1959), 179, 299–301n; *Viva l'Italia!* (1960–1), 166, 167, 293n; **Vanina Vanini** (1961), 15, 19, 20, 22, **167–81**, 213, 214, **297–302**n, 314n; *The Iron Age* (*L'età del ferro*, 1964), *The Struggle of Humanity for Its Survival* (*La lotta dell'uomo per la sua sopravvivenza*, 1964–70), *The Acts of the Apostles* (*Gli Atti degli Apostoli*, 1969), *Socrates* (*Socrate*, 1970), *Pascal* (*Blaise Pascal*, 1972), *Augustine of Hippo* (*Agostino d'Ippona*, 1972), *The Age of the Medicis* (*L'età di Cosimo dei Medici*, 1972), *Cartesius* (*Cartesio*, 1974), *The Messiah* (*Il Messia*, 1975) – all 296n
– Texts: *A Free Mind* (*Un esprit libre*, 1977), 167, 295n, 296n, 302n; *Quasi un'autobiografia* (posth.), 295n, 301n; *My Method* (*Il mio metodo*, posth.), 293–4n, 296n, 301n

Rossi, Monica, 285n

Rousseau, Jean-Jacques, 43, 102; *Émile*, 36

Rubini, Sergio, 45, 49–51

Rumble, Patrick, 272n, 273n, 275n

Russia, Russians, 4, 12, 17, 60, 69, 74, 78, 81, 88, 149–52, 156; Russian literature and culture, 13, 17. *See also* names of individual authors

Russian Formalists, 6, 8

Russian (October 1917) revolution, 149–51, 153–6, 290n

Sacher (misc.), 143, 285n

Sade, Donatien Alphonse François, marquis de, 16, 17, **101–21**, 209–11, **267–72**n, 317n, 318n; *Aline and Valcour, or Philosophical Novel* (*Aline et Valcour, ou roman philosophique*, 1795), 102, 269n; *Philosophy in the Dressing Room* (*La philosophie dans le boudoir*, 1795), 101, 106, 268n; *The New Justine* (*La nouvelle Justine*, 1797), 106; *Juliette's Story* (*Histoire de Juliette*, 1797), 106; *Idée sur les romans* (in *Les crimes de l'amour*, 1801 / an VIII), 106, 270n; *Dialog of a Priest and a Dying Man* (*Dialogue d'un prêtre et d'un moribond*, posth.), 106; **The 120 Days of Sodom** (*Les 120 journées de Sodome*, posth.), 16, 17, **101–21**, 210, 211, **267–72**n, 318n

Saïd, Edward, 139, 278n

Salò, republic of (1943–5), 109, 114, 211

San Miniato (prov. of Pisa), 88

Sant'Angelo, 162, 171

Sanzio, Alain, 312n, 318n, 319n

Sartre, Jean-Paul, 284n

Savonarola, Girolamo, 118

Savoy dynasty, 164, 166

Scala theatre (Milan), 59

Schiller, Friedrich, 304n, 306n, 307n, 317n

Schlegel, Friedrich, 238n

Sciascia, Leonardo, 271n

Scirocco, Alfonso, 292n

Scola, Ettore, 227n, 278n

Second (French) Empire, 127

Second World War, 60, 164, 165, 189, 190, 199

Sédan (France), 127

Selbmann, Rolf, 229n

Serceau, Michel, 299–301n

Sereni, Emilio, 293n

Sesti, Mario, 220n, 230n, 267n, 284n, 285n, 287n

Setschkareff, Vsevolod, 243n

Seville (Spain), 131, 132, 134, 140

Shklovskii (Shklovsky), Viktor (Victor), 6, 221n, 255n
Siberia, 81, 94, 96, 151, 153
Siciliano, Enzo, 275n
Sicily, 134, 165
Sierra Nevada, 153
Silone, Ignazio, 262n
Singer, Irving, 312n
Siniavsky, Andrei. *See* Terts, Abram
Sinyard, Neil, 312n
Slonimskii, Aleksandr, 248n, 249n
Socrates, 157, 186
Solinas, Franco, 180
Sollers, Philippe, 271n
Sorlin, Pierre, 220n, 267n, 294n
the South, Southerners: of Europe, 129, 139, 185, 187, 189, 194, 209; of Italy, 90, 94, 135, 139, 165, 282n, 305n. *See also* Italy, Mediterranean, Meridionalism
Soviets, Soviet Union, 143, 146, 154, 155, 199
Soviet semioticians, 206, 221n
Spain, 125, 128, 141, 151, 153, 155
Spence, G.W., 256n
Spila, Piero, 259n, 275n
Spilka, Mark, 236n
Squitieri, Pasquale: *And They Called Them Brigands* (*E li chiamarono briganti*, 1999), 263n
Staël-Holstein, Anne Louise Germaine de Necker, baronne de, 118
Stalin [Djugashvili, Iosif Vissarionovich], Stalinism, 9, 154, 155, 224n
Stam, Robert, 7, 222n, 223n, 238n
Starobinski, Jean, 237n
Stendhal [Henri Beyle], 16, 19, 43, 118, 126, **161–3**, 166, 168, **174–81**, 209, 213, 214, **291–2n**, **297–302n**; *Rome, Naples and Florence* (*Rome,*

Naples et Florence, 1827 [1817]), 19, 297n; *On Love* (*De l'Amour,* 1822), 19, 297n; *Promenades dans Rome* (1829), 162, 291n, 300n; *Vanina Vanini* (1829), 16, 17, 19, **161–3**, 166, 168, **174–81**, 213, 214, **291–2n**, **297–302n**; *Red and Black* (*Le rouge et le noir,* 1830), 19, 175, 297n, 298n; *The Charterhouse of Parma* (*La Chartreuse de Parme,* 1839), 19, 297n, 299n; *Chroniques italiennes* (1839), 161
Stirling, Monica, 308n
St Mark (Venice), 186, 189
Storia d'Italia, 229n, 293n
St Petersburg, 60, 62, 65, 66, 68–70, 78, 208, 248n, 252n, 311n
Striedter, Iurii, 226n, 318n
student movement (esp. in 1968), 119, 120, 199, 200, 278n, 315–16n
Sulmona (prov. of L'Aquila), 87
Swales, Martin, 230n
Switzerland, 155

Tambling, Jeremy, 279n
Tartu (Estonia), 6, 206, 221n, 316n
Tasso, Torquato, 127
Tassone, Aldo, 238n, 245n, 247n, 259n, 262n, 266n
taxonomy/typology of films analysed, **13–21**
Taviani, Paolo and Vittorio, 14, 15, 18, **77–97**, 210, 227n, **257–67n**, 292n; *A Man to Be Burned* (*Un uomo da bruciare,* 1962), 85, 89, 258n; *The Subversives* (*I sovversivi,* 1967), 85, 258n; *Saint Michael Had a Rooster* (*San Michele aveva un gallo,* 1971), 77, 85, 89, 258n, 260n, 265n; *Allons enfants* (*Allonsanfàn,* 1974), 85, 89,

258–60n, 264n, 265n; *Padre padrone* (1977), 14, 85, 89, 258n, 262n; *The Meadow* (*Il prato*, 1978), 258n; *The Night of the Shooting Stars* (*La notte di S. Lorenzo*, 1982), 258n, 262n; *Kaos* (1984), 258n; **The Night Sun** (*Il sole anche di notte*, 1990), 15, 18, 21, 77– 97, 210, **257–67n**; *Floréal* (*Fiorile*, 1993), 257–8n; *Elective Affinities* (*Le affinità elettive*, 1996), 258n

technology, 167, 168, 180, 294–6n

television, TV, TV stations, 96, 120, 140, 145, 149, 153, 154, 164, 180, 214, 266n, 267n, 284n, 294n, 295n

Terts, Abram [Siniavsky, Andrei], 65, 243n, 250n, 251n

Testa, Bart, 272n

Testa, Carlo, 16, 222n, 226n, 227n, 244n, 245n, 258n, 278n, 282n, 288n, 289n, 297n, 298n, 311n

Thirard, Paul-Louis, 312n, 318n, 319n

Third (French) Republic, 128

Third World, 117, 277n, 296n

Thomas Cook Travel, 186

Thompson, Howard, 226n, 281n

Thompson, Kristin, 15

Tibet, 13

Ticino River, 60, 62, 67

Tieck, Ludwig, 126

Tinazzi, Giorgio, 254n

Tolstoi (Tolstoy), Lēv (Leo) Nikolae-vich, 4, 16, 17, 18, **77–97**, 167, 181, 208–10, **255–62n**, **264–5n**, 296n, 317n; *What Is Art?* (*Chto takoe iskusstvo?*, 1897–8), 78, 181, 296n, 302n; *Resurrection* (*Voskresenie*, 1899), 78, 81, 96, 255–6n, 296n; *The Forged Note* (*Fal' shivyi kupon*, 1903), 4; *The Divine and the Human* (*Bozheskoe i chelovecheskoe*, 1906), 77,

78; 'Gogol'' (1909), 243n; *And Light Shines in the Darkness* (*I svet vo t' me svetit*, posth.), 78, 88, 96; **Father Sergius** (*Otets Sergii*, posth.), 16, 17, 18, **77–97**, 210, **255–62n**, **264–5n**, 296n

Tomasi, Dario, 220n

Tomasi di Lampedusa, Giuseppe, 7, 165; *The Leopard* (*Il Gattopardo*, 1958), 165

Tornatore, Giuseppe: *Everybody's Fine* (*Stanno tutti bene*, 1991), 141

Torri, Bruno, 259n

Trahan, Elizabeth, 243n

translation theory, 205, 316n

Trombadori, Antonello, 180

Tsarskoe Selo (by St Petersburg), 85

Turgenev, Ivan Sergeevich, 4, 10; *Bez-hin Meadow*, in *A Hunter's Sketches* (*Bezhin lug*, in *Zapiski okhotnika*, 1852), 4, 10

Turini, Patrizia, 259n, 262n

Tynianov (Tynyanov, Tynjanov), Iurii (Yuri, Jurij), 16, 215, 226n, 318n

Ughi, Stefanella, 286n, 287n, 290n, 291n

Ukraine, Ukrainians, 58, 208

Ungaretti, Giuseppe, 60

United States of America, 35, 42, 44, 45, 53, 165, 172, 241n

Ural mountains, 152

Vaget, Hans Rudolf, 303n, 304n, 312n, 315n

Vancini, Florestano: *The Events at Bronte* (*I fatti di Bronte*, 1972), 292n

Venice (Venezia), 17, 183–5, 187, 188, 195, 214

Venturi, Franco, 289n
Venuti, Lawrence, 316n
Verdone, Mario, 237n
Verga, Giovanni, 119, 287n, 292n
Verlaine, Paul, 22, 23, 228n
Viano, Maurizio, 255n, 275n
Vienna, 128
Vietnam, 120, 315n
Viganò, Aldo, 237n
Villari, Rosario, 293n
Virgil (Publius Vergilius Maro), 108,
    109, 111, 293n
Visconti, Luchino, 4, 7, 8, 13, 14, 19,
    21, 22, 33, 59, 75, 76, 119, 120, 164,
    166, 180, **183–201**, 214–17, 222n,
    227n, 301n, 303n, **308–16n**, 318n,
    319n; *Ossessione* (1943), 198, 314n;
    The Earth Trembles (*La terra trema*,
    1948), 13, 119, 198, 287n; *Senso*
    (1954), 14, 75, 76, 164, 166, 180,
    195, 198, 255n, 292n, 298n, 301n,
    311n, 315n; *White Nights* (*Le notti
    bianche*, 1957), 195, 198, 311n, 314n;
    Rocco and His Brothers (*Rocco e i suoi
    fratelli*, 1960), 75, 119, 198; *The Leop-
    ard* (*Il gattopardo*, 1963), 4, 7, 13,
    198, 292n; *Sandra* (*Vaghe stelle
    dell'Orsa*, 1965), 312n; *The Damned
    (La caduta degli dèi*, 1969), 197, 198,
    313n, 314n; **Death in Venice** (*Morte a
    Venezia*, 1971), 19–21, 33, **183–201**,
    214, 215, 272n, 303n, **308–16n**;
    Ludwig (1973), 314n; *Conversation
    Piece* (*Gruppo di famiglia in un inter-
    no*, 1974), 314n, 315n; *The Innocent
    (L'innocente*, 1976), 314n

Vitti, Antonio, 285n
Vollmann, Benedikt, 244n

Wagner, Geoffrey, 313n
Wagner, Richard, 128, 129, 280n
Wangermée, Robert, 281n
Wasson, R. Gordon, 310n
Waugh, Patricia, 238n
Wedekind, Frank, 280n
Weisbein, Nicolas, 256n
Welsch, Janice R., 238n
Wertmüller, Lina, 15
the West, Western countries, 155
Whelehan, Imelda, 222n
Whittock, Trevor, 286n
Wicks, Ulrich, 238n
Wilhelm II, Kaiser, 183
Winckelmann, Johann Joachim, 126
Wolfe, Peter, 274n
Wolff, Rudolf, 303n
women filmmakers in Italy, 226n

Yalta, 75
Yasnaya Polyana (Iasnaia Poliana), 78
Yourcenar, Marguerite, 274n
(ex-)Yugoslavia, 141

Zaccaro, Maurizio: *The Article 2*
    (*L'articolo 2*, 1993), 141
Zagarrio, Vito, 247n, 254n, 267n
Zambetti, Sandro, 282n
Zavattini, Cesare, 60, 61, 225n, 246n,
    248n, 264n
Zola, Émile, 128, 129; *Nana* (1879–
    80), 128